VIRGINIA HISTORICAL SOCIETY DOCUMENTS

Volume 3

WILLIAM FITZHUGH
AND
HIS CHESAPEAKE WORLD
1676-1701

THE FITZHUGH LETTERS AND OTHER DOCUMENTS

William Fitzhugh (1651-1701)

Copy by John Hesselius in 1751, owned by Mrs. Robert H. Stevenson of Boston.

WILLIAM FITZHUGH

AND

HIS CHESAPEAKE WORLD

1676-1701

The Fitzhugh Letters and Other Documents

EDITED WITH AN INTRODUCTION BY

RICHARD BEALE DAVIS

Published for

THE VIRGINIA HISTORICAL SOCIETY

By

THE UNIVERSITY OF NORTH CAROLINA PRESS · 1963 · CHAPEL HILL

Acknowledgments

This study of a significant colonial American and his time and region has been made possible through the generous assistance of a number of individuals and institutions. Dr. Thomas Fitz-Hugh, Jr., of Philadelphia, placed in my possession for a period of several months the original letter book of his ancestor. The American Philosophical Society, through its Executive Officer Dr. L. P. Eisenhart, made a grant in 1958 for research and photographic materials. The University of Tennessee English Department, through its chairman Dr. John C. Hodges, gave secretarial assistance, especially for a preliminary transcript of the letters.

Assistance on a smaller scale came from many directions. Among Fitzhugh descendants to whom I am indebted for photographs of family portraits, silver, and records I wish to thank especially Mrs. Conway (Edmonia Fitzhugh) Chichester, of Fredericksburg, Virginia; Mrs. Robert H. (Alice Lee Thomas) Stevenson, of Boston, Massachusetts; and Eppa Hunton IV, of Richmond, Virginia. Other members of the family who have been helpful are Miss Margaret W. Fitzhugh, of Richmond, Virginia; Mrs. Lucy W. F. Faison, of Arlington, Virginia; and Douglas Gordon, of Baltimore, Maryland.

George H. S. King, of Fredericksburg, Virginia, has been generous in sharing his extensive knowledge of persons and places in seventeenth-century Virginia. Others to whom I am grateful for information include: The late James W. Foster, director of the Maryland Historical Society, himself a Fitzhugh descendant; Associate Librarian Francis L. Berkeley, Jr., of the Alderman Library of the University of Virginia; Director John M. Jennings, of the Virginia Historical Society; Professor C. William Miller, of Temple University; Professor Richard L. Morton, of the College of William and Mary; Mr. and Mrs. Frank Marvin Murphy, of Kinsale, Virginia; Professor Charles E. Noyes, of the University of Mississippi; and Mrs. Chichester Tapscott Peirce, of Nuttsville, Virginia; also the staffs of the Hoskins Library of the University of Tennessee; the Manuscript and Legal divisions of the Library of Congress; the Rare Book Division of the Folger Shakespeare Library; the Henry E. Huntington Library; the Connecticut Historical Society; the New Hampshire Historical Society; the Maryland Historical Society; the Virginia Historical Society; the Hall of Records, Annapolis, Maryland; and the Virginia State Library.

Knowledge of William Fitzhugh's English origins and connections has been increased considerably through the care and courtesy of several persons in Great Britain, especially the Reverend John H. King, Vicar of St. Paul's, Bedford; Miss Joyce Godby, County Archivist, Bedford; G. F. Simmonds, Town Clerk, Bedford; J. P. Brooke-Little, Esq., Bluemantle Pursuivant of Arms, the College of Arms, London; A. H. Hall, the Guild-hall Library, London; Mr. E. B. P. Gillett, Headmaster, Queen Elizabeth's Hospital, Bristol; Miss Elizabeth Ralph, Archives Department, the Council House, Bristol; and the staffs of the British Museum and the Public Record Office. I am also most grateful to William M. E. Rachal, editor of publications for the Virginia Historical Society, for his excellent sugges-tions and painstaking efforts in seeing this book through the press. And equally I am indebted to the members of the staff of the University of North Carolina Press, for their care and patience in the same process.

University of Tennessee   Richard Beale Davis
Knoxville
June 1962

Contents

Illustrations

Abbreviations

Abbreviations Used in Footnote References in Introduction and Letters

Andrews, *Col. Period of Am. Hist.*   Charles M. Andrews, *The Colonial Period of American History.* 4 vols. New Haven, 1934-38.

Archives of Md.   *Archives of Maryland....* Maryland Historical Society, Baltimore, 1833——.

Beverley, *History*   Robert Beverley, *The History and Present State of Virginia.* Edited by Louis B. Wright. Chapel Hill, 1947.

Bruce, *Ec. Hist. Va.*   Philip A. Bruce, *Economic History of Virginia in the Seventeenth Century.* 2 vols. New York, 1896.

Bruce, *Inst. Hist. Va.*   Philip A. Bruce, *Institutional History of Virginia in the Seventeenth Century.* 2 vols. New York, 1910.

Brydon, *Va.'s Mother Church*   George MacLaren Brydon, *Virginia's Mother Church and the Political Conditions under Which It Grew. An Interpretation of the Records of the Colony of Virginia and the Anglican Church of That Colony 1607-1727.* Richmond, 1947 [Vol. I of a series].

Burk, *Hist. of Va.*   John Daly Burk, *et al., The History of Virginia from Its First Settlement to the Present Day.* 4 vols. Petersburg, 1804-16.

Cal. St. Papers, Col., Am. & W.I.   *Calendar of State Papers, Colonial Series, America and the West Indies.* 10 vols. London, 1860-1908.

Campbell, *History*   Charles Campbell, *History of the Colony and Ancient Dominion of Virginia.* Philadelphia, 1860.

xiii

Eaton, *Hist. Atlas Westmoreland*   D. W. Eaton, *Historical Atlas of Westmore-land County, Virginia.* Richmond, 1942.

Exec. Journ. Council Col. Va.   *Executive Journals of the Council of Colonial Virginia.* Edited by H. R. McIlwaine. Richmond, Vol. I, 1925; Vol. II, 1927.

Fothergill, *Wills of Westmoreland County*   Augusta B. Fothergill, *Wills of Westmoreland County, Virginia, 1654-1800.* Richmond, 1925.

Freeman, *George Washington*   Douglas Southall Freeman, *George Washington: A Biography.* Vol. I. New York, 1948.

Harrison, *Landmarks*   Fairfax Harrison, *Landmarks of Old Prince William.* 2 vols. Richmond, 1924.

Harrison, *Va. Land Grants*   Fairfax Harrison, *Virginia Land Grants, a Study of Conveyancy in Relation to Colonial Politics.* Richmond, 1935.

Hening, *Statutes*   W. W. Hening, *The Statutes at Large, Being a Collection of All the Laws of Virginia from the First Session of the Legislature in the Year 1619....* 13 vols. Richmond and Philadelphia, 1809-1823.

Jamestown 350th Anniv. Survey Reports   *Virginia 350th Anniversary Celebration Corporation, Colonial Records Project, Survey Reports.* Virginia State Library and University of Virginia Library, 1955—

Journals H.B. 1659/60-1693   *Journals of the House of Burgesses of Virginia, 1659/60–1693.* Edited by H. R. McIlwaine. Richmond, 1914.

Journals H.B. 1695 ... 1702   *Journals of the House of Burgesses of Virginia, 1695-1696, 1696-1697, 1698, 1699, 1700-1702.*

Lee, *Lee Chronicle*   Cazenove G. Lee, Jr., *Lee Chronicle: Studies of the Early Generations of the Lees of Virginia.* Compiled and edited by Dorothy Mills Parker. New York, 1957.

Legisl. Journ. Council Col. Va.   *Legislative Journals of the Council of Colonial Virginia.* Edited by H. R. McIlwaine. 3 vols. Richmond, 1918-19.

McGrath, *Merchants*

Patrick McGrath, *Merchants and Merchandise in Seventeenth-Century Bristol.* Printed for the Bristol Record Society. [1955]. Vol. XIX of the Bristol Record Society's Publications.

McGrath, *Records*

Patrick McGrath, *Records Relating to the Society of Merchant Venturers of the City of Bristol in the Seventeenth Century.* Printed for the Bristol Record Society. [1952]. Vol. XVII of the Bristol Record Society's Publications.

Meade, *Old Churches*

Bishop [William] Meade, *Old Churches, Ministers, and Families of Virginia.* 2 vols. Philadelphia, 1857.

Minutes Council and Gen. Court

Minutes of the Council and General Court of Colonial Virginia, 1622-1632, 1670-1676, with Notes and Excerpts from Original Council and General Court Records, Into 1683, Now Lost. Edited by H. R. McIlwaine. Richmond, 1924.

Owings, *His Lordship's Patronage*

Donnell M. Owings, *His Lordship's Patronage: Offices of Profit in Colonial Maryland.* Baltimore, 1953.

Prince Wm. WPA

Prince William, the Story of Its People and Its Places. Compiled by Workers of the Writers' Program of the Work Projects Administration in the State of Virginia. American Guide Series. [Manassas, Va.], 1941.

Stanard, *Col. Va. Register*

William G. and Mary Newton Stanard, *The Colonial Virginia Register.* Albany, 1902.

Va. Col. Abstracts

Virginia Colonial Abstracts. Compiled by Beverley Fleet and L. O. Duvall. 1st series, 34 vols.; 2nd series, 1937——.

Wright, *First Gent. Va.*

Louis B. Wright, *The First Gentlemen of Virginia: Intellectual Qualities of the Early Colonial Ruling Class.* San Marino, 1940.

Titles of bound photostat volumes and of microfilm "volumes" of County Records in the Virginia State Library are italicized for convenience, to differentiate them from mere citations of date and place. All such citations, unless otherwise noted, are to materials in the Virginia State Library.

All periodicals for which symbol short-titles are given follow the form for such citations as used in E. G. Swem, *Virginia Historical Index* (2 vols., Roanoke, Va., 1934-36). For example, 1 V 32 represents *The Virginia Magazine of History and Biography*, I, 32; 2 W(1) 84 is *William and Mary Quarterly*, first series, II, 84.

The William Blathwayt Papers in the Manuscript Division, Henry E. Huntington Library, are referred to as HEH, Blathwayt Papers.

Introduction

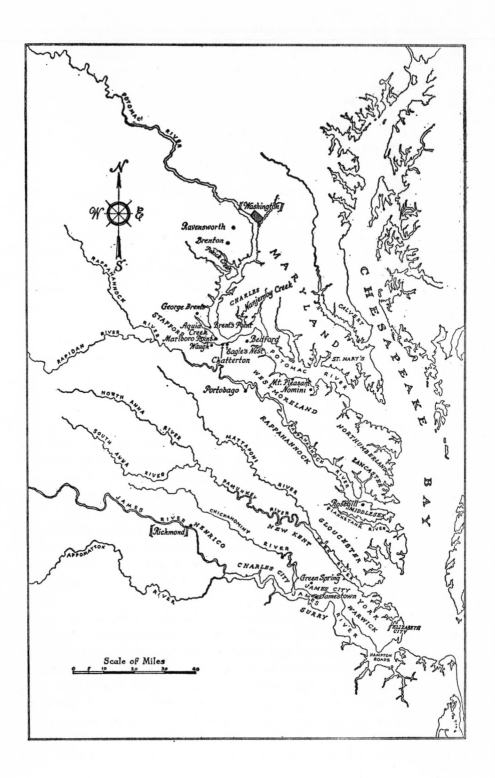

Introduction

It is not strange that a number of seventeenth-century Englishmen should settle on the shores of a great blue bay along the North American coast. Here seemed fitting places for the testing, and in some instances the resting, of their ambitions. These shores were for a seafaring people the most easily accessible portion of that territory which Queen Elizabeth of Blessed Memory and her captains a generation before had claimed as Britain's own in the struggle of western European nations for space in the New World. Great half-tidal rivers, smaller deep-water inlets, and navigable creeks formed a network of pathways into a green-wooded, richly topsoiled, pleasantly temperatured land. And this Chesapeake country was enough like the island their Saxon ancestors had seized a thousand years before for these people to be able to adjust themselves to it with comparative ease. It was enough different to offer excitement, adventure, and material opportunity such as their race had not known since they had sailed with Hengest and Horsa. Their Viking ancestors had conquered a romanized and civilized Celtic people and intermarried with them to produce a sturdy folk which had been slowly maturing for ten centuries. They found on this new continent only a primitive people, a people they were at first inclined to sentimentalize a little. Then because these primitives became a nuisance by insisting upon their own title to the land they inhabited, the newcomers began pushing them west. It rarely occurred to the invaders that all difficulties might be settled by intermarriage. Difference in levels of culture, in color of skin, prevented. The natives' natural resentments their conquerors dealt with sternly, almost always without qualms, though with some fear of the physical consequences.

In the early decades of the century these Englishmen established a stockaded village as headquarters on the banks of the James, the southern-most of the great rivers, and above and below it on the river banks a few dozen straggling plantations. At the same time some of them began clearing land for themselves on the two great capes forming the pillars of the gateway to the bay, settlements partially intended as outposts against foreign enemies of European origin. After periods of discouragement from

3

pestilence, starvation, and massacre, they began to reach out in scattered farms along the other great rivers to the north of the James—the York, the Rappahannock, and the Potomac—or on beautiful promontories along the bay proper, where navigable water was close inshore. The dark brown-green of forest vegetation was now broken at intervals by clearings containing a few cultivated fields, tobacco sheds, and rough frame houses, with rougher wharves jutting out into the salt water.

Soon a second chartered group established their central village farther north up the bay, and Maryland came into existence beside Virginia. For some years most of the farms of this second colony were along or near the north bank of the Potomac, facing the Virginia clearings across the river. Then Maryland extended its tentacles much as its older sister had done, building tiny settlements and clearing farms up to and around the head of the bay and its northernmost tributary, the Susquehanna, and down the eastern peninsula which formed the outer wall of the Chesapeake itself.

By the third quarter of the century there was a thinly populated, yet carefully organized, world around all the shores of the bay. In most aspects it was a unified world. Only in religion, with Virginia strongly Anglican and Maryland a mixture of Roman Catholic and Anglican and other Protestant sects, was there an easily discernible difference. Economically this microcosm was forming in an agricultural-mercantile pattern, which would become firmer and clearer for the next century and a half and eventually in its extension through the Old South would affect profoundly the whole history of American civilization. There were parliaments and courts and sheriffs as in the England from which its inhabitants came. But there were also Indian wars and labor systems and agrarian practices such as the mother country had never seen, and never would see. It was a dependent world, dependent on European markets and British business agents and on rain and sun and depth of topsoil. But already it was beginning to find England and some of Continental Europe dependent upon it. Primarily agricultural in practice, but also strongly mercantile in spirit, restless and greedy and yet dignified and sturdy, it was northern Europe's first great colonial experiment.

Colonial experiment, outlet for the restless, significant economic factor in an expanding western civilization, it was more than all these. Its people had begun to assume a social and moral character of their own, a character strongly English to be sure, but tempered and accentuated by a new climate, strange tensions from new dangers, and new hungers growing with the awareness of the tremendously abundant means of satisfying them. Already they were pointing out that the English law and legal systems could be only partially adopted here, for conditions were very different. They believed that they had already within sight the fulfillment of a hope their ancestors had expressed in 1610, more than two generations before.

Let England knowe our willingnesse, for that our worke is goode;
Wee hope to plant a nation, where none before hath stood.

MIRRORS OF AN AGE

Our knowledge of this Chesapeake world comes largely from surviving official documents, the records of the executive and legislative and judicial branches of the central government, of the county courts and tax assessors' offices, and of the parish registers. All these are scanty in Virginia because of fire and plunder during the Revolutionary and Civil Wars. We have added other records to them where we could. There is still not a great deal, however, for a people absorbed in laying foundations and surviving took little time to testify on paper as to how they fared, or what their impressions of their experiences were. But occasionally a colonist, who in another age might have become poet or novelist, in this late seventeenth century did put pen to paper. Usually the result was partly history and partly propaganda, designed to encourage emigration from Europe. But sometimes inadvertently it was the graceful expression of an artistic mind. Occasionally these works could be sardonic or even satiric in tone. Frequently they relied for their circulation more on European interest in the strange and marvelous than in the attractions of emigration. Such books were Ebenezer Cooke's satiric poem *The Sot-Weed Factor* (1708) and *The Present State of Virginia* 'histories' of Robert Beverley (1705 and 1722), Hugh Jones (1724), and Hartwell, Blair, and Chilton (written 1697, published 1727), books by men who lived in one or both of the colonies. All four volumes indicate their authors' sense of style, belletristic consciousness, and complexity of motives for writing.

But the clearest picture of the personal life and character of the Chesapeake colonists in this period comes from their surviving letters, most of them addressed to officials, friends, factors, or families in the mother country. Besides the epistles on official business sent through official channels (which may be included with the public papers mentioned above) there were a number of almost purely personal letters. These cover a multitude of subjects, from advice to a son or daughter and conjugal affection and hysterical fear of the Indians to descriptions of naval battles with the Dutch, of explorations in the mountains, of houses and farms and servants, or to philosophizing on the idyllic existence one might live on these shores. Most of these letters have survived by accident, and in the majority of instances only single letters survive, though occasionally there are two or three by the same person.

At least two methodical colonists of the later seventeenth century, however, one of whom lived on the James and the other on the Potomac, seem to have kept in bound volumes copies of outgoing letters, and at least retained and preserved these letters over a period of years. One of the men was William Byrd I (1652-1704), father of the polished Queen Anne gentleman who was the most distinguished writer of the colonial South. The elder Byrd preserved a series of letters, principally to the London merchants who were his agents, which afford us considerable information about trade with the Indians and tobacco growing, packing, and shipping, and incidentally a picture of the writer as a wise, practical man of considerable sophistication, a man who laid the foundations for what was to become in his son's time the finest of colonial libraries, for what was to be the great estate of "Westover" on the James, and for the distinguished American family that today bears his name.

The other methodical colonist was William Fitzhugh, who lived on the Potomac and practiced law as well as raised tobacco. When he died at the age of fifty he left to his descendants more than fifty-four thousand acres of land and a reputation for ability in many lines of endeavor. His surname alone and in combined form through the marital alliances of his children and grandchildren with Washingtons and Lees and Masons, among others, has had a notable place in American history from his time to ours.

Fitzhugh preserved some 212 of his letters to his clients, his London agents, his family in England, his law partner and other business associates, officials of the colony, and several personal friends. In addition to these there survive two letters addressed to the Commission of the Peace and preserved in the Stafford Court records; several of his speeches delivered before the House of Burgesses and copied verbatim into the records of that body, a most unusual procedure; his long and detailed will; and a number of land-transaction documents in several courthouses of the Northern Neck of Virginia. Of these, all the letters with extant enclosures and three of his more significant speeches are here reproduced. The letters were published in considerably garbled and sometimes unintelligible form, with several omissions, in the 1890's in the now rare earliest volumes of *The Virginia Magazine of History and Biography.*

Because of the value of the picture of the world they present and of Fitzhugh's significance as an individual and as a representative colonist, they have been here brought together in the earliest surviving text form and extensively annotated. But even with annotation the letters do not present all phases of Fitzhugh's career or of the activities of the colony with which he was associated. He left his traces in a variety of official records from parish vestry to colonial office in Whitehall. The letters, the man, and his world become clearer if we first employ all surviving evidences to trace his life chronologically and to survey briefly each of the facets of his versatile career. His is the story of the making of a leader and of the founding of a family, but it is also the story of the development of an economic system and a governing system. Fitzhugh goes far towards explaining the character and actions of his descendants of two and three generations later who led in the founding of the republic.

FITZHUGH BEFORE 1676

Though a great deal has been written about the personal backgrounds of the group who were the early leaders of the Chesapeake colonies, biographical details for most of them have been difficult to uncover. The social status of the immediate families from which sprang the first American Lee, Mason, Washington, even Byrd, has not been very satisfactorily determined, primarily because these emigrants appear to have paid so little attention to it themselves. Fitzhugh is not an exception.

Actually the little that is known of William Fitzhugh's family would indicate that they were substantial and leading burghers of the town of Bedford, allied not too remotely with county families of the same name. His father has been said to have been a barrister, but the most recent data rather conclusively determines that he was a woolen-draper.[1] The woolen-draper, born in 1614, was named Henry. His American son owned a portrait of him painted in 1634 at age twenty. This Henry was in turn the son of an earlier William, a maltster, and that is as far back as the ancestry has been traced with absolute surety.

But the Fitzhughs or FitzHughs were clearly among the town's prominent citizens for at least two centuries. A William FitzHugh had been

---

1. For genealogical materials concerning the Fitzhugh family, see 1 V 269, 411-45; 7 V 196-99, 317-19; 8 V 91-95, 209, 211, 314-17, 430; 9 V 99-104; 40 V 187-204; *Visitations of Bedfordshire ... 1566, 1582, and 1634* (1884), Harleian Society Publications, XIX, 26-27; H. W. Howard Knott, "William Fitzhugh," in *D.A.B.*; F. A. Blaydes, ed., *Genealogia Bedfordiensis Being a Collection of Evidences Relating Chiefly to the Landed Gentry of Bedfordshire A. D. 1538-1700 Collected out of the Parish Registers. The Bishop's Transcripts: Early Wills ...* (London, 1890), pp. 36, 37.

mayor of Bedford in 1487. A Henry had held the office in 1548, and another Henry, perhaps the emigrant's father, had been mayor in 1649. Robert FitzHugh, almost surely the emigrant's uncle and correspondent, was mayor in 1656, and again in 1679, and alderman until 1689. Then at least two generations of FitzHugh women married into the equally important Paradine family, which held the mayoralty several times during the seventeenth century. It is significant that after these names there frequently appears the suffix, "Gent.," indicative of their armigerous quality.[2]

Henry, the emigrant's father, married Mary, daughter of the Reverend Giles King of Tempsford in Bedfordshire, and they had at least two sons and several daughters who survived into maturity. Henry's brother Robert lived "at the Greenhouse in Bedford." The brothers seem to have had at least two sisters; for an aunt, Mrs. Margaret Porter, is addressed from Virginia, and an Elizabeth was the wife of John Paradine, mayor of Bedford.

Henry Fitzhugh died in Ireland in 1664. The only other personal information about this woolen-draper is that in the Bedford Court of February 26, 1657/58, he suffered a judgment for £1,200,[3] which may or may not mean that he was at least at this time in straitened circumstances. Certainly his widow later was. But the St. Paul's parish register indicates the baptismal dates of several children of Henry and Mary: Margaret, baptized November 12, 1640 (and mentioned in these letters below); Susan, 1642; Mary, 1643; Elizabeth, 1645; Dorothy (see letters below), January 24, 1645; Henry (see letters below), April 28, 1650; and William, January 10, 1651. Thus the emigrant appears to have been the youngest child, and younger son, in a family of average size and some provincial prominence.

That these Fitzhughs were entitled to armorial bearings the Virginia planter and his English brother Henry assumed without question. The interesting and puzzling thing is that the brothers did not agree as to what constituted their proper arms, as the letters below indicate. That the Virginian and his descendants employed the arms of the Barons Fitzhugh and of the Fitzhugh family of Wolcott in Oxfordshire, "*Az. three chevrons interlaced in base or, a chef argent*," is indicated by William Fitzhugh's letters, by a Fitzhugh bookplate his son or grandson had engraved in the

---

2. Guy Parsloe, ed., *The Minute Book of Bedford Corporation, 1647-1664,* Publications of the Bedfordshire Historical Record Society, XXVI (1949), *passim;* letters from the County Archivist, Shire Hall, Bedford, June 26, 1958, and from the Town Clerk, Town Hall, Bedford, of May 9 and April 29, 1958. For the children of WF's grandfather William Fitzhugh, see 7 V 196 ff., etc.

3. Information from G. F. Simmonds, Town Clerk, Bedford, May 9, 1958.

eighteenth century,[4] and by several surviving pieces of silver plate once owned by the emigrant which bear either the full arms or the appropriate crest.[5] A recent statement by an English Fitz-Hugh proves rather conclusively that the planter's cousin William Fitzhugh of London (see letters to him below) had a quite different arms, *"Quarterly, 1 and 4 ermine, on a chief gules, three martlets or [Fitzhugh]. 2 and 3 argent three chevrons sable each charged with a bezant."* This English writer feels that William was wrong about his arms and that probably his brother Henry, who sent what William considered the wrong seal, was right, though what arms or crest Henry sent we cannot be sure. Also this recent writer states positively that there was no connection between this family and the Barons Fitzhugh of Yorkshire. With this verdict the present Bluemantle Pursuivant of Arms (1958) agrees. This is all the more confusing because, a generation after William Fitzhugh's death, his descendants gave the name of "Ravensworth" (that of the baronial seat) to William's famous tract of 21,996 acres in upper Stafford County.

All this is hardly much ado about nothing, for the question of right to bear arms and the claim of kinship with gentle and noble families is part of the colonial planter tradition which has come down to us. That the Fitzhughs were entitled to arms, as many another family in trade was, is without question. There is nothing among the fragmentary records of Oxford and Cambridge to indicate that he attended those universities, nor among the remaining lists of the Inns of Court to suggest that he studied law at one of them. Yet by the age of twenty-five he was an established lawyer and member of the colonial parliament, and by the age of twenty-eight (when he wrote his first surviving letter) he possessed a depth of legal learning and dignity of epistolary style which hardly came entirely from self-training. He could have studied his law in the office of some mature and perhaps distinguished English barrister, as he could have done in Virginia down into the twentieth century. And he could have received the bases of his liberal education in the classical grammar school at Bedford. Certainly he received both before he came to America.

Though it has been stated several times that William Fitzhugh arrived in Virginia in 1670 or 1671, the first documentary record of his presence in the colony which has been located is a power of attorney granted him by his future mother-in-law Rose Gerard dated February 25,

---

4. See copy in Virginia Historical Society; listed in Charles Dexter Allen, *American Book Plates* (New York, 1896), p. 203. See also 7 V 196 ff.; ltr. to Henry Fitzhugh, January 30, 1686/87, note 2.

5. See ltr. to Henry Fitzhugh, January 30, 1686/87, note 2.

1673/74.[6] Whether anything other than a younger son's desire to try his fortune in a new environment, combined with the other attractions of Virginia noted above, brought him to the colony, one cannot now say. His sister Margaret, who died in Virginia in 1676 and left a daughter behind, may have been with her unidentified husband the personal means of bringing him to the colony. By 1685 he wrote that "I have lived a long time in a strange land, strugled hard with fortune's adverse hand, but thank God in the end, by God Almighty's blessing upon my mean endeavours, (having no friend or relative to lend a helping hand), have overcome...." Elsewhere he states that his sister lived "poorly." In other words, he did feel that he had made his own way. It is perhaps more than coincidental, however, that he settled in the Westmoreland-Stafford area, where at least two of the most prominent citizens, Dr. Edward Helder, the physician, and Nicholas Spencer, the Virginia Secretary of State, were Bedfordshire men who would have known his family at home. Spencer was to be a friend and adviser up to the time of his death in 1689. Helder, who died in 1678 before the period of Fitzhugh's letters, may also have had a personal relationship with the younger man.

That he had arrived with money in his pocket is probable from his early land acquisitions, though these may have come through his marriage. And the fact that he was surprised at the economic hardships which his mother and sister suffered when he renewed contact with his family in 1686 may imply that when William left home they were in at least comfortable circumstances. None of this answers the question as to why he did not communicate with his family for fifteen years, and then with every show of interest and affection.

But to turn to the marriage. On August 26, 1674, six months after he became her attorney, Rose Gerard settled property on William Fitzhugh in recognition of his marriage contract to her daughter Sarah Tucker and entered the settlement in the Westmoreland County records.[7] Thus at the age of twenty-three he was established in the Northern Neck of Virginia, the Proprietary located between the Rappahannock and Potomac rivers, and married into one of the settled and prominent families of the region. Fitzhugh probably lived first in the somewhat older and more settled Westmoreland before he built a home for himself and his bride in adjacent frontier Stafford. But the Stafford records for the period are missing and those of Westmoreland exceedingly fragmentary.

The young immigrant seems to have married an eleven-year-old girl,

6. 40 V 187-204.
7. *Westmoreland County Deeds, Patents, etc., 1665-1677*, folios 177 and 200.

for records indicate that Sarah Tucker was born August 2, 1663. Family tradition insists that the young husband sent his wife to England for two years of education before the marriage should be consummated.[8] This may well be true, though it would seem strange that there was no effort made for her to become acquainted with the English Fitzhughs while she was there. But in 1674 young Fitzhugh was marrying the elder daughter of the already twice-married Rose Tucker Gerard (whose third husband was soon to be, in March, 1676/77, John Newton),[9] a wealthy woman with good family connections in both Virginia and Maryland. In the marriage settlement William Fitzhugh received a Negro man and woman, three cows, six ewes and a ram, a number of hogs, a bay gelding, a necklace of pearls, and enough dishes, household furniture and kitchen equipment to set up housekeeping at once. Probably Mrs. Gerard was turning over to them half the personal estate of her first husband John Tucker, for Sarah and her younger sister Rose were her only children by this marriage. Even if Fitzhugh had nothing, which is hardly likely, he and his wife would start out with more worldly possessions than the average planter's family did. And Sarah had been left in the will of her father 5,000 pounds of tobacco and an equal share with other children of his two marriages in the rest of his estate, which she was to come into when she was seventeen.[10]

Two and a half years after the marriage the young lawyer-planter was elected to the Virginia House of Burgesses from Stafford County.[11] During the years between his marriage and this date, his name appears several times in the Westmoreland County records (those of Stafford not surviving probably included similar entries) showing him as attorney for his mother-in-law and for Thomas Mathews and as witness in land suits involving persons whose names appear in his later letters.[12] Probably some time before 1674 he had secured the tracts of land he was always after-

---

8. 1 V 268. Henry R. Eubank (*Touring Historyland: the Authentic Book of Historic Northern Neck of Virginia* . . . [Colonial Beach, Va., 1934], p. 16) tells the two-years-of-education story, but it is also a part of family oral tradition.

9. 36 V 296-97. Rose Newton lived into her eighties. Mr. George H. S. King has seen a family Bible which gives the date of William Fitzhugh's marriage as May 1, 1674.

10. Will of John Tucker, May 5, 1671 (proved May 31, 1671), *Westmoreland County Deeds & Wills, No. 1, 1653-1671;* also 1 V 269. On February 26, 1672/73, Thomas Gerard, Rose's second husband, bestowed on his four Tucker stepchildren (John, Gerard, Sarah, and Rose), to be received on their day of marriage or when eighteen, certain Negroes and cattle, and upon the two girls the "household furniture which did belong to their decd father John Tucker equally divided betwixt ye two daughters." *Westmoreland County Deeds, Patents, etc., 1665-1677,* folio 142.

11. *Journals H.B. 1659/60-1693,* p. ix.

12. *Westmoreland County Deeds, Patents, etc., 1665-1677,* folios 174, 207, 208, 257, etc. The names of Nathaniel Garland, John Gerard, and Samuel Bonum or Bonam are among those appearing. In 1675 he sold two Negroes to his mother-in-law (*Ibid.,* folio 257).

wards to consider his home place.[13] They are situated in Stafford County on the Potomac and touch on Chotank Creek,[14] the parish originally having been called Chotank. Apparently he began with a simple dwelling house of timber, which he added to through the years as he also added other buildings. The plantation is described in detail in one of the letters.

If his young wife did go to England in 1674 for two years of further education, she probably did not remain much over the time planned. For in 1686, Fitzhugh informed his brother Henry of the five "pledges of our conjugall affection" who had already been brought into existence, of whom two, a boy and a girl, were left to him, with another who would soon "come into the world." The living boy, he said, was his eldest son named William, some indication of the age of that child who was to succeed the father in the House of Burgesses of 1700 as Captain William Fitzhugh. But in 1676/77 the first American Fitzhugh was taking his seat in that legislative body, and public life for the family, hereafter rarely far removed from it, was beginning.

FITZHUGH'S PLANTATION LIFE, 1677-1701

Stafford County about 1670 was the sort of region ambitious young immigrants have settled in during most of our national history. The county had just been formed in 1664 from Westmoreland, which in turn had been separated from Northumberland only the year before. Stafford's northern and western borders were undetermined. They extended a vast distance into the interior of the continent. The whole of the neck of land between the two great rivers Rappahannock and Potomac was all relatively frontier country, for even Northumberland, the parent county, had been organized as recently as 1648. In 1673 this great territory called the Northern Neck contained six counties including, besides the three just mentioned, Lancaster, Middlesex, and Rappahannock, the last broken up into more counties in 1692. In all these shires Fitzhugh was to be engaged actively in legal practice and land speculation for the rest of his life.

The lower and eastern parts of this territory were easily available to water-borne commerce. The two major rivers and dozens of their tributaries afforded access to seagoing vessels or at least to the more shallow sloops. Even the upper reaches of the two great rivers were accessible to, though not so frequently visited by, British ships. They were less thickly populated. Along the river banks, spaced according to the amount of adjacent land their owners had acquired, were the great houses

---

13. Stafford records are missing for this period. Means and manner of securing the property must therefore remain unknown.

14. Eubank, *Touring Historyland*, p. 16.

of the leading gentry and occasionally the simpler dwellings of the small farmers. Though these small farmers were in the great majority, because their property was inland, or more often because they did not have wharves of their own, most of their crops exported and materials imported were handled at the seats of the larger landholders.

For, as Louis B. Wright has illustrated so clearly,[15] by this last quarter of the seventeenth century there was not only a landed gentry in Virginia, but a distinguished section of that gentry had established itself in this newer portion of the colony. Fitzhugh had among his friends, colleagues, and clients the large-scale planters Robert Beverley, Ralph Wormeley, and Christopher Robinson of Middlesex; Isaac Allerton, Richard Lee, Nicholas Spencer, and William Hardwick of Westmoreland; Thomas Mathew(s) and Leonard Howson of Northumberland; and Arthur Spicer of Rappahannock. In his own county were the two George Masons, George Brent, James Ashton, Samuel Hayward, Martin Scarlet, Thomas Ousley, and Thomas Youle, among others. All these men were at some time burgesses, sheriffs, county clerks, justices of the peace, militia officers, or customs officials, frequently holding several offices at the same time. Even the obstreperous clergyman John Waugh dabbled in land speculation and got himself elected to the House of Burgesses, though he was never allowed to serve.

Fitzhugh and his neighbors had friends too in the counties of York and Gloucester just south of the Rappahannock, men like John Buckner and Robert Peyton. And because they had frequently to visit the colonial capital, Jamestown gentlemen like Philip Ludwell, Edward Chilton, Henry Hartwell, and Thomas Clayton were a part of their society and returned their visits. Across the Potomac in Maryland they had close friends and alliances by marriage. Fitzhugh's law partner George Brent married as his second wife the stepdaughter of Lord Baltimore. William Digges and Samuel Chew were well-known names in the history of both Maryland and Virginia. Kenelm Chiseldine, sometime Maryland Attorney-General, had married a stepdaughter of Fitzhugh's mother-in-law, and Nehemiah Blakiston, Chief Justice of Maryland, married Mrs. Chiseldine's sister. These Maryland friends lived closer to the Stafford County people than did any Virginians from south of the Rappahannock.

Most of these landed proprietors were fairly well-educated sons, often younger sons, of English professional men, farmers or lesser country gentry, and merchants, with here and there the son of a knight or baronet like Robert Peyton, and more rarely a knight himself. Before they died most of them held military titles through their commissions in the colonial

15. In *The First Gentlemen of Virginia* (San Marino, 1940) and others of his writings.

militia. Many of them signed indifferently after their surnames the suffix "gentleman" or "merchant." For they had not then developed the later southern agrarian disdain for trade. And they actually were engaged in commerce of varying kinds, from "storekeeping" to gristmill operation to cargo-commissioning. Some of them were sons or brothers of ship captains who traded in the Chesapeake, and an appreciable number, including Fitzhugh's stepfather-in-law, John Newton, had been master mariners themselves. Some of them were second-generation, a few third-generation Americans, but most had been born in England. Some, like Fitzhugh's friend Ralph Wormeley, had been students at Oxford or Cambridge or the Inns of Court. Most of them probably had a classical grammar-school education such as we may assume Fitzhugh had. Even in this new land education counted for something.

It has been estimated that the whole of Fitzhugh's county of Stafford, even as late as 1724, hardly contained more people than the average Virginia county seat in our day.[16] Yet Stafford then included territory since divided into Prince William, Fairfax, Fauquier, Arlington, and (in part) King George. In pattern it was probably much like American frontier communities have been almost up to our own time, with relative concentrations of population in the older and eastern portions, defenses against and alarms of enemies such as Indians along the western borders, subsistence primarily of its own production, and the majority of its people plain, hardworking, a mixture of the restless and the ambitious, thinly spread out, and generally isolated from their neighbors. But the pattern is not entirely a typical one. These people were more purely English in origin than most pioneer communities later would be. Then because of their relative proximity anywhere in the county or whole Northern Neck to deep water, they were not nearly so isolated from their neighbors, their capital, or Europe as later frontier groups would be. Finally, almost from the beginning certain persons acquired extensive acreage and engaged in large-scale agricultural operations that produced, more quickly than was to be usually the case later, a clearly recognizable well-to-do class.

Perhaps Fitzhugh's description of his home plantation in his letter to Dr. Ralph Smith of April 22, 1686, a description admittedly designed to attract an English buyer, is the best surviving outline of a seventeenth-century plantation we have. Considering that the owner was at the time a prosperous man, but by no means the wealthiest man of his region, one

---

16. "Tithables" in Stafford in 1692 were 317; in 1698, 679; in 1699, 708. "Tithables" were all males of sixteen years and upwards, and all Negro, mulatto, and Indian women of sixteen and more who were not free. Harrison, *Landmarks*, I, 121 ff.

may add to or deduct from this picture to visualize almost any plantation of the period: a thousand-acre tract seven-tenths wooded and the remainder fertile, arable land; three units of "quarters" for the Negroes equipped with all necessary houses, fences, and livestock; a thirteen-room main dwelling containing four large rooms hung with tapestries, nine in all well furnished; this and all smaller "dependent" houses equipped with good brick chimneys; four good cellars, the deep-freezes of the period; a dairy, a dovecote, a stable, a barn, a henhouse, a kitchen, all rather new; nearby an orchard of twenty-five hundred apple trees enclosed entirely with a locust fence; a fenced one-hundred-foot-square garden, and a great palisadoed (perhaps as a protection against Indians) yard enclosing most of the dependencies; also cattle, hogs, sheep, horses, and household servants; about a mile and a half away a gristmill that more than paid its own way; and two storehouses of food and textiles and farm equipment enough to last for two or three years.

What Fitzhugh does not mention are the indentured white servants, many of them skilled artisans, and perhaps the valuable bluecoat schoolboy who could keep accounts. When he died Fitzhugh had six men and an old woman in this status. One of the indentured servants was his own cousin, a not unusual practice among those who could afford to pay the passages over of indigent or mettlesome young kinsmen. Other servants mentioned in his will are a carpenter and a glazier, men undoubtedly hired out to his neighbors when he did not need their services. A fourth bondservant, John Nicholson, was one of the witnesses signing Fitzhugh's will.

So was situated a thirty-five year old planter who had made his own way in the new land for fifteen years. He desired then and later to return to England. He was always a little homesick, apparently after his renewed contact with his English kin in 1686 in accentuated degree. As he explained to Nicholas Hayward (January 30, 1686/87) "Our Estates here depend altogether upon Contingencyes, & to prepare against that, causes me to exceed my inclinations in worldly affairs, & Society that is good & ingenious is very scarce, and seldom to be come at except in books. Good Education of children is almost impossible, & better never be born than ill bred, but that which bears the greatest weight with me, for now I look upon my self to be in my declining age, is the want of spiritual help & comforts, of which this fertile country is every thing else, is barren and unfruitfull, which last Consideration bears the greatest weight in my desires of Exchange & removal. . . ."

Contingencies did continue to keep him at worldly affairs, and steadily he added to the worldly possessions which were his at this time.

Charged against his tobacco credits with Bristol and London and Liver-pool merchants were necessities of life and luxuries of gracious living. For plantation operation he ordered cart wheels, harnesses, saddles, two stills, a pewter cistern, cider "racks," and smaller things such as stone jugs and nails. For the great house he wanted tapestries, leather hangings, beds and bed furniture, curtains and valances, matching chairs, leather and Turkey carpets, dressing boxes, diamond-shaped leaded panes for his windows, iron and brass andirons, iron backs for chimneys, an escritoire, picture frames, and a large looking glass. Of gastronomic and potable com-forts he particularly wanted spice, fruit, sugar, Gloucestershire cheese, and cases of claret. For his wife and himself he ordered clothing of many kinds, including in his last years a black crepe gown and petticoat and pair of gallooned shoes for her and a calico quilted morning gown, winter and summer suits, and two Carolina hats for himself. Over a period of years he tried to secure a vehicle known as a callash. Soon after he finally secured it he had to order new gears, but it is one of the two coaches mentioned in his will.

But what Fitzhugh was most interested in importing after 1687 for his household was silverware. Perhaps by this time he despaired of selling out with credit and returning to England. Certainly he was growing more and more prosperous. Silver, he thought, was a good investment for him and for his children; moreover, among distinguished guests at table it would make the proper impression. From 1687 to his last letters of 1698 he ordered candlesticks, snuffers, saltcellars, "basons," forks, (silver hafted) knives, castors, various sizes of spoons, porringers, bread plates, serving plates, chafing dishes, sugar bowls, and ladles, all to be engraved with his arms or crest, though in the last years he had a man among his servants who could do the engraving. In a codicil to his will he mentions more silver which he brought out of England with him, probably on a voyage made the year before he died and not on his first arrival. By this will his wife and children divided the silver, and several pieces have come down to our time. In Fitzhugh's time it must have on many occasions made a brave display. The reader will note that one newly arrived ship-ment was all brought forth on the occasion of Lieutenant Governor Francis Nicholson's visit to his estate in 1690, when that official and his company "first hansell'd it." [17]

So William Fitzhugh provided against the turns of that fickle wheel of Fortune and made himself more and more comfortable. More impor-tant than material comforts, he had said, was the lack of a congenial society of thoughtful men, a lack for which only good books could begin

17. To N. Hayward, July 10, 1690.

to compensate. Thus over the years he ordered a variety of volumes, from those concerned with his legal profession on to history and philosophy and chemistry and the classics. But he also said that the deepest source of his dissatisfaction with life in the colony was the lack of spiritual comfort. Though there seems to have been a church on or near his home, it was frequently, perhaps most of the time, without a clergyman. Several times Fitzhugh begged English assistance in securing a sober and learned man for his parish. One of the two men most troublesome to him in Stafford was the Whiggish Anglican minister John Waugh who, Fitzhugh felt, had disgraced his cloth. The absence of a good parson he felt keenly. An ideal society, or indeed any decent society, would never be complete without one.

Yet even thus early the amenities of social life were observed as they perhaps were not in most colonies. At General Assembly and General Court time in Jamestown, Fitzhugh consorted with his fellow lawyers and their wives, with his fellow burgesses, and with the Governor and Council, sometimes drinking a little too much, as he confesses in one letter. On his rounds of the Northern Neck courthouses, he saw a great deal of the families of other country gentlemen, and even in Gloucester and York he had intimate acquaintances. At home he frequently drank more than he liked when he negotiated a contract or land purchase with a client or neighbor, or friend from across the Potomac in Maryland. And every ship departing with a cargo of tobacco had to be sped on its way by a round of toasts with the embarking captain.

Perhaps the most attractive picture of the lighter side of Fitzhugh's life is contained in the travel account of the Frenchman Durand, who stayed in the Chesapeake country from September, 1686, to the middle of March, 1687. Durand, a Huguenot gentleman who traveled with his valet, was partially motivated by a desire to find suitable land on which his religious compatriots might settle. After spending some weeks in the Hampton Roads area, on December 17 he started northwest toward the Potomac. At "Rosegill," where Governor Effingham was living and meeting with his Council at the time, and at "Port Tabago," both estates of Ralph Wormeley, he was graciously entertained. The "Parliament" (Council) was at "Rosegill," and there he saw "fine-looking men, sitting in judgment booted and with belted sword." He was amazed that people of quality should handle money. For after supper these gentlemen began gambling and were still at it the next morning when the Frenchman awoke. Durand was most impressed by four men he met—Governor Effingham, a young baronet incognito whose real name was Sir Robert Parker, and two famous Virginians, Wormeley and Fitzhugh. Parker, a liberal

Catholic, wanted to spend Christmas among his co-religionists in Maryland. In a holiday spirit most of the gentlemen present at "Rosegill" decided to accompany him, and two days before Christmas they rode on to "Colonel Fichoux, whose houses stand along the banks of the great Pethomack river." Durand's account of their reception is the only one known of this side of Fitzhugh's social life. The good colonel's sour comment later covering Durand's book in a letter to Nicholas Hayward may at first glance seem churlish, for Durand is warm in his admiration for the master of "Eagle's Nest." But one should remember that Fitzhugh was agreeing complaisantly at the moment with Hayward, whose projected asylum for Huguenots in Stafford County was not reported on with quite the warm approval shown Fitzhugh, though Durand's book generally was designed to attract Huguenots to Virginia.

... so we rode twenty strong to Colonel Fichous', but he has such a large establishment that he did not mind. We were all of us provided with beds, one for two men. He treated us royally, there was good wine & all kinds of beverages, so there was a great deal of carousing. He had sent for three fiddlers, a jester, a tight-rope dancer, an acrobat who tumbled around, & they gave us all the entertainment one could wish for. It was very cold, yet no one ever thinks of going near the fire, for they never put less than a cartload of wood in the fireplace & the whole room is kept warm. ... The next day, after they had caroused until after noon, we decided to cross this river. The Colonel had a quantity of wine & one of his punch-bowls brought down to the shore; he lent us his boat.[18]

TOBACCO PLANTER AND BUSINESSMAN

The more than easy circumstances indicated by the accommodations for twenty guests, the flowing bowl, and the gleaming silver had been earned by hard work and clever management. No one can read Fitzhugh's letters without realizing that here was a busy, practical man, not the leisurely lord of a transposed English manor. Fitzhugh was active in many things that brought him income, including his avowed profession of law, but he spent the greater part of his time in growing and selling tobacco and in the enterprises that were the concomitants of that industry, the acquiring of land, the securing of labor, the bargaining for incoming cargoes of English goods. For tobacco was almost the only path to real wealth in seventeenth-century Virginia, and then by no means a sure path.

18. Gilbert Chinard, ed., *A Huguenot Exile in Virginia; or, Voyages of a Frenchman exiled for His Religion with a Description of Virginia & Maryland* (From the Hague Edition of 1687; New York, 1934), p. 158. The book includes as an appendix Hayward's come-hither pamphlet "Propositions for Virginia" concerning Brent Town tract.

Colonial administrators and governing bodies at home in England had in the first decades of the century tried to encourage the planters to grow "the staple commodities" and develop silk culture and other industries. But by 1685 not only had the King and Governor officially given up this attempt to diversify the economy; they were bent upon making this single crop profitable to England. Long before this time the colonists had fought for the freedom of a world market, for they realized by the beginning of the Restoration that the only hope of the maintenance of prosperity in the tobacco industry was to expand markets beyond the British Isles. The Lords of Trade and Plantations, the British merchants, and the King had united in what seems now a blind selfishness in refusing to permit the colony to sell directly to foreign nations. The result was that, as the cleared lands grew in number around the shores of the bay, tobacco was grown in such quantities that it was a glut on the English market, and large- and small-scale grower alike often found himself in desperate circumstances. When he asked for a cessation or at least voluntary curtailment of planting, he was refused because the home government and merchants feared they would lose by this arrangement more than by lowered prices. Fitzhugh quite clearly favored this cessation in the period from 1680 to 1682 and was considerably involved in the consequences of a rebellious group's plant-cutting. For he was Robert Beverley's attorney when Beverley was jailed and charged as the suspected ringleader in the movement. But more of this later.

The largest number of Fitzhugh's letters addressed to any group are those to the merchants who handled his shipments of tobacco and to the captains of their ships. To John Cooper, his London factor, Fitzhugh wrote from 1681 to his last letters of 1698, discussing the quantity and quality of his hogsheads of tobacco, his credit balance, and the purchase of all sorts of goods to be sent to him. To his London friend and agent the notary Nicholas Hayward he also addressed many letters concerning the tobacco, the prices, and potential markets. To several other London merchants, to Bristol merchants such as George Mason, to merchants in Liverpool and Belfast and Lyme Regis, he addressed himself. To ship captains from all these ports and others he wrote, sometimes addressing them at places along the Chesapeake and sometimes at their home ports in England. Many became in the course of years his personal friends. He drank with dozens more. These letters, with those of William Byrd I, reveal much of what is known about the Virginia tobacco trade in this period.

It is clear that Fitzhugh considered his lands good for the most popular kinds of tobacco, both Oronoco and Sweet-scented, though Stafford was generally considered as being in the Oronoco belt.[19] He himself, like most of his contemporaries, thought Sweet-scented the better tobacco but because of the nature of his soils cultivated both. In the earliest years he was shipping from his home plantation. Later he added tobacco from one of the plantations he owned up the river, probably from what came to be called "Ravensworth."

Because of his absorption in large-scale tobacco growing, Fitzhugh developed one of the first slave-labor-operated plantations of Stafford. Actually the kind of operation he conducted from the beginning was more like what his neighbors in the older county of Westmoreland were doing. We know from the surviving Stafford record books that there were few Negro servants among the farmers of that county.[20] His extensive operation demanded this kind of labor to be profitable and was profitable because this kind of labor was secured.

Overproduction, underproduction occasioned by drought, inter-colonial competitions, all of these affected the Chesapeake planters as they have always affected the agriculturist. Fitzhugh followed the habit of growing tobacco in newly cleared land and then developing more land as the old wore out, a habit the Reverend John Clayton in this same period tried to do something about by suggesting manures, draining of fertile swamps, and other husbanding processes.[21] This wasteful system accounts of course for Fitzhugh's and his friends' voracious land acquisitiveness: they looked forward not only to their immediate futures but to the futures of their numerous progeny.

Methods and habits of shipment are made evident in these letters. Sometimes the planter filled a whole ship, but more often he divided his tobacco into groups of from six to thirty hogsheads sent by different vessels: This was not so much from fear of possible wreckage and loss as from hopes of getting more return from the divided cargo. When he sent a few hogsheads to a new merchant, he was usually experimenting to see what prices he could get. It is no wonder that Fitzhugh felt that financial well-being in the New World depended too much upon contingencies. Yet he prospered steadily and laid the foundations for the prosperity of his five sons.

Fitzhugh and his immediate neighbors had some special problems as well as those they shared with the rest of the colony. The upper branch of the Potomac, farthest away of all navigable streams from the mouth of

19. Hugh Jones, The Present State of Virginia, ed. Richard L. Morton (Chapel Hill, 1956), p. 198; 48 V 141-153; Bruce, Ec. Hist. Va., I, passim.
20. Harrison, Landmarks, I, 168-69.
21. Bruce, Ec. Hist. Va., I, 432-34.

the bay and least thickly populated along the banks, received the least number of ships.[22] Fitzhugh often had to send to York or Gloucester to ask a friend to buy him some likely Negroes before they were all picked over, as they surely would be before the ships arrived in his neighborhood, if they ever did arrive there. And the Stafford County people frequently had to have their casks loaded on sloops and carried to central points, sometimes on the lower Maryland shore, to be taken aboard the seagoing vessels. This was expensive, hard on the tobacco, and not always satisfactory for bargaining. Then too it meant that incoming shiploads of trade goods such as household necessities rarely even came into the river. When they did, the captains or supercargoes asked high prices because they had to spend great amounts of time going slowly from one planter's wharf to another. Again and again Fitzhugh proposed to English merchants and ship captains ways of remedying the situation, and his proposals were of such a nature that he would have made a neat profit if they had been accepted. He proposed at various times to John Cooper and others to gather casks of tobacco at central points, presumably his own wharves, and exchange them for complete cargoes of storekeeper's goods, which he would sell on commission or under some other agreement. This would reduce the costly months the ships usually spent in disposing of manufactured goods and in gathering tobacco. On at least one occasion Fitzhugh offered "Dutch trades" to Liverpool merchants, shipload of tobacco for shipload of goods. Another time he wrote his English correspondents inquiring for men interested in setting up in one of the proposed "trade towns"—central points for exporting and importing—which the Governor and home government, against the wishes of the English merchants, several times tried to establish.

Fitzhugh persuaded some of his neighbors to ship through his favorite captains, for he mentions to certain merchants that George Mason or Samuel Hayward or George Brent will probably or positively consign their tobacco with his the following season. He himself bought up tobacco from the small growers around him or at least handled it for them, probably partly because they lacked wharves. He often speaks of certain tobaccos as his own, with the clear implication that much of what he sent abroad had not been grown by him. Or he may sometimes have

22. Governor Nicholson to Commissioners of the Customs, August, 1700, *Cal. St. Papers, Col., Am. & W.I., 1700,* p. 499, and Harrison, *Landmarks,* I, 121. In Henry E. Huntington Library, Blathwayt Papers, Box IV, is a 1698 "List of Ships & Vessels which have Entered & cleared in ye Upper District of Potomack River from ye 25 March 1697 to ye 25 March 1698." This list, signed by Richard Lee as Collector of the Customs, contains the names of only nine ships, of which four acknowledge Bristol as their home port, one London, one "Exon," one Bidiford, one New England, and one Newport, Rhode Island.

bought up tobacco late in the autumn to speculate with the next season. Occasionally he disposed of his leaf in Westmoreland, probably to some planter who was getting together a shipload there, or possibly to Scots merchants who may have partially processed their purchases in the colony. Most of the tobacco he shipped was already stemmed, for at least once he mentions as unusual a pair of hogsheads containing unstemmed leaf.

Tobacco led Fitzhugh and others of the large planters into commission-merchant and storekeeping work, as his proposals to English firms suggest. Though the early merchants had sent supercargoes with their ships to Virginia, by the later seventeenth century they entrusted most of the buying to the ship captains themselves. This frequently meant an agent in the colony, and in his double capacity as lawyer and planter Fitzhugh appears to have acted for certain merchants. Though this agency may have been fairly profitable, it probably formed only a minute part of his income. The British merchant, who had discouraged the setting up of towns, preferred the direct producer-disposer relationship by which the leaf went directly from farmer to English warehouse. In other words, he gave as little middleman profit as he could. Incidentally, all this does much towards explaining why towns failed to develop in the Chesapeake country.

Other facets of the situation are evident in these letters. The frequent lack of sufficient ship space is attested to by both Fitzhugh and the Byrds.[23] It is clear that a tobacco factor in London was inspired to be most pleasant in his relations with a planter who kept a good balance as Fitzhugh did. Also it is evident that the factor occasionally thought the orders of his planter too extravagant and refused or neglected to comply with them. Fitzhugh's sharp rebuke to Cooper for exceeding his authority in not shipping certain items is a case in point. Again, these letters afford evidence that by this period the larger tobacco plantation demanded, not simply preferred, Negro slave labor to white indentured labor; the latter in such establishments was reserved for household or skilled-artisan employments.

The county records of the Northern Neck contain many entries of Fitzhugh's purchase and sale of tracts of land, more often purchase than sale. Most of this activity was in Stafford and Westmoreland, but in 1691/92, for example, he acquired a great many tracts in Richmond County, newly formed from Rappahannock. And there are other entries. Some purchases were probably pure speculation. Others he held on to

---

23. J. S. Bassett, "The Relation between the Virginia Planter and the London Merchant," *Annual Report of the American Historical Association for the Year 1901* (Washington, 1902), I, 568.

and tried to enlarge by acquiring neighboring tracts. One thing he wanted to do was enlarge his home place, and he was disappointed when his friend Nicholas Hayward in England purchased the Ashton plantation adjacent from the English heir. In 1683 he proposed to buy the whole of his own parish from Lord Culpeper, the Proprietor of the Northern Neck as well as the Virginia Governor at the time. In 1689 he offered to purchase one hundred thousand acres of the Northern Neck Proprietary through the agent, his neighbor and friend Nicholas Spencer. Though he never suceeded in securing one of these gigantic tracts, in attempting to secure them he was anticipating the kind of land speculation which went on in the next century. After 1693, when he and George Brent were themselves the Proprietary agents, he was especially busy having lands confirmed to himself. Fitzhugh bought from all sorts of people, including his old enemy Parson Waugh and several small farmers, tracts of a few hundred or a thousand or twelve hundred acres.[24] Those he wanted to hold and did hold are listed in the deeds to his children in 1700 and 1701 and in his will. In some instances he bought land in partnership, as a letter of 1679, his own will, and the will of his stepfather-in-law John Newton attest.

Fitzhugh was always interested in the possible mineral values of his lands, read all he could on geology and ores, and sent specimens of what he found to England to be assayed. From his forest wealth he had pipe staves and walnut plank made to export to England.

How much sense of disinterested public service, and how much business acumen, entered into his undertaking to supply provisions for the Potomac River garrison is difficult now to determine. In 1681 he and his law partner George Brent appeared before the council and offered "to provide and furnish Potomk Garison with provision . . . rather than the Garrison should be unprovided of men, to supply the said Fort with provisions as aforesaid. . . ."[25] This fort was the outpost against the Indians for their own territory, corresponding to similar strongholds on the Rappahannock and other rivers. Tobacco was levied on all tithables in the whole colony to support these frontier garrisons. Brent and Fitzhugh received considerable sums of the leaf from all the Northern Neck counties and even counties as far away as Nansemond, Gloucester, and Accomac, and Northampton.[26] All of it added up to hundreds of thousands of pounds of tobacco. That the whole thing should become involved

---

24. For example, Beverley Fleet, *Va. Col. Abstracts, Richmond County, 1692-1704* (Richmond [1942]), XVI, 4, 9, 10, 60, 65, etc.
25. *Exec. Journ. Council Col. Va.*, I, 14.
26. *Journals H.B. 1659/60-1693*, pp. 171, 178, 181, 182, 183.

in politics and Fitzhugh be accused of claiming too much tobacco is not surprising. But this is part of another side of Fitzhugh.

The letters reflect Fitzhugh as businessman in yet another way. Those especially to Nicholas Hayward are full of listings of the bills of exchange drawn by various colonists, usually for fairly small amounts, which Fitzhugh sent to his English agents to deposit to his account or used within the colony as payment for Negroes or other merchandise. Some of the bills came to the colonists, including Fitzhugh, from English factors. They were payable in coin in England, but the currency rarely found its way back to the colonists. The names on many of these bills, of drawer and drawee, are interesting because they designate with whom he did business or for whom he acted as attorney. Even those bills for which he was not payee and which came to him probably through several hands are often of some historical interest because of the names they bear. For another thing, they indicate that a very considerable number of people in Virginia fattened on, or at least were kept alive by, their tobacco exports.[27]

LAWYER

Much of Fitzhugh's fame as well as a substantial portion of his fortune came first from his abilities as a lawyer. Though we can only guess as to the exact nature and place of his legal training, by the time of his earliest extant letter of 1679 he was sought by several kinds of colonists as an expert in the field. Perhaps too his even earlier election in 1676 to the House of Burgesses reflects a considerable legal reputation. As noted above, by February, 1673/74, he was already attorney for Thomas Mathews, the son and brother of two most distinguished colonial Virginians, and for his wealthy future mother-in-law. In public and private causes he was to continue to enhance this reputation until his death.

Fitzhugh's very first letters give legal counsel to great planters like Richard Lee II and Ralph Wormeley, and to brother lawyers like William Sherwood, Robert Beverley, and Thomas Clayton. For the next six or seven years he wrote to these men and others of their kind, usually concerning specific cases, but displaying considerable legal erudition. He could cite precedent after precedent, quote a wide array of authorities, and then theorize as to the general principle involved or conclude as to the specific case. Always he had much to say on the place of English common law in Virginia legal practice. These early letters now give the feeling of deliberate attempts to impress, to show these planters who knew

27. Bruce, *Ec. Hist. Va.*, II, 516-20.

some law themselves, and the lawyer-planters who were his colleagues, that their young fellow-colonist knew a great deal. Certainly he was successful in this, for in private cases Virginia secretaries of state and governors sought his advice, and in the General Assembly his interpretations of the law were listened to with the deepest respect. Eventually he was to be chairman of the committee for revisal of all of the colony's laws.

Actually, as notes on the letters below will indicate, Fitzhugh's citations from varied and ancient sources can be traced almost without exception to legal works that must have been familiar to all his colleagues—the *Statutes at Large* and Sir Robert Coke's *Reports* and *Institutes*. Fitzhugh's citations of Bracton, Britton, Dyer, Fleta, and Keilwey can be traced usually to the margins of Coke or the *Statutes,* not at all necessarily to the original works, though he may have owned several of the latter. What is more impressive today than the variety of his citations, and it also must have been impressive to his contemporaries as well, is the ability to locate historical precedents and authorities and weave them into a logical and convincing pattern of legal argument.

It has been said that Fitzhugh made his name in Virginia when he acted as counsel for his friend and fellow-barrister Robert Beverley in the plant-cutting and Assembly-records case, which extended over a considerable period from 1682 to 1684/85. To Beverley, at various times prisoner, free on bond at his home, and at large by escaping his jailors, Fitzhugh wrote long comprehensive surveys of the whole history and principle of individual liberty and of *habeas corpus,* which he invoked for Beverley but apparently never obtained by writ. As attorney for Wormeley in a great land case, as legal adviser to Madam Sarah Bland, of England, in a long-drawn-out and complex suit regarding her once-confiscated properties in Virginia, as agent for Lord Culpeper in the sale of the Brent Town tract, Fitzhugh was acting for the leading colonists of his time. His "Traverse of an Escheat" in the Wormeley case of 1684 (included with a letter on the subject below) is a good example of his abilities in enormously complicated argument supported by legal learning. He theorized on divorce laws in behalf of his mistreated Maryland sister-in-law, he was executor for the extensive Ashton estate involving English heirs, he was agent for a Lyme merchant in recovering tobacco due. His instructions of June 5, 1682, to John Withers as to a projected journey through the Northern Neck to collect legal fees owed and transact some other business, are illustrative of the quality of his clientele, for the names of Fantleroy, Buckner, Robinson, Walker, and Peyton were already distinguished in Virginia. That his practice was not confined to such people is indicated by lesser-known names in these instructions, and even more by the deed, will, and court records of these counties which show Fitzhugh as attorney for many humbler folk.[28]

During at least a large part of his professional career Fitzhugh had a law partner, the influential Roman Catholic George Brent. They acted both independently and together. That Brent was a very able barrister is indicated by his appointment at one time to the post of Attorney-General for the colony and perhaps by the fact that he too was at times a burgess. Together the two became in 1693 the resident agents for the Culpeper heirs and Lord Fairfax in the Northern Neck Proprietary, perhaps the ultimate compliment to their legal abilities.

Though the extent of Fitzhugh's practice in later years shows that he had become a good courtroom attorney, his early letter in which he tells Wormeley that he is glad that the latter has employed Beverley as Fitzhugh's aide in a case, glad because Beverley is so well versed in the practical side of legal practice in Virginia, points up what perhaps was always Fitzhugh's forte, his scholarly knowledge of the law and his ability to formulate law and legal principle on historical precedent. The French and Latin of the hoary annals of jurisprudence he cites frequently, and he always worked on the assumption that the common law was "only to be learned out of ancient authors (for out of the old fields must come the new corn) contrary to the opinion of the generality of our judges and practicers of the law here." In his career as burgess this historical perspective was one of the things which was to distinguish him.

BURGESS AND POLITICIAN

Fitzhugh's activities in the colonial legislative assembly receive relatively little attention in his letters. Yet a full comprehension of what he says in these letters can come only from some knowledge of the details of his legislative career. These details are fortunately available in the records of the House of Burgesses already published and in the additions in manuscript in the Effingham (Lord Monson) Papers recently deposited in the Library of Congress.[29] These records show that between 1677 and the end of 1693 Fitzhugh was burgess in several sessions and that he grew steadily

---

28. See, *e.g.*, *Stafford County Court Order Book*, 46 V 131-33; 47 V 23-26, 342-45, and other Stafford and Northern Neck Deed and Will Books (photostats in Virginia State Library): *e.g.*, *Westmoreland County Court Order Book, 1675/6-1688/9* and *Stafford County Microfilm Reel 5*.

29. H. R. McIlwaine edited several volumes of the *Journals of the Virginia House of Burgesses*, including the two pertaining to Fitzhugh. The Effingham Papers, the property of Lord Monson, now in the Library of Congress, include copies of records of the burgesses, Council, and administrative offices retained by Lord Effingham for the years of his administration. Many items have not been published.

in influence and prestige. And these records form also another of the explanations of the later high quality of personnel and of legislation in the Revolutionary period. The tradition was already established.

The Virginia House of Burgesses, the Commons branch of the General Assembly, the oldest representative legislative body of English-speaking America, had been established in 1619. It had a long history of constructive law making and of struggle to maintain and secure rights against the Governor and Council on the one hand and against the King and the Lords of Trade and the Plantations on the other. Just before Fitzhugh first entered the House, it had sat without dissolution for fourteen years, from 1662 until 1676, and had it not been for the troubles culminating in Bacon's Rebellion in the latter year, might have continued in session until Governor Berkeley's death.[30] It had in these long years been on the whole a loyal and almost complaisant body, such as it had not been before and was not to be later. There was a short-lived new Assembly in June, 1676, usually considered a pro-Bacon Assembly, in which Stafford County was represented by Thomas Mathew(s) and George Mason. Both Mathew and Mason were to some extent identified with the Bacon forces.[31] Under the just-arrived Lieutenant Governor Herbert Jeffreys, a new Assembly convened on February 20, 1676/77, showed for the first time the name of William Fitzhugh as the delegate of Stafford County. Though there were by law two burgesses from each shire, frequently there had been only one, and in this instance Fitzhugh's name stands alone. The records are fragmentary, however, and one cannot be positive that the twenty-six-year-old burgess was the sole representative of his county. But he is listed again alone for the October, 1677, and immediately following 1679 sessions, with Martin Scarlet as his county-colleague in the 1680-1682 session, and with George Mason in the 1684 session.[32]

It was not until 1680, when the home government demanded copies of all journals of the Assembly, that the records began to be kept with regularity and in detail. We have therefore at present very little knowledge of what went on at these 1677-1680 sessions.[33] Fitzhugh's first Assembly did repudiate all that had passed at the preceding 1676 session, which as noted above had been considered a pro-Bacon group. Despite orders from Jeffreys and the Commissioners sent to investigate the Rebel-

---

30. Bruce, *Inst. Hist. Va.*, II, 432.
31. W. E. Washburn, *The Governor and the Rebel* (Chapel Hill, 1957), pp. 3-4, 21, 183. Washburn has used some unpublished materials in his account.
32. *Journals H.B. 1659/60-1693*, pp. ix-xi.
33. Washburn, *Governor and Rebel*, states that he intends to publish many new documents of the Rebellion period which may include some of these.

lion, the Assembly followed superseded Governor Berkeley's last rec-
ommendations [34] and finally issued a defiant testimonial to Berkeley's
integrity and impartiality.[35] It was an Assembly of stated county grievances, not all of them pertaining to losses and outrages of the Rebellion
period. Fitzhugh in due course must have presented the grievances of
Stafford, though they do not survive in the detailed record that those of
some other counties do.[36]

In this representative body of the leading men of the colony Fitzhugh
found himself in 1676/77 seated beside planters like Richard Lee II, John
Washington, and Isaac Allerton from neighboring Westmoreland. In
the next several Assemblies he associated with these men and others such
as William Byrd I of Henrico, Edward Hill of James City, Francis Page
of York, William Randolph of Henrico, and his clients John Buckner of
Gloucester and Christopher Robinson of Middlesex, among others. In
1680 Stafford paid him six thousand pounds of tobacco for "Burgesse
Charges," as it did his colleague George Mason.[37] This is all we know of
his first three years as legislator. How he came to be elected we can only
guess. The House included a number of young sons of the established and
well-to-do—William Byrd II and William Fitzhugh, Jr., were to take their
seats just after they attained their majority—but as suggested above there
were also old colonists like Edward Hill and John Buckner and a group
like Byrd I, Lee, and Robinson within ten years of Fitzhugh's own age.
Though the existence of political parties in colonial Virginia has been
emphatically denied by historians, in Stafford at least throughout Fitzhugh's career there seem to have been campaigns for election, and action
within the Assembly, along party lines, or something approaching it. The
two George Masons and Martin Scarlet always seem to have been on the
opposite side of everything from Fitzhugh, George Brent, and perhaps
Samuel Hayward and John Withers, of whom more later. Actually events
within Stafford far more than legislative voting indicate this, as will be
shown. But Fitzhugh's alliance with conservative and royal Stuart interests,
and often with Governor and Council, is suggested if not proved in many
situations. This political bias, if that is what it is, by no means prevented
him from championing on occasion the causes of his humbler constituents,
and of the rights of the Assembly and burgesses in particular against

34. *Ibid.*, pp. 118-20.
35. *Journals H.B. 1659/60-1693*, pp. 79-80.
36. *Ibid.*, p. 89.
37. Va. State Lib., *Stafford County Microfilm Reel 5* and *Stafford County Court, Records,
Deeds, etc., 1680-1681*. Since Scarlet is listed in the *Journals* only for the second session of the
1680-1682 Assembly, this probably means that Mason was burgess in 1680 rather than in 1679.
In either case his holding a seat is not recorded in *Journals H.B. 1659/60-1693*.

executive encroachment in the form of "Instructions" from the Lords of Trade and Plantations.

By June, 1680, after three years and more in the House, William Fitzhugh was beginning to assume a position of some prominence.[38] He was a member of one important committee after another; he was one of two burgesses designated to inform the Governor regarding the House's progress; he was appointed to meet with the Council on urgent joint concerns; thus early he was one of a three-man committee appointed to draw up an amendment to the most important of bills, "An Act for raiseing a publ Revenue &c." He was one of a committee to look into provisions for the soldiers in garrison, interesting in that a year later he became one of the commissioned providers of these provisions. By April, 1682, he was one of the five leading members to accompany the Speaker when he conferred with the Governor, and in the same session he became a member of the most important of all committees, that on Grievances and Propositions, as its junior member. Eleven years later he was to become its chairman.

Two days after his appointment to this last committee he made two speeches, both recorded in full, an unusual proceeding in the journals of the House of Burgesses. They both were spoken to significant questions. For this reason, and perhaps because Fitzhugh had himself written them out, they were spread on the record. The first, concerning the status of laws passed by the Assembly for which no assent from the King had been received, was heard by his colleagues with enthusiastic approval and his recommendation therein—that their status be immediately investigated— was unanimously passed. The second was part of a debate as to whether members of the Council, the upper house, should be added to a committee appointed by the Speaker of the House for "Private Causes," many arguing that in England members of the House of Lords did not sit on Commons' committees. Fitzhugh here brought into use his knowledge of legal and political history and procedure, pointing out that two bodies were alike only as far as their legislative functions were concerned, and that the General Assembly in trying these "Causes" acted in a judicial capacity. He went on to point out that in the latter capacity the English and Virginia bodies were entirely dissimilar, for in England the House of

---

38. *Journals H.B. 1659/60-1693*, pp. 120-39. Fairfax Harrison (*Landmarks*, I, 128 ff.) states that WF was beaten in the 1680 election by Martin Scarlet and that hereafter the two alternated as delegates from Stafford, showing party feeling in their campaigns. Evidence of alternation is not extant in the journals of the burgesses, which show WF present in June, 1680, and in April, 1682, when the second session of the 1680-1682 Assembly convened. Harrison may have had access to some county records not easily available, but his generality about alternation is obviously mistaken.

Lords was the supreme court of the land but in Virginia the General Assembly as a whole was. Thus he was adding to the records another colonial observation of the differences between government in England and America.

By November, 1682, Fitzhugh had moved up from last place to third place on the Grievances-Propositions committee, just below Colonel Isaac Allerton, chairman, and Colonel John Lear.[39] Elected again to the next Assembly, that of 1684, in April of that year he took the oaths and almost immediately was a candidate for the Speakership against the senior member, Colonel Hill.[40] Though he was defeated, his very nomination was a compliment of some significance. In this Assembly he began a practice he continued as long as he was a burgess, that of reading "at the Table" addresses drawn up by the House to be presented to the Governor,[41] and the replies of His Excellency. He also, probably as author or as committee chairman or both, was more often than anyone else the reader of bills reported. By April 26, 1684, his name appears immediately after that of the Grievances-Propositions chairman on the roster of that committee.[42] But on May 9 he was excused from attendance by the House because of "some extraordinary and Emergent Occasion" [43] at his home. He participated no more in the deliberations of the House until nine years later, in 1693.

In 1685 the colony was beginning to reflect the political unrest in England already stirring before the death of Charles II on February 6 of that year. The Whigs, opposed to Catholic James II and emboldened amid the confusion, spoke up in Virginia as well as at home. Whether Whig opposition was the immediate cause of Fitzhugh's defeat for the House in that year we cannot be sure. But his long-time rival and political enemy the Whig Martin Scarlet was elected as one of the two burgesses from Stafford, and the other seat was disputed by Whiggish George Mason [44] and Fitzhugh. Both went to Jamestown and claimed election. After some investigation, perhaps inspired or directed behind the scenes by the already-seated Scarlet, Mason was declared elected and Fitzhugh was told to go home.[45] Fitzhugh's friend John Withers, then sheriff, was repri-

---

39. Effingham Papers, L.C.
40. *Journals H.B. 1659/60-1693*, p. 188. April 17.
41. *Ibid.*, p. 192, and Effingham Papers, L.C., April 18, 1684.
42. *Journals H.B. 1659/60-1693*, p. 202.
43. *Ibid.*, p. 218.
44. Family tradition says George Mason I fought on Charles's side at Worcester and then escaped to America. Kate Mason Rowland, *The Life of George Mason, 1725-1792* (New York, 1892), 2 vols., I, 1. Actually one can do no more than say that the first George Mason (1626?-1686) was Whiggishly inclined, for the terms did not come into use until *c.* 1679. There is more evidence that George Mason II (1670?-1716) was a real Whig.
45. *Journals H.B. 1659/60-1693*, p. liii.

manded for the confusion and "error" made in the election, perhaps another sign of party strife. There is still confusion in the record of this matter. The Effingham Papers date this dispute November 18, 1685. But McIlwaine *(Journals of the House of Burgesses)* shows Scarlet and Fitzhugh's friend Samuel Hayward as burgesses for 1685-1686. Perhaps Mason resigned after the first session, as he did in 1688,[46] and Hayward succeeded him.

Already in October, 1685, accusations had been made in the House, clearly by Scarlet, that Fitzhugh had in 1682 cheated the county of Stafford of several hundred pounds of tobacco by misrepresenting the amount of the claim due him and George Brent in their capacity as providers of the Potomac garrison.[47] The House, spurred by Scarlet and perhaps other Whiggishly-inclined gentry, demanded that the Governor issue a warrant to have Fitzhugh appear and answer charges at an impeachment trial at the next session and that meanwhile the Governor suspend him from all offices. Later in the second session of this Assembly, in October, 1686,[48] added was the charge that Fitzhugh had collected from the county four thousand pounds of tobacco as a burgess for the preceding session, in which he had not been present. All during October and early November the charges were discussed and resolutions drawn in the House. On October 30, Fitzhugh through his friends presented counter-charges against Scarlet, almost a sure sign that most or all of the original charges had been politically inspired. As Fitzhugh commented to Nicholas Hayward, all of this led to nothing but to his being detained longer than he liked at Jamestown. Apparently Effingham was on his side, for the Governor refused to remove him from various offices (by now he was Lieutenant Colonel of Stafford militia) and never brought the case to trial, either as impeachment or as an ordinary trial before the General Court.[49] The whole episode is significant generally, however, as showing the feeling of the House of Burgesses that it must champion personal grievances of the people, and as being the first American case of an impeachment proceedings. Apparently it reflected not at all on Fitzhugh's integrity.

This annoyance and the troubled times of James II and the Revolution of 1688 led Fitzhugh, however, to keep out of major politics from 1685 until 1693. George Mason II and Martin Scarlet of his rivals and George Brent and John Withers of his friends, as well as Thomas Ousley

---

46. *Ibid.,* p. xiv.

47. 5 V 60.

48. *Journals H.B. 1659/60-1693,* p. 266. For later records of the case, see *Cal. St. Papers, Col., Am. & W.I., 1685-1688,* Items 482, 963, 1927.

49. *Journals H.B. 1659/60-1693,* pp. liii, 266, 268, 271, 282, 300-5; *Exec. Journ. Council Col. Va.,* I, 509-10; *Legisl. Journ. Council Col. Va.,* I, 125, etc.

(political leanings undetermined) served the county as burgesses during the years between 1686 and 1693.[50] But for the session of October and November, 1693, Fitzhugh again took his seat, alongside George Mason II and such veteran colleagues as John Buckner of Gloucester, William Randolph of Henrico, and Arthur Spicer of Richmond.

Even in 1693 he clearly had his enemies. He had been earlier a known supporter of the Stuarts, and more recently had been accused in Stafford of papistry.[51] Like other loyal Jacobites in a period when it seemed that the political pendulum might yet swing the other way, he was not too careful to keep his opinions to himself. On April 29, 1693, the Virginia Governor and Council, in consideration of what was intimated to them in a letter from the government of Maryland, ordered that Fitzhugh be required to take the Oaths of Allegiance and Supremacy, and "subscribe the Test" and give bond to appear the fourth day of the next General Court. On May 26 it was reported that Colonel Fitzhugh had taken the oaths prescribed instead of those of Allegiance and Supremacy (which had been done away with on the accession of William and Mary) and had subscribed to the Test.[52] Accordingly, in October, at a time when he was the most important man in the House besides the Speaker and was appearing before Governor and Council as Proprietary Agent demanding certain rights for his owners, he had to appear before Governor and Council to answer these political charges. He was in good company, for his friend Colonel William Digges,[53] of a family distinguished in both England and America and himself owner of extensive lands in both Virginia and Maryland, had to answer the same charges with him.

Coll William Diggs & Coll William Fitzhugh Appearing before his Excelly in Councill, persuant to an Ordr of Councill of the 26th of May to answer to what may be objected agt them on their majts behalfe for words by them spoken in Maryland (viz) that King James had another son borne by his Queen, in France & Invited over thither several of the Lords wth a Safe Conduct to

---

50. As noted above, WF's friend Samuel Hayward had served during some part of the 1685-1686 session.

51. See section on WF as "County Justice and Militia Officer" below.

52. Bruce, *Inst. Hist. Va.,* I, 500-1.

53. Digges, a Protestant, had a Catholic wife and children (D. M. Owings, *His Lordship's Patronage* [Baltimore, 1953], p. 127) as WF had a Catholic law partner. In this nervous period any such affiliation was suspect. Of course religion was in the popular mind inextricably entangled in the Whig-Tory struggle. C. M. Andrews (*The Colonial Period of American History* [New Haven, 1934-38], 4 vols., II, 376) shows Digges's wife Elizabeth's connections and Digges's own important positions in the Maryland colony. Incidentally, both amusing and puzzling is the claim made by one Edward Ross to the Virginia Council that, on their orders, he had gone to Fitzhugh's home and brought the Colonel to Jamestown, for which he wanted his pay. This is puzzling because WF must already have been present in Jamestown for the session of the Assembly. See W. P. Palmer, ed., *Calendar of Virginia State Papers . . . Preserved in the Capitol . . .* (Richmond, 1875), I, 45.

see the Queen brought to bed, upon wch some did goe over, & saw a Son borne, who was Created Duke of Gloucester, & the said Fitzhugh said, he wondred what they would have to say now against the legitimacy of that Prince, all wch Coll Diggs also (coming over to Maryland affirmed) & further Added, that King James sent over Proclamacons to England in print, declaring a Genll Free pardon unto all Excepting only the Bishop of London, & my Lord President, & that Coll Diggs said Capt Purvis should say, he expected an Alteration before he Gott to England, & that this & the like discourse was publickly talked on in England and Virginia, & that Sr Edmo Andros himselfe ye Govr of Virginia, did Freely & openly talk of the same, amongst his Council, who also did the same without the least Notice taken & ca all wch being denyed by the sd Diggs & Fitzhugh & no Evidence therein, but the Deposition of Garett Van Sweringham of St. Maries in Maryland, & the Attorney Genll Acquainting his Excelly & Councill, that he had inquired of the Attorney Genll in Maryland, butt could find no other Evidence, & that the words were spoken in another Governt, & being butt one Evidence to prove ye would not be sufficient in Law to Convict them.

Upon wch they were discharged from further Attendance.[54]

By this time Fitzhugh must have been growing philosophical about accusations. Certainly he was busy about more important matters. Again he was the unsuccessful candidate for the Speakership (Thomas Milner being elected), but he had received the next most honored post, the chairmanship of the all-important committee on Propositions and Grievances. At this session his committee was entrusted with an even more important task than usual.

For some years both Council and House had been convinced of the need of a complete revisal of existing laws. The House over the past several sessions had rightly insisted that this was a long-term matter to extend over several years. Governor and Council had felt otherwise. Despairing of having their own plan adopted, the House at the beginning of this session agreed to follow a plan proposed by Governor and Council, that the bills of individual laws should be passed one by one by the House in the usual manner and sent to the Council for approval.[55] The House immediately made Fitzhugh's Grievances-Propositions committee a committee of revisal, who were to report the bills to the House as rapidly as they could be prepared. Sixteen bills were reported the next day. But the necessarily long-drawn-out procedures of three readings, possible rejections or amendments by the Council leading to return of the bills to the House, and resultant joint conferences then and later proved the utter

54. *Exec. Journ. Council Col. Va.*, I, 302 ff.; *Cal. St. Papers, Col., Am. & W.I., 1693-1696*, Items 298, 371, 643 (pp. 93, 109, 191).
55. *Journals H.B. 1659/60-1693*, p. lxx.

impracticability of the Council's plan. Finally it had to be abandoned, after long and tedious sessions concerned with complicated matters. It led to good results, however, for in 1699 a joint committee on revisal, to sit between sessions of the Assembly, was constituted, and in 1705 a revised code was adopted.[56]

Fitzhugh as committee chairman and as leader in special projects did notable service in this Assembly. As chairman of a small committee appointed to investigate alleged disrespect to the House, he showed himself zealous in guarding the rights of that body, for the offender was compelled to make abject apology on his knees.[57] Again and again he reported the revised laws, which he himself as the legal expert had formulated, before the House. Again and again he conferred with the Council on amendments.[58] As shown in one of his letters, he always regretted the failure to revise in this session. And elsewhere in his correspondence his tremendous interest in the Virginia code and its revisal is intimated by his plan to publish a complete and accurate edition of the colony's laws.

Practical, thrifty man that he was, the Colonel with the assistance of certain friends of the House tried to secure for himself additional recompense for his special labors on the laws. The House sent a recommendation to this effect to the Governor and Council. To the modern reader the reply is ironic in tone, perhaps induced by Fitzhugh's known enthusiasm for a project which the Council did not consider so favorably. "As to the 10800*li* of Tobacco presented to Coll *ffitzhugh*, for his great trouble, in Collecting & preparing the Laws in Order to a Revisall, we think fitt that, that be likewise rejected, for if Coll *ffitzhugh* thereby has meritted any thing from the Countrey ye reputation wch he will accquire therein, is a Sufficient & ample Sattisfaction for his Services...." [59]

More and more Fitzhugh was making speeches. Some of them represented the joint opinions of his Grievances-Propositions committee as addressed to the Governor, as one of October 30.[60] Some he prepared and gave as answers to the Governor's addresses, as the eight-line speech of November 11,[61] or the longer one of November 8 disagreeing with the British Privy Council's suggestion that Virginia aid New York in men and money against the French and Indians. Fitzhugh doubted New York's need and even more Virginia's ability to help.[62] The Governor replied,

56. *Ibid.*, p. lxxi.
57. *Ibid.*, pp. 475-76.
58. For example, *ibid.*, p. 492. November 15, 1693.
59. *Legisl. Journ. Council Col. Va.*, I, 206. Nov. 15, 1693.
60. *Ibid.*, p. 470.
61. *Ibid.*, p. 487.
62. *Ibid.*, pp. 482-83. Text below.

and in turn Fitzhugh rejoined for his committee, reiterating and enlarging upon previous arguments and adding that Virginia itself had never had aid from other colonies.[63]

On the last day of his last session as a burgess Fitzhugh must have been pleased at the unusual nature of the usual address to their Majesties. For at this time both Council and Burgesses united in thanking their sovereigns for the royal charter for erecting the College of William and Mary "for the education of youth and a Seminary for Church of *England* Ministry" and for their donations to the institution. For here was something that might supply two of the great needs of the colony, an intellectual society and a learned and spiritual clergy. Fitzhugh himself was one of the College's governors elected by virtue of the charter.[64]

Valuable as were Fitzhugh's direct and individual contributions to colonial legislation, perhaps he contributed most as a burgess in a less tangible way. For the legal learning and legislative dignity he exemplified raised the level of and ability in the General Assembly over a period of almost twenty years. One is tempted to feel that it raised it once and for all, that the ordinarily educated planters and provincial attorneys who had hitherto filled its benches were not hereafter to be enough. From Fitzhugh Virginia legislative history goes on to Sir John and Peyton Randolph, to Edmund Pendleton and a later George Mason, to John Marshall, James Madison, and Thomas Jefferson.

COUNTY JUSTICE AND MILITIA OFFICER

As Fitzhugh indicates in his letter to the Stafford County Court of June 10, 1691, he did not become a justice of the peace until 1684. In the same year he was designated as Lieutenant Colonel Fitzhugh,[65] indicative of his status as commander or deputy-commander of the Stafford militia. Both of these honors came after he had served in the General Assembly from 1677, and after his notable work as attorney in the Robert Beverley case. Immediately he began to sit on the Commission of the Peace next to the presiding justice, Colonel George Mason I, and during at least five of the seven years was himself presiding officer. To begin with, his prestige or

63. *Ibid.*, p. 490.
64. *A List of the Parishes, Ministers, Tithables, Clergy &c together with the Trustees, Govern'rs, Officers, & Number of Scholars of her Maj'ts Royal College of William and Mary, in Virginia, July the 8th, 1702,* Virginia Board of Trade, IX, 375. Here he is listed as "Wm. ffitzhugh, dead." See also, *Journals H.B. 1659/60-1693,* p. 353 (May 8, 1691).
65. On May 6, 1684, WF appears still in the burgesses' journals as "Mr," but on June 17 his name in the executive journals of the Council (I, 57) appears after "Lt Coll." In the latter case he is listed after "Coll George Mason" as one of the two Stafford justices in charge of the rangers then being raised to protect the colony. Mason died in 1686 and WF remained senior officer as well as senior justice for some years, the former until the year before or year of his death.

favored position must have come from the fact that he was Stafford's burgess, for councilor or burgess from a county always took the honored seat or seats.

The county court was the most important of seventeenth-century tribunals for the administration of local justice. It was no mere court in the modern sense. The county Commission of the Peace was responsible for the mercantile use of standard weights and measures, for the licensing of taverns, and for the enforcement of price regulations set by the General Assembly. It had to certify departure for England or removal from one county to another. The senior member of the commission had been earlier military as well as civil commander of his county, and even in Fitzhugh's time and in his case, the presiding magistrate and colonel seem to have been frequently the same man. As a court of record the commission was vital to present and future government. Details of original grants, escheats, and transfers appear on the pages of the books kept by the clerk of this court.

Its membership was chosen by law from the most able, honest, and judicious citizens, in practice from the wealthiest, most respected, and most capable. The number of justices varied. Beginning about 1677, ten was the usual number, though eight was frequently the total.[66] The court met at first monthly, then six times a year, at other times five. There were other variations. The Stafford records for 1690, for example, when Fitzhugh was presiding justice, indicate that the court met in March, April, June, July, September, October, November, and December,[67] several days at a time in each instance, though these records may not be complete. A quorum was constituted of four justices elected from the larger group. Any one of these and three other members of the bench constituted a valid court. The court of March 13, 1689/90, included besides Fitzhugh, six other justices, among them Samuel Hayward, George Mason II, and John Withers. On June 11 only four of the six appeared, making with Fitzhugh five members of the court. On June 10, 1691, when Fitzhugh refused to sit, George Mason presided over three other members.

As far as normal court functions go, this body considered only "minor" cases, and appeal could always be made to the General Court of the colony. Most of its cases concerned land titles and deeds. It is hard for us to conceive of the possibility of impartial justice in such a case as that of Sebastian *vs.* Ashton executors of March 13, 1689/90, tried before a court over which Fitzhugh presided, when Fitzhugh himself was chief

---

66. Bruce, *Inst. Hist. Va.,* I, 494.

67. 55 V 296-311; 45 V 11-27, 171-85. Campbell (*History,* pp. 331 ff.) observes that in 1681 Lord Culpeper reported that county courts were held three times a year.

executor of the Ashton estate. Even more potentially unfair to us seems the case of Fitzhugh *vs.* Dade, heard before Fitzhugh on June 11, 1690, a case in which he complained against Francis Dade for trespass. He was still on the bench when judgment was rendered, in his favor, on September 9.[68] It seems less strange that the General Court reversed the county decision, much to Fitzhugh's embarrassment. He pointed out to Hayward, however, that the real question was colonial central government's *vs.* Proprietary's rights, and that the Virginia government controlled the General Court, or was the General Court. That Fitzhugh took no part in judicial discussions concerning his own profit is probable, but his very presence must have been a psychological factor of great weight. It may be observed, however, that it would have been almost impossible to gather a county court in the seventeenth century in which an occasional case would not involve a justice of that court. Actually there are few charges of partiality in such courts.

Fitzhugh's petition-letter of June 10, 1691, stating his injured dignity and reputation from Scarlet's accusations, assumed that participation in the Commission of the Peace was a responsibility of leadership. Waugh had said that there was no law nor justice in Stafford except what Fitzhugh said would be. Fitzhugh may have been thin-skinned here and elsewhere, but he was clearly sincere in his claim of "faithfulnesse and Integrity" in the management of "the affairs of our Countie soe committed to me." What he was upholding, as he averred, was the dignity of the court as well as of himself. In his second letter or petition, that of November 10, 1691, he was clearly even more disturbed. The Whiggish trouble-making parson John Waugh had recently been involved in the "tumult" in which George Brent and other Catholics were accused of treason and Brent had on orders of the Virginia Council taken refuge in Fitzhugh's own house.[69] Waugh had been reprimanded and punished by the Council. Now, while abusing generally the Commission of the Peace to their faces, he had declared that Fitzhugh was a papist. Fitzhugh ironically suggested that the Attorney-General and Lieutenant-Governor had probably heard rumor of Waugh's behavior but refused to believe that the clergyman could be so foolish or so knavish, and pointed out correctly that the personal accusation exposed Fitzhugh to danger from the "Rabble." [70] The

68. 44 V 302; 45 V 19. Virginia county records elsewhere indicate many parallel situations. For example, Ralph Wormeley sat on the Middlesex court in the 1680-1685 period in cases in which he was concerned.

69. Harrison, *Landmarks*, I, 128 ff., and "Parson Waugh's Tumult," 30 V 31-37. This whole matter was closely related to the "Protestant Revolution" in Maryland, just across the river, at this period.

70. 45 V 253-56 and given among letters below.

Commission took the none-too-gentle hint and forwarded Fitzhugh's letter to the Lieutenant-Governor, but there is no record that Waugh was ever punished. There is every indication that Fitzhugh lived up to his declaration here made and never sat again as a county justice. There is good evidence, however, that he flew the county standard, symbol of the ranking justice, at his home plantation for many years after this if not until his death.[71]

It should always be borne in mind that Fitzhugh had frequently met both Martin Scarlet and John Waugh in land litigation in county and perhaps General Court, and that he usually had bested them. Also that Waugh was or was soon to be George Mason II's father-in-law. How much High and Low Church opinions, Stuart and anti-Stuart loyalties, personal finances and blood or marital relationships enter into these clashes we cannot be sure; but it seems not unreasonable to suggest that they all did. That feuds might be almost purely political, or at least did not endure forever in this Tidewater country, is indicated by the marriage in the next century of two of Fitzhugh's younger sons to two of Mason's daughters. After all, they were all Stafford gentry.

While many of Fitzhugh's friends among the Northern Neck gentry held military commissions as he did, most of them had gone through the grades of captain and major before becoming lieutenant colonels or colonels. Perhaps because he was not given the rank until about May, 1684, when he was a prominent member of the House and had been since 1681 a provider for the Potomac garrison, he was made at once a lieutenant colonel. At the same time George Mason I was listed as colonel,[72] a title he had held earlier. The two together were to organize and direct the rangers who were to defend the frontier. Though Mason and Captain George Brent, among others, had seen service along the frontier, there is no evidence that Fitzhugh was ever anything other than administrative staff officer for his county and the upper frontier generally. In 1700, when William Fitzhugh, Jr., was a militia captain, George Mason II was appointed lieutenant colonel and commander-in-chief of the Stafford militia. The documents showing this are official notes addressed to and from "Colonel Fitzhugh." [73] Perhaps at this time Fitzhugh assumed the full colonelcy the elder Mason had held before his death in 1686, a title not too frequently bestowed upon those below the political rank of councilor.

---

71. For example, 46 V 20, and Harrison, *Landmarks*, I, 136.
72. *Exec. Journ. Council Col. Va.*, I, 57.
73. *Cal. St. Papers, Col., Am. & W.I., 1700*, Item 68 lii, p. 454, and Rowland, *Life of George Mason*, I, 27. By 1698 Major Mason had been commander of the Stafford Militia. 49 V 307.

It is more probable, however, that Fitzhugh was on the way to or was in England at this time (see below) and was not too much concerned with such a matter. The duties of militia officer he considered one of the responsibilities of his general position, and he performed them quietly and efficiently.

PROPRIETARY AGENT

In his one other major activity his employment from 1693 to the end of his life with his friend George Brent as resident agent for the Proprietors of the Northern Neck, William Fitzhugh was to have what is probably his most definite influence upon the pattern of American economic history. It was the land-grant and patenting system practiced by this agency that the later land speculations and territorial developments employed. It became, for good or bad, the system of the expanding frontier.

The great territory between the Rappahannock and Potomac rivers, from the Chesapeake Bay on the southeast to the headwaters of these rivers on the northwest, was a world within a world, an economic and political entity within the larger unit of Virginia. Its size is variously estimated, but the minimum given is about one million acres.[74] In 1649 the exiled Charles II rewarded a group of seven of his loyal followers by granting to them this territory on the frontier of Virginia, a not unusual reward to deserving soldiers. Within this domain they were to possess all the rights of court barons in England, for they could build towns, castles, forts, create and endow colleges and other schools, and enjoy the patronage of churches. Among other privileges they could "give, grant, or by other means sell or alienate" acreage within the territory. Lands sold or leased were to be held by the usual tenures used in England, with the important stipulation that rents and "other lawful reservations" be paid to the Proprietors, not to the colony or Crown. The freeholder, then, could bequeath or alienate his real estate according to the law of the colony, but he would pay an annual quitrent to the Proprietors. Though if the Proprietors saw fit to make grants "in free and common socage by fealty

---

74. C. M. Andrews (*Col. Period of Am. Hist.*, II, 234) estimates five million acres as the size for the territory as it stretched back to the actual head springs of the rivers. The best and most recent study of the territory is Douglas Southall Freeman, "The Northern Neck Proprietary in 1745," in *George Washington: A Biography* (New York, 1948), I, 447-513. More details regarding the Brent-Fitzhugh agency occur in Harrison, *Va. Land Grants*, pp. 87-93, 125-27. See also Robert Beverley, *The History and Present State of Virginia* (mod. ed. by L. B. Wright; Chapel Hill, 1947), p. 94, and 6 W(1) 222-25. The acreage estimate of one million is of the minimum for the original grant of 1649, when "heads" of the two rivers probably meant a shorter distance from the mouths than it did in the different phrasing, "first heads or springs," in the 1688 charter. See Freeman, "Northern Neck Proprietary," pp. 481, 489.

only," they could relieve the purchaser of all obligations to pay the quitrent.[75]

There was little activity on the part of Proprietors or colony about the Northern Neck until after 1660. In 1662, when Bristol men offered to lease the whole property, Governor Berkeley and the Council opposed the lease because they were afraid that the lessees might not honor 576 grants of "headright" lands made in the Proprietary before 1661. After some dispute, the colonial officers won their point, for there was no lease. In 1669 the King made a new grant to the Proprietors, this time for only twenty-one years and for such tracts as they "inhabited or planted" within the period. Also this grant stipulated that the Proprietary be subordinated to the colonial government in military and general tax matters. In 1670 the Proprietors made halfhearted attempts to collect quitrents, levies never before collected by the Crown from original settlers. The landholders tried to and generally did get out of paying. The officials of the colony protested the attempts to collect and sent representatives to England to suggest that some way be found to return the territory directly to the Crown. This went on through the 1670's. During this time, in 1675, Lord Culpeper, a principal Proprietor, was granted succession to Governor Berkeley's office. He came into it on Berkeley's death in 1677. Culpeper himself arrived in Virginia in May, 1680, with instructions from the King that quitrents for the colony generally be collected, a matter to which Fitzhugh seems to make reference in a letter given below.

Upon returning to England late in the same year, Culpeper obtained all the shares of the other Proprietors except those of his cousin, Alexander Culpeper. Ordered back to Virginia, he reached Jamestown for the second time in December, 1682. After severe punishment of several of the tobacco plant-cutters, he again returned to England in 1683 without the King's leave. Culpeper was deprived of the governorship and was succeeded by Francis Howard, Lord Effingham. But Culpeper continued to try to collect the quitrents in the Northern Neck and Effingham supported him in the attempt. Charles II died and James II ascended the throne when Culpeper's grant had about five more years to run. After some trouble and delay, Culpeper secured from James a new grant to the Proprietary in perpetuity, this grant of 1688 setting the western limits farther back.[76] When James fled, Culpeper as a member of the temporary commission acting for William and Mary before they arrived was able to ingratiate himself with his new rulers. But not for long, for on January

---

75. Freeman, "Northern Neck Proprietary," p. 452. The first patent is printed in Freeman, pp. 513-19.

76. *Ibid.*, p. 481.

27, 1689, he died. His neglected widow and her daughter Catherine inherited the Proprietorship. In 1690, Catherine married Thomas, fifth Lord Fairfax, who became a sharer in the Proprietary, and the Northern Neck entered a new phase of its history.

In 1677, Daniel Parke and Fitzhugh's old friend Nicholas Spencer, soon to be Virginia Secretary of State, had been made agents for the Proprietary. Parke died in 1679, and from then until his death in 1689 Spencer was the sole agent, though he in turn had deputies. Fitzhugh years later comments in his letters to Roger Jones on Spencer's degree of efficiency in the post. Philip Ludwell succeeded Spencer and usually acted as absentee agent, employing two deputies to do the work. Ludwell proved quite autocratic in insisting on Proprietary rights, especially in escheats and estrays. The Virginia Council protested that through the frontier rangers he was seizing livestock of all kinds to the great prejudice of peace. Alarmed at the protests, Ludwell urged the Proprietors to get the grant again confirmed. This they did on December 15, 1692. Thereafter applications for grants increased enormously and Ludwell was attacked for his absenteeism. Finally in 1693 he opened a land office in the Northern Neck. At almost the same time he was ordered to Charleston to assume in person his post as governor of the two Carolinas, of one of which he had been absentee governor for some time. A few months later Alexander Culpeper, who owned one-sixth of the grant, died and left his share to Lady Culpeper, widow of the erstwhile colonial governor. Thus Catherine, her mother, and her husband became sole Proprietors. Another confirmation was made to them by Order in Council in 1693 which was to endure until American independence.

Ludwell's deputies had proved most inefficient. At this point they were removed and George Brent, like Ludwell a remote kinsman of the Culpepers, and his law partner William Fitzhugh were appointed agents for the owners. Fitzhugh's friend and correspondent Captain Roger Jones, who had been with Culpeper in Virginia and was in 1693 a London mercantile agent, recommended them for the post. Brent's family connections, his experience as Virginia attorney-general and burgess and generally good legal reputation must have been strong factors in his appointment.

As far as Fitzhugh is concerned, there is also some background to this appointment. The only large sale in the territory during Spencer's agency had been that of the Brent Town tract, secured by George Brent, Nicholas Hayward, Robert Bristow, and Richard Foote, through grant of February 10, 1687,[77] a transaction in which Fitzhugh had acted as attorney for

77. 17 V 309.

Thomas, Lord Culpeper.[78] Even earlier, in Fitzhugh's letter to Culpeper of January 8, 1682/83, it is evident that he and the Governor had been on good terms and that Culpeper respected the lawyer's judgment and influence. This would have prejudiced Jones in his favor. Then in a letter to George Luke in October, 1690, Fitzhugh complained that the Lieutenant Governor (Francis Nicholson) was suspicious of him because during the preceding summer he had entertained Ludwell at his house. Nicholson thought Fitzhugh had been instrumental with Ludwell in opposing the Governor and Council's attempts to secure the Northern Neck for the Crown. Though Fitzhugh disclaimed part in the affair, this implication of sympathy with Proprietary rights would not have hurt his chances when the time for a successor to Ludwell came. The Fitzhugh vs. Dade case referred to above and in the letters also seems to show Fitzhugh on the side of the Proprietary. And perhaps it should be observed in passing that one of the larger grants of Ludwell's agency was made to John Newton and William Fitzhugh of a tract lying in Stafford containing 2,150 acres.[79]

On November 3, presumably of the year 1693,[80] Brent and Fitzhugh received their powers and instructions from the Proprietors. From then on until Brent's death in the spring of 1699 they had their troubles. They were busy for a time appointing receivers for the quitrents in the form of tobacco, and some they collected, but so little in proportion to that due and expected that they were accused of cheating the Proprietors, as Fitzhugh's letters testify. Brent is usually given the blame for being too highhanded. Fitzhugh is said to have been more tactful.[81] Neither had been involved in previous quarrels between governors and agents, as Fitzhugh suggests in his comments on Nicholson's suspicions. They had been strongly supported on January 11, 1693/94, by the Order in Council which made all hopes of the colony's taking over the Proprietary utterly void. These things and others were in their favor, yet the contemporary historian Robert Beverley, son of Fitzhugh's old friend and client, recorded that they "succeeded no better than their Predecessors." [82]

In the autumn of 1694, following the Order in Council, Fairfax

---

78. Harrison, *Va. Land Grants*, p. 74.

79. *Ibid.*, pp. 84-87. *Northern Neck Land Patents, Book I, 1690-1692* (Va. State Lib.) indicate that on September 22 and 23, 1690, patents for various tracts were granted to George Brent and WF(1), to John Newton and WF(3), and to WF alone(2), by Philip Ludwell as agent.

80. WF to Roger Jones, n.d., p. 324 below. Later WF mentions that he had been lawful agent of the Proprietors by date of January 6, 1692. *Stafford County Will Book, Liber 2*, pp. 24-27.

81. Freeman, "Northern Neck Proprietary," pp. 487-88, and Harrison, *Va. Land Grants*, pp. 87-93.

82. Beverley, *History*, p. 84.

secured from the Lords of Trade a letter to the Virginia Council requiring that the agents be fully supported. The agents bestirred themselves. On October 1, 1694, they opened their land office in Stafford.[83] When Brent asserted firmly the title of the Proprietors to all escheats and found difficulty in getting the holders of headrights to accept tenancy under the new Proprietors, he threatened to double the quitrents.[84] An aroused General Assembly found a leader in Robert Carter, one of the largest landowners of the Northern Neck. In an address to their majesties of May 10, 1695, as chairman of a committee to look into the matter, Carter made a savage attack on the agents.[85] Under six heads he listed the "abuses" practiced, accusing the agents of demanding double the rent allowed by the King in the charter, of altering the forms of tenures by changing patents into conveyances, of selling the lands at full value and sometimes more, of granting lands already escheated and even lands that might be escheated *in Futuro,* of reserving a clause of re-entry upon the non-payment of rent for two years, and of allowing men to hold as much as fifty thousand acres by secure title without any seating or building thereon despite the clause as to lapsing for want of seating. Carter went on in general terms as to the ruinous state of the old inhabitants of the Proprietary.

Even Fitzhugh was moved to anger [86] by what were acknowledged to be in the main unfair accusations. The irate agents adopted such a lofty tone in a conference with the Council that Governor Andros reported to the Lords of Trade on June 4, 1695, perhaps to excuse his own failure to comply with the Order in Council. "I must assure you that Lord Fairfax's agents, being negligent of their business in order to colour their failures, become insolent without cause, and that the respect towards their employers procured them an easy censure as the offence would admit." [87]

A little later, in a letter to Jones of May 11, 1697, Fitzhugh compared the situation to a game of cards, saying that their opposers have the best cards and trumps to boot, but that if Lord Fairfax would take his turn at dealing and shuffling to see that the agents were not cheated in the game, that the agents might win the set. In other words, Fairfax should see that they were represented fairly before the Lords of Trade. On July 7, 1698, Fitzhugh grew more indignant, defending the agents'

83. Harrison, *Va. Land Grants,* pp. 87-91.
84. Freeman, "Northern Neck Proprietary," p. 487; Harrison, *Va. Land Grants,* p. 89.
85. *Journals H.B. 1695-1700,* pp. 27-29.
86. Harrison, *Va. Land Grants,* pp. 87-89.
87. *Cal. St. Papers, Col., Am. & W.I., 1693-1696,* Item 1871.

honesty and pointing out from what disreputable sources came the scandal about them which reached the Proprietors' ears.

But Brent and Fitzhugh beat off Carter's attack. From at least 1695 on they made valiant attempts to get the principal landowners to attorn, or acknowledge. On July 24, 1695, they even petitioned the Virginia Council complaining that they could not get common process against Colonel Richard Lee II, Fitzhugh's personal friend.[88] Meanwhile they were busy confirming lands to each other, "being their own best customers." [89] There was nothing legally wrong in this, for they paid what anyone else did. And in pointing out that Fitzhugh took title to one huge tract of 21,996 acres, the historians have often failed to recognize that this was land he had held since 1684, the famous "Ravensworth" property, and that he was merely reaffirming his title, and practicing what he preached. Actually most of Fitzhugh's other properties in the Northern Neck counties were bought from individuals, as the county records, the Proprietary records, and his will testify. For example, of some 27,316 acres Fitzhugh had confirmed to himself by Brent while they were joint agents, 21,996 he had first patented as noted above in 1684; 1,000 acres had been bought from Rice Hooe; 600 acres from Nicholas Spencer in 1688; and 200 acres from Malachy Peale in 1691. Several smaller ones came after escheats. Brent had only some 5,486 acres confirmed to himself, in tracts of various origins. To state simply that Brent and Fitzhugh died great landowners, with the implication that they obtained most of their property from unassigned or escheated lands in the Proprietary, is very misleading and unfair.

After Brent died in the spring of 1699, Fitzhugh continued as sole agent until his own death in October, 1701.[90] It has been several times pointed out that in this period the fortunes of the Proprietors took a turn for the better. Fairfax Harrison thought Fitzhugh's greater tact, efficiency, and generally strong character were responsible for this.[91] Beverley gives the only surviving contemporary explanation: "At last Colonel *Richard Lee,* one of the Council, an Inhabitant of the Northern Neck, privately made a Composition with the Proprietors for his own Land. This broke the Ice, and several were induced to follow so great an example; so that by Degrees, they were generally brought to pay their Quit-Rents into the

---

88. *Exec. Journ. Council Col. Va.,* I, 333-34.

89. But not solely this. For other activity of WF as agent see *Westmoreland County Records, Vol. II, 1690-1699,* pp. 112-13, 143 (2 V 277), and *Northern Neck Land Patents, Book 2, 1694-1700, passim.*

90. Not, as Freeman's "Northern Neck Proprietary," says (p. 488) and Harrison's *Va. Land Grants* says (p. 93), in 1700.

91. Harrison, *Va. Land Grants,* pp. 92-93.

Hands of the Proprietors again." [92] Since this arrangement made no grant necessary, the land books remain silent as to circumstances. Fitzhugh's "more adroit mind" may have prepared the minds of both parties for the compromise that Lee negotiated directly with Lord Fairfax, as Harrison thought, but some personal associations may also have entered into the settlement.

Fitzhugh signed his last grant under date of June 18, 1700.[93] Two months before that, on April 10, he had given power of attorney in this and other affairs to his son William, Jr., with power to appoint attorneys under him.[94] The son, burgess in the same year, soon county clerk, before long a member of the Council and from before the spring of 1697 clerk of the Proprietary office,[95] married (date undetermined but probably about this time) Ann, the daughter of Colonel Richard Lee. There is also considerable evidence pointing to the possibility that Fitzhugh visited England between July 1700 and the middle of 1701, of which more later. He may have carried Lee's proposals for "composition" with him. At any rate, a combination of ancient friendship between Lee and Fitzhugh, of family alliance, and of tactful maneuvering may well have brought about this coup.[96] Robert Carter, the agents' critic, himself soon followed them in office and pursued the course Fitzhugh seems to have helped to develop of securing many tracts for himself and his friends. But Carter carried the policy much further and secured much more from his agency than his predecessors ever did.

This land policy pursued by Fitzhugh and his successors, some phases of it introduced as long before as Spencer's time, of confirming large tracts or groups of smaller tracts to one individual or partnership, was to have far-reaching effects. Whether units of large grants came from purchase, after escheat, or from unassigned lands did not so much matter in its final result. Fitzhugh's acquisitions were actually quite modest compared with those of some of his successors, and they were acquired certainly by more scrupulous methods. But as Dr. Freeman has said, the Brent-Fitzhugh policy of multiple grants to themselves and of large tracts

---

92. Beverley, *History*, p. 94.

93. Harrison, *Va. Land Grants*, p. 93.

94. *Stafford County Will Book, Liber 2, 1699-1709*, pp. 24-27. Va. State Lib. Photostat.

95. *Richmond County Deed Books, No. 3*, p. 80; *No. 4*, p. 132. As early as Feb. 11, 1695/96, WF Jr.'s name appears as a witness (*Westmoreland County Deeds & Wills, No. 2, 1691-1699*). A Fitzhugh family chart in the Va. Hist. Soc. shows WF Jr. as marrying Ann Lee *c.* 1692. This is much too early. She was probably born about 1683. Her first child to survive was not born until *c.* 1705/6.

96. After WF's death and before the appointment of Robert Carter as Proprietary Agent, Richard Lee acted as assignee for the Fitzhugh agency in bringing action against various persons. See *Westmoreland County Order Book, 1698-1705*, p. 235.

to friends such as William Sherwood and Isaac Allerton who had no intention of living on them,[97] of ignoring the non-occupancy of even larger tracts granted in their predecessors' time, was full of "evil potentialities." [98] It set a precedent or prepared the way for even larger grants, in some instances retarding settlement and a more even economic growth, and certainly leading to the abuses of speculation in large tracts of land both before and after the American Revolution. For it was among the frontier policies which remained prevalent in the United States through several generations of independent national existence.

HEART AND HEAD

It has been noted that William Fitzhugh and his brother Henry disagreed as to what the family's proper armorial bearings were. One who has surveyed the American Fitzhugh's life is hard put to it today to decide which of the mottoes accompanying the two coats of arms more fittingly represents him, for in very definite senses both do. The arms used by William's sons bear the inscription *Pro Patria Semper*, "For Country Always," a most appropriate indication of the public side of the careers of William Fitzhugh and many of his descendants. But the other arms, now claimed by English FitzHughs as those he should have borne, carry the English motto "In Moderation Placing all My Glory." Anyone who has read Fitzhugh's letters will be conscious of his emphasis on the Aristotelian mean, the middle way, as his declared aim and practice in personal life. To him moderation in personal behavior was the natural way. To his suffering brother barrister Hartwell he wrote as to why he had never had the gout: "I'll tell you, Sir, I never much frequented Bacchus' orgies and always avoided Ceres' shrine, and never was one of Venus' votaries. To speak (plainly) to you, I never courted unlawful pleasures with women, avoided hard drinking as much as lay within my power, and always avoided feasting and consequently the surfeits occasioned thereby." But he carried moderation into other things as well.

This latter motto was of course a Renaissance as well as a classic ideal. Fitzhugh, whose family was allied to and yet was not directly of the English country gentry, was perhaps a little self-conscious in his desire to live the ideals of that gentry in both outward form and inward thought. Obviously the golden mean was not the only quality demanded. And among the required qualities were some that seem in our time incongruous mixtures of pretense and reality.

---

97. *Northern Neck Land Patents, Book 2, 1694-1700.* To Sherwood were confirmed 2,109 acres; to Allerton 1,950. Sherwood lived in Jamestown and Allerton in Westmoreland.
98. Freeman, "Northern Neck Proprietary," I, 488-89.

One personal quality characteristic of Fitzhugh and English country families is a real feeling for blood kin, a depth of tribal affection. Though why he lost sight of his English relatives for fifteen years we cannot now know, it is evident that he more than made up for any possible neglect on his part in the past by his warm personal letters to his mother, sister, and brother, his financial assistance to the two women, and his anxiety to secure for his brother a lucrative government post in the colony. When he invited his sister to come to live with him, he was careful of outward appearances. For the sake of his present standing and her future one in the colony, she must appear to be paying her own passage, she must be well dressed, she must be accompanied by a maid. Honor, position, family love and pride too all enter into his letter to George Luke's father and uncle explaining that their young relative had made a good match in marrying his sister Dorothy. His affection and deep solicitude for his "beloved" wife and their children is evidenced in his will and in certain letters to English relatives.

Religion was for him an important public institution and a deep personal belief. A staunch and orthodox communicant of the Church of England, he was eager over a period of years, as we have noted, to get a sober and learned clergyman for St. Paul's parish, one of the church buildings of which in his time stood very close to his home. He thanked Nicholas Hayward for his substantial gift to the parish, probably communion plate or altar furnishings. He wrote to his mother that his sister died "a true penitent of the Church of England." Yet he was not intolerant of other forms of Christianity. His close personal friendship for Roman Catholics such as George Brent, and his protection of them, is an instance. His attempt over many years to settle French Huguenots on his "Ravensworth" tract was largely a commercial venture, but so kind was Fitzhugh to those exiles that when he died a neighbor described him simply as the Huguenots' friend.

Personal piety was genuine. He was most grateful to his mother for the Bible she sent him, and he confided to her his religious feelings. Near the end of his life, in 1698, he reminded her: "Before I was ten years old as I am sure you very well remember, I look'd upon this life here as but going to an Inn, no permanent being [.] by God's [help] I continue the same, good thoughts & notions still. therefore am always prepared for my certain Dissolution, wch I can't be persuaded to prolong by a wish." In breaking the news of his sister's death to his mother he mentioned his own desperate illness at the time, "but God Almighty by his great goodness, was pleased to restore me again, to prepare myself for his service, & for eternall Beatitude hereafter, to whom be the glory thanks & praise I hope

God almighty will be pleased to store me with such a stock of his Grace, that I may make a pious & profitable use of his abundant mercies towards me."

Though his will and sometimes his letters indicate his personal interest in and human sympathy for his white indentured servants, among them a cousin, there is little evidence that he really gave consideration to the Negroes and Indians as human beings. The whites were part of his plantation family; the Negroes were chattels. At his wife's instigation, as he acknowledged, he stipulated in his will that one woman should not be put out to field work. But the later individual interest in particular slaves and in their plight as a group evident in Washington's and Jefferson's letters and wills did not occur thus early. When Fitzhugh asked a friend to secure for him likely servants from an African ship, he was but ordering merchandise. When he found he had been cheated by having been sold a slave known to be physically handicapped, he was angry only at the deception. No hint of pity appears. That there might be moral questions involved in the slave traffic apparently never entered his and his contemporaries' heads. They had discovered that the African was the answer to their agricultural problems as machinery or fertilizer might be in another day.

Similarly, there is no hint of personal humanitarian interest in the red aborigines. Stafford was frontier country all during Fitzhugh's lifetime, and he saw Indians frequently. His friends fought and killed or were killed by them. A careless and brutal massacre of friendly Indians, partly by mistake, had occurred only a few miles from his home and may have been the beginning of Bacon's Rebellion. At another time Fitzhugh sent to higher colonial authorities a long account of an investigation of "an Indian murther"; he commented calmly on several occasions concerning the relative quiet or tumult occasioned by Indian raids or the absence of them. But he never showed the sympathetic interest in them the historian Beverley and even William Byrd II displayed, nor the active hostility or fear shown by other frontiersmen of his own or later times. The Indian was a nuisance to be lived with and protected from. That was all.

"Better never be born than ill bred," Fitzhugh had remarked in a casual aside when he was giving reasons for wanting to sell his property and return to England. Education for his sons was always a major problem with him. He had been about to send William, Jr., to England for training when he happened upon a French minister (probably John Bertrand, a clergyman in Anglican orders) who took the boy into his own home and tutored him in French, the classics, and probably mathematics. Later he sent his second son Henry to the French schoolmaster. When Henry, eleven and a half years old, was sent to England to school and to the care of the Bristol merchant George Mason, the father wrote that his son could not read or write English, but did both in French, and knew something of Latin grammar. He wanted Henry to be placed in a French school near Bristol of which Captain Jones had told him. And in his will William spoke anxiously of the future schooling of the younger children, of whom none could have been more than twelve in 1700 when it was written.

To his two older sons, of whom the younger Henry was probably the better educated, William left his "study of books" mentioned above, unfortunately without the detailed inventory that would indicate what it contained. Years before, the owner of this study had intimated that the most stimulating society in Virginia was to be found in printed pages, agreeing exactly with that first speaker of the House of Burgesses, Master John Pory, in resolving "to have some good book always in store, being in solitude the best and choicest company." [99] The religious works chosen by his wife and listed in her "Relinquishment of Dower" [100] and the titles given in his letters, of books to be procured in England, are our only clues as to the content of this library. It was probably as large or almost as large as the collections of his friends Ralph Wormeley and Richard Lee II, concerning whose individual titles we know more.[101] The titles we do have indicate that in the main his interests were parallel to theirs.

Legal works, including legal history, and general history were naturally the volumes Fitzhugh sought most. Rushworth's *Historical Collections* he had to borrow before he ordered them for his own. The "secret histories" of various reigns he ordered in some instances within a year of their first appearance. Thomas Burnet's *The Theory of the Earth* (1684), Robert Boyle's *The Skeptical Chemist* (1661), and José de Acosta's *Natural and Moral History of the East and West Indies* (translated in 1604) indicate the variety of his interest in modern science and history. He also ordered Cornelius Agrippa's *Occult Philosophy*, Tacitus, Polybius, Virgil, Horace, Juvenal, and Persius in Latin and/or English. Though he pre-

---

99. S. Myra Kingsbury, ed., *Records of the Virginia Company of London* (Washington, D.C., 1933), III, 222.

100. *Stafford County Will Book, Liber Z, 1699-1709*, pp. 104-7.

101. See Wright, *First Gent. Va.*, pp. 187-234 and the same author's lists and analyses in the *Huntington Library Bulletin* and *Huntington Library Quarterly* (*e.g.*, [1938-1939] II, 1-35). Also George K. Smart, "Private Libraries in Colonial Virginia," *American Literature*, X (1938), 24-52. Dr. Wright in *The First Gentlemen of Virginia* regrets the disappearance of the inventory of Fitzhugh's books. It almost surely never existed. The inventory of other things is included in *Stafford County Will Book, Liber Z, 1699-1709*, pp. 180-83. This inventory refers simply to "a study of books," as the will does. Sarah Fitzhugh's "Relinquishment" list names seven books, including a Bible, Book of Common Prayer, *The Whole Duty of Man, The Practice of Piety*, Smith's Sermon Book, and *The Queen's Closett Opened*.

ferred English translations when available, he clearly had no trouble with Latin or French. He wanted Francis Bacon's *Remains* (1648) and Cotton's *An Abstract out of the Records of the Tower Touching the King's Revenue* (1642). A large Bible in quarto, a prayer book in folio, and all of the works of the author of *The Whole Duty of Man* were fairly staple items for the moral and religious edification of the Virginia family. Some of his books other than the legal ones were put to practical use. Boyle's *Skeptical Chemist* gave him some information about what he might do to assay the ores found on his property. Other volumes, grammars and classical authors, were school texts for his children. In his displays of legal erudition he refers to a number of works, though chiefly to the general English *Statutes* and to Coke's *Reports* and *Institutes*. As noted above, when he refers to legal authorities such as Keilwey, Bracton, and Britton, he is usually but quoting from the marginal notes of Coke and the *Statutes*. Occasionally Fitzhugh borrowed and lost a book, for which he was properly contrite. But this ability or opportunity to borrow must have considerably increased the variety of his reading matter.

PEN IN HAND

Like many another contemporary possessed of considerable intellectual curiosity, William Fitzhugh enjoyed taking pen in hand. Like others, he liked to communicate with his friends and family. Also he wanted to combine into a book a record of his impression of the world in which he lived with material that would be useful to others in his own profession. Therefore he wrote letters, and he wrote a brief history of the present state of the colony as an introduction to a compendium of its laws. Only the letters have come down to us. But what he was trying to do in his projected book, stated in detail in his letters, is another facet of the engaging character of this Virginia planter.

Letter writing for Fitzhugh was to be sure first of all a means of business communication, a utilitarian practice. Even in writing on business, however, he interjected much of a personal nature, of his philosophy of living, his enthusiasms, and his antipathies. In his personal letters these subjective expressions are naturally even more evident. And like other thoughtful and educated men of his time, he never forgot that every letter was artistic expression, a representation of the gentlest of all the arts, the epistolary.

Reared as any man of his time was on the epistolary manuals, really rhetorical manuals, in his letters he is always the conscious stylist, though he is always aware of his shortcomings in this respect when he becomes too involved in business detail. To Nicholas Hayward he modestly wrote: "I must confess I want abilitys, to polish & adorn my expressions with that Elegance & sweetness of Stile your two letters I this year receiv'd are full freighted with, yet I'll endeavour to supply that defect, with a true sincerity & ardent zeal. ..." That he was conscious of the style of others too is evidenced in a letter to Wormeley (February 1, 1680), in which he doubts that the alleged author ever composed a will in question, "considering the meanness of the Stile, & unmethodicall penning thereof," for that gentleman had been "so good a master of his pen" that the document could not be his.

Fitzhugh's own style, though somewhat sententious, can be pleasant and graceful. He enjoyed figures, such as "Necessity as 'tis the Mother of Invention, so it is the Nurse of Industry," or "I am more afraid of falling upon Scylla to avoid Charybdis," or (regarding a letter received) "which I am as joyfully pleased myself with, as the most miserly Usurer is in the enjoyment of his full bags, & with the same prosperity shall endeavour the continuance, as he does his adored golden Mammon." In one flight to his friend Hayward, himself apparently a moral essayist, Fitzhugh unburdens his feelings in real rhetoric:

I ... do fully agree with you in your Philosophical sentiments of ye Simpathy of absent friends, as you in Laconick expression aptly deliver in your last, for which reason the first Inventor of letters deserves eternal Commendations, by whose means I have not only the opportunity, of the first acquaintance with so worthy & judicious a friend, but a continued Communication & Society, which I as really enjoy, whilst I am reading your most endearing letters, or answering them, as if happily present with you.

But neither the communication with absent friends nor the adornment of its expression fully satisfied Fitzhugh's auctorial yearnings. As early as 1697 he told Hayward that he had in his thoughts

to write a small treatise, or History of Virginia, describing its Scitation Temperature, & fertility, nature of its present inhabitants, with their method & manner of living, the plenty of iron mines, almost everywhere in the Country, & probable conjectures of the Discovery of others (more profitable though perhaps not so usefull) together with the prodigious quantity of wood to manage the same, the plenty of all sorts of provision the easir & profitable living of the people therein. It's regular easie & even Government in its severall Courts of Justice, together with their respective powers & methods of proceeding, with divers other heads too many to be enumerated, & to observe that brevity as I proposed in the first part of my letter.

A year later, he commented that Durand's book on Virginia and Maryland was "a most weak impolite piece, having neither the Rules of History, nor method of description, & taking it only as a Private Gentleman's Journal, 'tis as barren & defective there too, when I come out in print I intend to appear more regular & therefore as yet am not provided for such an undertaking."

Either he was very busy for the next five years, or the effort to appear "more regular" required long and painstaking work, for it was not until December, 1693, just after his last term in the Assembly, that he wrote Hayward that "the full & methodicall digest of our Laws" together with a previously completed "summary discourse of Virginia" was ready to be sent to him. What the relation of this digest was to the revised laws he prepared for the General Assembly at this time is an intriguing question. Actually he did not get the manuscript off to Hayward until July 9, 1694. In a letter of that date he mentioned the encouragement he had received from various Virginia gentlemen. He suggested that the book be printed in quarto. And he made it plain that he did not want it printed bearing his name or at his cost. On July 25 he informed Hayward that a second copy had been sent to him, both copies having been dispatched via Bristol. He also noted that his "method" fitted well with the intended Revisal of the Laws by the Assembly, as the journals of that body's last session would show. Things moved slowly, however, and it was not until early 1696 that Fitzhugh received Hayward's opinion and a letter from the potential publisher, the bookseller Hugh Newman. Fitzhugh replied to Hayward late in 1696 or in early 1697. He accepted Newman's offer for the manuscript, to be paid in copies of the book. He enclosed further laws to be added, and he again urged that his name be kept secret even from Virginia merchants then in London. In an enclosed letter to Newman he explained some apparent discrepancies and incidentally revealed that the manuscript must have been completed in at least one draft before the 1693 "Revisal Session" of the Assembly. Then he went into meticulous detail as to the proper form for printing each section. But Hayward died within the next year or two, and there is only one further mention of this manuscript Fitzhugh so much wanted to see in print. On June 30, 1698, he asked his London factor Cooper to look into the matter for him. He enclosed for Cooper a copy of his detailed letter of instructions to Newman, which he rightly thought would be self-explanatory. There is no evidence that the book was ever published. Had it been, the students of Virginia history would surely have come upon it.

EXIT

Fitzhugh's last letter is dated April 26, 1699. Yet he lived on for two and a half more years. In the spring of 1700 he planned to go to England, as evidenced by the words of his will and the sweeping powers of attorney he gave his son William, Jr. He may still have been in Virginia in early July of 1700. On June 18 he had signed his last land grant. Though the records are not clear, apparently he transmitted an order from the Governor to the new Stafford militia commander, Lieutenant Colonel George Mason II, between July 2 and July 10.[102] Evidence to indicate that he had recently returned from England lies in the October, 1701, codicils to his will, which refer to various pieces of silver "I brought with me from England," probably not pieces going back to 1670 or 1671. Thus he probably did make the voyage this once during his Virginia years—a voyage his neighbor Samuel Hayward, for example, made several times.

Perhaps he hoped to see his mother before she died, to straighten out his accounts with the sons of his deceased friend Nicholas Hayward, to get the "Summary View" and "Laws" published, and to see his old home. It is hardly likely that he now sought an estate in England, though his will does dispose of any lands in England he might be heir to, a fairly usual procedure. His family was now deeply rooted in the New World. When he sat down to draw this last testament on the eve of his projected venture back across the sea, the words he put down naturally formed themselves into the cadences of the great prose of the Book of Common Prayer. To this last witnessing of his faith he added a characteristic request, a request that dignity and decorum accompany him to his last resting place.

So the colonial planter, to be cut off a score of years short of the span allowed by Scripture, prefaced his enumeration of the considerable estate he bequeathed to his wife and five sons. No daughter is mentioned.[103] Bishop Meade says that he had one daughter named Rosamond, who married a Colonel Oberton of Westmoreland and died without issue.[104] This was almost surely a misprint for Allerton, for several family records in the Virginia State Library and the Virginia Historical Society indicate that she

---

102. Nicholson's note to Mason of July 2, 1700, is addressed from "Col. Fitz-hugh's" (*Cal. St. Papers, Col., Am. & W.I., 1700*, Item 681 ii) and Mason's reply from Stafford Court House refers (as printed in Rowland, *Life of George Mason*, I, 27) to "your Excellency's commands from Colonel Fitzhugh [*sic*] have been received," which could easily have been "from Colonel Fitzhugh's." That is, WF was not then necessarily at home. *Westmoreland County Court Order Book, 1698-1705* shows WF Jr. on August 28, 1700, acting for his father; *Richmond County Misc. Records, 1699-1724*, shows WF Jr. on Oct. 2, 1700, and March 6, 1700/1, acting for his father; *Northumberland Land Order Book, 1699-1713*, shows on Oct. 17, 1700, brief entries of "Coll ffitzhugh agt" for two persons, suits perhaps carried over or handled by WF Jr.; *Westmoreland County Court Order Book*, Oct. 31, 1700, simply records a judgment granted WF of Stafford. In other words, there is no real evidence that WF was in Virginia between June, 1700, and a few weeks before his death in October, 1701. Of course it might be argued that his son's agency was the result of the parent's debility. But the will suggests otherwise.

103. The text of the will is included after the letters below.

104. Meade, *Old Churches*, II, 193.

married Colonel Willoughby Allerton, son of Fitzhugh's good friend Colonel Isaac Allerton (q.v.). Even if she outlived her father, she had probably been provided for in her marriage contract or dowry. The laws of primogeniture and entail which Thomas Jefferson was later to battle against were not yet established. The oldest son, William, did receive the largest share, but not a great deal more than the next son Henry. The three younger sons, Thomas, George, and John, were amply provided for in lands, horses, cattle, household furnishings, and silver plate. William and Henry shared equally in the great "Ravensworth" tract and received other lands as well. The three younger boys also received a number of separate tracts each. These lands, originally bought from a variety of folk including Parson John Waugh and Doctor Richard Bryant, were in 1700 in most instances leased or occupied by tenants. This total of some fifty-four thousand acres was by no means all Fitzhugh had owned at various times.

His wife and four younger sons received seven Negroes each, William eight. To William went his father's and mother's portraits and those of six of his relations as well as the large map in the study. There was much more. Silver, coaches, mourning rings, and dozens of other things are enumerated. Fitzhugh's cousin David Abbot, a newly indentured servant, received his whole seven years' time as his legacy.

Fitzhugh died on October 21, according to George Mason II, from a bloody flux contracted from the French refugees he had befriended.[105] On November 18 his wife entered (in the Stafford records [106]) her "Relinquishment of Dower," in which the property she received in lieu of dower rights is itemized, including a number of household items not individually listed in the will itself. The inventory of the estate was not entered until August 11, 1703.[107] By then there were fifty-one "Negroes and Mulattoes," 122 pieces of silver plate, a gold snuff box and two gold rings, an enormous amount of cotton, linen, and wool textiles in the two stores, horses and mares, six indentured servants (not including Abbot), cattle, sheep, hogs, and a great deal of household furniture and furnishings; of ready cash one guinea and one mill shilling; certain jewels in the widow's possession, the study of books, one calash and gear and two horses (one coach had disappeared!); and among other things the sixteenth share in a ship and cargo. So had prospered a man who had cultivated his talents in the Chesapeake world.

There can be no doubt that William Fitzhugh, the son of a Bedford woolen-draper, would have been pleased could he have known of the mar-

---

105. George Mason to Governor Nicholson, in Harrison, *Landmarks*, I, 189.
106. *Will Book, Liber Z, 1699-1709*, pp. 104-7.
107. *Ibid.*, pp. 180-83.

riages of his younger sons and the future of their descendants. Almost surely he had seen William, Jr., and Rosamond married to a Lee and an Allerton. Without exception all the children married into the leading families of the bay area. Thomas and George married daughters of George Mason. Henry married a daughter of Mordecai Cooke of Gloucester, and John a McCarty of Westmoreland. William in a very few years achieved the social eminence never accorded his father, a place on the Governor's Council, but it is clear that this high seat was set upon foundations laid by the parent. Henry was high sheriff of Stafford and a burgess. The descendants of all these sons in Virginia and Maryland, and later through the whole United States, have been distinguished in many fields. But perhaps no one of them has combined in himself the many-sided ability of his first American ancestor.

Foreword to the Letters

Foreword to the Letters

Though students of history have known of the bound volume of William Fitzhugh's letters for more than a century, information concerning it has been curiously misleading and mistaken during all of this time. Actually no scholar during the century worked directly from it, though selections were published. As early as 1848, the editor of the *Virginia Historical Register* (I, 165-69) recognized his indebtedness to a Fredericksburg, Virginia, correspondent for four Fitzhugh letters he published therein. The correspondent, who signed himself J. M., said that he was in temporary possession of a manuscript volume containing letters written by a certain William Fitzhugh between 1679 and 1699. Eight years later, Bishop William Meade, a descendant of Fitzhugh, mentioned (in *Old Churches, Ministers, and Families of Virginia*, [Philadelphia, 1857], 2 vols., II, 193) "a large manuscript volume of his letters, a copy of which was some years since gotten from the library of Cambridge, Massachusetts, by one of his descendants, and which is now in the rooms of the Historical Society of Virginia." Various writers down to the present time have referred to the "copy" in Richmond, and the original at Harvard, as they translated "the library of Cambridge." When Professor Howard Mumford Jones of Harvard was writing his *Literature of Virginia in the Seventeenth Century* (Boston, 1946) he searched for the original but could discover no evidence that it had ever been in that institution. Further investigation in that direction by the present writer through the Director of the Houghton Library (Harvard Manuscript Collections) still yielded nothing.

From Bishop Meade's comment it may be presumed that at some time before 1857 the Virginia Historical Society had a transcript of the letters. They may have received another later, for Mr. Douglas Gordon of Baltimore has informed the present writer that his relative John M. Gordon sent copies to the Society about 1870. At any rate, beginning with the first issue of the first volume of *The Virginia Magazine of History and Biography*, the Society published over a period of six years and six volumes the Fitzhugh letters from transcripts. Evidently the editor was troubled at what he recognized as undoubted errors in transcription, for he stated firmly that he had copied accurately from what was probably an inaccurate copy. His printers, however, did make a few more errors.

Some four or five years ago the present writer, in gathering Virginia colonial materials for another purpose, became interested in the Fitzhugh letters and the correspondence concerning them in the files of the Virginia Historical Society. He discovered two things: that an "original letterbook" still existed about 1926 in the hands of a member of the Fitzhugh family, and that the Library of Congress had a bound photostatic copy of this letterbook. Though this information was about thirty years old, after some search he located the letterbook in the hands of Dr. Thomas Fitz-Hugh of Philadelphia, a native of Virginia and direct descendant of the writer of the letters. Through Dr. Fitz-Hugh's generosity and that of another physician who agreed to accept the care and responsibility, the letterbook was brought to Knoxville. A careful examination of this volume revealed the great discrepancies between the published letters and these more intelligible versions and the consequent need for a new edition of this most significant material. Dr. Thomas Fitz-Hugh presented the manuscript letterbook containing the correspondence of William Fitzhugh to the Virginia Historical Society in November, 1962. All interested scholars may now consult the manuscript letterbook from which the text for most of the present volume was taken.

Conversations and correspondence with Fitzhugh descendants has brought out the family tradition that there was a second letterbook, lent within the memory of living man to a relative (no longer living) who never returned it and may have allowed it to burn with other possessions when his residence was destroyed a generation ago. No present Fitzhugh can hazard a guess as to what it contained. Since the known manuscript letters cover almost all Fitzhugh's active life, it is hard to believe that it contained more letters of his. And all references to letters during the past century have clearly been to those of the volume we now have. The last collection may have included business documents, or letters of other Fitzhughs, or, more probably, copies of these same letters, for reasons to be discussed below.

For the manuscript volume from which the present letters are printed is not a daybook or any other kind of file kept by William Fitzhugh himself. It is a tall, narrow "ledger," 6 x 1.15 x 16.2 inches, bound in boards, with the word *Bos[c]o[b]el* written in a large hand across the back board. The handwriting is definitely of the first half of the eighteenth century, not of the seventeenth, though a few seventeenth-century survivals, such as the *ff* capital *F,* may have been influenced by the originals from which it was copied. Now "Boscobel" is the name of a Fitzhugh plantation in Stafford County established by William Fitzhugh's grandson Thomas (1725-1768), son of Henry, second son of the immigrant. This ledger type of book was probably copied from an earlier book, or from the letters themselves, in either case perhaps when the originals were already deteriorating. It may have been copied because Thomas, recognizing the family and general historical value of the letters, was resolved to have a copy even though the original belonged to an older member or senior branch of the family.

This "Boscobel" volume is in a good clear Italian hand, though the writer did not always read carefully. As the reader will note in the letters below, there are omissions (sometimes supplied in brackets) and misreadings, probably those of the eighteenth-century copyist, but in some instances just possibly those of Fitzhugh or of the secretary who copied for him.

The book contains in the first and last unnumbered pages lists of the correspondents, with page numbers by each. There are 277 numbered pages, beginning with the first letter of 1679 and ending with the last of 1699. Between the two extremes in years, however, the letters are not entirely in chronological order. Sometimes there is a group on some subject or to a certain correspondent covering several months or even years, and then following another group or sequence of single letters which has jumped back a year or two or month or two in date. In other words, whoever first transcribed the letters into a book took them in some sort of subject-and-chronology order, not just chronological order, probably as filed or kept by William Fitzhugh. In a few instances, from context or from location or both, it looks as if a letter has been misdated in year, either by Fitzhugh or by the copyist. All in all, the letters seem clearest if read in the order in which they have been preserved. So they are here printed.

Perhaps more should be said of one of the principal reasons for republishing these letters, the inaccuracies of *The Virginia Magazine of History and Biography* versions. There are actually hundreds of errors in punctuation—periods, commas, semi-colons. Spelling and capitalization were unnecessarily and sometimes inaccurately modernized. There were new misspellings, and there are dozens of examples of other kinds of errors: Latin words such as the manuscript *quaere* was printed *quelre;* *quae cunque* as *guaring; tollitur* as *tolliten,* thus rendering unintelligible the law Latin. Ordinary English idiom is badly misread: the manuscript "I were able" was printed "Jureable"; "in timely" (clear in context) printed "time big." In proper names there were many misreadings: "Donnan" for "Dorman"; "Mangemoy" for "Nangemoy." There are also a few omissions, one short letter and an enclosure or two.

Equally important as a reason for publishing in the present form is the need for context for these letters to point up their significance. There are few explanatory notes in the 1890's printed versions, and no discussion of Fitzhugh's place in his world. These deficiencies have been, it is hoped, remedied in the present presentation of the life and mind of this man and his age.

The Correspondence and Speeches, 1679-1699

The Correspondence and Speeches,
1679-1699

To Major Richard Lee [1]

Honrd. Sir   May 15th. 1679

The Story mentioned in your letter [   ]* first year of
his Reign did itso happen to all the Justices except Sr. Willm. Thorning
chief Justice of the common Bench & two of the King's Serjeants Hankford
and Brinkley, for their detestable opinions given to Richd. the second in
the twenty first year of his Reign in the Declaration of high treason to the
great destruction and Disherison of many Lords &c.[2] Upon hearing of your
letter I rememberd something of it but my memory being deceitfull, and
my Account not Certain I durst not venture upon an information, considering whence it was & for fear of Censure, yet blush'd to my self to let
slip such an easie Quære in a Profession I intended to get money by. Last
fall I receiv'd a Demand of your book [3] which I neither then was, nor now
am capable of restoreing, because lost but will honestly satisfy you for
them in your reasonable Demands. And to Demonstrate my readiness
therein, & that I may be in what I were able, gratefull have inclosed sent
you an Account of some old Statutes what time they were made & by
whom because I remember once you seemed [to] doubt thereof, & were
pleased also to thin[k] (or tell me so) they were obsolete & out o[f] use,
which occasioned me to take the more especial notice in my collecting &
do find they are most of them in forc[e] at this day. I intended to have
given you an Account, which of them were introductory of new Laws, &
which declaratory of the old, & which mixt, but doubting the length of
such a particular account would rather seem prolix th[an] pleasant, therefore have referred it till I know farther your desire by your especial
Commands. How necessary the knowledge thereof is, I will demonstrate
by two Examples, the first is the Statute of Glo. Chap. 6.[4] gives treble
damages & the place wasted, in an Action of Waste   Now to know what

---

* Blank in letterbook.

65

Costs is to be given in that Action you must know what the Law was before the making that Statute, because where any Statute doth give treble damages, where damages by the common Law were given, there the Cost also shall be trebled, but where treble damages are given by a Statute, where no damages were formerly recoverable, there the damages shall only be recovered & no Costs. And because there were no damages given in the said Action of Waste before the said Statute, therefore only the Place wasted & treble damages shall be recovered & no Costs. The second is the Statute of 8. H: 6. of forcible Entry, which giveth treble damages in this case treble damages & treble Costs shall be recovered, because they should have recovered single damages at the common Law, before the making that Statute. By this you may see what precipitate judgment may be given upon any Statute, without understanding the common Law, before the making thereof, which is the only guide, & which is only to be learn'd out of antient Authors, (for out of the old fields must come the new Corn) contrary to the opinion of the generality of our Judges & practi[s]ers of the Law here. There are severall [ot]her old Statutes that I have not given [yo]u an account of, because I am not [su]re these will be chearfully accepted [be?]ing only done for the satisfaction of your former doubts. If this pleases Command more from

To The Honble.   Sir Your   W ff.
Majr Richd. Lee

[LB, pp. 1-2]

1. Richard Lee (1646-1715), of the second generation of Lees in Virginia, lived at "Mount Pleasant," in Westmoreland County. The rebel Nathaniel Bacon had named him as one of Virginia's unjust rulers. Councilor since Governor Berkeley's time, Collector of Customs and Naval Officer for the Upper Potomac, he was a man of considerable learning and fine character. A Tory, he was intensely loyal to the Stuarts, as noted in a letter below. See Louis B. Wright, "Richard Lee II: A Belated Elizabethan," *The First Gentlemen of Virginia* (San Marino, 1940), pp. 212-34.

2. Here and later WF refers to the great collections of and commentaries upon English law. In many places he probably refers to *The Statutes at large, Conteyning All Such Acts which at any time heretofore haue beene extant in Print from Magna Charta, vntill the sixteenth yeere of the Raigne of our most gratious Soueraigne Lord Iames. . . .* Divided into Two Volumes. . . . LONDON. . . . Printed by Bonham Norton, and Iohn Bill. . . . M. DC. XVIII.

WF's references are more often to Sir Edward Coke (WF, like many of his contemporaries, spells the name Cook or Cooke) and his two great legal works, the *Institutes* and the *Reports.* They appeared in many editions in the seventeenth century. References in the present notes are primarily to Huntington Library copies of the two works, in the following editions: *The First Part of the Institutes of the Lawes of England. OR, a Commentarie upon Littleton, not the name of the Lawyer onely, but of the Law it selfe . . . ,* The Second Edition . . . (London, 1629); *The Second Part . . .* (London, 1641); *The Third Part . . .* (London, 1644); *The Fourth Part . . .* (London, 1644); his thirteen *Reports,* in Law French, appeared separately for the first eleven parts 1600-1615, for the last two, posthumously in 1656 and 1659: *e.g., Le Second PART des Reportes del . . .* (London, 1618); *Le Sept Part . . .* ([London], 1608); *Le Neufme Part . . .* ([London], 1613); *Le Dixme Part . . .* ([London], 1614).

WF's references to Coke and to the *Statutes* are a trifle careless. Some volumes of Coke's *Institutes*, for example, use page numbers and some folio numbers. WF calls them all by folio numbers. Sometimes WF read fast and copied a reference from the *Institutes*, which in turn referred to the *Statutes*, as a reference to the *Statutes*. Naturally these secondhand references are sometimes a bit garbled. There is not too much of this, however.

For the detestable opinions given in Richard II's time, see *Statutes*, p. 168.

3. Probably a law book, though Lee had a considerable library of other materials as well. For an inventory of the Lee library, recorded December 8, 1715, see 2 W(1) 247-49 and (with identification of titles) *Huntington Library Quarterly*, II (1938-39), 1-35.

4. Coke, *Institutes*, II, 304-5, under Ch. V (not VI) of Gloucestershire.

To William Sherwood [1]

Mr. William Sherwood   June 10th. 1679

Sir   The Report I sent last between Barton & Merrideth [2] happening in your hands to discuss wherein I wrote the opinion of others on both sides which needed not to one so acquainted and [co?]nversant in the common & municipal Laws of the Land, which I understand was accepted & approved by you, more than really it deserved, has encouraged me more particularly to recommend this person & his Cause to your Conduct. I cannot report it, because never adjudged, neither needs there much Law or Argument because it is so plain & notoriously known. I have plainly set down the Case, lest he should mistake in the relation. You need no Armour to fend off the Opposite Arguments, because so weak they are not able to defend themselves, & his so palpably strong they are not to be undermined by any fallacy.

His desire is to be forthwith seized as according to Law & Equity he ought, for the greatest Plea they have, is by dilatory Evasions to keep him out this year, which I presume will not be admitted when the Court shall be acquainted, how long already they have continued trespassers to him, & how much they have damnifyed him thereby, he having forewarned them off above half a year since the finishing the last Crop, since they alledge that as they have sown they ought to reap. I must confess that Rule holds where they are in by a rightfull title & then sow their Land, & their Estate determined by the Lot of God, but not to trespassers Despisers &c. I could have enlarged more upon this point but relating farther to you would be carrying Coals to new Castle. I refer you to the relatio[n] of the person himself   I am

Sir   Your   W. ff.

[*LB*, pp. 2-3]

1. William Sherwood (d. 1696/97), at this time attorney-general of the colony, was a resident of Jamestown and a prominent barrister. He was a native of White Chapel Parish in London. As a clerk in the office of Sir Joseph Williamson, secretary to Lord Arlington of the Committee on Trade and the Plantations, he had committed a robbery of some sort but had been pardoned through Williamson's intervention. He lived a useful and honorable life in Virginia for thirty years. His past followed him, however, for from 1680 to 1682 he was refused a seat in the House of Burgesses because he had committed a felony. He was sitting in 1682. His house in Jamestown was used as a meeting hall by Governor and Council. Sherwood's letters indicate that he remained throughout his life a repentant and a humble man. He directed that his tombstone at Jamestown should bear the legend that here lay "a great sinner waiting for a joyful resurrection." 20 V 18 and Swem, *Va. Hist. Index*.

The New York Public Library contains the original manuscript of Sherwood's important account of Bacon's Rebellion entitled "Virginia's Deploured Condition; Or an Impartial Narrative of the Sufferings of his Majesty's Loyall Subjects under the Rebellious outrages of Mr. Nathaniel Bacon Junior to the tenth of August Anno Domini 1676." Though Sherwood was at this time a defender of Berkeley, later he turned against the Governor. Mr. W. E. Washburn promises an extended study of Sherwood. Washburn, *Governor and the Rebel*, pp. 171-72.

2. In a ltr. of April 7, 1679, WF writes of Thomas Barton's plantation. In 1700, Thomas Barton, who lived in upper Stafford, was away from home when Indians killed his three children and the neighbors who were staying with them, in "the horriblest [murder] that ever was in Stafford." The Indians used arrows and wooden tomahawks. Rowland, *Life of George Mason*, I, 25. This was probably Thomas Barton, Jr., who was assigned one hundred acres on Quanticutt Creek in Stafford by his father on July 6, 1697. *Northern Neck Land Patents, Book 2.*

Barton's suit to recover a plantation is discussed in more detail in a ltr. to Sherwood of June 10, 1679.

To Major Robert Beverley [1]

Majr. Robt. Beverley   Septr. 11th. 1679

Sir   I remember you were instancing to me one point of Law that you could understand no reason for, why the Cousin should inherit before the brother of the half blood, although you was satisfy'd the Law was so, neither could you meet with any one that could give you the Reason thereof. What reasons I had then in my memory, I acquainted you with though not so fully as you required and I desired. It is an antient point, and therefore the reason must be sought for in old Authors, which remain in their original Language to say French and Latin, & have purposely sent this to give a Professor in the Science satisfaction, as also to acquaint you that we here esteem no more our's than we are able to give the reason of, observing that old Rule Constante Ratione legis, Constat ipsa Lex[.] [2] In Bracton, Britton, & Fleta [3] you shall find these words no man can be heir to a fee simple by the common Law but he that hath sanguinem duplicatum the whole blood both of the father & of the mother so as the half blood is no blood inheritable by descent, because he that is but of the half blood cannot be a compleate heir for that he hath not the whole & compleate blood, & the Law in Descents in fee simple does respect that which is compleat and perfect. Also these foresaid Authors give these reasons for the Law in this point, first Every one that is heir to another aut est haeres jure proprietatis aut jure representationis, as where the eldest son dieth in the life of his father his issue shall inherit before the younger son, for although that the youngest son is magis propinquus yet jure representationis the issue of the eldest son shall inherit for he doth represent the person of his father. And it is great reason that he who hath full & whole blood should inherit before him that hath but a part of the blood of his Ancestor, for Ordine naturæ totam præfertur vincini%, parti. Secondly As none can be begotten but of a father & a Mother, & he must have in him two bloods Blood of the father & the blood of the mother, these bloods commixed in him by lawfull Marriage, constitute & make him heir, so that none can be heir to any if he hath not in him, both the bloods of him to whom he will make himself heir, & therefore the heir of the half blood cannot inherit, because he wanteth one of the bloods which should make him inheritable for parte quaecun%, integrante sublata, tollitur totum, as in this case the blood of the father & of the mother are one inheritable blood, & both are necessary to the preservation of an heir, & therefore deficiente uno, non potest esse haeres. Thirdly For avoiding of Confusion, for if as well the half blood as the whole blood shall be equally inheritable, then in many Cases Confusion & uncertainty will follow who shall be the next heir. I could in my third reason have instanced many Examples but that I think it needless, because they will appear of themselves. Thus Sir for your satisfaction, & in honour to the noble Profession, I have (I think) given you an account that the Law appoints nothing but what is grounded upon very great reason, although perhaps without further search it may not immediately correspond with every man's reason, if this be not satisfactory please to give me notice, & I will very much enlarge upon these reasons, & illustrate them by Examples.   I am

Sir   Your   W. ff.

[*LB*, pp. 3-5]

1. For Beverley, see ltr. to him of Sept. 6, 1679, note 1.

2. Many of WF's legal references are in Latin, others in Latin and French, others English and French. As even in certain English words, the transcriber of the letterbook was careless in some of the Latin phrases and clauses. One should remember too that "Law Latin" is hardly Ciceronian Latin.

3. These are standard legal reference works: Henricus de Bracton, *De Legibus & consuetudinibus Angliæ libri q[ui]uque; in varios tractatus distincti*. . . . (London, 1659), etc.; Britton, on the laws of England, had appeared in black letter [in French] as early as 1540 (WF probably had the "second Edition, corrected according to divers ancient Manuscripts of the same Booke," [London, 1646], still in French); Fleta, *Seu Commentarius Juris Anglicani sic nuncupatis, sub Edwardo Rego primo . . . ab Anonymo conscriptus . . . Subjungitur . . .] . . . Seldeni ad Fletam Dessertatio Historica*. . . . (London, 1647, new ed. with same pagination in 1685).

Though there is some indication in WF's letters that he owned these volumes, most of his references to them could have come secondhand from Coke, *Institutes*, for there are marginal references to these authorities on almost every page of Coke.

To Major Robert Beverley [1]

Majr. Robt. Beverley   Septr. 6th. 1679

Sir In my former by my brother George Brent [2] I endeavoured your private satisfaction. This I have recommended a[t] my Clients request to the Retainer I had advis'd him to. The Case is plain & easie. Thompson sues Owzley [3] upon a bond of 4000£b. of Tobo. Conditional, to pay a Servant at such a time, the Condition not being performed he recovers judgment upon his bond after which judgment the Defendant craves an Injunction in Chancery to whose bill (I being retained) Demmurred & pleaded these Precedents & reasons I have here inclosed for my Demurrer, which after some Argumts. the Court allow'd of & accordingly enter judgment for us, grounding their judgment upon the former quotations, from which judgment the Attorneys of Owsley appeals: I have given the full quotations though not the precedents there inserted but enough I think to give the Court satisfaction. I have also taken the most material Reasons out of the afore-recited Authors why Injunctions are not to be granted after judgments at the common Law obtained which I presume will be sufficient & satisfactory. And have further instanced that one of the Articles exhibited against that great Prelate Woolsey, was for such illegal Proceedings, which I hope none of our Courts in Virginia will be guilty of, for fear of the punishment, which is præmunire, as appears by the Statute I have likewise quoted to you. I have farther to urge that as servants are our way, together with the cheapness of Tobo. & the long time lapsed, before suit for it, after it became due, 4000£b. of Tobo. is but a reasonable rate, he having paid his Tobo. for it almost two years ago. This I have only intimated not doubting the failure of so clear law, Sir Because I advis'd him to you therefore for my Credit & his Inter est, your carefull management of this Cause is desired by

Sir Your   W. ff.

[*LB*, pp. 5-6]

1. Robert Beverley (*c.* 1641-1687), clerk of the House of Burgesses, major of militia, arrived in America about 1663, probably from Yorkshire. Beverley lived in Middlesex County near the present Urbanna. A planter and attorney of prominence, he had been most active in supporting Governor Berkeley during Bacon's Rebellion. *Cal. St. Papers, Col., Am. & W. I., 1677-1680, passim; Exec. Journ. Council Col. Va.,* I, *passim; Journals H.B. 1659/60-1693, passim;* Hening, *Statutes,* III, 547-71; John McGill, comp., *The Beverley Family of Virginia: Descendants of Major Robert Beverley (1641-1687) and Allied Families* (Columbia, S.C., 1956).

2. Here "brother" apparently meant "partner" or brother in the legal profession, for Brent was WF's law partner. There is no evidence of relationship by blood or marriage between the two families for another generation or so. For more of Brent, see pp. 120-21 and 210-11.

3. There are many gaps in the County and General Court records of this period, as noticed in the Foreword above. Stafford County records of all kinds skip from 1668 to 1689, for example. Nor do the General Court records survive for the years before, during, and immediately after this letter.

A Matthew Thompson in the 1690's was a justice of the peace in Stafford County and a considerable dealer in real estate. 1 V 231, 251; 5 V 278; 9 W(2) 182; *Exec. Journ. Council Col. Va.,* I, 370.

Thomas Owsley or Ouzley or Owzley emigrated from Lyme Regis to Westmoreland County *c.* 1677. By the 1690's, perhaps earlier, he was a prominent citizen of Stafford, in 1699 becoming clerk of the court. In 1692 he was seated on Little Hunting Creek in what was later Fairfax County, trading with the Piscataway Indians. 38 V 326-27; *Exec. Journ. Council Col. Va.,* I, *passim.*

To Thomas Clayton [1]

Mr. Thomas Clayton   April 7th. 1679

Sir   I have sent you the Report of One Cause of Action twice presented in our Court [2] I being both times retained by the Defendant. First before the Court themselves as triers of the fact, & Dispensers of the Law arising from that fact which found the Defendant & Plaintiff was nonsuite. Secondly upon the renewing the suite again the Plaintiff prays a Jury may be impanelled to enquire into the fact, who were accordingly summoned & sworn, who find for the Defendant. Upon which Verdict the Court gave judgment against the Plaintiff for ex facto jus oritur,[3] from which judgment the Plaintiff appeals. Now Sir I apprehend by the Law of England that when a Jury who are sworn tryers of the fact have found it, the fact that in that Case is no more to be enquired into without attainting the Jury, by reason Jurys are so strongly bound, both by their oath administer'd to them upon the tryal, as also for fear of Attainder being so severe & dreadfull by the common Law. Quod committantur Gnotæ Domini Regis, et quod omnia terræ et tenementa, capiantur in manum Domini Regis, et deratentur et extirpentur, et uxores et liberi eorum ammoventur, et omnia bona et Catulla foris faciunt Domino Regi et Amado amittunt liberum legem in perpetuum   My Lord Cooke in the first part of his Institutes folio 294 [4] says that this judgment imports eight great & generall punishments, & in the third Institutes divides into five parts as folio 222.[5] see Kelwayes Reports fo: 83.[6] Second Institutes fo: 130 & 237. 238 [7] & in the first recited place, gives the reason of the said judgment, because all Actions depend upon the oath of twelve Men, prudent Antiquity instituted so severe a punishment, but since the Statute of 23 H: 8. chap: 3.[8] hath something mitigated the punishment (See the Statute well expounded in Dyer) [9] fo: 81. and Cooke's Reports Lib: 3. fo: 4. & Lib: 10. fo: 119. yet not made it so slight, as that another Jury shall go out upon the same matter of fact, & bring in a contrary Verdict, which is both against Magna Carta & the fundamentall Laws of England, by which Law we are or ought to be governed, to condemn men unheard, how dangerous a thing it is, to change an antient Maxim of the Law   See the second part Cooke's Institutes fo: 97 & 98.[10] for as Cicero saith Major hæredit[as?] venit unicui᷒., rostram a jure et legibus, quam a parentibus, & as my Lord Cooke saith in his Commentary upon magna Carta fo: 56.[11] the Law is the surest Sanctuary that a man can take, & the strongest fortress to protect the weakest of all. But where is this Sanctuary & fortress, if the Law shall be so wrested, & contradictory Verdicts so taken, whereby innocent & honest men unheard & unseen, shall be lyable to Infamy and beggary, Infamy by being gulity of Perjury, and beggary if a legal scrutiny shall be made therein. And besides by the Law of England, all Jurys ought to be of the Neighbourhood, & in this Country I think the Constitution may very well permit it, in the same County, for the Rule is, Vicini Vicniora facta presumtur scire. This I have written with as much brevity as I could, because I am informed they generally so proceed at James Town, it rather requires a small treatise than a letter to discourse thoroughly upon it, but refer you to the quotations, where you may see it learnedly discussed, & hope there may be no occasion of urging it, for I take an Appeal to be the removing the matter in Law before a higher Court & better Judges, for the words of the Appeal be the judgment of the Court, & not from the Verdict of the Jury, that is, that the Judges are mistaken in point of Law in giving their Judgment which may be easily collected from the words. Thus Sr. I have adventured though unknown to recommend my Client & his cause which I have truly reported as it was argued here, & hinted what inconveniencies will follow, if Verdicts which are dictum Veritatis should be destroyed, without proceeding according to Law by Attaint, which is the particular remedy given by the Law, which point as I before intimated, requires rather a small treatise than a letter fully to discourse upon   I am

To. Mr. Thos. Clayton   Yr.   W.   ff.

[*LB*, pp. 7-8]

1. Thomas Clayton, attorney, represented James City County in the House of Burgesses from 1680 to 1682. He was probably of the family of Clayton of Fulwood, Lancashire, England. He was probably also a relative of the Thomas Clayton, merchant in Liverpool, to whom WF wrote on April 8, 1687. 1 V 225-53, 399; 3 V 275, etc.; *Journals H.B. 1659/60-1693, passim.*
2. "our Court" would mean the court of Stafford County, the records of which, as noted above, do not survive for this period.
3. That is, "the law arises out of the fact."
4. Reference correct to *Institutes,* I, folio 294. A number of these references have been checked and annotated by the present editor so that the reader may see the degree of WF's accuracy in reference and the method of his legal research.
5. *Institutes,* III (1640 ed.), Cap. 8 "Of Releases." Actually page 222 rather than folio 222.
6. Robert Keilwey's *Reports* appeared in both Latin and French editions, *e.g., Relationes quorundam casuum selectorum ex libris ... Regis Henrici Septimi, et ... Regis Henrici Octavi, emerserunt. . . .* (London, 1602, 1633 and 1638 eds. have identical pagination). WF has given us here, however, what appears to be a confused secondhand reference. *Institutes,* III, 222, gives reference to "Judgement, 109. 21 H. 7. 83. Kelway, a good president of a judgement given in an attaint."
7. Correct.
8. Also referred to in *Institutes,* I, folio 222. *Statutes* (1618 ed.), p. 491, gives this reference. If a petty jury give untrue verdict, every member of said jury is fined twenty pounds. etc.
9. Sir James Dyer (editions from sixteenth century on), *e.g., Les Reports des divers select Matters et Resolutions des Reverend Judges et Sages del Ley ... en le several reignes. . . .* (London, 1688).
10. On legitimacy or inheritance.
11. *Institutes,* II, 56. Cap. 29.

To William Sherwood [1]

Worthy Sir   April 7th. 1679

Once more at the instance of Bur Harrison [2] I take opportunity to write to you, I think the poor man is very much troubled in the delay of his business, for if Matthews had any title to land,[3] by the Law he ought to have Commenced suite & had a legal tryal, for by Magna Carta Chap: 29. & Cooke's Commentary's thereon fo: 46.47 [4] No man shall be disseised of his lands or tenements, or dispossess'd of his goods, without Action or Answer contrary to the Law of the Land. But here Harrison is kept out of his Right, that is Thomas Barton's plantation wch. he hath sufficiently made appear to be his,[5] without either Action or Answer, contrary to the Law of the Land, only under the colour of a pretended title, Matthews lays to it, which if it were true has no relation to that Controversie of Thomas Barton because Barton was possess'd by & held under Harrison's feofee, & not by any title or claim from the said Matthews, & consequently is a trespasser to the said Harrison. But as far as I can understand, Matthews has hardly the shadow of a title, for he grounds it, upon a grant from the Council when himself was Governor in 1657 & their Patents bears date & were confirmed in 1654 what a pretence that is the meanest Capacity is able to apprehend. A Grant without a Pattent obtained three years after a Pattent solemnly Signed, Sealed & confirmed

Sir I trust to your Care in that Concern of mine & three others partners,[6] & hope to hear something of it by this opportunity   I am

To Mr. William Sherwood   Your   W. ff.

[*LB*, pp. 8-9]

1. For Sherwood, see ltr. to him of June 10, 1679, note 1.
2. Burr Harrison [Harrys or Harrs] (1637-1706), born in the parish of St. Margaret's, Westminster, settled in Stafford about 1669. He lived in the Chopawamsic area and owned lands along a tributary of the Occoquan and in other sections of old Stafford. He was later involved in Waugh's "Tumult" (q.v.) and in 1699 was the colony's "ambassador" to his neighbors the Piscataway Indians. Harrison, *Landmarks*, I, 129-38; *Prince Wm. WPA*, p. 98; *Exec. Journ. Council Col. Va.*, 1, 104, 519; 23 V 215; 30 V 33-37.
3. Apparently this refers to the part of a 5,211-acre tract which in 1680, the following year, Harrison formally "purchased" from John Mathews, a tract originally patented by Samuel Mathews. Here WF is concerned with a fairly typical land case, in which Harrison appears to have claimed and held the land for a considerable time without challenge and apparently without knowledge for some time that Mathews later had once had it granted to him. Included here are problems and overtones of the Commonwealth-*v.*-Restoration period and governments, of Cavalier and Puritan. Incidentally, all of this, including the reference to Governor Mathews just below, seems further proof that Samuel Mathews (or Matthews), Junior (who probably died *c.* 1670), and not his father (1600-1660), was governor of Virginia in 1657. See also 14 W(2) 105-10. Samuel, Jr., was the brother of WF's friend Thomas Mathews (q.v.). Why WF uses present tense "has" and "grounds" in referring to former Governor Mathews is difficult to conjecture, since presumably Mathews had been dead for nine years.
4. *Institutes*, II, 46-47. Cap. 29. "Magna Charta" is the more usual spelling for WF and for Coke.
5. Barton's plantation was probably in upper Stafford, now Prince William County. See note 2, ltr. to Sherwood, June 10, 1679.
6. Sherwood as attorney-general of the colony may have been handling this matter for WF and his partners before the General Court. It was probably a land-grant matter; for, even

though the Northern Neck counties were a part of the Proprietary and their lands not to be granted directly by the Crown or its representatives, disputes over land and many other things went to the colony's General Court. See the later Fitzhugh *vs.* Dade case.

To the Honourable Nicholas Spencer [1]

Honoured Sir   Septr. 9th. 1679

I am informed by Burr Harrison [2] that you tax me of rashness in counselling him, phaps it might seem so to you, for want of a thorough information of his just Right, & a false information of a feigned Right, the first pretension of a title to the Land in Controversie, was by old Capt. Brent [3] who upon his pretended Right settled severall Tennants to say Burr Harrison Thomas Barton & one Bennet, whose widow this woman is, that makes such an exclamation about the house pull'd down; Afterwards Collo. Washington as Guardian to Gerrard Broadhurst sues & tries title about this Land, in Stafford County & recovers,[4] & the said tennants all turned to him, & became his Tennants as Guardian aforesaid. After the Tennants sue Giles Brent as Son & heir of his father deceas'd for their said Eviction & trouble & recovers agst him.[5] Afterwards Burr Harrison buys the Land of Gerrard Broadhurst being of age, so that by this it may appear, that Gerrard Broadhurst had a Title by Pattent, Possession, & the Judgment of Stafford County Courts, & consequently Burr Harrison is in Possession & the Rule is In equali Jure melior est Conditis possidentis And by magna Charta Nulli vendemus, nulli negabimus, nulli deferremus justitiam aut rectum & my Lord Cooke's Commentary thereupon fo: 46-47,[6] whose words are these, No man shall be disseised of his Lands or Tenements, or dispossess'd of his goods or Chattels without Action or Answer or contrary to the Law of the Land. But here Harrison is kept out of his Right, that is Barton's Plantation, which he hath sufficiently made appear to be his, without either Action or Answer & then contrary or only under the colour of a pretended title Matthews lays to it, which if it were true, yet Barton is a trespasser to Harrison, because Barton was possessed & held under Harrison's feofee, & not by any title or claim from the said Matthews. But as far as I am informed Matthews has hardly the shadow of a title, for he grounds upon a Grant from the Council when he himself was Governour in 1657, & the Pattent Harrison holds by, bears date & was confirmed in 1654. Now in my apprehension, a Grant without a Pattent, obtained three years after a Pattent solemnly signed, sealed & confirmed, cannot be very efficacious in destroying a title granted by that Pattent. Thus Sir I have run over the heads of the whole business, that I might make it perspicuous, that my counsel in advising them to pull down the house, after lawfull warning given them to depart, was not rash & inconsiderate, but grounded upon good reason & Authority in Law   For more than all I have before informed you, this widow Bennet after Harrisons Purchase did not only atturne & acknowledge her new Land-lord, but delivered up her lease into his hands, & after she & a freeman that lives with her, took the Plantation from that time till the fall, for the Rent of one hhd. of Tobo. At the expiration of which time, Harrison gives them two month's notice to provide for themselves, & before wit-nesses severall times forewarned them off, but their answer was they would neither go off nor pay the Rent. Then & not before I advised him to pull down the house, having found a Paralel Case adjudged intermino Hilarie 34. Eliza: inter Wigford & Gill in Banco Reginæ Cooke Eliza. fo: 269.[7] when the same thing was done, & after both Arguments at the Bar & solemn Argument at the Bench allowed of & justified. The man's importunity & my own vindication has drawn the letter to this prolixity, Yet I hope your Honour considering the occasion will pardon it in

To The Honble. Nics.   Honrd. Sr. Yr.   W. ff.
Spencer Esqr. Secretary

[LB, pp. 9-11]

1. Nicholas Spencer (d. 1689), second son of Nicholas Spencer of Cople in Bedfordshire, came to Virginia about 1659. In this year he is referred to by Nicholas Hayward the elder (q.v.) as a London merchant. Spencer settled in Westmoreland County at Nomini, and the parish of Cople was named in honor of his family seat in England. He was a burgess from 1666 to 1676; Indian commissioner in 1675/76; Secretary of State from 1679 to 1689; acting Governor and President of the Council from 1683 to 1684. He is generally said to have been the most powerful man in the colony for more than a decade. Apparently he and WF were always close friends. The question may well be asked as to whether Spencer's origin in Bed-fordshire and his relationship with WF's London friends the Haywards does not point to Spencer as the means that brought WF to Virginia.
   Spencer's blood kinship with the Culpeper family may have been the reason for his settling in the Northern Neck Proprietary and for WF's early association with the Proprietors as legal agent. 2 V 32-34; *Exec. Journ. Council Col. Va.,* I, *passim.*
   2. See ltr. to Wm. Sherwood, April 7, 1679, note 2, and content of ltr.
   3. Giles Brent (d. 1671) the elder, of a famous Virginia-Maryland family, had been in the 1630's and 1640's a councilor and even Treasurer of the Province of Maryland. Between 1648 and 1650 he and his sister Margaret (see *D.A.B.*) quarrelled with the Maryland government and moved across the river into Westmoreland County and settled at "Peace." He married the sister of an Indian chief; his half-breed son, Giles, Jr., is mentioned later by WF. Giles the elder was apparently an uncle of WF's law partner George Brent. *Archives of Md.,* I, *passim; Md. Hist. Mag.,* XXIX, 212-23; *Prince Wm. WPA,* p. 20.
   4. Walter Broadhurst died in 1658, leaving patents to land in Chopawamsic to his son

Gerard. The same property or another five hundred acres was patented to Gerard by Governor Berkeley in 1668. Since Gerard's mother married as her third husband John Washington, he is probably the Colonel Washington referred to as her son's guardian. This is John the immigrant. Freeman, *George Washington*, I, 21n; 4 T 332; 3 W(2) 100; Harrison, *Landmarks*, I, 53.

 5. Giles Brent, Jr. (1652-1679) married Mary, a sister of his cousin George Brent of "Woodstock." 16 V 99; 19 V 445; Harrison, *Landmarks*, I, 75.

 6. *Institutes*, II, 45.

 7. *Ibid.*, I, folio 269, contains a considerable discussion of "Releases" but this particular parallel has not been located.

To the Honourable Nicholas Spencer [1]

Honrd. Sir   Novr. 2nd. 1680

 Thomas Dutton [2] was recommended to me by the Honble. Ralph Wormley Esqr. [3] to manage his business about Prescot's lands, upon view and examination of all his papers, I find him to have no longer an Estate than for life in those lands if the Will made by Prescott in new London were here authentickly proved. [4] Yet upon a farther consideration, waving all thoughts of any real Interest of any Estate of Inheritance in the lands, I considered the Equitable Right of the Escheat to appertain to him, & considering also you are pleas'd to grant an Escheat, to those who in Equity, had the most seeming right, I was intended to have waited upon your Honr. with Thomas Dutton, so soon as I should have an account of your safe & desired Arrival to communicate this to you, & sollicite yor. Honour in the poor man's behalf. While these thoughts & intentions were thus in my mind, Thomas Dutton brings me a letter he receiv'd from your Honr. considering his equitable Right, wherein you appear not only willing to grant him the Escheat upon his Petition, but are pleased to offer him the Escheat, & direct him to petition & compound for the same. Immediately upon view of this your Honour's charitable offer, I directed him to go to his Tennants in whose behalf he now busies himself, & for whose interest he begs the benefit of Escheat, that he may now confirm what he before so foolishly sold to them, & they as simply bought of him To see what they would do in his behalf. Some of them agreed to stand by him & assist him in the payment of the composition money & Escheat fees; but being yesterday at Mr. Bridges [5] and understanding by Collo. Allerton [6] his Majestie's Escheator. That your Honour would not be paid in Parcel, but would have it in one intire sum. I discoursed some of the

Tennants who with Thomas Dutton intreated me to become security or paymaster for the whole, to say for that six hundred Acres. I was willing upon their request & Counter security, which they then promised me, to engage to you for the payment of the whole, if you will accept of my Security. Capt. Lord [7] Mr. Bridges & the rest of the petitioners seem pleased to tax me of self Interest upon these my offers; to acquit my self of that, I will acquaint your Honour, how I direct him in his Proceedings. Those Tennants that are willing to pay their proportionable rate of his Escheat, according to the quantity of land they hold, shall enjoy their former Purchase, & for this new imbursement will have their Estate ascertained and enlarged; which will be more to them, than the money they'll be out about it, those that are willing to reimburse any more, I'll take care with Dutton they shall not be turned off their Land Losers, but shall have reasonable satisfaction   If I had any self Interest (which I'll assure your Honour I have none) it must be esteemed very modest where the sole business that I aim at (in Dutton's behalf) is the continuing of former purchasers, the reimbursing those that are willing to continue, & keeping Dutton from endless litigious & expensive Suites, which must inevitably fall upon him, if the Escheat be elsewhere granted, & the Tennants be either turned off, or put to new Purchases

Sir

To. The Honble Nics. Spencer   Your   W. ff.
Esqr. Secretary

[*LB*, pp. 11-12]

1. For Spencer, see ltr. to him of September 9, 1679, note 1.
2. Another good evidence of WF's reputation as a lawyer by this date. Thomas Dutton appears in the Westmoreland records in depositions indicating he was born *c.* 1633-1635. Apparently he was a planter of that county. *Westmoreland County Deeds, Patents, etc., 1665-1677,* folio 312; *Deeds and Wills, No. 1, 1653-1671,* p. 147.
3. The Honorable Ralph Wormeley, Esq. (1650-1700) of "Rosegill," Middlesex County, was WF's client and friend over many years. Onetime student of Oxford, planter, burgess, member of the Council and, in 1693, Secretary of State and President of the Council, he was in the years after Spencer's death often referred to as "the most powerful man in Virginia." Wormeley was Collector of the Rappahannock district. He had a fine library. Wright, "Ralph Wormeley: a Cultivated Gentleman-Planter," *First Gent. Va.,* pp. 187-211; Swem, *Va. Hist. Index.*
4. The Connecticut Historical Society informs the editor that no will of any Prescot or Prescott shows in New London in this period.
5. Perhaps Anthony Bridges, one of the earliest attorneys of Stafford County. He received his license from Governor Berkeley in 1666. He is described as a man of ability and integrity. His name appears again and again in the Westmoreland County records. Bruce, *Inst. Hist. Va.,* I, 582; *Westmoreland County Court Order Book, 1675/6-1688/9, passim.*
6. Isaac Allerton (1630-1702) of Northumberland, second of the name in Virginia, was

the son of a Pilgrim who came on the *Mayflower* and of a daughter of William Brewster. Father and son arrived in Virginia between 1655 and 1663. Isaac II had three children by his first wife in New England and several more by his second wife Elizabeth (Willoughby) in Virginia. In 1686 he and WF were to be connected by marriage when Allerton's daughter married John Newton, Jr., son of WF's step-father-in-law. Some years later WF's daughter Rosamond married Allerton's son Willoughby. Allerton was a leading planter of the Northern Neck. At various times he was sheriff (of Northumberland), burgess, and councilor. With Thomas Gerard, Henry Corbin, and J. Lee he agreed in 1670 to build a banqueting house at the common joining of their properties. In 1686/87 he (and WF later) was called a papist by Parson John Waugh (q.v.), merely an indication that he was probably a loyal supporter of the Stuarts. Through Allerton the blood of two Pilgrim "saints" entered a prolific and prominent Virginia family and made thousands of Virginians *Mayflower* descendants.

An escheator was always a prominent citizen of the county, usually a councilor (though Allerton had not yet attained that rank). Apparently Allerton represented Northumberland and perhaps other counties. It was the escheator's duty to see that land of one dying without heirs be investigated and inquested by a jury of twelve. Certificate of the inquest went to the secretary of the colony (in this case Spencer), where it remained for nine months; then a patent was issued to the person for whom the inquest was made. Bruce, *Ec. Hist. Va.*, I, 566.

Confusing as most of the early grants and patents are, this one seems fairly clear. Prescot of New London, who had originally held the property, died and his will was not filed in Virginia, thus invalidating any heirs' future claims to the lands. Dutton had held the land for some time; Spencer, like most secretaries of state, was willing to grant Dutton the escheat because of his equitable right. What agreement Dutton had made with his tenants is to be inferred. They had secured long-term leases, perhaps for several lives, from him; yet without the escheat he may have held, as WF says, only his own life interest. For terms of tenancy, see Bruce, *Ec. Hist. Va.*, I, *passim*.

7. Probably John Lord of Mattox in Westmoreland County. He like Allerton had migrated from New England, where his father Thomas Lord was an original proprietor of Hartford. A Captain John Lord was living in Westmoreland as early as 1668. By a 1687 deed we know that he owned five hundred acres in Stafford at that time, "near Giles Brent's mill." At one time he was high sheriff of Westmoreland. 1 V 200; 8 V 409; 9 V 69; 16 W(1) 291. Also in 1692 a Captain John Lord commanded the Bristol ship *Jamaica Planter*. *P.R.O., C.O. 5/1306*. 119Vᵛ, L.C. copy. Presumably Lord, Bridges, and others had themselves petitioned for the land or certain rights thereof.

To Captain Francis Partis [1]

Sir   April 7th. 1680

That I may correspond with your desires & mine own inclinations, have by this opportunity sent you an account that I have receiv'd yor. Letter, & shall do my utmost endeavour, to the full accomplishment of your Deserts & desires therein. When I was on board, you may remember I entreated you to take me twenty hds. freight certain & thirty uncertain, you told me I need not because you would secure it me, upon which I rely. As I do'nt question your care & endeavour, in the Disposal of my

Tobo., so I doubt not you'll endeavour to furnish me with those necessary things I sent for by you, As also give me an Account of them by the first opportunity, & how all affairs stand in in [*sic*] England, which I shall assuredly expect from you, as you may do the station of all affairs in this Country from me, by all opportunity. I have omitted one thing in my Particular, which I desired you to buy for me, that is a Riding Camblet Coat,[2] if my money holds out, buy it, if not use your Discretion. In my note of Particulars I did not forget it, only omitted for fear of overcharging my accot. & your trouble. A prosperous Voyage, a lucky Market, & a happy Returne is wish'd by

Sir Yr.   W. ff.

To. Capt. Fras. Partis at the
Hermitage near East Smithfield London

[*LB*, pp. 12-13]

1. One of the ship captains with whom WF was on intimate terms. There are several letters to him below, and many references to him and to his brother Captain Charles Partis. A Matthias Partis also is mentioned below.
2. The word *Camblet* or *Camlet* originally referred to a costly eastern fabric, and then later to substitutes which were various combinations of wool, silk, hair, and sometimes linen or cotton.

To Captain Francis Partis [1]

Sir   June 11th. 1680

I promis'd you by all Conveniencys to give you an Account of the affairs of the Countrey, to comply therewith I have taken this opportunity, I am not able to inform you of any new matter, but only to tell you that we are at present very quiet from our Indian Enemies. I believe no great crop will be this year made, by reason of our great drought, not having had one good Shower since your departure, which is now almost a month, so that every thing is kept under thereby. I have drawn bills of Exchange on you for £ 7 .. 13 .. 4. payable to Mr. William Law[2] of London Merchant, if those bills comes to your hands please to give them due acceptance: for I had rather that part of my Pr. ticulars that I sent for by you, were let alone than the Discredit of the Protest of those Bills, which by no means let be protested. I am now a great distance from home & cannot be so large as I would, but shall refer you to my next Letter by some of our own Ships, for a more ample information I am,

Sir

To Capt. Fras. Partis at e&c.   Your   W. ff.

[*LB*, p. 13]

1. For Partis, see ltr. to him of April 7, 1680, note 1.
2. Law is unidentified. Presumably he is one of those from whom WF purchased household and agricultural equipment. By drawing a bill of exchange on Partis, WF apparently indicates that Partis was himself something of a merchant and at least the authorized agent. WF may have been drawing on an account already owed him by Partis or on anticipated returns from tobacco of that year.

To Captain Francis Partis [1]

Sir   June 11th. 1680

By my former I gave you what account I could how affairs stood then, there's little alteration has since happened, I have not now the Copy by me, being above one hundred miles from home, but take this opportunity to give you an account, that I advis'd by my last that I drew bills of Exchange for £7 .. 13 .. 4 which I did then & do now desire you to accept and make punctual payment. I did then also request you to let alone sending me some of my goods, rather than refuse the payment of those bills, but now I desire you to send or bring in every particular I have sent for, because I have here inclosed sent two bills of Exchange one for £20 sterling, the other for £3 I have also inclosed sent you a letter of Advice, to be delivered with that bill of £20. to Sr. Robert Peyton [2] upon sight of which I believe there's little doubt of receiving the money. I hope I shall have occasion to transmit near 100 £ sterling next Shipping, therefore please to give me an Account timely of your intentions whether you intend for Virginia next year or to stay there, that I may accordingly order my affairs. I expect to hear from you by all Conveniencies, wherein I hope I may have a particular relation of my own affairs, & a generall account of the proceedings there. This is the needfull from

To Capt. Fras. Partis at e&c.   Your   W. ff.

[*LB*, p. 14]

1. For Partis, see ltr. to him of April 7, 1680, note 1. At this time WF was attending the General Assembly at Jamestown and was very busy in its work. *Journals H.B. 1659/60-1693,* pp. 120-23.

2. Sir Robert Peyton was probably a relative of Major Robert Peyton of Gloucester County, Virginia, mentioned several times below. Other Peytons had lived and died in Westmoreland County and were connected with WF through his marriage. Eaton, *Hist. Atlas Westmoreland,* p. 55; Lyon G. Tyler, *Encyclopedia of Virginia Biography* (New York, 1915), 35 vols., I, 304; John B. Burke, *A Genealogical and Heraldic History of the Extinct and Dormant Baronetcies of England, Ireland and Scotland* (2nd ed.; London, 1844), *passim.*

To Captain Francis Partis [1]

Sir   The above is Copy of my former June 11th. 1680 I have no new matter to add, only I would have you be very carefull of my flax, hemp & hayseed, two bushels of each of which I have sent for, because we now have resolved a cessation from making Tobo. next year, We are also going to make Towns,[2] if you can meet with any tradesmen, that will come in & live at the Towns, they may have large priviledges & immunitys. I would have you to bring me in a good Housewife, I do not intend or mean to be brought in as the ordinary servants are, but to pay for her passage, & agree to give her fifty shillings or three pound a year, during the space of five years, upon which terms I suppose good servants may be had, because they have their passage clear, & as much wages as they can have there, I would have a good one or none: I look upon the generality of wenches you usually bring in not worth the keeping. I expect to hear from you by all conveniencys, for I assure you I let slip none to tell you I am &c. I would have you bring me two large Paper books, one to contain about fourteen or fifteen Quire of Paper, the other about ten Quire, & one other small one

July 1st. 1680   W. ff.
Capt. Fowler

To Capt. Fras. Partis at &c.

[*LB,* pp. 14-15]

1. For Partis, see ltr. to him of April 7, 1680, note 1.

2. Seeing the need for ports of entry other than Jamestown, soon after the arrival of Lord Culpeper as governor in May, 1680, the General Assembly in June passed an elaborate bill "for the encouragement of cohabitation." Ostensibly this act was brought about by the

low prices of tobacco and the belief that there would be great advantages in central storehouses at convenient places for the reception of all merchandise imported and tobacco to be exported. Each "town" was to be of fifty acres, one in each county. Sites selected in WF's neighborhood were Tyndall's Point in Gloucester, the Wormeley plantation in Middlesex, Corotoman in Lancaster, Chickacony in Northumberland, Hobb's Hole (now Tappahannock) in Rappahannock, and Peace Point in WF's own Stafford. As inducement to build, one-half acre was granted in fee simple to anyone on condition he build a residence and store on it, and pay one hundred pounds of tobacco to the county.

All forms of merchandise and all English servants and Negro slaves imported into the colony were to be landed and disposed of only in these towns. The planter was to bring his tobacco in a sloop to the town. This would have proved most expensive to many planters, perhaps a boon to those who lived nearby. English merchants opposed it because it introduced a distinct middleman between them and the planters. Many captains of ships ignored it from the beginning. It was eventually suspended. Governor Nicholson tried it again in 1691 in his Act for Ports, with a smaller number of ports. In 1691, WF's friends William Digges and John Buckner, among others, invested in lots in a town at York they hoped might become the Virginia metropolis. This Act was suspended, too, in 1692/93. Tried again in 1705, it was again unsuccessful, this time largely because of the opposition of the merchants trading in Virginia.

Many of the principles behind these acts were in WF's mind at various times when he attempted to make his own wharf the center from which he and his neighbors could operate. Beverley, *Hist. of Va.*, pp. 88, 100; Bruce, *Ec. Hist. Va.*, II, 547-62; Hening, *Statutes*, II, 471, 478; *Exec. Journ. Council Col. Va.*, I, *passim*; *Journals H.B. 1659/60-1693*, *passim*.

To Captain Francis Partis [1]

Sir   Decr. 4th. 1680

Both your's I have receiv'd by Capt. Paine [2] am glad of your health, sorry you came to no better a market. I hope this year Tobo. will rise by reason there's but small Crops made throughout this Country and Maryland too. I have got ready the Tobo. I owe you, which when your brother comes or any one by your order may receive, we now look out every day for his Arrival, by whom I intend to ship thirty or fourty hhds. Crops are so small & debts comes in so badly that I cannot send so much as I thought by twenty hhds. But what I do send is pretty good. What friend, I can advise shall assuredly secure you. Mr. Scarlet [3] has promised me to consign you twenty hhds. and I believe shall get you some more this year. Sr. I kindly observe two passages in your letter, one is that if I have occasion for fourty or fifty pound sterling you will pay it, though you have none of my effects in your hands, the other that you paid my last bills of £7 .. 13 .. 4 at sight. The one gives me credit the other honour for both which I thank you. I understand by the said letter that you have sent me all I sent for which you inform me comes to something more than you have in your hands. Yet being encouraged by your letter & assured of money, that I shall remit home if my Tobo. should either miscarry or come to a bad market, for I shall certainly remit home a hundred pound sterling certain, if not more from good hands & sure paymasters. I have ventured on a bargain of 29£ sterling for two Negroes of Mr. Vincent Goddard [4] for which I have drawn bills of Exchange upon you which please give due acceptance I know not yet what to inlarge, by the first opportunity after your brother's Arrival, shall give you a larger account, & therefore at present shall only tell you that I shall always continue

Sr.

To. Capt. Francis Partis   Your   W. ff.

[LB, pp. 14-15]

1. For Partis, see ltr. to him of April 7, 1680, note 1.
2. Unidentified.
3. Captain Martin Scarlet of Stafford County was from this time on WF's principal rival for a seat in the House of Burgesses from Stafford County. In 1685/86 they presented charges against each other in the General Assembly; in 1691 they presented accusations against each other in the Stafford County Court (below). Scarlet was usually a burgess when WF was not, though occasionally both were elected together. Both were justices of the peace. Scarlet was allied with the Waugh-Mason Whiggishly-inclined group of gentry (see Introduction above). On a grave near Dawson's Beach, near Occoquan, is a worn inscription bearing the decipherable words "M.S. 1695. Here lyes Martin Scarlet, Gentleman." *Journals H.B. 1659/60-1693*; *Journals H.B. 1695-1702, passim*, and *Prince Wm. WPA*, pp. 83-84.
4. Unidentified. There had been a person of this name in the colony as early as 1624. In the eighteenth century there were Goddards in Prince William (formerly Stafford). 27 V 292; *Prince Wm. WPA*, p. 34.

To the Honourable Ralph Wormeley [1]

Honoured Sir   February 1st. 1680

Your's I receiv'd together with one from the Honble. Mr. Secretary [2] & another from Collo. Allerton [3] who acquaints me the 14th. february is the day he hath appointed a Jury to meet for the finding an Office for your Grant.[4] At which time or before (if sickness &c. doth not prevent) I shall wait upon you to tender you the utmost of my service in that affair & anything else you shall please farther to command me, shall endeavour in the mean time throughly to understand the Case, & learn how the Law directs that is whether it be a will, considering the meanness of the Stile, & immethodicall penning thereof, when the party speaking (or which ought to speak) was a person of such known abilitys, if the discovery of the fraud fails in the consideration of the stile then he that was known so good a Master of his pen, should in the last act of his life affix his mark, is almost irrationall to imagine. Secondly If it be a will whether it be good in whole or in part, that it is not good in the whole, the first part Argument makes manifest, by affixing his mark &c. Thirdly if it be good in part, in which part, That it cannot be good in that part that concerns the Land, this late Statute hath provided, for the title of the Statute is to prevent frauds & perjury, the preamble or key of the Statute pursues the same, then the body of the Act declares the manner how this shall be avoided, when such considerable bequests as Lands & tenements, that is by three or four witnesses at the least, but here is but two, then for this part void, & all thoughts of Equity banished, by reason of the probable presumption of fraud in the whole, but more especially in this part. Fourthly & Lastly Admit that it were a Will good in all its parts, & fully supply'd with all the ceremonies that the Law requires, whether his lands & Tenements should pass by these words real & personal Estate, admits I think considerable Dispute. These Sr. are the heads of the Argument, that I at present apprehend, are to be managed in your just Cause, & which I shall take pains to my Ability to inform my self in, where I hope I may assure you I am

To The Honble. Ralph Wormley   Sir Yr. W. ff.

[*LB*, pp. 15-16]

1. For Wormeley, see ltr. to Nicholas Spencer of November 2, 1680, note 3. This is the first of a series of letters to Wormeley extending into 1684 concerning a suit in both the Middlesex and General Courts concerning certain land formerly the property of Colonel John Burnham, bequeathed by him to Leroy Griffin and Lewis Burwell (qq.v.), and granted to Wormeley when the will was declared invalid because it had only two witnesses.

2. For Nicholas Spencer, the Secretary of State, see ltr. to him of September 9, 1679, note 1.

3. For Allerton, see ltr. to Nicholas Spencer, November 2, 1680, note 6. Though a resident of Northumberland County, he may have been escheator for several counties of this northeastern part of Virginia.

4. Proceedings to prove the rights of Griffin and Burwell began in Middlesex County and consume many pages of its records. The "finding an Office" for the grant is apparently used in a legal sense generally referring to the King's rights to land, "to return a verdict showing that the king is entitled to the possession of lands or chattels." *Shorter Ox. Dict.*

To Stephen Watts [1]

Mr. Stephen Watts   March 30th. 1681

Sr.   By the Bristol men [2] that have used our parts I have heard of you, but by Mr. Richard Gotley [3] this year dealing in these parts, I have had more particular account, of your honest & faithful dealings, which induced me at this time to consign you eight hhds. of Tobo., an Invoyce whereof I have inclosed sent you, this only [a]s an invitation to correspondence if the market gives encouragement, I shall consign you more next year & a greater quantity. The commodity is grown so low here & in England too, that I am affraid the present necessity of my affairs, forcing me to send home with my Tobo. bills of Exchange for £12 .. 10 .. 00 of their acceptance. Therefore Sr. I shall only desire you to proceed in this method for me, if my Tobo. meets a good market, make ready acceptance of the Bills, & send me the remainder in such things as I shall after mention, but if my Tobo. should not clear the money drawn for, please to pay as much for them as you shall have in your hands, & let the remainder be only protested. You are much a stranger to me but I much more to you, therefore dare not make an Overture of paying more money than you have effects, nor of sending me any thing without I had mine own with you to pay, the things I want are a pair of Cart wheels horse harness for three horses, a pack Saddle & two dozen shoes. I shall enlarge by the latter Ships

[no signature]

[*LB*, pp. 16-17]

1. Stephen Watts, member of the Bristol Society of Adventurers from at least 1665, was a merchant of prominence. He imported a great deal of tobacco from Virginia and exported it again to Spain and northern Europe. A list of the articles he exported to Virginia in 1679 in the *Bristol Factor* includes shoes, "stockins," "Woosted hose," 14 pds. of "haberdashery," one "Ferkin" of butter, cloth, 4 dozen "bodices," 10 suits of "Apparell," English fustians, nails, wrought iron, one feather bed, blankets, 150 English glass bottles, 2 "quarternes of Mault," butts of sack, and 150 "soape." McGrath, *Records, passim; Merchants, passim.*

2. As this correspondence and the notes indicate, Bristol seamen and merchants were most active in Virginia in the later seventeenth century. For details of their operations from the English point of view, see McGrath, *Merchants,* and *Records.*

3. Richard Gotley (or Gostley), a Quaker Bristol merchant, was probably the person of that name who as early as 1667 had the benefit of a Virginia General Assembly act "granting seven years Liberty after the date of the patent for seating" land. In 1675, Gotley granted power of attorney to his brother Peter then setting out for Virginia. Later he was an

executor of the will of Thomas Pope of Bristol and Virginia. He is one of the better examples of the Bristol merchant who personally and through relatives and close friends had direct experience in and with the Virginia colony. He is mentioned several times later in WF's correspondence. McGrath, *Merchants; Journals H.B. 1659/60-1693*, p. 50; 3 W(2) 102; 3 V 424; 17 V 346.

To John Cooper [1]

Mr. Jno. Cooper   April 4th. 1681

Sr

By the Reccomends of Capt. Norrington [2] & some little knowledge I have of your honest & fair dealing, by Inspection into some Returns of Sales of Tobo. & purchase of goods, has occasioned this letter, wherein you'll find the Invoice of eight hhds. of Oronoko Tobo.[3] & bill of Loading for the same consigned to yor. self which I hope you'll help to the best market. The inclosed Bills of Exchange I desire you to present & receive. By the latter Ships shall enlarge & give farther Directions, & perhaps consign you more Tobo. & send you some more bills   I am

[no signature]

[*LB*, p. 17]

1. John Cooper was a London merchant with an office, as we are told later, in "the Virginia Walk" along the London waterfront. This letter marks the beginning of an extended correspondence and factor-planter relationship over most of the remainder of WF's life.
2. Captain William Norrington appears frequently in WF's letters. As a ship captain, he enjoyed the confidence of the Virginia government as well as of individual planters. As commander of the *Barnadistance* in 1692, he brought in gunpowder and other ammunition for the colony. *Exec. Journ. Council Col. Va.*, I, 134, 230; *Journals H.B. 1659/60-1693*, pp. 384, 401.
3. In *The Present State of Virginia* ([orig. ed., 1724] new ed.; Chapel Hill, 1956), the Reverend Hugh Jones distinguishes (pp. 77-78) between "Oroonoko the stronger, and sweet-scented the milder; the first with a sharper leaf like a fox's ear, and the other rounder and with finer fibres: but each of these are varied into several sorts, much as apples and pears are." Though Jones believed that the lands between the York and the James were those best suited for the growth of sweetscented, WF claimed (ltr. to James Bligh of 1697, below) that his sweetscented was as excellent as the same kind of York. Oronoco was usually grown in the Chesapeake Bay region and the back settlements in the rich land along the rivers. Though his soils were a determining factor, WF seems to have sometimes been influenced as to which he planted in greater quantity by what he anticipated would be the demand in England. For a firsthand intelligent observation of Virginia tobacco-growing in the 1680's, see John Clayton's letter in *Miscellanea Curiosa* ..., III (London, 1707), 304-7. Also Bruce, *Ec. Hist. Va.*, I, 432-36; G. Melvin Herndon, *Tobacco in Colonial Virginia: "The Sovereign Remedy,"* Jamestown 350th Anniversary Historical Booklets, no. 20 (Williamsburg, 1957).

To the Honourable Ralph Wormeley [1]

Hond. Sir   May 21st. 1681

I intended to wait upon you as I came from Town to give you an account of Collo. Griffins &c proceedings about Collo. Burnham's land, for which you have had an office found. By your former letter & my answer thereunto, I thought my self oblig'd to your part, & to my utmost to hinder the probate of the said Will, but hearing nothing from, & being threatned by mutuall bonds, given & taken between you & the others, I could make no Defence, in your behalf nay durst not own my self concerned on your side, yet was troubl'd to see such proceedings, & such large fees given by them, to the value of fifty pound Sterling which I certainly guess'd was for a farther end than to secure the personal Estate & accordingly so it happened, for at the latter end of the Court they petition for a day to be assigned them this next Court to traverse the Office found,[2] pretending a right by virtue of the said Will with some reflections upon their first Delay in the probate at your County Court.[3] I have sent this Gent. Mr. Hickes [4] purposely with this letter to advise you thereof & receive your Commands & instructions therein, whereby I am assured it will appear with a better countenance, at the next Court, to their trouble & loss, & to your quiet & content wch. is truly desired by

To. The Honble Ralph Wormley Esqr.   Your   W. ff.

[*LB.* pp. 17-18]

1. For Wormeley, see ltr. to Nicholas Spencer of November 2, 1680, note 3. This letter is the second concerning the Wormeley *vs.* Griffin and Burwell land case. See ltr. to Wormeley of February 1, 1680, above and several ltrs. below.
2. The text of the arguments before the higher court and Council are included in 18 V 129-60 and *Exec. Journ. Council Col. Va.,* I, 479-85; Hening, *Statutes,* II, 563-64; *Middlesex County Deeds, No. 2, 1679/80-1694,* pp. 27 ff.; *Middlesex County Order Book, 1680-1694,* pp. 10-12, 48, 54-55. WF and Robert Beverley (q.v.) were Wormeley's counsel, and other lawyers in the case before the general court included Thomas Clayton, William Sherwood, and Arthur Spicer. Though the decision has not come down to us, there is an opinion of William Jones, attorney-general of England, on this very case in "Barradall's Reports," p. B 1 (Vol. II, R. T. Barton, ed., *Colonial Decisions* [Boston, 1909]). Jones fully sustained the contention of the plaintiff's counsel that the will was good. A note in Barradall (p. B 2) observes that Lord Culpeper showed this opinion to all the judges in England and they pronounced it good

law, and that on Culpeper's second arrival in Virginia, about November, 1682, he in the General Court pronounced judgment accordingly. Thus, despite what might be called the high-powered team of Fitzhugh and Beverley, it would seem that Wormeley lost his case. This was a battle of giants on both sides, for Wormeley, Burwell, and Griffin were leading planters and the lawyers of the opposition were among the ablest of the colony.

3. The probate in the Middlesex County Court has not been located. The first full extant record of this court is of September 30, 1681. *Middlesex County Deeds, No. 2, 1679/80-1694; Deeds, etc., 1687-1750; Order Book, 1673-1680; Order Book, 1680-1694; Wills, etc., 1675-1698*, Pts. 1 and 2.

4. Perhaps this was John Hicks, doorkeeper of the House of Burgesses during some of the years between 1682 and 1701.

To Captain Francis Partis [1]

Capt. Francis Partis   May 31st. 1681

Sr.   Till the Receipt of your's by Capt. Shepard [2] I was fully intended to write you at large, but by that understanding, that you intend certainly in this next year I refer a larger discourse till then, but yet must now tell you, I am sorry the Initiation of a Correspondence with you, should by your unkind dealing be so soon broken off. Your brother Capt. Charles Partis is able to give you an account thereof & to him I'll refer, who has endeavoured as much as in him lies to palliate the matter, by perswading me that it was not really & intentionally done by you, but by mistake or some other accident, which in truth by his perswasions & my own charitable inclinations, I am no Infidel to, yet could do no less than stop the Current of all farther dealings, till these mistakes & Errors if they be so, already committed be regulated, which I suppose may not be difficult upon your Arrival. What of your Tobo. is paid & why not all paid, & the care & provision I had taken therein, your brother can, & will I dare say fully inform you. I hope I shall see you in timely this next year in your first Rate Merchantman which I shall be very glad of who am

To Capt. Francis Partis in London   Sir Yr.   W. ff.
℈ his brother Capt. Charles Partis

[*LB*, p. 18]

1. For Partis, see ltr. to him of April 7, 1680, note 1.
2. Shepard is unidentified. He may be the George Sheppard mentioned in WF's will as one from whom he secured land.

To Captain John Lucum [1]

Mr. John Lucum   May 31st. 1681

If nobody should come from me or by my order, to take the bills of Exchange for the Pipe Staves, & the bills of loading for the eleven hhds. of Tobo. consigned to Mr. John Cooper [2] of London Merchant, I am so far satisfy'd of your Integrity & fidelity, that I request you to do it your self, that is to pass bills of Exchange for your full debt, according to the number of Pipe Staves you receive, & bills of Loading for the eleven hhds. Tobo. according to the agreement, & yr. receipt for the other one hhd., consigned to your self, which I would have you thus order. Inclose one of the bills of Loading & one of the bills of Exchange, in this letter to Mr. Jno. Cooper which you have open, & write a letter your self to me, & inclose the other two bills of Loading & the two bills of Exchange, & your Receipt for the hhd. Tobo. well sealed up, & leave them either with Mr. William Hardidge [3] or Mr. Secretary [4] & deliver them to themselves with request to keep them, till I send for them for fear of miscarriages, if they should chance to convey them up to me by an uncertain hand.

Also I farther request you to acquaint Mr. Cooper, the reason that I could not indorse the bills of Exchange to him, which upon your information will give him the opportunity of demanding & receiving it without Indorsement. I hope you'll keep this letter by you, for your Instructions & follow it, if I have not the opportunity of sending one to do it for me which will oblige

To Capt. Jno. Lucum on   Sir Yr. W. ff.
board his Ship

[LB, p. 19]

1. John Lucum is unidentified. Apparently his home port was London. He is mentioned several times in WF's letters.
2. For Cooper, see ltr. to him of April 4, 1681, note 1.
3. William Hardidge (or Hardwick) (d. c. 1697/98) was probably the son of William Hardwick "of Nominy, Westmoreland Co., Virginia, Gent., and now of Bristol, England," who made his will in 1668 (probated 1669). The will mentions a son William, who is to continue his education in England until he is twenty-one. The younger Hardwick returned to Virginia and married Frances, daughter of Dr. Thomas Gerard, Hardwick being her fifth husband. This meant that Hardwick was a relative by marriage of WF, whose mother-in-law

had married as her second husband Thomas Gerard. Hardwick was burgess several times and a captain of militia in Westmoreland County. In October, 1692, he is mentioned as living at Nomini and was therefore a neighbor of Nicholas Spencer.

Presumably Lucum's ship was on its way down the Potomac and would pass Nomini, an important port in that region.

4. For Nicholas Spencer, see ltr. to him of September 9, 1679, note 1.

To John Cooper [1]

Mr. John Cooper   June 2nd 1681

This is Copy of my former by Capt. Jno. Lucum bearing date 31st. May last, I have sent another by the said Lucum, of the same date & of the same purport but open, for a bill of loading & a bill of Exchange to be inclosed therein, for the above Tobo. Sr. In my particulars mentioned & here inclosed, you'll find I send for a feather bed & furniture, curtains & vallens. The furniture Curtains & Vallens I would have new, but the bed at second hand, because I am informed new ones are very full of dust. The Curtains & Vallens I would have plain & not very costly. I desire you to take notice in the purchase of these things in the Note of Particulars here inclosed, & if it should so happen by accident, or some other mischance, I should not have the opportunity of giving you farther advice please to take care to send those particulars, by the first ships, by Capt. Norrington [2] if he comes forth early

[no signature]

[*LB*, pp. 19-20]

1. For Cooper, see ltr. to him of April 4, 1681, note 1.
2. For Norrington, see ltr. to Cooper of April 4, 1681, note 2.

To John Cooper [1]

Sir   June 7th. 1681

By Mr. Lucum & Mr. Lymes [2] bearing date 31st. May & 2nd. June I have given you an account of eleven hhds. Tobo. consigned to you, together with several bills of Exchange to the value of £31 sterling, besides Mr. Lucum's bills of Exchange for what value I know not yet, which according to my order receive of him. I desire your Care in sending me in those things I sent for, & do now send for, which are for my own particular use, therefore I desire you to take care in the goodness of them, & what my money comes to more than I have given you advice of, please to send me it in Linnen, of which let gentish holland be finest except, one piece of Kenting, & let there be two pieces of white Dimmity, & one piece of colour'd. I refer the sorting the linnen to your self, being mindfull of blue Linnen in the Parcel. If you could possibly procure me a Bricklayer or Carpenter or both, it would do me a great kindness, & save me a great deal of money in my present building, & I should be willing to advance something extraordinary for the procuration of them or either of them. If you send in any tradesmen be sure send in their tools with them. Sr. My small acquaintance begs my excuse for not giving you an account of news stirring. Although I have sent none yet I hope to receive some from you, together with the present transactions of affairs in England, if the market gives any encouragement, you may be sure to hear more from me for the future I am

To. Mr. Jno. Cooper in Londn.   Your   W. ff.
Mercht. 𝄪 Capt. Lymes

[*LB,* p. 20]

1. For Cooper, see ltr. to him of April 4, 1681, note 1.
2. Lymes was a London ship captain, as the inside address at the bottom of the letter indicates.

To the Honourable Ralph Wormeley [1]

Sr.   June 19th. 1681

Yours I receiv'd by Mr. Hickes [2] whereby I am now throughly acquainted with your business, & have communicated the same to Mr. George Brent,[3] & have also sent him your inclosed Guinea, the bond I must take notice to you, is not so well as it should be, for in the obligation it is something superfluous at least, if not amiss to name them Executors of Mr. Burnham,[4] it might have been more excusable, if it had been so mentioned in the Condition, yet the most sure way had been, to Condition with them as Legatees to Burnham, not to interrupt your Possession, or traverse the Office, for by that name comes their Pretensions, & not as Executors, for as they are Executors only, they have nothing to say to any lands or tenements of the Testators.

I shall take what care I can, & shall use my utmost skill to defend your most just Cause, to clear you from this unjust molestation. The Course you give me account, you have taken to put the bond in Suite is grounded upon good counsel   Sr. I am heartily glad of Major Beverley's association & assistance in this affair,[5] who is in my Esteem the best acquainted with the practic part in Virginia. If terms of treaty or Complyance should ever more come to be offered, take not this Course by bonds to oblige them, but rather Confirmations, Releases, or Deeds of Conveyance, well penned, by good Advice, which I presume Major Beverley is able to assist you in, & that will utterly disable them, from any Pretensions to a Suite for the future, & if not strengthen your title, yet I am sure quiet your Possession.

Sr. I understand there are some Negro Ships expected into York now every day, I am so remote, that before I can have notice, they'll be all dispos'd of, or at least none left but the refuse, therefore Sr. I request you to do me the favour, if you intend to buy any for yours self, & it be not too much trouble to you, to secure me five or six whereof three or four boys if can, & please to send me word of it, & shall readily come down, & thankfully acknowledge the favour who am

To. Ralph Wormley Esqr.   Honrd. Sr. Your   W. ff.

[LB, pp. 20-21]

1. For Wormeley, see ltr. to Nicholas Spencer, November 2, 1680, note 3, and subsequent letters to Wormeley.
2. For Hickes, see ltr. to Wormeley of May 21, 1681, note 4.
3. George Brent (d. 1699), WF's law partner and the Virginia colony's most distinguished Catholic, had come to Virginia about 1650 and settled in Stafford County. He was the son of George Brent and grandson of Richard Brent and Sir John Peyton of Doddington. He held various county offices, was in 1683 Receiver-General of the Rappahannock, in 1684 Attorney-General of the colony, and in 1693 with WF agent for the Northern Neck Proprietary. He, like WF, was a great landowner. His home estate of "Woodstock" (see the Herrman map of 1673 for its location on Acquia Creek) and "Brenton" (of which more later) were the most famous of the tracts he patented. In a later letter to Wormeley (June 10, 1684), WF included a "State of your Case" done by Brent as well as one done by himself.
4. In Wormeley's series of suits mentioned above and below, Leroy Griffin and Lewis Burwell declared themselves both legatees and executors of John Burnham's estate.
5. For Beverley, see ltr. to him of September 6, 1679, note 1. Though Beverley was himself an active lawyer, WF acted as his counsel and personal adviser in many legal matters. In this association it is quite clear that WF is the legal scholar and theorist, Beverley what we might call a good trial lawyer.

To Major Robert Beverley [1]

Majr. Robt. Beverley   June 19th. 1681

I receiv'd your's inclosed in Esqr. Wormley's wherein you write down that branch of the Statute relating to his Case, with your interpretations & opinion succinctly & pithily, with which I fully agree, & doubt not if Statutes be of any force, (which is doubtless) is sufficient to quiet his Possession, & clear him of trouble, which I believe is rather occasioned, by their Advisers to get money from them, than out of any probability of obtaining the land for them. Instead of Bonds ha[d] Configurations, Releases, or Conveyances &c. been well drawn they could not possibly have contrived any trouble now, which is the best Course to be taken if any Overtures of Quiet & Cessation from Arms should more be offered. Sr. The business would not admit me to write less, & hast will not suffer more to be added by

To Majr. Robt. Beverley   Sr. Your   W. ff.
in Rappahannock

[LB, pp. 21-22]

1. As noted in the letter to Wormeley of this date, WF and Beverley were to act together as counsel for Wormeley in the Wormeley vs. Griffin and Burwell case.

To Henry Hartwell [1]

Mr. Henry Hartwell   June 19th. 1681

I cannot miss this opportunity to beg my Excuse for parting so rudely without taking leave, I am sure some of the company were equally concerned, in the Bacchanalian Banquet, & those that were not cannot deny an Excuse to the great absurdity, or Solecisms committed by Bacchanals, who have Priviledge for them by Bacchus himself, the first Institutor of the Order. I desire you'll give my service to all friends there, & mind Mr. Clayton [2] to provide Institutions for our intended Society, & to take care that none be admitted therein but Loyalists,[3] & then I don't question, but we shall continue in order & obedience as Loyalists. Sr. I desire you'll send me by the bearer, a Writ at the suite of William Balthrope against George Thorne,[4] in an Action of Trespass, directed to the Sheriff of Westmoreland, also a Dedimus Potestatem for Collo. Mason [5] to examine Evidences in the Appeal betwixt him & Mr. Lincolne [6] (for which our clark intends to kiss your hand next Court) directed to Mr. James Ashton,[7] Majr. Andrew Gilson,[8] and Doctr. William Bankes [9]

To. Mr. Henry Hartwell　　　　　　Sr. Your　W. ff.
at James City

[LB, p. 22]

1. Henry Hartwell (d. 1699), a Jamestown lawyer trained in England, came to Virginia before 1672, for he was in that year appointed clerk of the Council, the beginning of an official career which continued for twenty-seven years. He was later a burgess and in 1692 a councilor. In 1695 he departed for England on colony business and never returned. WF addressed letters to him in London in 1698. With the Reverend James Blair and barrister Edward Chilton (q.v.) he was the author of *The Present State of Virginia, and the College*, written in 1697 and published in 1727. *Journals H.B. 1659/60-1693, passim; Exec. Journ. Council Col. Va.*, I, *passim*; H.D. Farish, ed., *The Present State of Virginia, and the College* (Williamsburg, 1940), pp. xxviii-xxix.

2. Thomas Clayton, another prominent practicing attorney, represented James City in the House of Burgesses from 1680 to 1682. He was probably related to the Liverpool merchant of the same name with whom WF later corresponded. Both seemed to have been related to the Claytons of Fulwood in Lancashire, one of whom (William) was mayor of Liverpool from 1698 to 1702. 1 V 225-53, 399; 3 V 275; *Exec. Journ. Council Col. Va.*, I, 503; *Journals H.B. 1659/60-1693, passim*.

3. Presumably WF refers to a society of lawyers, or some sort of bar association. By "Loyalists" he may mean supporters of the Stuarts, of whom there were great numbers in Virginia, especially among the leading planters and lawyers. WF was certainly such a person. He may mean here, however, a society of surveyors, for many of the lawyers were also surveyors. And he mentions such a society in his ltr. to Richard Lee II, April 13, 1683, below.

4. *Writ*, legally, "a written command, precept, or formal order issued by a court, directing or enjoining the person or persons to whom it is addressed to do or refrain from doing some act specified therein." *Shorter Ox. Dict.*

Though the court records, general or county, for the Balthrope *vs.* Thorne case have not survived, William Balthrope's name appears several times in other cases in Stafford and Westmoreland. *Stafford County Court Records, 1689-1693*, March 13, 1689/90; *Westmoreland County Deeds, Patents, etc., 1665-1677, passim*.

5. *Dedimus potestatem*, Latin "we have given the power," legally "a writ empowering one who is not a judge to do some act in place of a judge." *Shorter Ox. Dict.* George Mason I (c. 1629-c. 1686), sheriff, clerk of the Court, burgess, and county lieutenant for Stafford, was the founder of the family in America. According to tradition, he commanded a troop of horse at the battle of Worcester and, escaping, embarked for Virginia. He patented land as early as 1655, and later gave Stafford its name, calling it after his native shire; these first lands were on Potomac Creek, at the mouth of Accokeek, and here he was buried. Though he seems to have in the main been loyal to Berkeley during Bacon's Rebellion, he fought for a time with Bacon against the Indians and was a burgess in the pro-Bacon Assembly of 1676.

Later he was WF's fellow burgess and, in 1685, he was victorious over WF in a disputed election. In his later days, one may surmise from his opposition to WF and his part in the Bacon Assembly, that he was "Whiggishly enclined." His son George Mason II was active in the Whiggish interest. *D.A.B.;* Rowland, *Life of George Mason,* I, 1-23; Swem, *Va. Hist. Index.*

6. Probably Garrett Lincolne, for whom WF was attorney in 1680-1681. *Westmoreland County Court Order Book, 1675/6-1688/9,* pp. 194, 230.

7. The three men named together here were with Mason the Stafford Commission of the Peace, or part of it, at this time. James Ashton, WF's neighbor, died in 1686, naming WF one of his executors and bequeathing to Rose, WF's daughter, two heifers and two calves. His estate was called "Chatterton." There is more about his bequests in later letters.

8. Andrew Gilson (*c.* 1628-*c.* 1698), a large landowner, married as her second husband Behethland Bernard Dade, widow of Francis Dade (q.v.). 5 V 161; 38 V 181-84; 9 W(2) 60-63.

9. Dr. William Bankes (d. 1709) may have been at one time high sheriff of Stafford as well as justice of the peace at this time. He died in King and Queen County. In Ashton's will of August 18, 1686, he left 20s. for a ring for William Bankes. 5 V 104; 10 V 292; 21 V 66, 140, 281; 32 V 145; 4 W(2) 41.

To William Hardidge [1]

Mr. William Hardidge   June 19th. 1681

I have now by me two of your letters one by Mr. Gibson [2] which I receiv'd about 12th. June last, when Partis was ready to sail the other I receiv'd yesterday by Mr. Lincolne.[3] In the first you acquaint me you have sent me Partis bond, because he refus'd to deliver Bills, which I something admire, if ever you look'd upon the Bond, or the Assignment on the back side, the Bond is absolute for 50£ sterling, & no other Condition in it to save him from the penalty, but the payment of 25£ sterling the fourth of April, & the Claret & white sugar. The Assignment on the back side is also as clear & absolute, from [me to] * Mr. Gotley [4] with a Warranty that it is due, & [which is] every penny due. By your last you inform [me?] Partis tells you I have otherwise disposed of [the] Pipe staves, tis true I sold some Pipe staves, & [have] yet some to sell, but I never yet sold any of Capt. [Partis] [5] his Pipe staves, what staves I owe him he ha[s] bill for, if I have not performed according to the ten[our] thereof I am lyable to an Action, but yet that has [a] relation to Mr. Gotley's debt, if it had I should n[ow] have sent you bills of Exchange. I here inclosed you the Bond which I have nothing to do with excep[t] you can make it appear not to be due, had I [had] your first letter sooner, I should have advised [you] otherwise,

---

* All brackets in text indicate frayed edge of page on which words are partially or wholly obliterated, rather than worn away.

& secured your money of Partis, I desir[e] you'll shew the Bond & this letter of mine to the [Honble] Mr. Secretary [6] who I dare say will assure you [that] your being without that money, is your own, not [my] fault who am

To. Mr. William Hardidge   Sir Your   W. ff.
at Nomany

[*LB*, pp. 22-23]

1. For Hardwick or Hardidge, see ltr. to John Lucum of May 31, 1681, note 3. Hardwick lived at Nomini in Westmoreland.
2. WF later (ltr. to Wormeley, August 2, 1682) mentions a Richard Gibson, or Gypson, of Stafford. In 1691 a Richard Gibson built at Quantico what was probably the first watermill in Stafford. In 1693 he attacked George Brent as a papist. 17 V 311; 28 V 70-73; Harrison, *Landmarks*, I, 121, 141.
3. For Lincolne, see above ltr. to H. Hartwell, June 19, 1681, note 6.
4. For Gotley, see ltr. to Stephen Watts, March 30, 1681, note 3.
5. For Partis, see various references to him, especially in letter to him, of April 7, 1680, note 1.
6. For Nicholas Spencer, Secretary of State and resident of Nomini in Westmoreland, see ltr. to him of September 9, 1679, note 1.

To Kenelm Chiseldine [1]

Mr. Kenelm Chiseldine   June 8th. 16[81]

Sr. The Cruelty of Mr. Blackston towards my Sis[ter] * in Law [2] is grown so notorious & cruel, that there [is] no possibility of keeping it any longer private, w[ith?] the preservation of her life, his cruelty alread[y] having occasioned her to make two or three attemp[ts] to destroy her self, which if not timely prevent[ed] will inevitably follow, therefore Sr. in Relatio[n] of my Affinity to her, as also at the Instance a[nd] Request of Mr. Newton,[3] to propose some remedy I think there's some means to be used for a s[e]paration, because of his continued cruelty, whic[h] in England is practical, here in Virginia it i[s] [a] rare Case, of which nature I have known but o[ne] which was between Mrs. Brent & her husband Mr. Giles Brent; [4] the Case thus managed: She petitio[ns] the Governour & Council, setting forth his inhumane usage, upon which Petition, the Court orders her to

* Pages much frayed. Whole last line and more at bottom gone. Bracketed materials supplied from *VMH&B*.

live separate from him, & he to allow her a Maintenance, according to his Quali[ty] & Estate, & to make his appearance at the nex[t] General Court, before which Court he dyed, & so [no farther] [proceedings] therein Mr. [Newton can give you a full account of his cruelty and barbarity] * [towards h]er, & has evidences ready to prove, therefore [I] advised him to consult you for the manner of pro[ceeding] therein, & earnestly request you will assist him in [it] [It] cannot properly be called a Divorce but a separa[tion] rather, for I find in Cooke on Littleton folio 235 [5] [sever]al sorts of Divorces a Vinculo Matromonii, but [Div]orces propter Sævitiam & causa Adulterii are more properly Separations, because no Dissolutions a Vinculo Matromonii but only a Mensa et thoro, & the Cov[erture] continues, & consequently a Maintenance allowed [her] & Dower after his Decease, as is plentifully set [fourth?] by those that treat thereof. You may find one precedent in Cooke Car.[6] fo. 461.462 between Porter & his [wife?], where upon prosecution it was decreed, Quod propter Sevitiam of her said Husband &c. I question not but you [are] furnished with Precedents of like nature, therefore [your] assistance & Advice in this Affair is desired by

To. Mr. Kenelm Chiseldine   Sir Your   W. ff.
Attorney General of Maryland

[LB, pp. 23-24]

1. Kenelm Chiseldine (d. 1708), prominent in Maryland over a long period, was sworn in as Attorney-General of that colony in 1676. Later, as a strong Protestant, he was one of the committee which seized the government in 1689. In 1693 he was Commissary-General. WF was writing to Chiseldine on this divorce or separation matter for several reasons. As Maryland Attorney-General of course Chiseldine would have a say in the matter. But also he was connected by marriage with WF's wife and with the Rose Blackston (probably Blakiston) in question. For Chiseldine had married Mary, tenth child of Thomas Gerard, who in turn had been WF's mother-in-law's second husband. Owings, *His Lordship's Patronage*, pp. 118, 123, 130, 133; H. Chandlee Forman, *Jamestown and St. Mary's, Buried Cities of Romance* (Baltimore, 1938), pp. 230, 329; *Md. Hist. Mag.*, XLVI (1951), 202.

That this part of Maryland was a part of WF's world is clearly illustrated by Chiseldine's complaint in 1699 to the Virginia Council that Parson Waugh (q.v.), WF's longtime enemy, had gone into Maryland and married one of Chiseldine's daughters to a stranger without publication of banns or license as the law required, and contrary to the inclination of her parents. He prayed that Waugh be brought "to condign punishment for the same, In being a Notorious Offender in that kind." It was so ordered. *Exec. Journ. Council Col. Va.*, II, 31.

2. There are several Blackstons connected by marriage with WF's in-laws, including Col. Nehemiah Blakiston (d. 1693), who in 1669 married Elizabeth, another daughter of Thomas Gerard. He was therefore Chiseldine's wife's brother-in-law and the step-son-in-law of WF's mother-in-law Rose Tucker Gerard Newton (q.v.). His wife Elizabeth survived him and married twice more. It is probable that WF refers to Ebenezer Blackston or Blakiston (1650-1709) of Cecil County, Maryland, son of George and nephew of Colonel Nehemiah. Though the printed records indicate that Ebenezer's wife was Elizabeth, daughter of John James, she was probably his second wife. Of the three children assigned to the Ebenezer Blakistons in various records, Ebenezer (b. 1684/85), William (d. 1746), and Anna, probably only the last

was the child of the second wife. That Ebenezer's wife was Rose, younger sister of WF's wife Sarah, is indicated in WF's letter to his mother-in-law of June 8, 1681; also by a Maryland court record of 1700, which finds Rose, wife of Ebenezer Blakiston, guilty of having eloped with Edward Bathurst in 1697 and of having lived with him since that time (*Provincial Court Judgments*, Liber W.T. No. 3, folios 250-52, Maryland Archives). The sons Ebenezer and William each had a daughter named Rose (*Md. Hist. Mag.*, II, 64) or Rosamond, surely more than coincidence. And then there is a record of Ebenezer Blakiston's visiting at WF's plantation in Stafford on July 19, 1697, probably in regard to this very elopement (*Archives of Md., Proceedings of the Court 1696/7, 1698*, XXIII, 177). Apparently Rose endured her marital situation for sixteen years after WF's letter to Chiseldine.

3. John Newton (1639-1697), third husband of WF's mother-in-law Rose Tucker Gerard Newton, was a native of Yorkshire who had first settled in Maryland. He is earlier styled "Master Mariner." He came to Westmoreland County, Virginia, and married Rose some time before 1677, when his fourth son Gerard was born. His will (dated August 19, 1695; proved July 28, 1697) requests that his "loving friend, Col. William Fitzhugh," advise and assist his executors and in case of differences settle matters between them. His eldest son by a former marriage, John Junior, married a daughter of Isaac Allerton (q.v.), whose son Willoughby was to marry WF's only daughter Rose. 33 V 297-302; 36 V 293-97; 37 V 87, 183, 283; *Journals H.B. 1659/60-1693*, p. 69; Eubank, *Touring Historyland*, p. 111.

4. Giles Brent, Jr. (1652-1679), half-Indian, married a Mary Brent, sister of WF's law partner George Brent. She was allowed by Council and General Court separate maintenance May 8, 1679. 9 V 187; *Md. Hist. Mag.*, XXIX (1934), 212-23.

5. *Institutes*, I, folio 235, section 380, Lib. 3.

6. WF may have given the year after "Car." in the original.

To the Honourable Colonel Richard Lee [1]

Honrd. Sir   June 8th. 1681

The business of your brother's [2] & Mr. Charles Roane [3] [could] not proceed successfuly last Court for two reasons [One] was timely entering the Petition, the other he was [on]ly arrested at the Suite of Mr. William Lee. How they [both] happened I know not, & Collo. Kendall [4] pleaded Ignorance therein. I have here inclosed sent you a Writ [& Pe]tition against Roane, who is most willing to have [an end], & to have the legal Right known without delay, there[fo]re to begin with him will cause Expedition, & the Judgment in [h]is Cause will be a Precedent to the rest. I wish you much [jo]y in your young son now & Comfort hereafter [5]

To. The Honble. Collo. Richd. Lee   Your   W. ff.

[*LB*, p. 24]
[Edge of page worn away.]

1. For Lee, see ltr. to him, May 15, 1679, note 1.

2. William Lee (*c.* 1671–*c.* 1697) was the fourth son of the immigrant Richard Lee I. He was probably born in Northumberland, was educated at Stratford-Langton, Essex County, England, and was later high sheriff, captain of militia, and burgess for Northumberland. Apparently he is the brother who had the suit with Roane, though WF's wording does not make it clear here. Other Lee brothers were John (*c.* 1645-1673), Richard, Francis (*c.* 1648-1714), William, Hancock (1653-1709), and Charles (*c.* 1656—*c.* 1700). B. J. Hendrick, *The Lees of Virginia* (Boston, 1935), chart opposite p. 438.

3. A Charles Roane was in Gloucester County as early as 1664 and in 1670 a man of the same name was attorney for Captain Humphrey White. Many grants of land in 1664, 1665, 1667, etc., are recorded to him. He was a loyalist sufferer in Bacon's Rebellion. 10 V 379-80; 16 V 66-69; *Journals H.B. 1659/60-1693*, p. 181; Tyler, *Cycl. Va. Biog.*, I, 313.

4. William Kendall (d. 1685), frequently agent for Virginia in treating with the Indians, was WF's fellow burgess several times and was in 1685 speaker of the House. His son William was a burgess in 1695/96. *Exec. Journ. Council Col. Va.*, I, 503; *Journals H.B. 1659/60-1693*, *passim*.

5. Probably Philip (*c.* 1681-1744), third son and ancestor of the Maryland Lees. WF's son and namesake was to marry Ann, youngest child of Richard Lee II. Hendrick, *Lees of Virginia*, chart opposite p. 438. This may refer to Francis, the next son, however, for Cazenove G. Lee, Jr. (*Lee Chronicle* [New York, 1957], p. 348) gives Philip's birth date as 1678 with no known date for the next son.

To Mrs. Rose Newton [1]

Dear Mother   June 8th. 1681

To go to Rose [2] before you have provided means for her relief will rather Aggravate than alleviate her Misery, therefore this Course that Mr. Newton [3] advises to, will be safest & surest, & make your voyage comfortable to your self, & a Credible Relief to your Daughter which is heartily wish'd by

[To Mrs.] Rose Newton [4]

[*LB*, p. 24]

1. See ltr. to Kenelm Chiseldine just above, June 8, 1681, notes. Rose Tucker Gerard Newton (d. *c.* 1712) became the fourth wife of John Newton in 1676. She had two daughters by John Tucker, her first husband, WF's wife Sarah and the Rose Blakiston here referred to. 33 V 302, 393; 36 V 296-97. Rose Tucker was probably married to Ebenezer Blakiston (1650-1709) of Cecil County, Maryland. See ltr. to Chiseldine above, note 2.

2. As noted above in ltr. to Chiseldine, Rose lived in Maryland.

3. For Newton, see ltr. to K. Chiseldine, June 8, 1681, note 3.

4. Whole bottom line is missing and first inch of next-to-bottom line.

To Captain Thomas Mathews[1]

Sir   July 3rd. 1681

I have this Conveniency by Nat: Garland[2] to acquaint you that I cannot receive Answers to a third of the Letters I sent you   I believe there may be some miscarriages, but not so many but that one in three comes to hand. Friends at a Distance want the happiness of seeing one another, yet a friendly Communication by Letters is not barred, which I should much rejoice in, I assure you I let slip no opportunity, & should be glad you would use but a friendliness therein. I hope Distance has not occasioned forgetfullness. Nat Garland tells me you have made a great & profitable progress in your linnen Manufacture,[3] which I heartily congratulate, wishing that as you give good example to others, you may reap benefit thereby to your self. Sr. I have here inclosed sent a letter to Mr. Alexr. Broady[4] with his papers inclosed in it, I have left open for your perusal &c., after which I desire you'll seal it & get it a safe conveyance to his land. My Wife & self salute you & your good Lady, with our Respects & service I am

To Capt. Thos. Matthews at Cherry Point[5]   Your   W. ff.

[*LB*, p. 25]

1. Thomas Mathew or Mathews or Matthews, of "Cherry Point" in the parish of Bowtracy (really Fairfield) in the County of Northumberland, also owned lands in Stafford, including one estate eight miles above George Brent in the Acquia neighborhood. Apparently he was the son of early settler Captain Samuel Mathews, and brother of a second Samuel who was governor of the colony in 1657/58. Thomas was burgess for Stafford in the pro-Bacon Assembly of 1676. He had become such a Bacon partisan that he was exempted for a time from the general pardon. He is almost surely the "T. M." who wrote "The Beginning, Progress, and Conclusion of Bacon's Rebellion, 1675-1676" (first published in the Richmond *Enquirer*, September, 1804) for Sir Robert Harley in 1705. The manuscript was described by Thomas Jefferson and is now in the Library of Congress. It is an eyewitness account, though probably a prejudiced one. It has been said on good authority that Mathews was responsible for much of the Indian trouble himself. 1 V 91-92; Harrison, *Landmarks*, I, 74; Washburn, *Governor and the Rebel*, p. 183.
2. The name of Nat Garland of Cople Parish appears often in the Westmoreland County records. *Westmoreland County Court Order Book, 1675/6-1688/9, passim; Deeds, Patents, etc., 1665-1677*, folio 235. Garland himself paid in court (Feb. 13, 1683/84) for so many pounds of wax for spinning.
3. Linen manufacture had been tried in the colony as early as 1612, and Captain Mathews of Blount Point on the lower James (Thomas' father's place?) had been successful in employing spinners of flax about 1646. In 1682 a new law was passed at the instance of Lord Culpeper to encourage linen and woolen manufactures. This continued in effect until 1685. In 1693 a

new law encouraged such manufactures and remained in effect until 1699. WF's friend Wormeley was among those interested in the linen manufacture. All this is indicative of the spasmodic attempts throughout Virginia colonial history to encourage industry. Bruce, *Ec. Hist. Va.*, I, 454-57.

4. The name of Broady or Brodie, as agent for Paul Littlefield, appears in *Northumberland County Order Book, 1678-1698,* on (March?) 19, 1678, p. 31.

5. The probate of Mathews' will in England in 1706 lists him as "formerly of Cherry Point in the parish of Bowtracy, Northumberland county, Virginia." Tyler, *Cycl. Va. Biog.*, I, 286-87.

To Alexander Brody [1]

To. Mr. Alexr. Brody at Capt. Lend. Howson's [2]   July 3rd. 1681

This is the first & most certain conveniency I have had since my coming from Town to communicate to you how your business depends. When I receiv'd yor. letter with the inclosed supersedeas, I admired at that clause in it, you satisfy'd me by your letter, that it was neither at your Motion nor Petition. The Copy of the supersedeas together with the Copy of the Order,[3] & this inclosed Petition, I presented but to no effect, for the Governour & Council said they would not vacate Ordrs. of Court upon prayer only, without legal Process & proceeding; the said Seaborne being not arrested by the sd. Writ, nor any Return made therefore their Directions were, if the Court had injured you, you might have your remedy legally against them. So that what I can advise farther is, either to arrest one or two of the Court, that then was sitting, when the Order past against you, or wait with patience till Seaburn's Arrival,[4] & then return your Supersedeas, & so get a rehearing of the whole matter before the Governour & Council. I know no other means to get relief for you, but by one of these ways, if you take the former, I desire you to come up to give me account thereof & Instructions therein, if the latter, please to give me timely notice by the first opportunity, & in either you shall find me

Your   W. ff.

[*LB*, p. 25]

1. Broady or Brodie is mentioned in ltr. to Thomas Mathews just above, July 3, 1681.

2. Leonard Howson (d. 1689) was a merchant of Wicomico Parish, Northumberland County. His wife Elizabeth was a daughter of Colonel Richard Lee I. In 1678 he had been sworn high sheriff of Northumberland County. 31 V 354-56; 38 V 81; *Northumberland County Order Book, 1666-1678*, p. 361.

3. Latin *supersedeas*, "you shall desist." Legally, "a writ commanding the stay of legal proceedings which ought otherwise to have proceeded, or suspending the powers of an officer: so called because of the occurrence of the word in the writ," *Shorter Ox. Dict.*

Action on this matter does not appear in the Council and General Court records published. See *Exec. Journal Council Col. Va.,* I.

4. Unidentified. A Nicholas Seaburn appears in *Northumberland County Land Order Book I,* p. 53, on August 16, 1699. The Court referred to was probably a Northumberland one.

To Captain Thomas Mathews[1]

Sir   August 24th. 1681

Your's by Christopher Warner[2] bearing date 29th. July I have receiv'd, am glad to hear of your and Lady's health therein, which I have also been satisfy'd in by Mrs. Rogers,[3] who has been in our parts, & whom I have intreated to be the Conveyor of this.

I do not approve of your term project, for the advancement of a most usefull & advantageous Manufacture, which I believe in time, when necessity & use shall have reduced more to follow, will be found more profitable & advantageous to a generall Commerce, than the greatest probability can imagine from this superfluous staple, that at present custom hath render'd suitable to the generality, by reason one is of absolute necessity, the other a thing indifferent, & more obliged to the fancy than any real worth in it self. Absolute necessity of business calls me abroad so often, that I am glad when I can have some leisure at home, I am taking of some & assure your self, that you shall be one of the first whom when I get time I intend to visit. Necessity as 'tis the Mother of Invention, so it is the Nurse of Industry, which has so far been cherished here that there's little of any wool left in our parts not wrought up either in stockings &c, therefore no hopes of the purchase of any here. Mine & Wive's best Respects salute you & your good Lady, continuance of that health & happiness you at present enjoy is wished you by

To. Capt. Thomas Matthews   Your   W. ff.
at Cherry Point

[*LB*, p. 26]

1. For Mathews, see ltr. to him, July 3, 1681, note 1.

2. Christopher Warner was almost surely a member of the already prominent family mentioned elsewhere in these letters though he has not been individually identified.

3. Possibly this was Jane (Pressley) Rogers (b. 1664), who married Richard Rogers of Northumberland County first and then (in 1698) Christopher Neale. 34 V 191, 288; *Journals H.B. 1659/60-1693*, pp. 45, 417, 432, etc.

To the Honourable Ralph Wormeley [1]

Honrd. Sir   July 14th. 1681

I receiv'd your's by the Soldier wherein you give a farther discovery of your business in Mr. Kennon's relation,[2] which discovers such a palpable cheat, that I admire your perswasions should induce them, to proclaim their own scandal, especially when without interuption, things in your power to have avoided, you had been so obligingly Civil, to admit them to carry away the personal Estate. I doubt their catching at the land may occasion them the loss of the real Substance, I mean the personal Estate, which they may say, they were once quietly seised with, like the dog in the fable.

Sr. Your promise to assist me in the purchase of those Negros, I requested you to buy for me, only desire farther advice & more particular directions, which I shall now do, I desired you in my former to buy me five or six, whereof three or four to be boys, a man & woman or men & women, the boys from eight to seventeen or eighteen, the rest as young as can procure them, for price I cannot direct therein, because boys according to their age & growth are valued in price therefore Sr. shall refer that wholly to your self, & doubt not your Care therein, & if you please to hire a Messenger to come, either away with them, or to come immediately & give me notice thereof, I shall gladly pay the Messenger, & readily come down my self to make payment for the same. Sr. Mr. Brent & my self are resolved to wait on you, in our journey to Town, to be well advised & fully informed in the state of your affairs, which are grounded upon such just foundations that success is little doubted by

Yr. W. ff.

This letter I sent before the other on the other side but mistook the entering it [3]

To. Ralph Wormley Esqr.

[*LB*, pp. 26-27]

1. For Wormeley, see ltr. to N. Spencer, Nov. 2, 1680, note 3.

2. Possibly Richard Kennor, or Kenner (d. 1696), of Northumberland County, a burgess (1688-1691) or Rodham Kennor of Northumberland, sheriff (1699). 25 V 129; 14 W(1) 132-33; *Journals H.B. 1659/60-1693, passim; Exec. Journ. Council Col. Va.*, I, 444, 446. But since the name *seems* to be spelled Kenno*n*, it may refer to Richard Kennon, the 1685-1686 burgess from Henrico. Actually there were two Richard Kennons, one who died in 1688 and the other in 1696. 6 V 90; 24 W(1) 131; Tyler, *Cycl. Va. Biog.*, I, 271.

3. There is no letter to Ralph Wormeley on the preceding sheet nor on the back of this. The next letter to him, *LB*, p. 29, is dated Feb. 26, 1681/82.

To John Buckner [1]

Mr. John Buckner   Decr. 3rd. 1681

Sr.   I was intended the last generall Court to have waited on you, in order to have take care for your payment what I am indebted to you, but in my going was straitned in time, & in my coming home earnest to be here. I have now taken this opportunity by Mr. Jno. Withers [2] to send you bills of Majr. Robert Beverley's for £20 . . . 5 . . . 00. which I suppose before this time, he has taken care with you about, he promis'd payment in your hands at the passing of the bills, Esqr. Wormley likewise at the same time assured me, that he would take care to pay you £20. more upon my account, which I doubt not but before this he has done what remains I will hereafter take care honestly to pay but hope you will make me some abatement for your dumb Negro that you sold me, had she been a new Negro, I must have blamed my fate not you, but one that you had two years, I must conclude you knew her qualitys, which is bad at work worse at talking, & took the opportunity of the softness of my Messenger, to quit your hands of her. I will I will [*sic*] freely quit you the £3 . . . 5 . . . 0. Overplus of £20 that he gave for her to take her again, & will get her convey'd to your hands, or hope if my offer be not acceptable [of?] you will make me some abatement of so bad a bargain. I desire if you have not heard from Mr. Wormley & Majr. Beverley in order to the payment as above, Mr. Withers will not scruple to stay a day while you send to them, that thereby he may bring my Obligation with him & will pass himself for the Ballance which I'll see certainly paid. Sr. This Gentleman is come purposely to buy two or three Negro boys or girles, men or women, upon the Report the protested Bills has opened the Negro Market, I advised him to you for your Advice, & instructions there, as well knowing that if such a thing be, you can best advise him, I will also myself buy six or eight, if the market be slow as is here reported, in both which your Advice is desired by

To Mr. Jno. Buckner   Sr. Your   W. ff.
℔ Mr. Withers

[*LB,* pp. 27-28]

1. John Buckner (1631-1695) of Gloucester County, burgess in 1680-1682 and 1693, was a merchant and planter and perhaps lawyer, for he acted frequently as attorney for English merchants. He brought the first printing press and printer to the colony. In 1682, having printed in 1680 without permission the laws of the preceding Assembly, he and his printer were ordered to give bond not to print anything further without consulting the royal wishes on the subject. Also in 1682 he was one of the securities for Robert Beverley (q.v.) in the case discussed in some detail elsewhere in these letters and notes. 1 V 406; 2 V 410; 7 V 299; 10 V 236; 18 V 255; 31 V 232; 6 W(2) 173; *Journals H. B. 1659/60-1693, passim; Journals ... 1695 ... 1702, passim; Exec. Journ. Council Col. Va.,* I, 39, 493.

2. John Withers of Stafford County was sheriff (1685), burgess (1696/97), and captain of militia. He probably married first Frances Claiborne, daughter of Colonel William Claiborne of King William County (*King William Deed Book,* May 10, 1681; Va. Hist. Soc. MSS. 6: 1 W 276 "Washington," p. 9). He was the second husband of Frances Townsend (her first husband being Francis Dade [q.v.]) and her third Rice Hooe (q.v.). At this time he frequently acted as WF's agent. 6 V 310 ff.; 3 V 26; 11 V 146; Stanard, *Col. Va. Register,* p. 91; *Journals H.B. 1659/60-1693,* pp. xiv, 381; *Journals ... 1695 ... 1702, passim; Exec. Journ. Council Col. Va.,* I, 368; Meeting H. B., Nov. 18, 1685, Lord Monson Effingham Papers, L.C.

To the Honourable Nicholas Spencer [1]

Honrd. Sir   February 13th. 1681/2

At the Instance of my very good friend Doctr. William Bankes [2] this comes, not to sollicite any thing from you in his behalf, but truly what he is most capable of performing himself, but only to acquaint your Honr. what a great Sufferer his Predecessor Mr. Thomas Bunburry [3] has been in the late Distractions,[4] & chiefly in the Sheriff's office granted him by the Governor, without doubt for a help and furtherance in his Affairs, which those times made unprofitable, & his death after has render'd his fruitless labours therein, chargeable & troublesome to his Successor, &

ruinous to his surviving Children, by reason considerable sums have been taken by Law from the Estate upon that account, & the profits lie scatter'd up & down in parcels, not possible to be brought together for use or profit to the Children without a Repetition of the same favour, to their Successour - - - - , (as was thought at an ill time) granted Mr. Bunburry. He is now prepared to wait upon the Governour, if your Honr. please to grant your letter of Recommendation in that affair. The profits I dare say will go to the increase of that small Pittance of the Children their unhappy father left them

To Nics. Spencer Esqr.   Hond. Sr. Your   W. ff.
Secretary of Virginia

[*LB*, pp. 28-29]

1. For Spencer, see ltr. to him, Sept. 6, 1679, note 1.
2. For Bankes, see ltr. to H. Hartwell, June 19, 1681, note 9. It has been stated that Bankes became high sheriff of Stafford, and that the place was got for him by WF. This may be mere inference, however, from the letters of WF. 4 W(2) 41.
3. The will of James Ashton of Stafford proved Jan. 26, 1682/83, bequeathed to Thomas Bunbury and his wife £5. Though this may refer to a son, it probably refers to the already deceased Thomas mentioned in the present letter. As early as 1666, Bunbury had brought into Stafford court a servant of Colonel Peter Ashton's to have his age adjudged. 44 V 199.
4. Stafford, on the frontier in its northwestern portion, had suffered from the Indians, the loyalists, and the rebels during Bacon's Rebellion from 1675 to 1677. There had also been more recent Indian troubles.

To the Honourable Ralph Wormeley [1]

Honoured Sir   February 26th. 1681/2

This is the first opportunity since I had left the honour of your good company to assure you that I am not unprovided with Arguments (if the Assembly requires it) to prove that the Laws of England are in force here, except where the Acts of Assembly have otherwise provided, by reason of the Constitution of the place & people. The Gentleman the bearer is my Neighbor Doctr. Bancks whose health we drank at Majr. Beverley's, he is come to wait upon the Governor, to get a grant of the high Sherriff's place, whose predecessor Mr. Thomas Bunburry was a great sufferer, by his untimely death in the said Office, & he as his successor [2] has been a considerable Sufferer thereby, as he is able truly to inform you, & I dare say would esteem it an infinite obligation if your Honour would be pleased to introduce him into the Governor's knowledge, & second his Endeavours. Sr. I hope you have had an opportunity of satisfying Mr. Buckner [3] that sum you were pleas'd to promise at Majr. Beverley's. I have had a relation of your observations upon Collo. Griffin's Attorneys,[4] but no account what Evidence they had farther to produce, which if you think it worth your while, I should be glad to be informed from your self that thereby I might be throughly capable of assuring you I am

To Esqr. Wormley &c.   Hond. Sr. Yr.   W. ff.

[*LB*, p. 29]

1. For Wormeley, see ltr. to N. Spencer, Nov. 2, 1680, note 2.
2. This seems to imply that Dr. Bankes was already acting as sheriff. See ltr. to Hartwell, June 19, 1681, above, and other ltrs. below.
3. For John Buckner of Gloucester, see ltr. to him, Dec. 3, 1681, note 1.
4. As noted in several letters to Wormeley above and below, Leroy Griffin and Lewis Burwell had been bequeathed by John Burnham, before 1681, certain lands. Since Thomas Clayton, William Sherwood, and Arthur Spicer have been listed as among the attorneys taking part in the Wormeley *vs.* Griffin and Burwell action, it may be presumed that they were the Griffin attorneys, since we know that WF and Beverley represented Wormeley. For records of the several suits in the case, see ltr. to Wormeley, May 21, 1681, note 2, and "Traverse of an Escheat," June 9, 1683, below.

To the Honourable Nicholas Spencer [1]

Honrd. Sir   March 6th. 1681/2

Your's came to my hand yesterday by Mr. Fox,[2] this morning I sent him to Mr. Waugh,[3] where he forewarned him off the Plantation, spoke to him to desist from falling any more timber trees & from medling with any more of those Pipe staves already got, which I according to your Honour's Command seconded, & endeavoured to set forth to him the inconveniency & damage that would attend an obstinate refusal, but he was deaf to all, & did openly aver that the Promise of Surrender was upon

Condition to be repaid what money he hath already paid towards the Purchase, & to be reimbursed what charge & expences he had been at upon the Plantaon in building fencing &c. And did farther alledge that he had an Obligation from under your Honour's hand to assure him a title to the Land, which as soon as he has, he says he shall then be ready to pay the remdr. of the money, due to the purchase. The severall passages that happened Mr. Fox will fully relate to you to which I'll refer. But the Result of all was he would take no forewarning; And withall promised that he would wait upon your Honr. to accommodate the matter   Those two hhds. of Tobo. you were pleas'd to nominate to me for pay at Edward Washington's,[4] I have already dispos'd of, & indeed the remainder of my Tobo. in Westmoreland, except some at Mr. Newton's[5] & four more at Nomany[6] for which I have already taken freight. My Receiver told me this hhd. at yor. Quarter was as good as any he received, & before I receiv'd your Honour's letter I had a purpose to ship it off, but that Conveniency in payment hinder'd, I am sorry it will not answer your expectation in shiping off, now I have that Tobo. demanded for your use, but I dare assure you from my Receiver that it is good Tobo., & it is so late in the year I cannot contrive your Tobo. else where, which I hope will be excusable in

To. Mr. Secretary Spencer   Your   W. ff.

[*LB*, pp. 29-30]

1. For Spencer, see ltr. to him, Sept. 9, 1679, note 1.
2. Probably David Fox (d. 1702) of Lancaster County, burgess between 1677 and 1692/93. In 1683, Fox was a Receiver-General for the quitrents due the Northern Neck Proprietors in Lancaster County, the same position WF's partner George Brent held in Stafford. During the Fitzhugh-Brent period as agents for the Proprietors, Fox was one of the receivers of considerable grants. *Journals H.B. 1659/60-1693, passim;* Harrison, *Va. Land Grants,* p. 152; *Lancaster County, Wills, etc., Inventories and Wills, 1690-1709,* p. 111; *Northern Neck Land Patents, Book 2, 1694-1700, passim.*
3. The Reverend John Waugh of Overwharton Parish, later notorious as the prime instigator of the "Tumult" (see below and Introduction). Though the Stafford records for this period do not survive, this is the earliest evidence this editor has come upon of the long series of litigations involving Waugh and WF.
4. Not identified as to his relation, if any, with the John Washingtons of Westmoreland and Stafford. He was probably the ancestor of an Edward Washington described in 1792 as "yeoman and planter" whose breeding "escaped" Fairfax Harrison, as the latter acknowledges. Harrison, *Landmarks,* I, 275-76.
5. John Newton (1639-1697), WF's step-father-in-law (see ltr. to K. Chiseldine, June 8, 16[81], note 3), lived in Westmoreland County at Lower Machodock. 36 V 296-97.
6. Or Nomini. One of the ports established in 1691 by law, and apparently surveyed under the law of 1680 for ports, Nomini was located at the mouth of the Nomini in Westmoreland County. There were probably a few residences there. On at least one occasion the Virginia Council met at Nomini, probably because of Spencer's residence in the area. Bruce, *Ec. Hist. Va.,* II, 556; Bruce, *Inst. Hist. Va.,* II, 389.

Speech to Burgesses, 24 April 1682 [1]

[H. R. McIlwaine, ed., *Journals of the House of Burgesses 1659/60-1693*, Richmond, Va., 1914, pp. 165-166]

Mr *Speaker*

Among other the greiuances brought from euery perticular County I haue here the perticular greiuances of our County, and genll greiuances of ye Country which I now humbly offer to this houses consideration, the frequent practice of Parliamentary proceedings upon their first beginning is to looke upon and see after the proceedings of precedent Sessions and from thence to make the first stepp of their affaires grounded upon weighty reasons well to consider what was done, wt was left to doe, and what was necessary to be done, giues a great light for the present what is first fitt to be entred upon, how necessary and indispensably suitable to our affaires at present to looke a little back to the last Session, may be easily conceiued when we consider that most of the acts past were to pass the Royall assent before the full consummation thereof, or indeed before they could be said to be Lawes, as appeares by the words in all the sd acts, in order therefore to gaine that royall Assent, the genll Assbly then mett tooke care to have them fairly transcribed, and presented to his Majestie, as in the journall book of this house appeares of great advantage to us, if the King in his princely wisdome should haue thought fitt to haue granted the same, but now Mr. *Speaker,* although it is not two yeares quite since those were sent away, yett the Conveniency of two shippings comeing to us hath elapsed, and not one word from his most gratious Maty hath appeared in the Country to our knowledge in that affaire, I haue and dare say euery one here haue soe dutifull an esteem of his Maties most gratious fauors towards us, and Royall Condiscentions to anything requisite to our well being that we must immagine his Sacred Māty would upon the humble representation of the same, haue giuen a most favourable answer to the same especially to our Lawes sent home without whose Royall assent his Maty well knowes of what vigor and force they are off; I shall take upon me to enquire the reasons but dare averr it to be a thing indispensably necessary the consideration of this grand Assbly Therefore

THE LETTERS / 111

Mr. *Speaker* I humbly moue that a Committee may be appointed to inspect the whole Journall book of the Last Sessions, and that they may make report to the house of the same, and that a sure way be proposed and certain cares taken to represent the Same to his Matie Together with the State of the Countrey, as it now stands for I humbly Conceiue it to be as necessary to cleare all ambiguityes and doubts, and to take away all objections to Lawes formerly made, especially if they are found expedient for the Countrey as it is to make new Lawes, Therefore I hope this motion will not be thought unseasonable, but by this house thought most reasonable, and indeed theire prime Consideration, considering that the objectors doe not quibble or play upon the words or Letters of the Law or abiguously interprett any clause prouisoe or Limmitations therein but they strike at the root and very heart and essence of the Law doubting whether it be a Lawe or noe till the Royall Assent obtained and here promulgated, then the advantage we justly promised to ourselves in our addresses if his Māty should haue bin gratiously pleased to haue granted all or any of them, might if that *unum necessarium* I mencōned before about the Lawes, had not binn soe important, was worthy the Consideration of this house, to take into their serious consideration, and to take such care that his Maty may haue the same humbly represented to him together with the full remonstrance of the present State of this Calamitous Countrey. [continued thus:] This house approues of the motion and speech of Mr *William Fitzhugh* Seconded by seuerall other the members of this house and unanimously consented to by all and doe *order and resolue....*

1. This is the first of two speeches made by WF at the second session of the 1680-1682 Assembly, a session lasting only from April 18 to April 25, 1682. The Assembly met under unusual circumstances, having been called by the senile acting governor, Sir Henry Chicheley, at the instigation of the forceful Robert Beverley. Before the burgesses convened word came from the home government that no meeting should be held until November, when it was supposed that Lord Culpeper, the Governor, would be at Jamestown. The ship bringing this word also brought orders that the two companies of English soldiers then in Virginia should be disbanded unless paid for in future by the colonists. Under these embarrassing circumstances the Council, which had not been consulted about calling the Assembly, agreed that the session should be held but that only the matter of the soldiers should be allowed consideration. Beverley and his followers had hoped to pass a law prohibiting the planting of tobacco in 1682, since the King had not granted a previous request for a cessation of planting. At first the burgesses tried to proceed to the transaction of other regular business; when they were thwarted in this, they refused to do anything about the soldiers. The deputy governor then prorogued the Assembly on the twenty-fifth of April.

As McIlwaine has pointed out (*Journals H.B. 1659/60-1693*, p. xxxiv, note 42), the fact that this speech and the next by WF are recorded in full is most unusual. As he also points out, both questions of which WF spoke were of the greatest importance to the Assembly.

WF probably had in mind future legislation and the possibility of its approval by the home government as well as the pressing necessity of the Assembly's knowing within a reasonable time where it stood in relation to laws it had already passed. Here, as always in his legislative career, WF is championing the principle that the provincial Assembly should be allowed to make its own laws, for it knows the local situation, and what is "expedient."

Also there are pertinent suggestions of the calamitous state of affairs in Virginia, which only a "cessation" (he seems to imply) may remedy.

Finally, WF is here the legal scholar who knows that the colonial legislative body can never work effectively or indeed legally as long as the home government is so dilatory or indifferent in observing and remedying patent injustices.

Second Speech to Burgesses, 24 April 1682 [1]

[McIlwaine, ed.,
Journals H.B.,
p. 167.]

Mr *Speaker*

I humbly offer that Councill are absolutely necessary to be added to this Committee of priuate Causes, because the practice is soe continued from ye Beginning and first settlemt of Assemblyes in this Country yett I doe Concurr with the gentlem that before spake to us as to the Parliamentary proceedings in *Engld* wherein noe Committee appointed by the house euer did or euer will desire the assistance of any of the Lords, but I must begg this favor to distinguish betwixt the nature of this Comtee and all other Committees, for there was never such a Committee appointed by the Parliament in *Engld* because the house of Lords is the onely Court, and the prime and Supreme Court of Judicature in the naͨon and to which Court onely a writt of error from a judgment in the Kings bench lyes, the house of Commons are esteemed onely the grand inquest of ye nation and cannot administer an oath, thereore uncapeable of appointing such a Committee, is the onely deuiation which wee make from the Parliamentary proceedings of *Engld,* which method for a long time hath continued unaltered and truely I am of opinion hath bin rather indulged then allowed by reason of the State of our Country for that the genll Court is an honble body constituted of the Governr & Councill wch is the upper house in our genll Assbly and whoe stand here wth us in the quallity the Lords Spirituall and temporall are there, Now considering the state of our case the constant usage of appeales from that honble Court, it was requisite by the constant usage and continuall practice that those Causes by a Comtee composed of some prime members of the house of Burgesses who assisted wth some of the Councill should determine these appeales which makes them capeable to try them for exceṇtricall and irregular

Henry FitzHugh of Bedford, England, father of the emigrant William

Copy by John Hesselius in 1751, owned by Mrs. Robert H. Stevenson of Boston.

The arms used by the Virginia Fitzhughs

Reproduced from an example in the Virginia Historical Society.

would it seem to any rationall man that Causes of *Meum & Teum,* and of
such great consequence as doubtless most of these are should be tryed by
such a Court that haue not power in themselues to administr an oath, the
Lowest Courts in *England,* soe much as the Court of Byponders[2] haue
power to administer, Then would it not seem unreasonable that a Comtee
of some number of Burgesses should be esteemed a more Supreme Court,
and examine the causes pleadings and judgmts wch haue bin by the
Governr and Councill tryed, and yet in yr constituc̄on not Capeable of
administring an oath, then the very words in the appeale imports as much,
for if appeale is made to the Assembly then I demand by wt rule these
gentm can make the Burgesses the Assbly, for I conceiue ye Assbly to
consist of Gouernr Councill and Burgesses, then if the appeale be to all,
then all the tryall must be before a select number of such a body and not
by the Burgesses alone, because the appeale is genll

1. On April 24 a debate arose in the House of Burgesses as to whether or not members
of the Council had of necessity to be added to the Committee for Private Causes. The arguments of the burgesses opposed to their addition is not given, but it may be largely inferred
from WF's speech from the opposite point of view. His opponents apparently argued from
the analogy that since the General Assembly corresponded to the English Parliament, and it
was an unheard of thing for Lords to be added to Commons committees, councilors should
not be added to the burgesses' committee. WF here points out the distinction between the
legislative and judicial functions of the two legislative bodies, showing that in judicial affairs
Parliament and the General Assembly were quite different.

WF's argument was apparently so convincing that members of the Council were added
to other committees as well as to that of Causes. Ironically enough the Assembly did not
then know that all this was wasted endeavor, for the home government had already ordered
that henceforth no more appeals should be allowed to the General Assembly. See *Journals
H.B. 1659/60-1693,* pp. xxxiv-xxxv, etc.

2. Probably, as McIlwaine suggests (*Journals H.B. 1659/60-1693,* p. 167n), a mistake for
"Court of Piepowders," "a summary court formerly held at fairs and markets to administer
justice among itinerant dealers, etc." *Shorter Ox. Dict.*

To Major Robert Beverley[1]

Majr. Robt. Beverley   May 29th. 1682

Sr. This Messenger[2] who is faithful & intelligent, we have purposely sent
to be certainly informed from your self whether your Restraint continues,
the generall Report with us is, that your freedom was granted you, without any endeavour of Recrimination, which will add a greater lustre to
your Innocence, & assure the world of yor. Capacity that a small jealousie
of your Dissatisfaction may put great men in Dismay. Sr. Magna Charta,

the Petition of Right & the divers Statutes. made in Confirmation of the firs[t?] wth. the severall Commentarys & Expositions upon all, setting forth the liberty of the subject, together with the causes & occasions of this confinement, I am indifferently well furnished with, & assure your self shall not be wanting to one of the choicest of my friends, to communicate my utmost knowledge therein, did your business now re [sic] require it, nor should I scant my pains to do you service, or to give you any means of Satisfaction touching the same, which freedom assure your self is Candid, & if your occasions require it shall find it real from,

To. Majr. Robt. Beverley*   Sr. Your   W. ff.

[Also in pencil (same as clerk's hand) at bottom of page (under *Satisfaction*) is "Mr. John Withers vio[?] [. . . . .?] "

[*LB*, pp. 30-31]

1. For Beverley, see ltr. to him, Sept. 11, 1679, note 1. Beverley's arrest in 1682 had a long prelude and postlude. As early as April, 1677, as clerk of the House of Burgesses he had refused to deliver the journals of that body to Governor Jeffreys and the other Commissioners, on the ground of the rights of the House, and they finally took the records by force. Beverley's loyalty to the Berkeley cause during the Rebellion may lie behind his motives in this and behind the Commissioners' insistence. Among his other activities from 1675 to 1677, he had been a zealous plunderer of the rebels. At any rate, the House of Burgesses in 1677 supported Beverley by sending a vigorous protest to Governor Jeffreys of the "violation of our privileges." Charles II was angry when he heard of this "great presumption" on the part of the burgesses, and directed the new governor in 1680, Culpeper, to rebuke the Assembly and punish the authors and abettors of it. Actually even the Council in Virginia supported the House, and urged the Governor to suspend the King's command. Charles was persuaded to rescind the order, but he insisted that the declaration be erased from the "books of Virginia."

It is clear that then and later Beverley was supported by the "Green Spring" party of Colonel Philip Ludwell, Colonel Edward Hill, Colonel Thomas Ballard, and other old Berkeley adherents. But as time passed, Virginians of all parties became dissatisfied with their economic situation, directly due, they felt, to the low price of tobacco. Acting Governor Sir Henry Chicheley on April 18, 1682, at the insistence of Major Beverley, convened the Assembly for the passage of a law of cessation from growing the crop. As noticed above (note on WF's 1682 speeches), the House found that it was allowed to vote only on another matter. After a few bitter days (during which WF made two strong speeches) the Assembly was prorogued until November 10. Before dismissal, however, the burgesses voted that the journal of their proceedings should be read publicly in every county. Anger that nothing had been done to relieve the poor tobacco planter produced a defiance of authority. In Gloucester organized bands began the work of destruction of the overabundant crop then in the fields. Militia dispatched by the Governor captured several of the plant-cutters.

The gravest suspicion seemed to rest upon Beverley, for he had been the most zealous advocate of cessation and had inspired the convening of the Assembly. Behind this, Nicholas Spencer wrote to Sir Leoline Jenkins in London, lay in part the fact that Beverley himself had an overlarge supply of tobacco on hand (*Cal. St. Papers, Col., Am. & W.I., 1681-1685*, Item 495, May 8, 1682). Because Beverley was quite popular with the rabble, the Governor and

[* Written in pencil just below: "Beverley was at this time a prisoner on board the ship Duke of York in the Rappahannock."]

Council came to believe that he might lead a new insurrection. Although they had no real evidence against him, only "rudeness and sauciness," "general sauciness," and "evil influence," some time before May 28, 1682, they placed him under arrest in order to keep him from accomplishing further mischief. He was first kept in confinement aboard the *Duke of York,* where he was safe from rescue by the people. Actually by May 23 the authorities had grown uneasy and ordered his removal to the *Concord,* "now at York river." Thus things stood at the time this letter of WF's was written.

In the autumn Beverley through WF as his attorney demanded a legal trial and writ of habeas corpus. The writ was refused. But he was soon allowed to be released on bail, for fear of the insurrection was over. Actually he had escaped custody at least twice in the summer of 1682.

Though Beverley was not punished at this time, it was on orders from England that he was tried later and found guilty of certain offenses not directly connected with the plant-cutting but showing his defense of the rights of the House of Burgesses. A record of his misdemeanors was submitted to His Majesty in England. It was "proved" that Beverley had (1) broken open letters directed to the Secretary's office; (2) made up the journal and inserted His Majesty's letter there, where it was first communicated to the House of Burgesses at their prorogation (Hening, *Statutes,* III, 547); (3) refused to deliver copies of the journal of the House of 1682, saying to the Deputy Governor and Council "he could not do it, without leave of his masters." Not until May 9, 1684, was he found guilty of these "high misdemeanors." Probably because of his own high and respected position under the administration of Effingham and his own persuasiveness (as in the defense he made in 1683, Hening, *Statutes,* III, 557-60), he was allowed to escape with only the punishment of asking pardon on his bended knees and giving security for his good behavior. Later the House asked for his reinstatement as clerk. WF is many times mentioned as his attorney and adviser through it all (see Hening, *Statutes,* III).

Beverley was in office still in March, 1687, just before his death, though the King had ordered him (in August, 1686) prosecuted with the utmost severity for defacing the records of the Assembly.

It has been said that WF made his reputation as a lawyer through his defense of Beverley. If so, the details are now too obscure for us to follow. Beverley did not win even a qualified vindication in the eyes of authority, but he was released from confinement and his punishment was light. WF probably presented his arguments in favor of individual rights as cogently and as persuasively as he presented other legal principles in his letters and speeches.

Beverley has been a puzzle to many earlier historians, who have seen in him a conservative adherent of the tyrant Berkeley who became rather suddenly the champion of the common people and of colonial legislative rights. They have failed to consider all the crosscurrents of politics, the basic self-interest in the championing of plant-cutting, and the insistence on the "rights of Englishmen," which one finds all through Virginia colonial history, and frequently, from men otherwise the most loyal and conservative. Staunch Stuart adherent and Anglican, WF manifests the same feeling as to colonial legislative rights. Too often, men like Beverley and WF felt, governors and councilors and home government committees ignored and failed to understand the needs of freeborn men in a non-European environment.

2. As the penciled annotation at the bottom of the letter seems to indicate, this was John Withers (q.v.).

To John Burrage [1]

Mr. John Burrage   June 5th. 1682

Sir   Herewith comes bills of Exchange drawn upon you for £7 sterling, the whole with what was paid last year by Mr. Tucker,[2] for my fees in

managing your severall businesses in Virginia, both in the Generall &
County Courts, Mr. Bull [3] can certainly inform you, that I was equally
concerned wt. Mr. Brent in your business & last year & this year I demanded it of him, but he was unwilling to draw for any more, because he
said you had not receiv'd any quantity of your effects, where that fault lyes
I know not, but this I am sure, that your whole effects that I was concerned
in was due by Judgment.

Sr.   What I had last year was but small in respect of my Service for
you at the Generall Court, & this that I charge now is less in respect of my
Service at the County Court, for I can assure you & Mr. Bull well knows
that my County Court fees barely, according to Act of Assembly at 150 ℔
Cause, comes to above eight thousands pounds of Tobo., which I may demand, you can't deny, & the Law will give me, yet in respect your Employ
was something considerable, & I am something straitned for want of
money, I have made this small & modest Demand, in full of my whole due,
which I hope you will give due acceptance to, which I can assure you will
be to your own advantage & the satisfaction of

To. Mr. Jno. Burrage Mert. in Lyme   Sr. Your   W. ff.

[LB, p. 31]

1. Though Stafford records are missing, the very brief *Westmoreland County Court Order
Book, 1675/6-1688/9* show that in 1683 Burrage entered several suits for recovery of debts due.
    2. There are so many Tuckers thus early in Virginia that this one is difficult to identify.
He may have been a relative of WF's wife Sarah, daughter of John Tucker, even her older
half-brother. See Will of John Tucker, *Westmoreland County Deeds & Wills, No. 1, 1653-1671,*
May 5, 1671, proved May 31, 1671.
    3. The Bulls are as frequent as the Tuckers in early Virginia, or almost so, and we have
less here to go on than with Tucker. It is possible that WF refers to a merchant in Great
Britain, or even a sea captain.

To Madam Sarah Bland [1]

Madam Bland   June 5th. 1682

This comes with three bills of Exchange drawn upon you for £20
sterling the full ballance of your bill to me, which upon answer thereof,
I will take care to Cancell, & do farther signifie & oblige myself by these
presents to acquit & discharge you, from the sd. bill of £20 upon payment
of these bills. This letter comes only to advise, I have writ you something

concerning your business already, & by the next shall return your answer of your severall letters. which about a fortnight ago I receiv'd, together with a full account of your business, as far as it relates to me & have taken care with Mr. Blayton [2] & Mr. Minge [3] to give you the full State of your whole Affairs. I hope you will not fail in answering these bills to the full satisfaction of

To. Mrs. Sarah Bland in London   Madam Your   W. ff.

[*LB.* pp. 31-32]

1. Sarah Bland was the widow of John Bland and daughter of Giles Green, M.P. in Charles I's time. She was the mother of Giles Bland. Her husband was a nephew of Theodorick Bland of Westover, Virginia. John Bland had purchased large estates in Virginia, which were managed by his brother Theodorick until the death of the latter in 1671. After his uncle's death Giles Bland came to Virginia to take charge of his father's property. Soon after his arrival, a long suit was commenced, first by John Bland against the widow of Theodorick Bland, and afterwards by Sarah his widow against the same defendant, who by that time had become the wife of St. Leger Codd. Something about this suit may have caused the quarrel between Giles Bland and Ludwell which led to Bland's execution in 1676/77 with other rebels, and earlier to his being fined and removed from office as Collector of Customs. For many years thereafter Sarah Bland in England petitioned the King, Privy Council, Committee on the Plantations, etc., to get her property restored and to settle her suit against the Codds. There was a steady stream of petitions and appeals. From this date at least, and for many years thereafter, WF served as legal adviser to her and to her Virginia attorneys Blayton and Minge (just below). See the letters below. 20 V 238-39, 242; 350-53; 21 V 128-32; *Cal. St. Papers, Col., Am. & W.I., 1677-1680,* p. 545; *Journals H.B. 1659/60-1693,* pp. 199, 204, 209; *Exec. Journ. Council Col. Va.,* I, 1, 57, 58, 497-98, 501-3; *Jamestown 350th Anniv. Survey Reports,* No. 255, pp. 7 ff. (P.R.O., C.O. 5/1356, pp. 87-89, 119-20, 318-21).

2. The Charles City County lawyer Thomas Blayton. He had been a sympathizer with Bacon and had been exempted from pardon but later was pardoned by Berkeley. Tyler, *Cycl. Va. Biog.,* I, 188; 3 V 132-47, 239-52, 346-48; Washburn, *Governor and the Rebel,* pp. 50, 59; Wertenbaker, *Va. under the Stuarts,* p. 202.

3. James Minge, surveyor, burgess, clerk of James City County, clerk of the House of Burgesses in 1676, apparently had been a Bacon sympathizer. That Blayton and Minge as Bacon sympathizers should be acting for Mrs. Bland was quite natural, of course, in view of the fate of her son and her property. That WF, apparently always a loyalist, should be their and her adviser is somewhat more surprising. But WF was a lawyer working for fees, and in the years after the Rebellion all groups had been inclined to let bygones be bygones.

To Major Robert Beverley [1]

Majr. Robert Beverley   June 5th. 1682

Sr. This comes by the same Messenger [2] of the other of the 29th. May, & I hope will find you as well & as free as it leaves me, accompany'd with an assurance of my utmost Endeavour, to do you service to the utmost of my power. Sr. I have lately receiv'd a letter from Madam Bland,[3] by which I understand she keeps in her old way of Court Sollicitations, & assures me of doing me any kindness in her Circumstances therefore desire you to send me a fair Copy of the Journal of our last Assembly, to send to her who I doubt not upon receipt thereof, will be advantageously serviceable to us, & please also signifie whether I may that way be serviceable to you.[4] I hope you'll mind & hasten the expediting of your promise, in giving me a Copy of these Commissions, Instructions &c. you were pleas'd to assure me should be the first of your Care, upon your coming home. Sr. Those two bills Mr. Brent[5] & I took of you for £20...5...0 I cannot find & do doubt have lost them, therefore desire you to sign anew the bills herewith sent you, which have relation to the discharge of the former, if ever they should be found again, which I very much doubt, if you think these are not authentickly drawn, for a discharge of the former, please to draw others your self. My humble service to your self & good Lady   If you could draw bills of Exchange payable to Mr. Jno. Buckner[6] or order, for the whole sum, it would be very advantageous to me, & mightily satisfactory to him who I can pay no other way

To. Majr. Robt. Beverley   Your   W. ff.
c/o Mr. Jno. Withers

[LB, p. 32]

1. For Beverley, see ltrs. to him, Sept. 11, 1679, note 1, and May 29, 1682, note 1. The Virginia Council on June 19, 1682, ordered that Beverley, who had escaped and had been recaptured, be brought to James City. Apparently Beverley calmly went home each time he escaped. *Cal. St. Papers, Col., Am. & W.I., 1681-1685,* Item 574.
2. John Withers, as noted above, was at this period frequently "field representative" for WF. By 1685 he was sheriff and in 1696 burgess. See ltr. to John Buckner, Dec. 3, 1681, note 2.
3. For Sarah Bland, see ltr. to her, June 5, 1682, note 1.
4. Beverley had been brought on board the *Concord* on May 31, 1682. On June 15 he was ordered transferred to the Eastern Shore aboard Colonel Custis' sloop. On June 19 it was reported that he had escaped from on board the sloop. Presumably he was in custody at the time WF wrote this letter, but WF thought him at home. Beverley had taken the journals home. Presumably WF felt that Madame Bland had sufficient influence in England to be useful to Beverley and to the burgesses who sought their "rights" as against the Council and Governor. Hening, *Statutes,* III, 543-44.
5. George Brent (q.v.) was of course WF's law partner.
6. For John Buckner of Gloucester County, see ltr. to him, Dec. 3, 1681, note 1.

Instructions for John Withers [1]

Instructions for Mr. Jno. Withers his proceedings in his York
journey June 5th. 1682

First to Majr. Beverley [2] there's two letters, & two bills drawn for him to
sign for £20 ... 5. as ℞ the bills you'll see, which remember to take,
except he will give you bills of Exchange to Mr. Jno. Buckner for the said
Sum 2ndly. To take of Madam Hull, Roger Hull's widow [3] two bills of
Exchange for £3. each payable to Mr. Brent & my self. Thirdly to take Mr.
Fantleroy's [4] bills for £8 .. 10, if he will pass for so much, but be sure
for £6. or else tell him I shall sue him for his Protest   Fourthly To deliver
Mr. Brody's [5] letter, & take bills of him for £5 sterling, or ready money if
he pleases   Fifthly To deliver Herriot's [6] letter & take bills for £3. in
your own name, or else to receive the same in ready money, & deliver his
papers after paymt. Sixthly To Deliver Mr. Christopher Robinson [7] his
letter, & take bills for £7 .. 10. for Mr. Brent, & as much for me in my
own name, & to acquaint him that you are to pay them away as you come
up   Seventhly   To pass Leftidge's [8] bill away, though it be for fourty
shillings. Eighthly   To purchase what likely Negroes you can, either 1, 2,
3, 4, 5, or 6. what boys & men you possibly can, as few women as may be,
but be sure not above two, to purchase neither men nor women above
thirty years old, not to exceed £20 for the price of a man, unless he be
extraordinary likely, to buy Mr. Walkers [9] boy alone for £20 if you can, or
to give £54 for the three at most, what under you can, if you cannot purchase him alone. To proceed to £34 for Majr. Peyton's [10] two boys, if you
can't get them under or can't hear of a better purchase to do for me as
for your self in choosing & purchasing. Ninthly   To pass Haverton's [11]
bills away in the purchase of Negroes if you can. Tenthly   To pass George
Boyce [12] his two bills in the Purchase of Negros, or any other Swap to
advantage, nay though with loss. Eleventhly   To pass Corbets [13] bills of
£6 for any thing to my best advantage, though at halves, or for any truck
Twelfthly   To Deliver Gullock's [14] letter, & to take bills of Exchange for
Mr. Brent for £5 & the same for me in your own name, if you see occasion,

Your   W. ff.

[LB, pp. 32-33]

1. For John Withers, see just above, and ltr. to John Buckner, Dec. 3, 1681, note 2. Since all the persons mentioned cannot be identified with certainty, it is impossible to say whether or not WF mentions the names of persons in the order in which Withers should see them. The identifications that are possible, however, would suggest that WF's listings are in no precise route-order, if in any particular order.

2. For Beverley, see ltr. to him, Sept. 11, 1679, note 1, and other letters. Beverley lived in Middlesex County, on the south side of the Rappahannock.

3. Unidentified.

4. Moore Fauntleroy or Fantleroy, a burgess from Lancaster County from 1659 to 1660, left three children, William, Moore, and Elizabeth. William (1656-1686) married Catherine Griffin. He was a J.P. of Rappahannock County in 1684 and later. Juliet Fauntleroy, comp., *Colonel Moore Fauntleroy, His Ancestors and Descendants,* Typescript, Va. State Lib. (Alta Vista, Va., 1936), 2 vols., pp. 68-101, 164 ff. William seems the most likely to be the person referred to.

5. For Brody, see ltr. to Thomas Mathews, July 3, 1681, note 4. The earlier letter located Brody at Captain Leonard Howson's. Howson was a merchant who lived in Wicomico Parish, Northumberland County.

6. Unidentified. In 1703 and 1706 a George Heriott or Herriott lived in King William County. 25 V 175; 31 V 344.

7. Robinson (1645-1693), burgess for Middlesex, 1688, 1691, later member of the Council, and in 1692 Secretary of State, lived at "Hewick" on the Rappahannock near present-day Urbanna. In 1682 he was clerk of Middlesex County. He had been a bondsman for Robert Beverley. His second wife was the widow of Beverley. 2 V 411; 3 V 2-5n; 7 V 17-19, etc.

8. Unidentified.

9. Probably one of the descendants of John Walker, burgess for Gloucester in 1666. A John Walker was sheriff of King and Queen County in 1702. A Henry Walker lived in Stafford and died before 1693. John Newton and WF took up his tract of 550 acres on escheat from the Proprietors. *Journals H.B. 1659/60-1693,* pp. viii, 21, 25; *Journals H.B. 1695...1702, passim;* 47 V 342.

10. Robert Beverley's eldest son Peter married Elizabeth, daughter of Major Robert Peyton of Isleham, Gloucester County, Virginia, and granddaughter of Sir Edward Peyton, Bart. In 1674 a Robert Peyton was one of the two attorneys enjoying the largest practice in Middlesex County, probably the same man. 20 V 116; 32 V 48; Bruce, *Inst. Hist. Va.,* I, 579.

11. Unidentified.

12. Unidentified.

13. Unidentified.

14. The will of a Robert Gullock was proved in Rappahannock County, May 23, 1684. The inventory of a Thomas Gullock was returned in Westmoreland on August 31, 1698. William M. Sweeny, *Wills of Rappahannock County, Va., 1656-1692* (Lynchburg, Va., 1947), p. 105; Fothergill, *Wills of Westmoreland County,* p. 28. The references here are to old Rappahannock County, which stretched across the Rappahannock River and was abolished in 1692.

To George Brent [1]

Sir   June 20th. 1682

Mr. Herriout [2] being bound your way, I could not miss so fit an opportunity of saluting your self & good Lady also by the same to present mine & wive's humble service to you both. I am newly returned from my Nomany & Cherrypoint journey, which seemed to be more troublesome in

Imagination, than I found them in the Action. Lincoln [3] praised be Heaven & his good friends has all his pannick fears & fearfull petts &c. removed. Our good friend Mr. Matthews [4] spent that small time I had to converse with him, Rather in inquiring names &c. which I was fully capable of solving him, what use he can make of knowing men's names I know not, its too deep a reach for my shallow capacity. I am not yet able to acquaint you with Southern news, by reason Jno. Withers is not yet returned,[5] whom I every minute longingly expect, at his Arrival do hope we may be together to communicate. I desire you'll signifie what plank is ready for me, that I may take care to get it home, yet I must beg the favour of you, very speedily, if it not be not already done, to get down my Walnut Plank to Mr. Peyton's landing,[6] I shall not be ungratefull to the person that does it, & shall esteem it as a singular favour of your's to

To. Mr. George Brent   W. ff.

[*LB*, pp. 33-34]

1. For George Brent, see ltr. to R. Wormeley, June 19, 1681, note 3.
2. For Heriott, see ltr. of instructions to John Withers, June 5, 1682, just above. He is not really identified.
3. For Lincolne, see ltr. to Henry Hartwell, June 19, 1681, note 6, above. WF was employed as his attorney from 1680 to 1682.
4. For Thomas Mathews, see ltr. to him, July 3, 1681, note 1. He lived at Cherry Point in Northumberland. Though he did not write out his account of Bacon's Rebellion for Sir Robert Harley until 1705, it is just possible that he had such an account in mind thus early in 1682 and was gathering details, such as names of persons who may have participated.
5. That is, Withers had not yet returned from the journey projected in the "Instructions" of June 5, just above.
6. This might be Valentine Peyton of Westmoreland or Major Robert Peyton of Gloucester, more likely the former. Bruce, *Inst. Hist. Va.*, I, 583, 579.

To William Leigh [1]

Mr. William Leigh   June 27th. 1682

Sr. Your's bearing date 1st. June about a fortnight ago I receiv'd, wherein your taxing I must patiently bear & acknowledge my fault, yet with this extenuation, that want of health hinder'd my coming, want of horses my sending, & my dependence of finding them hinder'd an early care to provide another to send to you, which I hope by my friend will be admitted excusable, & sooner I could not effectually send to you, than this opportunity I now take, together with what effects I could raise for your satisfaction, which herewith I send you (viz) Mr. Robinson's bill for £7 .. 10.0 Mr. Fantleroy's for £8 .. 10. Mr. Storke's for £2 .. 10 & Mr. Herriot's for £2 .. 10 .. 6. which makes in all £21 .. 00 .. 6. which is all the ready money I can at present procure for you, that will be certainly paid,[2] Sr. I have sent & indorsed two bills more, one of Thomas Howerton [3] for £3 sterling which at the fall will be certainly paid, together with that bill of Coxes [4] for £5. which makes in all £29 .. 00 .. 6. I likewise send you Mr. Leftidge's [5] bill due & payable long since, which I am affraid is none of the best, I am sure to me at this Distance it is not, therefore have purposely sent it to you, well knowing your nearness may give you all opportunitys to secure it, which I desire you to take care in for me, & when obtained let it go to my credit in these bills, the remainder due is £1 .. 11.6. which at the fall I shall contrive to your conveniency together with what you want in those other bills (if any) which I hope not. Sr. I desire to know whether you continue your resolutions as to your Town practice I assure you I continue mine for the declining yr. of, therefore if your's continue, both Mr. Brent & my self shall recommend as before intimated at Town what Clients we can, together with our particular business to your Care & management, & please to acquaint me in what my self may be serviceable to you & you may command me. I have herewith also sent you an Account ready stated, which I desire you to sign & my Creditor's name, therefore have left a blank for it, which I desire you to fill up, which may be for my future justification upon the mortality of either of us. Sr. Here's a friend of mine in these parts has about £100 sterling by him, which he desires to lay out in Negroes if any good ones are to be purchased & reasonable in your Parts, please to signifie the same in your letter by the bearer, & I shall acquaint him therewith. Our Parts are so barren of News that I am able to inform you of none   I hope your's will, which I dare say you'll not be wanting in communicating. The Messenger goes to James Town therefore may be engaged to call as he comes back. I have herewith sent a letter to Mr. Buckner [6] with some considerable concerns in it, I request your favour of delivering it your self, or sending it by a safe Messenger, who may bring an answer back from him to you, which you may please to deliver the Messenger upon his return back

To. Mr. William Leigh   Your   W. ff.
in New Kent

[LB, pp. 34-35]

1. William Leigh was an attorney of Middlesex and New Kent (King and Queen after 1691) counties, later a burgess and a colonel of militia. He was one of the prominent attorneys of the colony. 1 V 363; 10 V 285; 22 V 245; 32 V 63; *Journals H.B. 1659/60-1693, passim; Journals H.B. 1695...1702, passim; Exec. Journ. Council Col. Va.,* I, *passim;* Bruce, *Inst. Hist. Va.,* I, 579.

2. All these men save Storke are mentioned in the "Instructions" to John Withers of June 5. Storke was probably "Thomas Storke of London, merchant," mentioned in various Stafford records and apparently at some time in the colony. Or it may have been Nehemiah Storke of Stafford, probably a relative of Thomas. 10 V 292; 9 W(2) 183; Harrison, *Landmarks,* I, 112-13.

3. In 1704, Thomas Howerton owned lands in King and Queen and Essex counties. 32 V 150; 33 V 363.

4. Unidentified.

5. Also mentioned in Wither's "Instructions." Otherwise unidentified.

6. Leigh in New Kent was not far from Buckner in Gloucester, just across the York River.

To John Buckner [1]

Mr. Jno. Buckner   June 27th. 1682

Sr. I have inclosed sent you bills of Exchange for £26..10.00 & bills that will be certainly paid, for the remainder that is due to you, I will next year betimes, make punctual payment. The reason that I did not this year comply & that sooner, was by reason of Majr. Beverley's money not being paid [2] for that money I purposely purchased for your conveniency, & drew bills to Mr. Brent for one half of it, which since has not answer'd with expectation nor your payment. I hope the next year, part of it may do for the Ballance now due, but if it should not, I will be sure fully to satisfie You to content. Also I have herewith sent you an account as it stands betwixt us, which I desire you to sign & send me up inclosed in your letter, which will manifest in case of Mortality, the true station of Accounts betwixt us, & if you please a little news will be acceptable to

To. Mr. Jno. Buckner   W. ff.

[*LB*, pp. 35-36]

1. For Buckner, see ltr. to him, Dec. 3, 1681, note 1.
2. Major Beverley's troubles at this time are discussed in detail in a ltr. to Beverley, May 29, 1682, note 1.

To the Honourable Ralph Wormeley [1]

Honrd. Sir   August 2nd. 1682

This Messenger's haste will not admit me to Copy out that Breviate for your Perusal, which I promis'd you, & therefore shall take the first Conveniency by some of Collo. Jones [2] his men, which will not be long first, for contriving you that, together with the most material of your other papers. Yet this Conveniency gives me this opportunity, of returning you thanks for your favours, especially your last which was accompany'd with a generous promise of lending me the second & third part of Rushworth's Historical Collections, & his tryal of the Earle of Strafford,[3] which I earnestly desire you will please send me by this bearer, who will take great care of them, & safely convey them to my hand.   Sr.   The bearer has with him from the Office a special Warrant ready drawn for the Governor's Signature in behalf of Mr. Richard Gibson against Matthew Thompson,[4] which Mr. Secretary [5] promised me last generall Court to get signed, & has since assured Mr. Gibson, to write to the Governor about it, but lest multiplicity of business might occasion his forgetting [yr.] of Mr. Gibson desired me to acquaint you, that there might be no scruple in signing it. My earnest desire of the perusal of those Books, makes me not fear the danger of Impertinency in Seconding my above Request about the Books wch. shall be carefully used, & safely returned to you by

To. Esqr. Wormley   Your   W. ff.

[*LB*, pp. 36-37]

1. For Wormeley, see ltr. to N. Spencer, Nov. 2, 1680, note 3.
2. Cadwallader Jones, son of a London merchant, in 1681 lived in Rappahannock County and owned tracts on Chotank Creek in Stafford and more in the Stafford backwoods (later Fairfax) near WF's "Ravensworth." He was made a lieutenant colonel of Stafford militia in 1680 for frontier service against the Indians, with whom he traded. He was too sanguine in his Indian trade and land speculations, however, and soon came to bankruptcy. See WF's correspondence below concerning him. Later he wrote "An Essay: Louisiana and Virginia Improved," with an early map of eastern America, and another on the Indian Trade. 30 V 323-40; *Jamestown 350th Anniv. Survey Reports*, No. 405 (P.R.O., C.O. 5/1310).
3. John Rushworth, *Historical Collections of Private Passages of State, Weighty Matters in Law, Remarkable Proceedings in Five Parliaments...The Second Part* (March 10, 1628/29 to April 13, 1640)...(London, 1680, in two volumes). *The Third Part* also appeared in two volumes, covering the period Nov. 3, 1640, to the end of 1644. The earliest edition of the latter printed in the seventeenth century was published in 1691, too late for WF's letter. Actually

THE LETTERS / 125

he must have meant volumes II and III of what was to be eight volumes in the complete *Collections*, though II and III contain only *The Second Part. The Tryal of Thomas Earl of Strafford, Lord Lieutenant of Ireland Upon Impeachment of High Treason* . . . was published in London as a separate volume in 1680.

4. Richard Gibson's name appears several times in Stafford County records in lawsuits and in accusations against George Brent. In 1702 and 1714 a person of his name was a J.P. 1 V 372; 17 V 311; 28 V 70-72; Harrison, *Landmarks*, I, 121.

Matthew Thompson, also of Stafford, was in 1699 and 1700 a J.P. In 1697 he was appointed a commissioner of oyer and terminer. 1 V 231-51; 5 V 278; 9W (2) 182; *Exec. Journ. Council Col. Va.*, I, 370.

5. Nicholas Spencer (q.v.) was Secretary of State in Virginia from 1679 to 1689.

To John Cooper [1]

Mr. Jno. Cooper   June 5th. 1682

Sr. In my last by Capt. Norrington,[2] I had only leisure to acquaint you that I had inclosed Bills Loading for 18 hhds. shipped in him & consigned to you; one of which upon my return home I find left behind, but three omitted in the bills of Loading which I hope you have since found out in the ship, notwithstanding that omission in the bills Loading for I have sufficient Evidence to prove that those hhds. of Tobo. so marked & number'd as are omitted in the bill Loading, were by Capt. Norrington's men taken away from the respective houses where they lay, upon view of my Notes given for the same by Evidence of two sorts. First I have Evidence that at such houses, so many hhds. of Tobo. of such a Mark & Number were received for me. Secondly The respective Housekeeper Deposes that Capt. Norrington's Seamen carry'd away that very Tobo. so mark'd & number'd, by vertue of my Notes given for the same. The Copys of which Evidence I hope to get ready to send here inclosed, that you may inform Capt. Norrington thereof, which may give him opportunity to enquire the truth thereof, & get me Righted without Charge to himself, which without his care there, may chance to fall upon himself here, the three hhds. left behind, were number'd 7, 11, & 14. that of 14. was really left behind, but those of 11 & 7 carry'd away tho' not put into the bills Loading. I have receivd your four letters dated 22nd. August, 14th. Septr. 21st Octr. & 17th. Decr. all which are now by me, in the first you give me an account of the receipt & mean Market for my Tobo., which I must submit to, its in vain for me to repine at the common calamity In that of the 14th. Septr. ℔ Capt. Norrington I receiv'd inclosed my Accompt Currant, Accompt of Sales, & Invoice of goods brought in by him, which goods were much abused on board, as you'll perceive by my receipt given upon the back of the Bill of Loading, what right I may have therein, I am not Merchant enough to know, but think it hard measure to pay freight for goods, to have them carelessly damnify'd, wch. without farther mentioning I refer wholly to you. Sr. The Tobo. I sent you, I can say little in Commendation of, for my skill in the Commodity is but small, but four hhds. No. 1, 2, 3, 4. were sweet scented & of my own Crop, & well handled in the opinion of the knowingest Planters, the Residue were Oronoko & the choicest my Receiver could pick out of 100 hhds. he received for me, how it will prove there with you I know not, but will not despair, & hope the Market may rise upon the news of the great destruction of Tobo. by Cutters & Pluckers,[3] who at the writing hereof have not yet desisted, the particulars I presume you have fully heard, therefore will not now trouble you with & for a farther lessening the quantity, the great frequent rains have largely contributed, especially to those living in low Grounds In your Accompt Currant & Letters in Octr. & Decr. £15 .. 18 .. 00. which I hope before the receipt of this, you have reimbursed your self & withall I find in my Accot. of Sales my self charged Dr. with six & three pence for 25lb. of damnified Tobo., which I presume to be a mistake, & I believe I ought to have Credit given me for that, which if so, will lighten my Accot. & if it be an Error to rectifie it. I have here inclosed sent you Bills of Exchange one drawn by Majr. Thomas Youle [4] upon your self for £5. one other of Mr. Chamberlain's [5] for £6 .. 10 another upon Mr. Burrage [6] of Lyme which I assure my self will be all paid, & another upon Mrs. Bland for £20. which I doubt not but upon sight she will comply with, which in the whole amounts to £38 .. 10 .. 08. Sr. I was intended to have sent you ten thousand Pipe staves, & four hundred feet of two inch black Wallnut Plank, but could not get freight for them, my remoteness from shiping & long absence from home hindering me from taking advantageous opportunitys therein, therefore if you find it may turn to my profit, please to signifie the same to me by the first opportunity, & if you can with conveniency, contrive me freight for the same, also I would desire you to enquire the price of Ship trunnells ⅌ thousand, & inform me thereof, & if you find that trunnels of two foot, a foot & half, & a foot in length, will clear one with another £25 or £30 ⅌ thousand, take me freight certain for 40, 50, 60. or 70 thousand, for the lowness of Tobo. has utterly discouraged me, & if the Market this year rises not, I have small encouragement to run so great a Risque, to have nothing considerable for my Tobo., nay less by one half, than I can have at my own Door, without either trouble, or hazard. I desire you to speak to Capt. Norrington or any of your friends being Master of a Ship, bound for Potomack River to bring me two or three couple of Rabbits.   Sr. My wants still continue the same for a Bricklayer or Carpenter, & should be glad to have either of them consigned to me tho' some of the goods were let alone   I am Sr.

To. Mr. John Cooper   Your   W. ff.
Mercht. in London

[*LB*, pp. 37-39]

1. For Cooper, see ltr. to him, April 4, 1681, note 1.
2. For Captain William Norrington, see ltr. to John Cooper, April 4, 1681, notes 1 and 2. He was apparently master of a ship owned by or contracted for by Cooper.
3. The plant-cutting in Gloucester and New Kent counties, a protest against the Deputy Governor's failure to allow the Assembly to enact legislation for curtailing production of tobacco, was thus about a month after the Assembly was prorogued at its height. As noted above, WF's friend and client Robert Beverley was suspected and arrested. See ltr. to Beverley, May 29, 1682, note 1.
4. Major Thomas Youle, Youell, or Yowell, of Westmoreland, a cousin of William Hardidge (q.v.), married Anne, daughter of Colonel Richard Lee of Dividing Creek, Northumberland County. He was a burgess in 1688 and 1692/93. His will is in *Westmoreland County Deeds & Wills, No. 2, 1691-1699.*
5. This was Robert Chamberlain of Westmoreland, against whom WF was awarded damages for a protested bill of exchange for this very amount, £6.10, in Westmoreland Court on Feb. 13, 1683/84. *Westmoreland County Court Order Book, 1675/6-1688/9,* pp. 321, 327.
6. Presumably a merchant of Lyme Regis, with whom WF and other Virginia planters did business.

To [John] Jackson [1]

Mr. Jackson   February 11th. 1682/3

As to your Proposal about the bringing in Negros next fall, I have this to offer, & you may communicate the same to your owners & Employers, that I will deal with them for so many as shall amount to 50000lb Tobo. & cash which will be about 120 hhds., under the Condition & at these ages & prices following, to say to give 3000lb. Tobo. for every Negro boy or girl, that shall be between the age of seven & eleven years old, to give 4000lb. Tobo. for every youth or girle that shall be between the age of 11 & 15 & to give 5000lb. Tobo. for every young man or woman that shall be above 15 years of age, & not exceed 24. the said Negroes to be delivered at my Landing, some time in Septr. next & I to have notice whether they will so agree some time in August next, And I do assure you & so you may acquaint them that upon your delivery & my receipt of

the Negroes, according to the ages abovementioned, & that they be sound
& healthfull at their Delivery I will give such sufficient Caution for the
payment of the Tobo., accordingly, by the 20th. Decr. then next following, as shall be approved of. The ages of the Negros to be judged & determined by two or three such honest & reasonable men here, as your self
shall nominate & appoint. The whole Sum of the Tobo. to be paid in the
Compass of twenty miles perhaps not so remote [2]   I am

To. Mr. Jackson of Piscataway   Your   W. ff.
In New England These

[*LB*, pp. 39-40]

1. Presumably John Jackson of Piscataway, or Piscataqua, New Hampshire, master
mariner, who made his will on January 24, 1690/91 (proved Feb. 28, 1690/91). He had a son
John, also a master mariner, who may have been the master of the ketch *George* of Piscataway
trading in Virginia in January, 1690/91. New England ships had been for some time taking
triangular or quadrangular courses from home to London to Africa to Virginia. There is no
evidence that Jackson had any connection with the Royal African Company which, according
to Culpeper, did not become active in the slave-trade in Virginia until after 1682. Bruce,
Ec. Hist. Va., II, 77, 80, 82; *Exec. Journ. Council Col. Va.*, I, 153; Albert S. Batchellor, *et al.*,
eds., *Probate Records of the Province of New Hampshire*, Vol. I. State Papers Series, Vol.
XXXI (Concord, N.H., 1907), 346; Nathaniel Bouton, ed., [*New Hampshire*] *Provincial Papers.
Documents and Records of the Province of New Hampshire from 1686 to 1722....* (Manchester,
N.H., 1868), II, 77.
2. The reader will notice the business-like objectivity of WF and, by implication, of his
addressee in this negotiation. This letter and that to Mrs. Cutt and Jeffries (just below)
would appear to indicate that the cargoes at this period were mixed ones of slaves and dry
goods, or that the New England ships alternated between the two. That they were mixed
cargoes is evident in a letter to William Byrd I in June, 1684. Bruce, *Ec. Hist. Va.*, II, 82n.

To Mrs. Eleanor Cutt & George Jeffries [1]

Mrs. Elear. Cutt & Mr. George Jeffries   Febry. 5th. 1682/3

At the Instance of Mr. Jackson [2] though unacquainted this comes to
acquaint you, that I apprehend you are mistaken in carrying on any trade
in our Parts, by your sending your goods to purchase her own Loading,
which puts a Necessity upon your Dealer, to sell for the speed of his
Market, a great deal cheaper than you need, if you could afford a stock
before hand, to lie in some factor's hands in this Country, & who would
then take the opportunity of his Market, & could reduce the whole Loading to lie in some certain places, to be immediately taken in upon the

Arrival of your Vessel, which those that come to purchase their Loading, are forced to go from place to place for, so that the profit of the Voyage, if you purchase very cheap (which is uncertain) is eaten up by the length of stay necessarily occasioned, by going from place to Place, to fetch the several parcels of wheat, besides the uncertainty of the Market; those things would be taken away, by settling a constant factoridge here, & whatever Commodity you had a mind to, or gave advice of, might be reasonably & certainly every year purchased, & the Vessel that comes for it quickly dispatched, so that the first Stock of money being dead, about five or six months gives these advantages a certain & sure Market, an easie charge & a quick Dispatch, which is the life & profit of every Trade.[3] What I have said is not to court your Employ but to satisfie Mr. Jackson

Your   W. ff.

[*LB*, pp. 40-41]

1. Mrs. Cutt succeeded her husband Captain Richard Cutt in merchant shipping after his death in 1677. She made her own will on July 12, 1684, and it was proved on July 29, 1684. She was a woman of considerable wealth, having a farm, a number of white servants, and several Negroes. *New Hampshire State Papers Series*, Vol. XXXI, *Probate Records, 1635-1717*, I, 164, 282.

George Jeffrey or Jaffrey of Portsmouth, merchant, is mentioned as "my good friend" in the will of Samuel Cutt in 1698. A son was granted the administration of the estate of Jeffrey on Feb. 20, 1706/7. *Probate Records*, pp. 439, 581, etc.

2. For Jackson, see ltr. to him, Feb. 11, 1682/83, note 1.

3. WF is certainly on solid ground economically in pointing out the chance and potential waste or loss in a ship with cargo having to peddle its wares over a considerable territory and time without surety of a return cargo. What he is proposing is that he (or some other) as individual act as Virginia factor or merchant, receive all the cargo, take responsibility for its disposal and supply loading of tobacco (or here, wheat). Though WF disclaims personal interest, that he wished to become a merchant-factor for various ships or companies is evident in several of his other letters.

It is interesting that thus early northern Virginia was exporting wheat as well as tobacco, the former particularly to New England. The region around the present city of Alexandria was to become an important wheat and flour center between the Revolution and the War of 1812.

To Major Robert Beverley [1]

Majr. Robt. Beverley   January 1st. 1682/3

Sr.   I suppose Mr. Robinson [2] before the receipt of this, has been so kind to acquaint you that your tryal will be easie, which will at present save me some labour, yet to correspond with yours & my word, I shall give you some matt [touchy] * in relation to your tryall which will be very suddenly. Multiplicity of business at present a little disorders me. First for Imprisonment see Cap: 26. Magna Charta   I refer you, for the words of of [*sic*] the Statute it self,³ I shall take notice of Conclusions drawn from thence, And first though the offence whereof he was accused was such, as he was not baylable by Law, yet the Law did so highly hate the long Imprisonment of any man, though accused of an odious & heinous crime, that it gave him this Writ of Inquisition for his relief. Secondly, There was a Mean whereby the common Law, before Indictments to protect the innocent party against false Accusation, & to deliver him out of Prison. And a farther Benefit was by this Law in favour of Prisoners, that he should have it without fee, or without Denyal or Delay, for more of this matter see the Mirror Cap. 5. Sect: 2 ⁴ But this Writ was taken away by the 28 Edw: 3, but within twelve years after. it was Enacted, that all Statutes made against magna Charta as this 28 Edw: 3rd. should be void, so that it is again revived. Nay the Justices have been so far from allowance of any one's being detained in Prison without due tryal, that it was resolved in the Case of the Abbot of St. Albans by the whole Court, that where the King had granted to the said Abbot to have a Goal, & diverse persons were committed to that Goal for felony, & because the Abbot would not be at cost to make Deliverance, he detained them in Prison long time without making lawfull Deliverance, that the Abbot had, for that cause forfeited his franchises &c. See Sta: Glo: Cap. 9. H: 8. 4. 18. 20 Edw: 4. 6. Brooke title forfeiture & Cooke upon Magna Charta fo: 43 many such like Cases.⁵ And it is provided by the Statute 5. H:4. Cap. 10 & Cooke's Reports Lib: 9 fo: 119 ⁶ that none be imprisoned by any Justice of Peace, but in the common Goal, to the end they may have their tryal at the next Goal Delivery. And this Statute extendeth to all other Judges & Justices for two reasons. First This Act is but declaratory of the common Law. Secondly Ubi est lex specialis et ratio est generalis generaliter accipiendum est. By the Statute Glo: Cap. 9.⁷ you may see what expedition ought to be used, for avoiding long Imprisonment, (viz) till the next Court for tryal. From whence it is to be observed that the Law of England is lex Misericordiæ for three Causes. First that the Innocent shall not be worn away & wasted by long Imprisonment but as hereby & by magna Charta speedily come to his tryal. Secondly That Prisoners for criminal cases when they are brought to their tryal be humanely dealt withal, for Severos quidem facit Iustitia in humanos non facit   Thirdly The Judge ought to

---

* This word appears above the line and may be an alternative for *in relation to.*

exhort him to answer without fear, & that Justice shall be duely administer'd to him. Magna Charta Cap. 29.[8] No man shall be taken, or imprisoned, or dispossessed of his Lands, livelyhood or libertys, unless it be by lawfull judgment of his Equals, or by due Course & Process of Law, & not Petition or Suggestion, nay though it were to the King & Council, see this notably explained, by these Acts 5 Edw: 3. 9. 25 Edw. 3. 4. 37 Edw. 3. 8 38 Edw. 3. 9. 42 Edw. 3. 3. 17. Rich. 2. 6. Cooke's reports Lib. 10 fo. 71.[9] All these Conclusions upon a Commitment do follow. First that he or they that do commit them have lawfull authority. That this Warrant or Mittimus be lawfull, & that must be in writing, under his hands & Seal. Thirdly The Cause must be contained in the Warrant, as for Treason, felony &c. Fourthly the Warrant or Mittimus containing a lawfull Cause, ought to have a lawfull Conclusion, & him safely to keep untill he be delivered by Law &c. & not untill the party committing to farther order. This & the former Conclusions do evidently appear, by the Writs of Habeas Corpus, By which writs it manifestly appears that no man ought to be committed but for some certain Cause, and these words in the Habeas Corpus ad subjiciendum et recipiendum, prove that Cause must be shewed, for otherwise how can the Court state Orders thereon according to Law. And this agrees with holy Scripture Acts Apostles Cap 25 v. ult.[10] It seems to me unreasonable, to send away one bound into Prison, & not to signifie the Cause thereof, So also the Petition of Right 3 Car.[11] Imprisonment doth not only extend, to false Imprisonment or unjust, but it is both false & unjust, if he be detained longer than he ought, although at first lawfully imprisoned Cooke Magna Charta fo: 53.[12] Good Judges and Justices abhor such Courses as the Centurion took against St. Paul Acts Apostles Cap: 22 v. 24. 27.[13] He commanded Paul to be bound & then asked who he was & what he had done. For Remedy for Injustice done in this nature See Cooke Magna Charta Cap. 29. fo. 55, & 56 &c,[14] there you will also find that Justice ought to have three qualitys, Libera, quia nihil est, iniquius, Venali justitia, Plena, quia justitia non debet claudicare, et Celeris, quia dilatis est quædam negatis. And then it is both justice & Right. Again in the Statute de frangendibus Prisonam, there you may see what a lawfull Mittimus is. First it must be in the writing, in the name & under the hand & Seal of him that makes the same, expressing his Office Place, & Authority, by force whereof he makes the Mittimus, & is to be directed to the Goaler or keeper of the Prison. Secondly In it must be contained the Cause, as it expressly appeareth by this Act, with such convenient certainty as it may appear judicially, that the Offence tale Judicium requirit. And this is proved both by Reason & Authority. By Reason first, for that it is in case of felony quæ inducit ultimum Supplicium, &

therefore ought to have convenient certainty as aforesaid. Secondly for that a voluntary escape is felony in the Goaler, & if there be certainty expressed. Thirdly If the Mittimus should be good generally pro felonia then as the [   ] * is Ignorantiæ Judicis foret calamitas Innocentis, & therefore in Reason in a Case of so high a nature concerning the life of Man, the convenient certainty ought to be shewed. By Authority for that the Indictment must rehearse the effect of the Mittimus. Thirdly & Lastly See the resolutions of all the Judges of England in their 21 & 22 Answers to the objections of Archbishop Bancroft in behalf of all the Clergy of England Tertio Jacobi.[15] They answer that upon complaint, they ought to send the King's Writ, for the Body & the Cause, & if in the return no Cause, or no sufficient Cause appear, that then they ought to set him at liberty &c. This to the 21. To the 22 They answer & resolve that upon Complaint made unto them if any one imprisoned without just Cause, we are to send to have the body, & to be certified of the Cause, & if they will not certifie us of the particular cause but generally without expressing any particular Cause, whereby it may appear to us, his Imprisonment to be just then we do & ought to deliver him. Hereupon it appeareth that the common Warrant or Mittimus to answer such things as shall be objected against him, is utterly void & against Law. Now as the Mittimus must contain a certain Cause, so the Conclusion must be according to Law (viz) The Prisoner safely to keep untill he be delivered by due order of Law, & not untill he that made it, give order or the like.

Sr. This is what at present occurs, & what is to be taken notice of, & what I dare & do avow to be good Authority, if you have farther occasion, please to signifie, & shall be ready to serve you therein. I question not your care about our Tobo. in your County & Gloucester, to urge your Diligence would seem to make doubt therefore as I said before proceed for us as for your self. My service to your good wife Esqr. Wormley, & all friends there

To. Majr. Robt. Beverley   Your   W. ff.

[LB, pp. 41-45]

1. For the situation in which Robert Beverley now found himself, including imprisonment, see ltr. to him, May 29, 1682, note 1. The reader should recall in reading this letter that here is one lawyer writing to another about the latter's own particular case, really the legal scholar writing to the practical lawyer, as we learn elsewhere.

A record of Beverley's "offenses" had been sent to His Majesty in England, and a reply was daily expected. This is probably why WF warns Beverley that his trial will be sudden—

* Blank space in line.

when the verdict comes in. What WF is talking about here is the refusal of the writ of habeas corpus he had asked for earlier, for no specified charges or evidence had been brought forward against Beverley. For the charges later made, see ltr. to Beverley, May 29, 1682, note 1. It is possible from this letter for the reader to see WF as the legal research scholar going through the *Statutes* and *Reports* and finding apt precedents and parallels.

Beverley appeared before the General Court on April 17, 1683, only to have the trial deferred first to the twenty-third and then to the twenty-fifth. On April 25, at the trial, the Governor, Lord Culpeper, "in friendly wise" advised Beverley to accept the terms offered for an easier bond. Hening, who gives this account (*Statutes*, III, 557-61), follows it with the speech Beverley intended to give in his own behalf but was prevented. Beverley spoke of his abode in this country for upward of twenty years, and claimed that "God knows my innocence." Hening's account concludes with many pages of testimonials, from Sir William Berkeley to more humble folk, to Beverley's loyalty. The case apparently was continued and Beverley was not brought up for judgment until May 9, 1684, at which time he was required to give good security for his future good behavior, having already made "humble and abject submission" (on his knees). The case of Beverley v. Home Government did not end here, however, for as late as August, 1686, a few months before his death, the King ordered that Beverley be punished with the utmost severity for having defaced (i.e., altered) the records of Assembly, and that he be held incapable of public employment. The order came too late to affect him. *Cal. St. Papers, Col., Am. & W.I., 1681-1685*, Item 1672; *idem, 1685-1688*, Items 563, 655, 1169, 1214.

2. As noted above ("Instructions" to John Withers, June 5, 1682, note 7), Christopher Robinson (1645-1693), Beverley's Middlesex neighbor, had been Beverley's bondsman. He married Beverley's widow. Later Robinson was burgess, councilor, and Secretary of State.

3. *Institutes*, II, pp. 45-47.

4. The reference is to the margin of *Institutes*, II (Cap. XXVI), p. 42 (1642 ed.), which notes "Mirror. Cap. 5 s 2." *Mirror* is *Mirroir des Justices vel Speculum Justiciarum*, a "worthless" thirteenth-century authority Coke has been criticized for using. Though some legal authorities deny that he ever owned or knew such a book, it is shown in *A Catalogue of the Library of Sir Edward Coke* (Samuel E. Thorne, ed. [New Haven, 1950], Item 304) as a manuscript volume.

5. "Sta: Glo: Cap 9" is in *Statutes* (Edw. I, 6th year), I, 24. "H: 8. 4. 18" possibly refers to Hen 8: 4-8 (last chapter is 8), concerning Richard Strode, held in a terrible dungeon. Apparently the eighteenth-century transcriber of WF's letters, or WF himself, miscopied some numbers. This holds also for "20 Edw: 4.6," for there is no twentieth year for Edward IV in the *Statutes*. "Brooke title forfeiture" probably refers to Sir Robert Brooke, *La Graunde Abridgement*, I, folios 341-44, "Forfeiture de terres & biens & offices." On 344v is a reference to "20. E. 4. 6," perhaps indicating WF's source for the above reference. Brooke, II, folios 256-58, concerns "Titles." "Cooke upon Magna Charta fo: 43" refers to *Institutes*, II, p. 43.

6. These are references to *Statutes*, p. 190 and Coke, *Le Neufme Part des Reports*, folio 119v.

7. *Statutes*, p. 24 [6 Edw. I, ch. 9].

8. *Statutes*, p. 2 [9 Henry III, ch. 29].

9. These references are, in order, to *Statutes*, p. 73; p. 94; p. 121 (though reference is possibly incorrect); p. 123 (this refers to complaints made to King—if one cannot prove them he goes to prison himself); p. 125 (false accusers to be punished); p. 166 (Chancellor may award damages); *Reports*, Pt. 10, fo. 711 & v.

10. Probably this exact reference is given in *Institutes*. Cf. note 13 below.

11. *Institutes*, II, p. 53.

12. *Ibid*.

13. This exact reference is in *Institutes*, II, p. 55.

14. *Institutes*, II, pp. 55-56.

15. Unlocated.

To Lord Culpeper [1]

May it please your Excellency   Janry. 8. 1682/3

Sr. That great Countenence you were pleas'd to favour me with at my last being in Town more especially at Green Spring, gives occasion to this, to assure your Lordship, that in my private Capacity, as I now stand in this Country (having had the happiness never to be dignified by an empty title) & quietness from all profitable employments therein. I have & shall strenuously endeavour to assure the people of our Parts of your Lordship's great & weighty Services done for them in England, particularly about your elaborate pains in answering such weighty objections from such powerfull Opposers, in that most necessary Concern of Towns,[2] which you were pleased to communicate to me, as also your just resolution for a regular Proceeding by the known Laws of England, which though set off with such poor abilitys as I am Master of, has given our people here so great & generall satisfaction, that they not only rejoice that your Lordship is happily arrived to the place of your Government, but always add their prayers for your Continuance therein, still with this respect—that the advantages as well as their dutys might fully answer your expectation. I must beg your Honour's Pardon if I have not given a full relation in your own more immediate concern of, the Quitrents, not want of will but a dullness in my apprehension,[3] not thoroughly understanding your Lordship is the Occasion thereof, esteeming it better be silent, than to give imperfect or but half relations. If your Lordship thinks I may be serviceable to you therein, please to give me but the least intimation, & the utmost of my endeavours shall not be wanting. This Gentleman the bearer hereof comes purposely to solicite your Excellency for the high Sherriff's place of our County,[4] I dare not presume to move in his behalf, yet I can give your Lordship this assurance that last year he had the promise of it & that no one can pretend a better Right, if a Right might be admitted, for his Predecessor died in the Place & Office, in the late unhappy troubles, his enjoyment of it gave him no profit, but abundance of trouble, & the unhappy inconveniency of contracting debts throughout the County out of his own Estate, which his poor Orphans now want. And his motion for the place is as much in behalf of the poor Children, (He being their Guardian) as for himself, by which means he would have the Conveniency of getting without charge or trouble those scattering debts to their advantage

Long may your Lordship quietly & happily govern us, under his most sacred Majestie is the prayers of

To. His Excellency Thomas Lord   Your Lordship's &c.
Culpepper ⅌ Doctr. William Bankes

[*LB*, pp. 45-46]

1. Thomas, Lord Culpeper (1635-1689), had been commissioned Governor of Virginia in 1675 and had spent four months in the colony in 1680. On the King's order he returned to Virginia a second time, arriving on Dec. 17, 1682, and remaining about five months. During Culpeper's first stay his attitude had been conciliatory and he became very popular with the colonists, but on his return his attitude had changed. He was apparently very severe, for example, with the plant-cutters, hanging several of the ringleaders among them, though some historians have claimed that he had no choice. He has also been said to have been largely responsible for the punishment of Major Beverley. *D.A.B.; Bruce, Inst. Hist. Va.,* II, 320.

WF here is being very tactful and diplomatic, perhaps for a combination of reasons. Culpeper was now sole owner of the Northern Neck Proprietary.

2. For the idea of and interest in "Towns," see ltr. to Captain Francis Partis, July 1, 1680, note 2. Culpeper seems always to have worked for the "Town idea," its opponents being the powerful English merchants who traded in Virginia.

3. The quitrent, a land tax, was one of the two kinds of taxes levied directly for any length of time in the seventeenth century. The quitrents had been granted at various times to various persons, and in 1673 to Culpeper and Arlington. There was an outcry in Virginia after this last grant. About 1678, Deputy Governor Chicheley submitted, through the Privy Council, a petition to the throne for the release of all quitrents unpaid, on the ground that they amounted now to so great a figure that, if a serious effort were made to collect them, it would fall with intolerable heaviness on every citizen, but especially on the poorer classes. That a large sum due on this account was still outstanding when Culpeper arrived in the colony was shown by his command that the quitrents should be collected during that year with the utmost strictness in order to throw a full light on the extent of the delinquency during previous years. But the results were disappointing because the value of tobacco had sunk to a low point and the charges for collecting the rents were very considerable. That such a large proportion of quitrents due were always in arrears seems to have been chiefly a result of the fact that great sections of land taken up under patent remained uncultivated. Culpeper's comments to the King as to what might be done in general are thoughtful and unbiased.

Culpeper's Forty-Seventh "Instruction" from the King had expressed the intention of "taking in" the patents that had permitted favored subjects to issue land grants or to receive the revenue from quitrents. Consequently, Culpeper had been told to see that "quit-rents which shall hereafter become due to us (the respective patentees being first fully satisfied) also the escheats, fines and forfeitures be applied to public use." Culpeper's sharp comment was that the patentees had never even been treated with, much less satisfied, and that there was no occasion to do anything with either of these instructions. He said that he had had the sheriffs in his Proprietary collect what they could; he also noted elsewhere that the escheats did not belong to the King but to the patentees. He thus asserted his rights in regard to the Proprietary and to a grant the King had made to him in southern Virginia. In the end, in 1684, Culpeper sold all his rights in Virginia to the Crown except those to the Northern Neck.

It is not entirely clear as to whether WF refers to Culpeper's quitrents for the Proprietary, in which case WF as a resident thereof might be very useful to him, or to the rents for the colony as a whole, most of which seemed legally due him. In the latter case, the more likely one, WF's advice would probably have been sought as a shrewd lawyer who could comment on legal aspects of the problem. WF says himself he is not sure what Culpeper wants him to do, if anything. For discussions of Culpeper and this quitrent situation, see Freeman, *George Washington,* I, 479; Bruce, *Inst. Hist. Va.,* II, 576; *Cal. St. Papers, Col., Am. & W.I. 1681-1685, passim.*

4. For Dr. Bankes, see ltr. to H. Hartwell, June 19, 1681, note 9.

To the Honourable Ralph Wormeley [1]

Honrd. Sir   January 8th. 1682/3

    This Gentleman my neighbour Doctr Bancks [2] is come purposely about the Sherriffs place, I assured him he need neither doubt nor question your assistance, & therefore I advised him to apply himself to you   If you have any time to spare with him you will find him an ingenuous Gentleman, & a boon facetious Companion, & one that will gratefully acknowledge your favours. Sr. I hope to hear from you by the bearer, in which I am sure to meet with a full satisfaction of all transactions there. My most humble service to your honoured Father, & a kind Remembrance of all friends else there, is all I can think of at present farther than to assure I am

To. The Honble. Ralph Wormley   Your   W. ff.
Esqr.

[*LB*, p. 46]

    1. For Wormeley, see ltr. to N. Spencer, Nov. 2, 1680, note 3. As a councilor, Wormeley could be most useful in getting the place for Bankes.
    2. For Bankes, see the ltr. just above and the ltr. to H. Hartwell, June 19, 1681, note 9; also I V 115n-16n.

To Roger Jones [1]

Mr. Roger Jones   January 8. 1682/3

    This day I had report of Blagg's [2] arrival   this Gentleman the bearer being bound directly down to your parts, & Blagg's house being not far out of his way, he assured me, he would purposely call in & give you a true & certain relation thereof. This Gentleman [3] is come to my Lord to move for the Sherriffs place of our County, I desire you in his behalf to give him what assistance you can in it, a small converse with him I am sure

will endear him to you, for you will find him as well supplyed with gratitude to acknowledge & when it lies in his power power [*sic*] to kindnesses,
as facetious & Jocose in boon jovial Company. Sr. Assure your self the
readyest ways & easiest shall be sought to do you service that thereby you
may be assured   I am

To. Mr. Roger Jones at   Your   W. ff.
Green Spring 🜄 Doctr. Wm. Bankes

[*LB*, p. 47]

1. Captain Roger Jones (*c.* 1625/35-1701) came to Virginia in 1680 with Lord Culpeper
and remained until about 1692. Commander of a guard sloop of sixty tons, he was once
suspected of collusion with pirates. He amassed a considerable fortune either in Virginia or
in London, in which he was a merchant. He is said later, in 1693, to have recommended WF
and George Brent to be agents for the Proprietors of the Northern Neck. WF corresponded
with him and about him through 1698. After 1692 Jones seems to have been an agent in
various concerns, colonial and otherwise, and to have retained the confidence of the Proprietors who succeeded Culpeper. Freeman, *George Washington*, I, 487; *Exec. Journ. Council
Col. Va.*, I, *passim*; Bruce, *Inst. Hist. Va.*, II, 179-81; Arthur Pierce Middleton, *Tobacco Coast*,
ed. George C. Mason (Newport News, Va., 1953), pp. 314, 423; 1 V 276n; *Westmoreland County
Deeds & Wills, Book 5*, p. 63.
2. A Colonel Thomas Blagg lived in the Potomac River neighborhood, perhaps in WF's
Chotank region, though here WF seems to suggest someone living near Jamestown and
Green Spring. By 1653 a Captain Thomas Blagg was one of the commissioners of the militia
in Westmoreland. An Abraham Blagg of Appomattox Creek in Westmoreland, "merchant,"
appears several times between 1678 and 1683/84 in Westmoreland records. His will was
recorded March 31, 1697. He was probably the son of Thomas. "Blaggs Place" may be at
present Rollins Post Office in King George County. Eaton, *Hist. Atlas Westmoreland*, p. 16;
Bruce, *Inst. Hist. Va.*, II, 21; *Westmoreland County Court Order Book, 1675/6-1688/9*, pp. 289,
317, etc.; *Westmoreland County Deeds & Wills, Book 2, 1691-1699*.
3. For Bankes, see the two ltrs. just above. WF is clearly leaving no stone unturned to
get Dr. Bankes appointed. Jones appears to be living at Green Spring as part of the
Governor's retinue.

To John Cooper [1]

Mr. John Cooper   March 10th. 1682/3

Sr.   This comes by Capt. Smith,[2] where you'll find 19. hhds. of Tobo.
Consigned to your self, as 🜄 bills of Loading will appear. I can assure you
it is as good a parcell of Tobo. as ever I saw of the sort, most of it of my
own Crop, which I my self took care to see well handled & sorted, the remainder which is 7 hhds., I saw them well pack'd, & therefore am sure it

is good, if this doth not suite the Market, & get a price, its in vain for me to think of shipping any more Tobo. Just as I am writing I have news of Capt. Norrington's [3] Arrival, by whom I expect to hear farther from you, all that I have yet this year receiv'd was one letter ₱ Capt. Harris.[4] Business & the small encouragement Tobo. gave. was the occasion I writ no oftner & larger to you last year, but this year being sure the first is something abated, & in hopes the latter is amended, I shall be more ample & frequent in my letters & advices   The first thing that I have of Necessity to advise you, is that I have charged bills upon you payable to Mr. Jno. Bourdon [5] for the use of Capt. Elisha Mellowes [6] of Barbadoes, for £35.02 .. 10. at eighty days sight which I hope you have effects of mine to comply with before the time of payments. I took so large a time that I might have a full opportunity of advising you thereof, & of remitting the effects. Sr.   I have a proposal of Trade if your self or any of your friends there approve it, the manner this, To send a small Vessel hither, of about 200. or 250 hhds. burden at most; which I will undertake to give her Notes for Loading, within a month at farthest after her Arrival, & that within twenty miles compass, which is but a small Distance here, upon this Condition, to have well bought goods, & bought with ready money, delivered at my Landing at 10 sh: ₱ Cent without any advance or if you think that not convenient, because of the uncertainty of the Market, then give me an allowance of 2 lb. Tobo. in the hundred weight of Tobo. more than the general Market goes at in our parts, upon the Arrival of the said Vessel, for my Commission, Expedition, Storage, & Insurance of the whole, & all other incident Charges that Traders here necessarily lie at, Provided the Ship comes not before some time in Decr. & I have Notice thereof, by the forward Ships in Septr. Octr. or Novr. though I desire none of the goods till her Arrival. By this trade here will be a great charge saved, in the long stay ships generally make here, being oftentimes forced to run from one end of the Country, to the other almost, which eats out the profit of a good Market, besides Sloop hire, the allowance to your factor & Merchants, the uncertainty of purchasing Tobo. & if purchased, many times lying out & behind & some bad debts never to be recovered, on the other side as soon as your Ship Arrives she may be taking in Tobo., her whole Loading certain, the Distance the Tobo. lies at small so that two or three flatts will presently load her, & by that means save Sloop hire.[7] About one third or near one half of the loading, will be in one place together, which she may well take in in four days. As soon as I see Capt. Norrington (which I now every day expect) I shall discourse him farther therein, & if he thinks the proposal will be approved, I shall then be more large by the next Conveniency, & withal manifest to him something of my Method to proceed therein, & shall desire him to give you an account, whether I am fully fitted & capable for such an undertaking   I am

To Mr. John Cooper   Sr. Your   W. ff.

[LB, pp. 47-49]

1. For Cooper, see ltr. to him, April 4, 1681, note 1.
2. This is probably Captain Thomas Smith, commander of the *Constant* of London, who wrote a letter to the Virginia Council (received May 19, 1684) asking whether his ship riding at anchor in Nomini Bay, in Potomac River, was under obligation to pay Maryland as well as Virginia duties and fees. Smith had just gone with a sloop to Maryland to get tobacco for his "loading." The letter from Smith was presented by Secretary of State Nicholas Spencer of Nomini, probably a friend of Smith, for the ship was near his plantation, "within the Governmt of Virginia." *Exec. Journ. Council Col. Va.*, I, 56.
3. For Captain William Norrington, see ltr. to J. Cooper, April 4, 1681, note 2.
4. In a ltr. of March 19, 1682/3 WF speaks of Captain Harris in the *Gerard*. In a ltr. to Cooper, April 18, 1687, WF refers to Captain Martin Harris. In 1692 a Captain John Harris was commander of the *James and Benjamin* of London. P.R.O., C.O. 5/1306V, L.C. copy.
5. Unidentified.
6. Unidentified.
7. Here WF is concerned with one of his favorite projects—to become agent for the cargo of a whole ship or of whole ships from London merchants. The ship captain usually had to hire a sloop to go up into the smaller creeks and coves to collect hogsheads of tobacco from the individual planters' wharves. The procedure was tedious and expensive.

To John Cooper[1]

Just as I was concluding my lettr. I recd. my lettr. on board Capt. Norrington,[2] one bearing date 25, & 28th. Octr. & the other 19. Decr. wherein I have so low account of my Tobo. that it is not worth shipping. I also find by them you have sent me none of my goods, & indeed had no effects of mine to procure them. Now I positively desire you to desist from sending me any but once again desire you to comply with these bills of £35 . . 2 . . 10. I have also shipped some Tobo. out of York from myself & Mr. Brent, from whom I suppose you will hear by the next Ship Capt. Harris in the Gerard,[3] & also from self too, we neither of us yet knew what to write in that affair, because we have not as yet any account what quantity of Tobo. is shiped nor on what Ship, nor what freight which we now every day expect, & then shall take the first conveniency thereof to give you an acct. The hopes of a better Market this year, makes me large now, & will encourage to write by all opportunitys. I desire you to take care of the inclosed to Madam Bland,[4] I have sent it open that you may see her mistake, & withall have writ to her, to pay you the whole or part of the money, as perusal of her letter you'll see, what you can get receive upon my Accot. Once again I desire your carefull Disposal of my Tobo.

To. Mr. Jno. Cooper in London   Your   W. ff.
Mercht. Capt. Thomas Smith
March 19th. 1682/3

[*LB*, pp. 49-50]

1. For Cooper, see ltr. just above and ltr. to him, April 4, 1681, note 1.
2. For Norrington, see ltr. to Cooper, April 4, 1681, note 2.
3. For Harris, see ltr. to Cooper, March 10, 1682/83, note 4, just above.
4. For Sarah Bland, see ltr. to her, June 5, 1682, note 1. Though WF was not her American personal agent, he acted for her as attorney and advisor in several matters. See letters below.

To Madam Sarah Bland[1]

Madam Sarah Bland   March 19th. 1682/3

By what miscarriage I know not you have not receiv'd that letter I last year sent you, wherein I gave you an account of yor. business, with reference to Mr. Blayton's[2] more particular relation, the sum of it was that I used my utmost endeavour in the management of all your businesses at the Generall Court, but after long Argument they concluded to enter Judgment as formerly, which you know was against you, from which Judgment I offered to Appeal, & it was allowed me, but then Security must be had, which I could not obtain, for Mr. Blayton utterly refused, & then I knew not who to apply myself to, to get security for want of which I could not have an appeal in my business. I know not how you left your business with Mr. Blayton, but this I was throughly sensible, that no Appeal here will be granted without Security, & how you became so remiss in your own business, as not to take care therein, know not, or whether you have been disappointed by Blayton. When I found I could get no Security, whereby to obtain the Appeal, I was forced to suffer what that I could not avoid, Judgment to pass against you in all but Collo. Codd's business,[3] which for gaining time I got to be Conditional, under pretence of making an amicable composure, but got my self to be one concerned in the composing thereof, together with Mr. Blayton & Mr. Minge [4] who I thought would be stiff to your Interest, that thereby I might have spun out time, till I could have heard farther from you, & receiv'd the King's Order: that I certainly expected well knowing that I could break all to pieces, and bring it again to the Generall Court, which course I reckoned would gain a year's time, whereby you might have your full opportunity to make your best advantage thereof in England. But Mr. Blayton unknown to me, or without the least Intimation or signification thereof, did afterward make up & compose the business with Codd, &, in your behalf, & as your Attorney gave him full, absolute, & generall discharge from the whole business, at which I was both troubled & ashamed, & questioned him about it, he answer'd me he thought it was to your advantage, & he had power sufficient from you to Justifie what he did, & farther told me I was no farther concerned in your business, but just to appear in Court for you, & for what he had done he would fully answer to you, & give you a particular relation thereof together with the Copy of all the proceedings therein, & truly did shew me a long letter, which he designed to send to you, endeavouring therein to justifie & vindicate his proceedings, which did not seem reasonable to me, how it will do to you, I know not. Thus Madam I have given a generall account of your business, the particular relation (& indeed very pernicious to your self), I refer to Mr. Blayton. I am sorry your business hath no better Success, it was not for want of will or endeavour in me, & that I might be well strengthened I got Mr. Brent to stand by it upon my own Account, which I hope shall not suffer in, & I am to assure you deserves your thanks. Had not your Plenipotentiary Mr. Blayton foolishly comply'd & ended Codd's business, & had either by himself for his Procurement got Security to prosecute the Appeal, you might have had them in England by this time. I have neither seen the King's Order, nor heard nothing of it from Mr. Blayton though I was at Town at my Lord's Arrival, & eight days after, but the Copy of it that came in with your Order dated 24 August 1682, & doubt that rash & foolish Composure of Mr. Blayton has utterly destroyed the good effect of that Mandate for he has as your Attorney, fully releas'd him, & enter'd the said Release upon the Generall Court Records, as I told you before unknown to me. I may present your bill drawn upon Mr. Blayton, but I believe he'll not answer it, because when I urged him to be Security in the Appeals alledging for reasons that he had sufficient Effects of your's in his hands, his answer was that he had nothing, & therefore could not with safety be your Security &c. I therefore desire it if you cannot pay the whole presently down with conveniency. Pay part to Mr. Cooper, & at your own leisure pay the Remainder, or if money be scarce with you, please to procure me a Suit of Tapestry hangings for a Room twenty foot long sixteen foot wide, & nine foot high & half a dozen Chairs suitable, & take your time to pay the Remainder. Madam I thank your kind Recommends to Mr. Blaithwait [5] & please to assure him in any thing I am capable to serve him, if he please to give me least signification of any particulars that he desires satisfaction in, relating to this Country, I shall be ready & willing to serve him with my utmost Abilitys.

To Mrs. Sarah Bland at the   Madam Your   W. ff.
Office in Broad Street London
Sub Cover Mr. Jno. Cooper

[*LB*, pp. 50-52]

   1. For Sarah Bland, see ltr. to her, June 5, 1682, note 1.
   2. For Blayton, see ltr. to Madam Bland, June 5, 1682, note 2. With James Minge, he was Madam Bland's agent and attorney at Jamestown in her various petitions.
   3. The complicated series of appeals and petitions of Mrs. Bland in attempting to have "relief" from sentences imposed in the courts of Virginia take up considerable space in the archives of the Privy Council and the Committee on the Plantations. She seems usually to have won in British appeals only to lose again in some way in the Council and General Court in the colony.
   "Colonel Codd's business" probably refers to the attempt to get restoration of property and money allegedly owed by Mrs. Codd and her former husband Theodorick Bland to Mrs. Sarah Bland. Codd, a burgess and prominent figure generally, seems to have had the Virginia Assembly generally, not just the Council, on his side. But there were judgments against him, and sometime in 1682/83 he appears to have fled to Maryland to escape them. 10 V 366; 23 V 313; *Exec. Journ. Council Col. Va.*, I, 1, 57, 497, 501-3; *Cal. St. Papers, Col., Am. & W.I., 1685-1688*, Item 782; *Jamestown 350th Anniv. Survey Reports*, No. 255, p. 7 (from P.R.O., C.O. 5/1356).
   4. James Minge acted with Blayton as agent and attorney for Madam Bland.
   5. William Blathwayt (1649?-1717) was from 1679 Secretary of the Lords of Trade and the Plantations. Colonial officials were writing to him as early as 1678. By 1682 he was a power in colonial administration. L. J. Cappon, "The Blathwayt Papers of Colonial Williamsburg," 4 W(3) 317-31; *D.A.B.*; Gertrude A. Jacobsen, *William Blathwayt, a Late Seventeenth Century Administrator* (New Haven and London, 1931).

To John Cooper [1]

Mr. Jno. Cooper   May 22nd. 1683

   Sr.   I shall only in this take notice that I have formerly wrote you ℞ Capt. Smith & Capt. Harris [2] at large, & in them given you full Instructions to proceed in my business, nothing hath since occurred, only one bill I have drawn upon you payable I think to Mr. Richard Gostley [3] & company which I desire you to give due acceptance. In my next shall be more large, at present I have not opportunity & conveniency, only take this opportunity to tell you, that this day I have ordered six hhds. Tobo. to you by Capt. Norrington [4] at £5 .. 10 ₱ Tonn, clear of Impost & Country duties. also that Capt. Norrington had of me 6240 pipestaves towards his Barbadoe's freight when designed thither this day I receiv'd his lettr. that he hath got a freight for England (which now I am sure of though I heard it long since ₱ report, & cannot reasonably carry my pipestaves at halves thither, as it was agreed he should do to Barbadoes, & therefore desires me to take a reasonable price for them, upon his request I am willing to take at the rate of 50 shillings ₱ thousand, & a hamper of Canary, under which rate I have never sold, & therefore desire you ₱ this (if I should not have an opportunity) to take his bills of Exchange for the money, & a note for the Canary, to demand & receive the same of him, which I am confident upon the first demand he will readily pay, I desiring no more of him in this Streight, than if he had endeavoured to beat down the lowest of the Market, Also if I should not have opportunity to get bills Loading for my Tobo., I desire you ₱ this my letter to take up the same, & dispose to my best advantage. I only write this lest I may want opportunity to get bills Loading for my Tobo. which I hope I shall not. I forgot to give you account of one single letter I sent you by one Capt. Davis of Lime,[5] who promised to take care to deliver it into the Post office, by which have desired you to send me 3 dozen Gallon Stone juggs. & two dozen two Gallon Stone Juggs, which I hope you will take care in, as in all the rest of my things I have sent for, to take care your self that they be good of the sort. Sir I hope you will give me a particular answer by the very first Ship to that Proposal of Trade, that I sent to you about in my former, if you or your friends approve of it, & are minded to begin this year, give me but timely notice, & Suite out a Cargo for the Ship in coarse goods, such as are usefull for the Country, especially remembering Iron ware, & it shall be fully comply'd with on my part. I know not at present what farther to add. 6240 Pipestaves at 50 shillings ₱ thousand is £15 .. 12 .. 00 & a hamper of Canary. 6 hhds. marked WF No. 1 to 6. I desire timely & frequent advice the fore part of this year I have farther to advise you of bills of Exchange I have drawn upon you for £8 .. 13 .. 00 payable to Mr. Josiah Bacon of London Merchant [6] which I desire you to accept, & would rather have you let alone some of my things sent for than protest, but if this should happen to be presented before Capt. Norrington's Arrival, in whose hands there will be money, & in his Ship Tobo. I desire you to get

so much time if possible till his Arrival, upon which I am confident you
will both accept & pay.   I am

To. Mr. Jno. Cooper of London Mercht.   Your   W. ff.

[*LB*, pp. 53-54]

1. For Cooper, see ltr. to him, April 4, 1681, note 1.
2. For Captains Smith and Harris, see ltr. to Cooper, March 10, 1682/83, notes 2 and 4.
3. Richard Gostley or Gotley of Bristol, apparently a Quaker merchant, had investments
in Virginia as early as 1667. He had a brother Peter in the colony in 1675. Gostley was very
active in overseas trade. 3W (2) 102; 17 V 346; 3 V 424; McGrath, *Merchants*, p. xxx;
Journals H.B. 1659/60-1693, p. 50.
4. For Norrington, see ltr. to Cooper, April 4, 1681, note 2, and ltrs. immediately above
this one.
5. Presumably of Lyme Regis, Dorset, whose merchants regularly traded in Virginia. In
1699 the ship of Captain Davis was saluted as it went down the James. In 1700 a Captain
Nathaniel Davis and his ship the *Sarah and Susannah* of London was in Virginia. *Exec.
Journ. Council Col. Va.*, II, 153; P.R.O., C.O. 5/1306, 1310, L.C. copy.
6. A London merchant with whom William Byrd I as well as WF traded. 26 V 389;
27 V 168.

To the Honourable Colonel Richard Lee[1]

Honoured Sir   April 13th. 1683

I presume you may have opportunity at Town this Generall Court to
have the opinion of the Society of Surveyors concerning the difference of
Land betwixt you & Burbridge,[2] Mr. Scarlet[3] is gone purposely to Town
to enquire therein, for which reason I thought fit to give you this Notice,
that he might not be beforehand with you in his Enquiry. Sr. I have here
inclosed sent you the Remainder of Nat Garland's[4] papers, the rest he has
himself that is, the Dedimus, & Examinations there upon, which I intreat
the favour to deliver him or his Attorney there, they object against the
legality thereof, which your Honr. will be there ready to assert, then they
object they had no notice. I have Deposed that fourten days at least before
the Examinations taken, I gave him notice, for I think it about three
weeks before that I ordered Nat Garland to go to your Honr. for a
Dedimus, & drew him out his interrogatorys, & immediately thereupon
gave the Parson[5] notice thereof, then a week afterward when Nat Garland
was preparing his business, & sent me an account what Evidences he had
prepared, & what they could say, and as near the time & place for their

Henry Fitzhugh (1687-1758), second son of the emigrant William

Portrait from life by John Hesselius in 1751, owned by Mrs. Robert H. Stevenson of Boston.

The Proprietors' Grant to Fitzhugh's friend William Sherwood, showing the
names of the two Agents for the Northern Neck in the lower left corner.

In Ambler Papers, Library of Congress.

examination as he could guess, I gave the Parson notice again, which was a fortnight before the Execution of the Dedimus, then again immediately upon the receipt of the Dedimus, I gave him farther notice, which I think sufficient to take away that scruple. I desire you will inform Nat or his attorney of this, I am forced to give your Honr. this trouble, because I am not certain what Attorney to direct it to, nor certain of his being in Town, & am very unwilling he should miscarry in so just a Cause, by such an egregious Baffler

To. The Honble. Collo. Richd. Lee   Sr. Your W. ff.

[*LB,* pp. 54-55]

1. Richard Lee (1646-1715) had risen in rank from major to lieutenant colonel or colonel since WF had written to him on May 15, 1679.
2. For this society of surveyors, see Bruce, *Inst. Hist. Va.,* I, 536. Scarlet (see note 3 below) lived in Burbage's Neck in Stafford County, the neck between the Neapsco and the Occoquan. Thomas Burbage of Nansemond County owned three thousand acres in this territory, and his tract was used as a key to all descriptions of property in the region. Perhaps some relative of his is here referred to. On November 26, 1660, Richard Lee I had patented land (four thousand acres) on the Occoquan. It is mentioned again in the will of Richard Lee II. Harrison, *Landmarks,* I, 46, 49, 50, 147, 171.
3. For Scarlet, see ltr. to Captain Francis Partis, Dec. 4, 1680, note 3, and WF's petitions to the Stafford Court given below.
4. For Garland, see ltr. to Thomas Mathews, July 3, 1681, note 2.
5. This is apparently the Reverend John Waugh, the man with whom WF had much trouble later, trouble brought on perhaps in part by WF's having to proceed against him as a squatter. See ltrs. below, WF's petitions to Stafford County Court, and Introduction above.

To the Honourable Ralph Wormeley [1]

Honrd. Sir   May 23rd. 1683

Just now receiv'd your's from your Quarter, & should have been glad if Mr. Brent's occasions,[2] could have afforded him so much time, to have had the Station of your Case ready for you now, to have sent. Mr. Brent did at his coming up acquaint me therewith & left my Breviates with me, to prepare the chief heads of the Cause which I undertook & have them almost ready, & Mr. Brent promised to be forthwith down with me, so soon as he had rested himself & settled his domestick affairs, since I have not heard from him we every day expect him, so soon as he comes down, or if he stays much longer, I'll send purposely up to him, at which time we shall take carefully to conclude it, & then I'll take care to give it an immediate conveyance to Jo: Mason's.[3] I hope it may be but I cannot promise before Rider [4] sails. Now Sr. I have given you an assurance of my ready devotion to your service. I must be sensible and take notice of those dubious words in your letter (will not deny) as if you doubted my complyance to your commands, which assure your self nothing but an unavoidable necessity shall ever make me neglect or disobey any the least of them. And I am confident you are both so good & just not to condemn any man unheard, or which is worse, upon uncertain report, notwithstanding your short but sharp reproof in your letter, when I shall make it plainly appear to you that I had not only a willingness but an earnest propensity to have afforded you my mean Service at the Generall Court but an unavoidable necessity prevented,[5] which as soon as I shall have time fully to inform you, then you'll esteem me (as heretofore I please myself to think) you have done.

To. The Honble. Ralph Wormley Esqr.   Your W. ff.

[*LB*, pp. 55-56]

1. For Wormeley, see ltr. to N. Spencer, Nov. 2, 1680, note 3. WF refers to the case of Wormeley *vs.* Griffin and Burwell, first mentioned in ltr. to Wormeley of May 21, 1681 (see especially note 2) and continued in a number of letters. See ltr. to Wormeley of June 10, 1684, and accompanying "Traverse of an Escheat."

2. WF and his law partner seem to have been working jointly on this case. Since WF mentions preparation of materials "before Rider sails," they may have been preparing an appeal to the Lords of Trade and the Plantations.

3. In Westmoreland County, Mary Mason, relict of John Mason and administratrix of his estate, was granted the administration on July 25, 1683. *Westmoreland County Court Order Book, 1675/6-1688/9*, p. 292.

4. Captain Mathew Rider, commander of the ship *Barnaby*, was in York River in 1679 and 1682, and again in Virginia in May, 1684. 18 V 246, 369; 24 V 363; *Exec. Journ. Council Col. Va.* I, 487, 499.

5. Since the General Court records do not survive, we do not know exactly what happened in the case at its 1683 meeting.

To Lord Culpeper [1]

May it please your Lordship   June 25th. July 10

I made an Overture to Mr. Brent your Lordship's Agent for our Parts, that I would if you pleas'd purchase out the fee simple of the Rents, profits, Commoditys &c. of this Parish wherein I live, which goes by the name of the lower Parish of Stafford, & contains in it about 28000 Acres,[2] I believe there's not [   ] * Acres more or less, it will not be long uncertain for Mr. Brent is now making a strict inquiry into every ones tenure and quantity of Land, & by that time you can send in your resolve to what I shall now propose, he will have made a full and perfect Discovery, & it being fully settled, there can be no addition or Increment of Land added to it, the whole having been upwards of twenty four years ago taken up & Pattented. I will give your Lordship eight years Purchase for it, according to the true Value as it now stands at the Rent of 28000 Acres at 12lb Tobo. ℔ hundred, which is the Rent that is & always has been paid comes to 3360lb Tobo. ℔ annum, so that the purchase in Tobo. comes to 26880, which I will pay in ready good choice Tobo., or if your Lordship had rather deal for money, I will pay it at the rate of six shillings ℔ Cent, which is the highest Rate (to our sorrow be it spoken) Tobo. in our parts bears, which amounts to £80 .. 12 .. 6, & will pay your Lordship an annual acknowledgement of an ear of Indian Corn &c. If your Lordship likes the offer, but should think the quantity too small, I am very willing to double the quantity at the same rate, that is, to take a like quantity on the north side of Rappahannock, which will be exactly contiguous to our Parish. I presume your Lordship knows that the whole that I propose to purchase comes near any land newly taken up or to be taken up &c.[3]

To The Right Honble. Thomas   Your Lps" W. ff.
Lord Culpepper Baron &c.

[*LB*, pp. 56-57]

1. For Lord Culpeper, see ltr. to him, Jan. 8, 1682/83, note 1.

2. George Brent was of course WF's law partner. He was at this time really an attorney for the Proprietor's interests; the official agent was Nicholas Spencer. The parish WF offered to buy was at the end of the century called Chotank from the creek which drained it. See the list of parishes in *Cal. St. Papers, Col., Am. & W.I., 1677-1680*, p. 557, and 1 V 243. By 1702 it had assumed the name of St. Paul's, probably from WF's home parish in Bedford, England. Harrison, *Landmarks*, I, 302.

3. Probably WF means that his lordship knows to what extent the land he proposes to purchase comes near land already taken up. This is puzzling, however, for there were already other persons settled on tracts in the parish. What WF is apparently after is a patent which will make him a sort of sub-proprietor of this whole parish.

---

* Space as shown.

To Richard Page [1]

Mr. Richard Page   July 10th. 1683

    According to my promise I take this opportunity to assure you, that what lies in my power shall not be wanting to serve you, especially in those concerns committed to my care & conduct, I question not but you will also be mindfull of your promise to me, in the Chairs, Carpet & good Ale.

    All affairs here stand just as you left them, only Doctr. Hall is not altogether so mad,[2] & Mr. Ashton constrain'd to be more sober for want of drink [3] neither have I heard any fighting news lately from Collo. Mason,[4] which gives me occasion to believe his stock is pretty well exhausted. This is to comply with my word, the next if I can meet with another opportunity this year, to give you a more ample account. Therefore now I will only assure you, you shall always find me,

Yor. W. ff.

Pray give my service to Mr. Warren [5]
& his good wife.   To. Mr. Richd. Page
Mercht. in
Belfast sub Cover Mr. Jno. Cooper

[LB, pp. 57-58]

1. A Richard Page as early as 1625 was a ship captain trading in Virginia. In 1704 a Richard Page owned 150 acres in York County. On March 25, 1685, John Cooper entered suit in Westmoreland against Thomas Pope, administrator of Richard Page. Thus this man was probably a ship captain, son of the earlier Page, with relatives in Virginia. 24 V 241; 31 V 70; *Westmoreland County Court Order Book, 1675/6-1688/9*, p. 386.
2. Unidentified.
3. Probably Major James Ashton (d. 1686), J.P. of Stafford, whose estate "Chatterton" WF was later to handle as executor.
4. WF and Colonel George Mason served for years together on the Stafford Commission of the Peace, as WF testifies in one of his petitions to the Stafford Court given below. Since Mason was colonel of the Stafford militia, WF as lieutenant colonel from 1684 was to serve directly under him. Though George Mason II and WF were later political enemies, the tone here regarding the father is certainly friendly. Mason was probably a relative of the Bristol merchant of the same name with whom WF was to correspond.
5. A Mr. Thomas Warren as captain of a ship in Virginia in 1672 had acted as agent for various London merchants. Bruce, *Ec. Hist. Va.*, II, 344.

To Major Robert Beverley [1]

Majr. Robt. Beverley   feb⁴ʸ 8th 1683/4

This messenger gives me the opportunity of of [sic] sending you your papers again, for except Jonas Rivetts [2] I cannot get one pound of the Remainder, Mr. Brent saith he hath or will satisfie your self. Westmoreland & Stafford discharge themselves by Collo. Jones, [3] Pinett [4] is uncapable of payment, & God knows when he will be better able, so in vain for me to keep it in expectation. Collo. Lee [5] says for what's your due he will agree with your self & make complyance. I am in hopes to get Rivetts and therefore have not sent that bill, as soon as I get it shall punctually comply with your Order. Sr. I know you have a full intelligence e'er this, concerning my Lord Howard our every day expected Governor. [6] I desire a line or two from you therein. Give my humble service to your good Lady, [7] Esqr. Wormley & other friends there. Please to deliver my receipt to the bearer, & this shall oblige me to be accountable for Jonas Rivetts thousand pounds of Tobo., when receiv'd or return the Bill. Upon Return of this Letter my Receipt was sent.

To. Majr. Robt. Beverley in   Your   W. ff.
Middlesex ♏ Thos. Maule [8]

[*LB*, p. 58]

1. For Beverley, see ltr. to him, Sept. 6, 1679, note 1. The "papers" probably were concerned with the tobacco levy made throughout the colony to support the garrisons of the forts along the frontier. Reference here is probably to supplies to be bought with the tobacco for the Rappahannock fort for which Beverley was "undertaker." WF himself and Brent were "undertakers" for the Potomac garrison, but as militia officer in Stafford WF probably had to collect for both, though, as he says the tobacco in Westmoreland and Stafford is to be paid to Colonel Cadwallader Jones (see note 3 below). Bruce, *Inst. Hist. Va.*, II, 90, 106, 110, etc.; *Journals H.B. 1659/60-1693*, pp. 171-83.

There had been a proposal to abandon the Potomac garrison in 1681, but WF and Brent, looking on this as a public calamity, offered themselves as substitutes for former "undertakers" now refusing to serve. It was estimated in 1680-1681 that support for garrisons at the heads of the great rivers would require that forty-seven pounds of tobacco be levied from every tithable in Virginia. In 1682 the accounts show that Beverley disbursed a total of 189,000 pounds of tobacco for the Rappahannock garrison alone. Bruce, *Inst. Hist. Va.*, II, 112.

2. Unidentified.
3. Col. Cadwallader Jones had already quarreled with Beverley in 1679 over the supplies

for Indian frontier garrisons. Jones as commander of the Rappahannock garrison may have received supplies directly, or at least the tobacco directly. Bruce, *Inst. Hist. Va.,* II, 106.

4. Unidentified.

5. Colonel Richard Lee II as militia officer and large landowner was responsible for some of these supplies of tobacco.

6. Francis, Lord Howard of Effingham, took the oath at a meeting of the Virginia Council on Feb. 21, 1683/84. He had arrived at Col. Pate's in Gloucester on Feb. 10, by his own testimony. See ltr. to his wife, Feb. 11, 1683/84, in Lord Monson Papers, L.C.

7. Catherine Beverley was the daughter of Theophilus Hone of James City County, and later the second wife of Christopher Robinson (q.v.).

8. There was a surveyor of this name active as late as 1710. But there was also a Thomas Maul, a New England merchant, who traded in Virginia between 1670 and 1685. 4 V 37, 39, 40; Bruce, *Ec. Hist. Va.,* II, 320.

To the Honourable Nicholas Spencer [1]

Honrd. Sir   Jane [sic] 11th. 1683/4

This Conveniency by Mr. Simpson,[2] gives me the opportunity not only of saluting your Honr., but returning you my humble thanks for your favour, in that worshipfull employment, which because it comes from your Honr. I shall readily, (& could wish that my ability &r. would admit me to say) & willingly accept, assuring myself you designed it a publick advantage (suitable to the rest of your endeavours for a generall good) & no particular prejudice to any Individual: & therefore do not question but your Honr. will be assistant to support me, in the charge you were pleas'd to confer upon me,[3] that Contempt (the worst of enemies to any in Authority & the certain & inseparable associate of poverty) (may not discourage me. And I shall endeavour to make use of the utmost, and as far as I can those poor Abilitys (it hath pleased God to bestow upon me) for the good & service of my Country.

To. the Honble. Nicholas Spencer   Yr.   W. ff.
Esqr. President of Virginiæ

[LB, p. 59]

1. For Spencer, see ltr. to him, Sept. 9, 1679, note 1. Spencer was at this time acting as President of the Council and administrator of Virginia until Effingham should arrive, as he did on Feb. 10.

2. Probably John Simpson, of Acquia in Stafford. On March 10, 1689/90, WF complained in Stafford Court that Simpson died owing him 679 pounds of tobacco; he brought suit

against John Withers as executor. 6 V 311; 8 V 211-12; 12 V 197; *Stafford County Court Records, 1689-1693*, pp. 13, 19.

3. Probably WF was acknowledging his appointment as lieutenant colonel of Stafford militia, for a few months afterwards his name first appears with this military prefix.

To the Honourable Ralph Wormeley [1]

Honrd. Sir June 10th. 1684

Herewith comes accompany'd all your Papers, a letter with State of your Case [2] drawn by Mr. Brent, the Contents I have not seen, till I had view of your papers I could not finish mine, I have also sent you the State of your Case done ℔ myself, as well as I could draw it, I have not had the happiness of seeing or discoursing Mr. Brent since his coming from Town but just half an hour, as he came up, his business constantly calling him abroad, so that I may not perhaps be so full, but I am sure what I want is fully supplyed by his better abilitys & better Judgment, I believe our drawing it separately may be for your advantage.

Sr. Be sure if possible to get Copys of those things I advised, as the Commissione &c. to send with the rest of your papers. Sr. My last for a sudden dispatch away (being hastened by Collo. Jones [3] as you may see ℔ his writing to help forward) will not suffer me to all any more, save to wish this successfull to you, & to assure you notwithstanding the false Calumnies & storys, that have been made to you of me, I shall always endeavour to manifest myself

To Ralph Wormley Esqr. Sr. Your W. ff.

[*LB*, pp. 59-60]

1. For Wormeley, see ltr. to N. Spencer, Nov. 2, 1680, note 3, and various ltrs. to Wormeley himself, especially that of May 21, 1681, note 1. "The Traverse of an Escheat," dated a year earlier, was clearly an enclosure with the present letter. The copyist or WF himself may have made an error in dating, for it seems probable that the "Traverse" was written only a short time before the letter.

2. Only WF's "Traverse" is here included. For citations of some of the many documents in the case, see ltr. to Wormeley, May 21, 1681, note 1. Among the documents surviving are Griffin and Burwell's "Traverse," and various answers and replications, including depositions of witnesses.

3. Cadwallader Jones is discussed in some detail in ltrs. to Wormeley, August 2, 1682, note 2, and to Beverley, Feb. 8, 1683/84, note 3.

For the Honourable Ralph Wormeley, Traverse of an Escheat [1]

Traverse of an Escheat inter Lewis Burrell & Lewis Griffin as Legatees to Collo. Jno. Burnham [2] Deceas'd, & Ralph Wormley Esqr. as Tennantts, & Purchaser of his Majestie, of a certain parcel of land lying in Middlesex County, after an Office found for the same, & by a lawfull Purchase of the King of the said land in fee by the said Wormley, now in his Possession. The said Burrell & Griffin set forth that the said land ought not to Escheat to his Majestie for that the Burnham made a Will, & by the said Will Demised it to them therefore &c. but it was answered on the part, that the said Will that they claim by, was not good de jure to pass Lands & Tenements, by reason there was not such & so many Witnesses to it, as the Law requires, & for that pleaded the Statute made in the 29th. year of his Majestie's Reign,[3] Intituled an Act to prevent fraud & Perjury &c., & farther that by the Ecclesiastical Law which reformed the Civil Law from seven to three Witnesses, whereof the Parochial Minister to be one, except in Demises ad pias Causas &c., where two was sufficient, it was not a good Will, but by the Generall Custom of the Realm, which is the Common Law, whereby two are sufficient provided they be free from all just Cause of Exception: But these two witnesses that were to his Will, were not clear from all just Cause of Exception, as appears by Mr. Kennion [4] and others. therefore &c. Secondly Admitting that those two Evidences by the common Law, according to the Generall Custom of the Realm, were sufficient notwithstanding the exceptions, taken to them & proved against them, yet by a late Statute made in the 29th. year of his Majestie's Reign, Instituted An Act to prevent fraud & perjury &c. It is there provided & Enacted, that for every bequest of land & tenements &c. for the future, no Will shall be good & effectual in Law, except there be three or more Witnesses attesting & subscribing in the presence of the Demiser &c. which is Introductive of a new Law & without doubt, the Parliament before they set down so precise a Law, had sufficient tryal of great Craft & Cunning practised in the making & proving of Testaments, & were inducted to it, upon the same Rule as Justinian was to approve of his solemn Testaments, (propter Testamentorum sinceritatem ut nulla fraus adhibeatur), Now for that the said Will had not such Witnesses so qualified as the Law requires (viz) free from Exception &c. or so many as the said Statute did require & appoint &

without which it doth invalid the Will, as to the passing of land & Tenements, & because it hath not a legall probate, therefore moved to be dismiss'd. To the first part they moved for a Jury to try it, which was admitted, who brought in a Verdict, that it was a lawfull Will. Now it was the business of a Jury, & by what Rule in Law a Jury try'd that will, I am wholly ignorant of, For the Probate of Testaments according to the Law of England, there are two sorts, the one the vulgar or common sort, the other according to the form of Law   Swin 6. 6 ℗ art S. 14 [5] The first is Presentation of the Will to the Judge, without citing any body, & producing witnesses to prove the same, who testifying upon their oaths viva voce, that the Testament exhibited, is the true whole & last Testament of the Party deceased, the Judge doth confirm the same. In the other, the Widow or next of kind ought to be cited, & in their presence ought the Presentation & probation of the same to be that they may have knowledge thereof, & conveniency of cross Examination, & then upon sufficient proof the Judge by his sentence or Decree doth pronounce for the validity of the Testament. neither of these, not so much as the vulgar form was observed, in the probate of this Will & therefore it ought not to be admitted as a good Will, for the passing of goods & Chattels, much more the passing of lands & Tenements, & how a Jury could proceed thereupon or give Verdict therein, to make that good & legal, who have nothing to do but with matter of fact, for ad questionem juris non respondent juratores, & how their Verdict should make that a good & lawfull Will, which was illegal ab initio & never hath receiv'd lawfull probate. As to the second, which is upon the Statute, they pleaded, that the Laws & Statutes of England were not binding to us here, except such Statutes where we are particularly named, & parallelled in with Ireland, saying that Ireland was not bound by any Statutes made in England Except particularly named &c. That the laws & Statutes of England are binding here we shall make appear, by these reasons. First there's no body will deny but we are governed by some Laws, or else we must be lawless, that we are not lawless, appears by all our Courts of Judicature, & Judicial proceedings, therefore we have Laws to proceed by. Secondly We have no Original Laws amongst us derived from the Natives here, for we found them at our first coming, (& they yet continue little better) so barbarous & rude that they had no other direction & Government amongst them but the Law of Nature, & what civility they since have, arrives to them from their Commerce with us. Secondly That we are not ruled by Laws made amongst us, is manifest, by reason what Laws we have made amongst us here since our first Settlement, are merely made for our particular Constitution, where the Laws of England were thought inconvenient in that particular, & rather disadvantageous & burdensome than any way for our advantage or benefit. For Example The Laws of England require a Jury of the Vicinage for the tryal of all offences especially of Capital offences, but because our constitution will not admit thereof, expressly by reason we have but one Court settled in one place for all such tryals & the fewness of our Inhabitants, & the great distance some live therefrom, would be very burdensome to us, to be summoned thither, we have made some alteration therein, that not only six of the Vicinage, & six more of the Inhabitants or people about the Generall Court to be joined with them, shall be held a good & lawfull Jury for such a tryal, & the rest of the Laws made amongst us are such like. Thirdly & lastly, Seing we have no Original Laws amongst us derived from the Natives, nor new Laws made amongst us, to direct guide & govern our judicial proceedings, & have Courts of Judicature we must consequently be governed by the Laws of England which is thus manifested. First from his Majesty's Instructions from time to time sent to us. Secondly from the severall Commissions granted to the Governors. Thirdly from all the Commissions of Oyer & terminer directed to the Governor and Council here. Fourthly from all the Commissions, of the respective Justices of the Peace, for the Countys made pursuant to the Commissions and Instructions, from time to time, granted to the several Governors, & particularly those to my Lord Culpepper. 5thly from all the Pattents granted since our first Settlements! Sixthly from our own Acts of Assembly, which we have priviledge & authority to make. Seventhly from the continual practice & usage of the Country, since its first Scituation. Eigthly & lastly from the inconvenience that would follow thereupon, if it should not be so. To the first his Majestie's Instructions from time to time, directed amongst other things, that all proceedings here shall be according to the Laws of England, as may be seen by the Instructions themselves. To the 2d, 3d, & 4 The several Commissions make manifest, In some of which it is expressed in these very words, according to the Customs & Laws of England, especially the first, & now in these latter Commissions by reason we have some Acts of Assembly, that make some small deviation from the laws of England, the respective Officers in the said Commissions, were directed & commanded in these express words, to proceed as near as may be to the Laws and Customs of England. To the 5th. All our Pattents join & unite us, to the Realm of England as parcel thereof, as ℔ the words of our Pattents doth plainly appear, the words of which are to be held as of the Mannor of East Green with &c. & now if we are a Part & branch of Engld. then consequently, we have a Right to, & benefit of the Laws of England. To the sixth That is our own Acts of Assembly, & these confirmed & allowed of by his Majestie. First the preamble to the body of our printed Acts doth declare that what Laws we make, must not be repugnant to the Laws of England &c.[6] Ergo 2dly. the 31st of our printed Acts, which appoints County Courts, to proceed in Causes of meum & tuum without limitation, for the which by the Laws of England, Justices of Peace cannot do in their Sessions, & therefore a particular Law was required for that, but then for direction of their Judgment, for management of that Jurisdiction thus by this Law given, it directs them to proceed according to the Laws of England & more particularly in one Act made in Octr. 1666. there it is directed & appointed, that every particular Court in Virginia, shall send for the Statutes at large, & in Especiall directs & appoints the getting those made in this King's reign, also orders the sending for Cooke's first Institutes, Swinburne of Wills &c. & the Law yields the reason of this. a Command & Charge (viz) for their guide & Direction to proceed to Judgment. Now if the Laws, Statutes & Customs of England were not binding here, this was an idle frivolous Law, & quite breaks a good Rule of reason lex neminem cogit, advana seu inutilia, but if the Laws of England were not in force here, the Court was forc'd to do an idle & unprofitable Act. To the 7th. Our continual usage & practice since the first Settlement, hath been according to the Laws & Customs of England, & all the precedents in the severall Courts both Civil & Criminal whereof there's above 10000 Precedents, nay some fresh ones that occurs to my memory last genll. Court, there was some tryed condemned & executed upon 13th. of this King for treason, in several branches of this very Statute of the 29th. of his Majestie, not only in the General Court, but in divers other County Courts. Now how far custom, Precedent & Practice Rules, may be seen Co: Lib 2. fo: 16.17.[7] in these words, For the customs & Courses of every of the King's Courts are as a Law, & the common Law for the universalitys doth take notice of them, & needed not be allowed or pleaded any usage or prescription to warrant the same, & so it is holden 5 Edw. 4.1, & 11 Ed: 4 & 2 that the Course of a Court is a Law, & 2 R. 3 & 9.[8] also in a Patent of H 7: four letters (viz) H: R: F: H: were left out, intending afterwards propter known to be drawn & limned in gold, but the great Seal was put to the Grant, leaving out those letters, & yet the Pattent was judged good, for the multitude of precedents. Co: Lib 2. fo: 6.[9] Upon view of severall precedents shewn by Mr. Brownlow, the Court suffered no farther arguments, but gave judgment according to them. Co. Lib. 4. fo: 41,[10] Precedents shewed to strengthen and Indictment & allowed. Quod nimia Subtilitas, injure reprobatur   In Rawlin's Case in the fourth Report fo: 53 54[11] All the Judges Commanded, that Precedents must be searched, because without Precedent Precedents [sic], it seemed to them the Law to be otherwise, & upon search of the Records many were shewed to the

Justices: And thereof the Justices & Barons una voce, in regard of the precedents which make a Law, adjudged the case according to them. Co: Lib. 4. fo: 93.94 [12] An Action of the case lyeth as well upon a Contract as an action of Debt, because of the divers Precedents for the same, in H: 6. Ed: 4. H: 4 & H: 8. to which precedents the Justices have always great regard, & therefore in the 11 E: 3. 32 it is holden that antient forms & manner of Precedents are to be maintained, & kept, & 34 A: T: 7 that which hath been according to usage shall be admitted And likewise in 39. H 6. 30 Reverend Judge Priscot & the rest of the Judges resolved, that they would not change the usages, notwithstanding their opinion was to the contrary, but gave Judgment according to the Precedents & usages & 4. Ed: 4. 44. it was adjudged that common Course maketh a Law, though perhaps Reason willeth the contrary, & further said they cannot change the usage now, for that shall be inconvenient, & thereunto agreeth the 5 Ed: 4.1 where it is said that the course of a Court maketh a Law, so also 2, 33. P & M. 120. Stat: W.2. Cap 12.[13] Quod Justiciarius coram quibus formatum est Appellum et terminatum, shall enquire of Damages where the Defendant is acquitted, Yet Precedents, expounds the Law against the express letter that Justices of Nisi prius, before whom the Appeal was not begun, shall do it. Eigthly & lastly Ab Inconvenienti How inconvenient would it be, if the Laws & Statutes of England were not binding here, may be seen by these Rules. First every Subject that is born out of the extent & reach of the Laws of England, cannot by judgment of those Laws be a natural subject to the King: The consequence will be this; All that are born in Virginia &c. will be out of the reach & extent of the Laws of England, & therefore cannot by Judgment of the Laws of England be natural Subjects to the King 2dly. That Subject that is not at the time, & in the place of his birth inheritable to the Laws of England, cannot be inheritable or partaker of the benefit & privileges given by the Laws of England, The consequence will be that all Virginians &c. in the place of their birth, were not inheritable to the Laws of England, & therefore not inheritable or to be partakers of the benefits & privileges of those Laws, & then we are no longer freemen but Slaves &c. 3rdly Whatsoever appeareth to be out of the Jurisdiction of the Laws of England, cannot be tryed by the same Laws, the consequence will be all that are born in Virginia, & are out of the Jurisdiction of the Laws of England, therefore cannot be tryed by the Laws of England. But admitting those Rules were not so consequential against us as they appear to be, Yet upon Consideration had of all our Judicial proceedings in all Causes civil & Criminal, what sad consequences would follow upon the denyal of the Laws & Statutes of England to be of force & binding here, may appear when we consider what malefactors have here suffered, & in civil causes how many hundred judgments & executions upon the same, to the death & destruction of their familys, & to the ruin & overthrow of others, which if not warranted & allowed of by the Laws of England (for we have no Law amongst us that directs therein) must be esteemed in the one Murther, & in the other the highest oppression, heigthened & aggravated to its supremest extent, under the colour of the Sword of Justice. Now Considering the constant Usage, continual practice, & multitude of Precedents for allowance of the Laws of England, & withal considering the many & great inconveniencys & mischiefs that would follow if it should be denyed. That all the Courts & more especially the generall Assembly, have submitted to & approved of, & as much as in them lay authenticated the same, that our Pattents makes us a part & branch of Engld., that his Majestie by his severall Commissions & Instructions from time to time sent us, Commands & enjoins the Ruling by, and governing according to the Laws of England that the subordinate Courts viz the County Courts, deriving their power from, & under the Governor by vertue of his Commission, from his Majestie are strictly charged & en-joined, to proceed in their Judicature in some, according to the Laws & Customs of England, & in other some, as near as may be, to the Laws & Customs of England, it must seem a great innovation in any one, that should deny to be governed by, & submit to the Laws of Engld Admitting the Laws & Statutes of England are not binding here, by what pretence can they lay claim to this Land, we have no Acts of Assembly, that ap-points the demising land by Will, & if they admit of the common Law of England to be of force here, then they have no title themselves by the Will, for before 32. & 34. H. 8.[14] the Generall Custom of the Realm did restrain men to Demise their Lands to any, if not that it were by some special Custom, in some particular place, & that appears by these words in the Act of 32 H. 8. Cap. 1 or otherwise, at his will & pleasure &r. for if they will admit some of those Statutes also to be of force here (for without that they cannot take ℈ the Will) then I demand why they admit some & not the Remainder, perhaps they may object, that this Statute of 29 King Charles was never promulgated, & so were the others of H. 8. & 13 of this King, to that I answer, that the promulgation of a Law, is not of the essence thereof, as may be seen in the 4th. Institutes fo: 26. for Cavendish in the 29 Ed: 3. being of Council for the Bishop of Chichester, who was sued upon the Statute of 29 Ed: 3.[15] objected two things first That the Act whereupon the Writ was grounded was no Statute. Secondly That if it were a Statute it was never published in the County. To whom Sr. Robert Thorpe Chief Justice answer'd, Although Proclamation be not made in the County, every one is bound to take notice of that which is done in Parliament, for as soon the Parliamt. has concluded anything, the Law intends that every person hath notice thereof, & this Will was made some years after the finishing the sd. Law of 29 Car. 2. Now as to the comparing us to Ireland & therefore concluding because Ireland is not bound by any Act of Parliament made in Engld., unless particularly named, or generally included, we are not neither. There is great difference between Ireland & us, they having the Kingdom of Conquered Christians, we of Conquered infidels. They were to be governed by their antient municipal laws, till an alteration made amongst them, ours if we had had any were ipso facto abrogated, because not only against Christianity, but against the Law of God & nature, contained in the Decalogue. For Infideli sunt Christi et Christianorum Inimica this Rule makes the Diversity betwixt the Conquest of them & us. First Our Establishment must be by the King himself, & such Judges as he shall appoint, who ought to judge us & our Causes, according to the King's direction, & how that has been the Commissions, Instructions, Patents &c. foregoing fully Demonstrate. Ireland after their Conquest, (which was first begun by King Edgar as appears by a Charger of his Ego Edgarius &c. but the Conquest was fully finished by H: 2 & therefore the honour thereof is attributed to him Co: Lib. 7. fo: 22.) [16] had municipal laws of their own, by which they were governed till King John introduced the English Laws, & afterwards H: 3 by Act of Parliament in England confirmed the same, as appears by this Pattent Roll. Quia pro Communi utilitate terrae Hiberniae et unitate terrarum Regis, Rex vult, et de communi consilio Regis promisum est, quod omnes leges et consuetudines quae in Regno Angliæ tenentur, in Hibernia teneantur &c., so that they had municipal Laws originally, we had none. Secondly They are a distinct Kingdom from England, but we a part or branch thereof, as appears by our Pattents before mentioned. For a Voyage Royal may be made into Ireland Co: Inst: 1₱t. [Part?] fo: 69. Co: Lib 7. fo: 23. And in the 33 Eliza It was resolved by all the Judges of England in the case of Oruck an Irishman who had committed high treason in Ireland, that by the Statute of 33 H. 8. 23 [17] he might be Indicted, Arraigned, & tryed for the same in England, according to the Purview of that Statute, the words whereof be, that all treasons &c. committed by any person out of the Realm of England &c. & there it was resolved that Ireland was out of the Realm of England. By a Record in 52 H.3. 26 [18] wherein the Lordship of Ireland is granted to his eldest Son Prince Edwd. Aurum Reginæ is granted to the Prince's wife, notwithstanding she was but Lady of Ireland, for untill the 33 H:8. C. 1 [19] they were never stiled Kings of Ireland, yet by that Act it appeareth, that the King & his progenitors had Kingly Jurisdiction & Royal Authority. Albeit this Royal Dominion and land of Ireland, was permitted of antient time to be granted de facto to the King's son, yet by the Law the King by his letters Pattents cannot grant so royal a Member from his Imperial Stile to any one, no more than he could do of his Kingdom of England, (See an excellent Record in R 2 time, well noted in Co: 4 Inst: fo: 357 Cap: Ireland), [19] nor if those Letters Pattents were authorised by Parliamt because it is against the Law & Custom of Parliament to assent to anything to the Disherison of the King Co: 4 Inst: fo: 13 & 14,[20] also because it is one of the titles & Stiles of his Royal Crown   Now by this plainly appears the great difference betwixt us & Ireland, for they are a distinct Kingdom, we apart of the Realm of England, their Kingdom cannot by Law be alienated or disposed, ours may, as appears by the severall Pattents & Grants of part of America as Maryland, New York, Carolina &r. & part of Virginia itself, to the Lord Pattentees. Thus Sir by myself, I have run over the chief Arguments of your Cause, what I have further to add, is only to advise you, to get Copys of those Acts of Assembly mentioned, Copys of Commissions to the Governors, to the Governor & Council, and Commission of Oyer & Terminer. Copys of his Majestie's Instructions, of Commissions to County Courts, especially those granted by my Lord Culpepper, Copys of Pattents, & if you could some few precedents of Judgments, if you can get any enter'd with their reasons, as I believe you may, & by them, those that you send them to, will understand more than my poor capacity is able to inform them.

To Ralph Wormley Esqr.   Sr. Your   W. ff
℥ Collo. Jones [21] June 9th. 1683

[LB, pp. 60-71]

1. For more on this case, see the various ltrs. to Ralph Wormeley above, including the cover letter just above. For details of the case, ltr. to Wormeley, May 21, 1681, note 2.

2. WF insisted, in a ltr. to Wormeley, June 19, 1681, that Griffin and Burwell should be referred to as "legatees" rather than as "executors."

3. In *Statutes at Large in Paragraphs* (London, 1681), under 29 Caroli Secundus, p. 1477, Cap. III, "An Act for Prevention of Frauds and Perjuries."

4. For Richard Kennor or Kennon, see ltr. to Wormeley, July 14, 1681, note 2. WF probably refers to Richard Kennon, the 1685-1686 burgess from Henrico; but he may refer to the Richard Kennor of Northumberland, his neighbor, in a sense, who was burgess in 1688. The name Kennion or Kenyon has not been located in Virginia records of the period.

5. Henry Swinburne, *A Briefe Treatise of Testaments and Last Wills....* (London, 1635), Part VI, "Who May Be Executor," § 14 (p. 69 of 1635 ed.).

6. In the Preamble to *The Lawes of Virginia Now in Force....* (London, 1662) is the declaration: "and have also endeavored in all things, as near as the capacity and constitution of this Countrey will admit, to adhere to those Excellent, and often refined Laws of *England*, to which we profess and acknowledge all Reverence and Obedience; and that the Laws, made by us, are intended by us but as brief Memorials of that, which the capacity of our Courts is utterly unable to Collect out of its vast Volumns [sic], though sometimes perhaps, for the difference of our and their Condition, varying in small things, but far from the presumption of contradicting any thing therein contained."

7. *Reports,* II, folio 16v, "car les customes & courses...des courts le roy sont come on [*sic*] ley."

8. In *Reports,* II, folio 16v, are all these references, though in slightly different form.

9. *Reports,* II, folio 6, concerns "Throughgoods Case," but the relationship is not clear. Certainly "the multitude of precedents" is not there. Actually this is probably an error for *Reports,* II, folio 16. All the section on the initials H: R: F: H: follows on folio 17r.

10. *Reports,* IV, folio 41, "Cases of Appeals & Indictments." Probably WF's reference is correct here.

11. *Reports,* IV, folios 52-54, "Rawlin's Case." Correct.

12. *Reports,* IV, folios 92-95, "Slade's Case." Correct.

13. Most of the references in the preceding six or seven lines are apparently to the *Statutes,* though they have not been checked.

14. Referred to in *Reports,* II, folio 17r and in *Statutes,* p. 656.

15. *Institutes,* IV, *p.* 26 rather than folio 26.

16. *Reports,* VII, folio 23r; also in *Institutes,* I, folio 69v.

17. The statute appears in *Statutes,* p. 757, "An Act to proceed by a commission of Oyer and Determiner against such persons as shall confess treason, &c." But Oruck the Irishman under 33 Eliz. or elsewhere has not been located.

18. This is taken from *Institutes,* IV, "Of Ireland" marginal commentary.

19. *Institutes,* IV, p. 357, contains reference to 33 H. 8. cap. 1.

20. *Ibid.,* IV, pp. 13 and 14.

21. Col. Cadwallader Jones (q.v.) was commander of the Rappahannock fort. As noted above, this date perhaps should be 1684 instead of 1683.

To Samuel Jefferson [1]

Mr. Saml. Jefferson   Febry 18, 1684/5

I have sent my boy purposely to you that you may reconcile the breach, which I suppose & do believe, your self may be throughly sensible of, by this time you inconsiderately made in our bargain, so long in bringing to perfection, for the things spent were only your beer sugar & brandy, which does not amount in the whole to above £10, or 12 five or six days lying runs out, that is the Vessels hire, & to assure you that I neither desire nor design to have so much Tobo. abated, I shall very readily accept the same either in money or bills, as also what small parcel of the goods may be wanting to compleat the sum, may be so paid: I will not repeat our bargain its very plain and easie, My part is to pay 50000 lb. Tobo. & either 800 or 4000. Your part is to deliver £358 sterling worth of goods, or what thereof is wanting to pay me in money, or otherwise to suit your own conveniency, & to deliver me either your own two servants or two Negros, that's the substance & whole of our Contract. I have been considering your well laid Design, of future years trade, & do so well approve thereof, that gives the occasion to this sudden Message, considering that if this Voyage miscarry, it may be a stop, if not an overthrow to that Design, which I earnestly design, & singularly approve of. My advice to you is seriously & considerately to weigh & debate the matter, & throughly look into all your Circumstances, & if upon the whole you think it convenient to close, then your best Course in my opinion is, to come directly away with your long boat, & bring what of the goods she can conveniently carry, & you may return with her Loading of Tobo. & your self staying, in two days time, may receive enough to keep your Ship in employment, this fortnight or three weeks, & then may take a horse, go up to the Collector,[2] enter your boat & so proceed in your business, & till you can have that conveniency, I will take care to expedite your business, & clear you of all trouble & Damage. If what's offered be acceptable, then I know my boy will have a quick & convenient passage home, but if it should not I beg the favour of you to give him a passage to the nearest Landing in the Virginia Side. My humble & hearty thanks for your & your Master's kindness when on Board, is justly render'd by

To. Mr. Samuel Jefferson on board   Sir Your   W. ff.
his ship in Nangemoy Maryland

[*LB*, pp. 71-73]

1. Jefferson was the merchant-owner or supercargo-contractor for the ship. Nanjemoy in Maryland was an esturial creek of the Potomac just opposite WF's home plantation.
2. The collector was probably Richard Lee II, who was certainly appointed naval officer and receiver of duties along the Potomac by Governor Andros. This was probably a re-appointment or continuation, for it was stated elsewhere that he was appointed by Berkeley in 1677. 1 V 244; Campbell, *History of Colony and Ancient Dominion of Va.*, p. 351n; Lee, Jr., *Lee Chronicle*, p. 56.

To John Cooper [1]

Mr. Jno. Cooper   March 30th. 1684

Sr. Your's ℔ Capt. Norrington [2] I receiv'd, together with all the things mentioned, except the Dutch nails & tacks, which I presume were omitted in packing up the goods, also two of the Citys to wit London & Amsterdam were utterly spoiled with the wet & all the Rabbits dead before they arrived, except the Buck Rabbit. I have ℔ Capt. Norrington shipped six hhds. Tobo. 3 No. 1. 2. 3 are Oronoko of my own Crop. 3 more

No. 4. 5. 6 are sweet scented, & of Collo. Jones[3] his Crop, I hope they will yield a good price, their freight being very low, the heigth is not to exceed £5..5. ℔ Tunn all charges clear perhaps lower, if any freighter on board has lower, then I am to have at that rate. By Capt. Norrington I shall be more large, & perhaps shall send you bills Loading, but to be sure the Copy of the Receipt for the Tobo. Sir My very good friend Mr. Newton[4] has sent to you about dispatching some business for him there, & had this year consigned some Tobo., but this business happened after the disposal of his Tobo., next year I am confident if this business hits, he will send you Considerable Consignments, towards the raising of the sd. money, & if not, yet will consign you some to pay you your reasonable Consideration, together with all charges & Disbursements, which if you doubt I will see you satisfyed. Mr. George Brent[5] I suppose this year will consign you some Tobo., & another in our parts did assure me he would send & consign to you ten hhds. his name Mr. Richard Gibson.[6] What service I can do you therein shall not be wanting. In my next which I believe will be by Capt. Norrington, shall be more large to which I refer you

Your W. ff.

[*LB*, p. 73]

1. For Cooper, see ltr. to him, April 4, 1681, note 1.
2. For William Norrington, see ltr. to Cooper, April 4, 1681, note 2.
3. For Cadwallader Jones, see ltr. to Ralph Wormeley, August 2, 1682, note 2. Apparently he inherited from his mother a plantation on Chotank Creek near WF's home place and also had patented large tracts in upper Stafford near WF's "Ravensworth." Presumably this is tobacco from one of these plantations, probably "Rich Neck." 30 V 323-40; Harrison, *Landmarks*, II, 608.
4. For WF's step-father-in-law John Newton, see ltr. to K. Chiseldine, June 8, 16[81], note 3. Newton was WF's partner in many land speculations, as both their wills testify. Newton refers in his will to his "loving friend" Colonel Fitzhugh.
5. For Brent, see ltr. to R. Wormeley, June 19, 1681, note 3. WF's law partner and friend lived at "Woodstock."
6. For Richard Gibson, see ltrs. to W. Hardidge, June 19, 1681, note 2, and to R. Wormeley, August 2, 1682, note 4.

To Samuel Hayward[1]

Mr. Samuel Hayward   June 3rd. 1684

I hope this will find you in good health, & the pleasant enjoyment of your most dear Brother,[2] & very good friend. I suppose e'er this you have presented, & I hope receiv'd that small note of mine upon Mr. Cooper,[3] The Country at present affords little news, this Assembly has done so little, that I know nothing worth while to write to you about. Your own particular business, I am informed by Robin,[4] is a little incumber'd with your brother Lewis,[5] but the particulars I cannot acquaint you with Robin intends to take a speedy & secure course with him as he tells me, what fair and just service I can do you therein, or in any thing else shall not be wanting. Robin has hitherto, & I believe will prove faithful & diligent in all your Concerns, & I am assured will approve himself a good servant, to so good a master. Sr. I have a great mind to try if Olives would not thrive in this Country, since I am well assured they grow & thrive well in the Streights, as far in the Northern Latitude as we are here, some of which sort you might procure in London: Therefore I would desire you to procure for me some of them, together with directions how to manage them. And I hope you will furnish your self with other raritys both for your own & your friends use, having now so pregnant an opportunity

To. Mr. Samuel Hayward &c.   Sr. Your &c.

[*LB*, p. 74]

1. Samuel Hayward, son of Nicholas Hayward the elder and thus brother of the Nicholas mentioned just below in note 2, had settled in Virginia in Stafford County, his home place being adjacent to WF's "Eagle's Nest" plantation, and close to "Bedford." In 1665 he became the second clerk of Stafford County, and in 1685-86, burgess. His will, made on December 3, 1684, and proved on November 11, 1696, left to WF "all ye books wch I shall leave in his hands att my Departure for England [i.e., in 1684]." Hayward's wife Martha was a sister of the immigrants John and Lawrence Washington. A photostat of Hayward's will is in Va. St. Lib., Archives Div.

2. Nicholas Hayward, from this time on WF's most frequently favored correspondent, was a London notary public and merchant. He was WF's legal adviser, confidant, and friend, as WF here indicates.

3. For John Cooper, see ltr. to him, April 4, 1681, note 1.

4. Unidentified.

5. A puzzling reference. No connection has been found with the Washington-connected Lewises, unless the fact that Hayward's wife was a Washington made it so. But in his will (see note 1 above), Hayward left to his nephew Philip Lewis one cow.

To John Cooper [1]

Mr. Jno. Cooper   June 28th. 1684

I have occasion for two pair of small Andirons for Chamber Chimneys, one pair of brass ones, with fire shovel & tongs, & one pair of iron ones well glazed, with fire Shovel & tongs, also two indifferent large Iron backs for Chimneys, wch I would have you send me by the first ships

Yor. W. ff.

[*LB*, p. 73]

    1. For Cooper, see ltr. to him, April 4, 1681, note 1.

To William Sherwood [1]

Mr. William Sherwood   May 10th. 1684

    Sr. In Collo. Jones [2] his business, please to follow the Order he has given me ℔ his letter, & secure Tobo. as near as may be according to his direction first taking out what's your own due in my name ℔ order of Collo. Jones, in what County you please, after that pay Mr. Secretary [3] upon my account out of the said Tobo. 2000lb. in Westmoreland County, or where else he shall direct, or you can procure it, & get the remainder to make up 8000 lb. Tobo. to be paid to me in Stafford County if possible, or at least in Westmoreland County & contrive to get the Remainder to Collo. Jones his best advantage, according to the direction of his Letter. Please also to use your endeavours to procure his claims, expressed in his letter, & I dare say he will not be ungratefull, but gentilely satisfie you

To. Mr. Willm. Sherwood at   Sr. Your W. ff.
James Town

[*LB*, p. 75]

    1. For William Sherwood, Jamestown attorney, see ltr. to him, June 10, 1679, note 1.
    2. For Cadwallader Jones, see ltr. to R. Wormeley, August 2, 1682, note 2. By this time Jones may have been approaching the financial straits he reached later and was anxious to dispose of his own crop. More probably, however, as commander of the Rappahannock garrison, or in consideration of the losses he had undergone in defending the frontier, Jones was collecting tobacco due him. WF as an "undertaker" for the Potomac fort, or as Stafford J.P. and burgess as well as friend, may have felt that he should help Jones collect. As "undertaker" with Brent for the Potomac garrison, he may be referring also to tobacco due him by various counties and persons.
    3. For Secretary of State Spencer, WF's friend and Westmoreland neighbor, see ltr. to him, Sept. 9, 1679, note 1. Spencer lived at Nomini.

To Captain George Brent [1]

Dear Brother   Octr. 2nd. 1684

I Just now receiv'd your kind letter by Mr. Bonam,[2] & take this opportunity by Mr. Minor [3] to return you thanks, He is now coming up to
Reckon, with some amendments in his accot., as I have Cursorily run it
over, & finds himself Dr. to us 13 or 1400lb. Tobo. after all charges put in,
to say, all notes allowed, the full deduction of Cask, & the payment of
Clark's & sheriff's fees, for us both, as he charged it in the generall (the
Particulars I did not enquire into) together with my note to Mr. Newton [4]
for 225 Tobo., I referred him to you for a full settlement, and therefore
did not curiously enquire into the returns of each Note, nor account of
fees, how much to your self, how much to me, assuring my self it would be
done by a more capable & dextrous Accomptant, & therefore refer my satisfaction to your particular Station. What news I know is, that your Writ
summoned him immediately up, who else perhaps would have been contented to have staid for his Tobo. (as he thought due) rather then be at
the trouble of reckoning &c. Mr. Secretary [5] who I saw, & can assure you
is well, & gives his service to you, acquaints me there's a Ship arrived in
James River, with thirty Servants & good store of goods, but neither news
nor letter from any body, but that Tobo. is good for nothing, if any one
will believe them. Tom Clayton [6] is very sick at Mr. Secretary's, & so
disabled that he will not have the advantage of writing, or Chamber
Council this Court, which I believe will prove to be his own greatest Loss.
Mine & Wives humble service salute your self & good Lady

To Capt. George Brent   Sr. Your   W. ff.
at Woodstock

[LB, pp. 75-76]

1. For George Brent, see ltr. to R. Wormeley, July 14, 1681, note 3. "Brother" apparently
refers to the fact that WF and Brent were law partners.
2. Samuel Bonam or Bonum of Yeocomico in Cople Parish appears many times in Westmoreland records. There was in 1702 and later a Thomas Bonam who was a Westmoreland
J.P. *Westmoreland County Deeds, Patents, etc., 1665-1677*, date June 13, 1677; *Westmoreland
County Deeds & Wills, No. 2, 1691-1699*, Jan., 1691; *Westmoreland County Court Order Book,
1675/6-1688/9*, Oct. 31, 1688; 2 V 14; 37 V 87; 27 W(1) 28.

3. Probably John Minor (d. 1699) of Westmoreland or Nicholas Minor, son of John, who flourished from 1680 to 1695. Nicholas also had a brother named John. Harrison (*Landmarks*, I, 344) thinks this reference is to Nicholas.

4. For John Newton, see ltr. to K. Chiseldine, June 8, 16[81], note 3.

5. Nicholas Spencer, Secretary of State, WF might have seen either at his home on Nomini Bay or at Jamestown.

6. Though WF also corresponded with a Thomas Clayton, merchant of Liverpool, he refers here to the Thomas who was burgess from James City County from 1680 to 1682 and one of the well-known lawyers of the colony. See ltr. to H. Hartwell, June 19, 1681, note 2. Also *Journals H.B. 1659/60-1693, passim.*

To John Cooper[1]

Mr. John Cooper   May 18th. 1685

Sr. Your two letters by Capt. Smith[2] & Capt. Partis[3] I have receiv'd, in your first you gave an account of Mr. Newton's[4] business, in your last of the acceptance of Mrs. Bland's[5] bills, & the receipt of the six hhds. consigned you last year, but no account of some old things I sent for, or of the receipt of any letter from me, which I admire at. I have shipped no Tobo. this year, it gave too good a Market here to admit thereof, for I had this year near £5 a hhd. for 150 hhds. bought with ready money, & clear of charge, as Custom, freight, package &c. Our River this year produces little Consignment of Tobo., & I suppose no great quantity will be carry'd from us to you thither, for other parts[6] have found an advantageous trade to themselves here, & profitable to us ꝑ the good prices they give for our Tobo., in which you might have been a Considerable sharer, if you had thought convenient to have accepted my Offers I made you about three years since.[7] I suppose this Crop, if Crops proves any thing like, I shall be Master of betwixt 5 or 600 hhds., what method I take for disposing part thereof, Capt. Smith & his Mate Burnham[8] can fully inform you, if you are willing to put in, might be readily receiv'd & accepted

To Mr. Jno. Cooper Mercht.   Sr. Your   W. ff.
in London

[*LB*, pp. 76-77]

1. For Cooper, see ltr. to, April 4, 1681, note 1.
2. Captain Thomas Smith, commander of the *Constant* of London, "now riding at Anchor in Nominy Bay, in Potomacke River, within ye government of Virginia," is mentioned thus

in an entry at the Council meeting, May 19, 1684. See ltr. to Cooper, March 10, 1682/83, note 2, and *Exec. Journ. Council Col. Va.*, I, 56.

3. For Captains Charles and Francis Partis, commanders of merchant vessels trading in Virginia, see ltr. to Francis Partis, April 7, 1680, note 1.

4. Probably John Newton's shipment of tobacco or his personal estate in England. See ltrs. above, and 33 V 300-2.

5. Mrs. Sarah Bland, WF's correspondent and client, certainly owed him fees which she probably paid in bills of exchange.

6. Harrison (*Landmarks*, II, 391) says that this refers to the Scots merchantmen, who were able at this time to take their tobacco into Scotland without the duty paid by English ship captains and were therefore beginning to undertake trade in Virginia.

7. In modern pencil, notice of footnote: "See p. 47."

8. Probably the same person as the Captain Burnham mentioned many times in the correspondence below. Burnham was a frequent visitor at WF's plantation.

To Nicholas Hayward [1]

Sir   May 18th. 1865

The welcome return of your Brother,[2] ushered in your generous gift to our Parish,[3] & highly obliging letter & favour to myself   Sr. The Parish by me return you their hearty thanks & wish their Capacity were as able as their inclinations & desires, are willing to gratifie so signal a favour, by a more lasting continuance than at present our paper built Temples will admit of, but do assure you what the Register & a gratefull remembrance & communication will contribute to the commemoration thereof, shall not be wanting. Sir To my self your obligations are so great & binding, that I am in despair either to render due acknowledgements to the one, or retribution to the other, yet what my poor power, & hearty abilitys are capable of shall upon the least intimation, be gratefully contributed, to the service of your self, or any of your friends by

To. Mr. Nichs. Hayward &c.   Sr. Your W. ff.

[*LB*, p. 77]

1. For Nicholas Hayward, see ltr. to Samuel Hayward, June 3, 1682, note 2.

2. For Samuel Hayward, see ltr. to him, June 3, 1684, note 1. According to Hayward's will, he did not leave for England until after its date, Dec. 3, 1684 (though since he writes it "Xber 3" he possibly might mean October 3, 1684). In either case, his return by May 18, 1685, meant that he had made a quick journey.

3. According to G. MacLaren Brydon (*A Sketch of the Colonial History of St. Paul's, Hanover, and Brunswick Parishes, King George County, Va.*, typescript photostat, Va. St. Lib. [1916], pp. 10-11) Nicholas' gift was probably recorded in now-lost parish registers. Samuel did bequeath to the parish a tract for a glebe called subsequently "Hayward's donation."

To Captain Roger Jones [1]

Dear Friend   May 18th. 1685

Our good friend George Brent with his most acceptable self, brings up your welcome letter, wherein you advise of your immediate Voyage for England, where I hope this will find you safe arrived, to your own satisfaction & wishes, & therein desire to hear from me, which I was always ready to perform, & can now more more [sic] readily to London, than formerly to James Town, & where conveniency admits, I'll be sure never to miss the congratulating so good a friend   Sr. If I had gone to England this year, as I once intended, amongst others I should have endeavoured two things, one was to get if possibly I could Letters Pattents for the high Sheriff's Place of our County, in fee or at least for life,[2] the other to have acquainted the Bishop of London, the advantages he might make in this part of his Diocess, by Probate of Wills, grant of Administration, charitable Dispositions of Intestates Estates, & other things as appertains to his jurisdiction, which at present I suppose might be worth 5 or 600£ sterling ℔ annum & in this growing Country, will with it every year encrease. Now Sr. for the Sherriff's place to be granted in fee, has been antiently practicable in England, & in one County, is still retained in the family of the Cliffords, & to this day is continued in the Kingdom of Scotland therefore the proposal is not illegall, & I suppose might neither be improbable nor impossible to effect, if it be not too much trouble to you, & you see any likelyhood of effecting it, I desire you in my behalf to negotiate therein, & if it can be performed, though it be at the charge of 40. 50. or 60 guineas, I will readily & thankfully repay them again. The other of the Bishops, can be no unwelcome News, nor make you unacceptable for the relation of it, if it be not laid hold of, but I suppose, if it should, you cannot miss for your Intelligence some mark of favour, if not some place of advantage (a great many of which profitable places I heartily wish you) besides the Obligation it will be to the Country in Generall, if this should give occasion to his Lordship's more immediate care of us, if this should give occasion of supplying us with plenty of able, & painfull, & sober Pastors,[3] which at present how greatly wanting your self is fully able to inform. Sr. I know your skill & Activity for business, therefore need not farther advise, but if I were, knowing your interest & acquaintance with my Lord Culpepper [4]

I should advise to consult him, before you embark therein, whose great Judgment & strong abilitys, together with his great Interest, is able both to advise & direct you in the management thereof, to whom if I be not wholly forgotten, please to present my humble service & best wishes. By this trouble Sr. you see I do not take your friendly letter merely complimental, but really as it is writ, & I am confidant as you intended, & please readily to command any thing, that lyes in my power to serve you, & you shall find it as readily obey'd by

To Capt. Roger Jones at &c.   Sr. Your   W. ff.

[*LB,* pp. 77-79]

1. For Roger Jones, see ltr. to him, Jan. 8, 1682/83, note 1. Though he is generally said to have returned to England for good in 1692, as noted above, this letter seems to imply that this date in 1685 is that of his resettlement in England.

2. Presumably WF now wants the high sheriff's place in fee or for life. It will be recalled that in 1682/83 he was supporting Dr. Bankes for the appointment under ordinary conditions.

3. WF is often quoted in regard to this matter, but there is much other evidence. Brydon, *Va.'s Mother Church,* I, *passim;* Meade, *Old Churches, passim;* Bruce, *Inst. Hist. Va., passim.*

The other suggestion to be made to the Bishop of London, concerning a Probate, etc., office such as that of the Archbishop of Canterbury in England, was clearly with the idea that WF might be put in charge of it.

4. As noted above, Jones had come to Virginia with Lord Culpeper. Culpeper had been back in England since the summer of 1683.

To William Fitzhugh [1]

Dear Cousin   May 18th. 1685

By a Stranger who had once occasion to buy some books of you, I had a relation of your living & thriving; therefore take this first conveniency of congratulating you, & together wt. you, of a respectfull, obedient, & loving remembrance, of all friends & relations there, and desire not only by you to hear how they all do, but intreat you to desire them to write to me, than which nothing would be more welcome or acceptable, especially from my Mother, brothers & Sister, Uncles, & Cousins &c. or as many of them as are living, & would be so kind to write I have a long time in a strange land, strugled hard with fortune's adverse hand, but thank God in the end, by God Almighty's blessing upon my mean endeavours, (having no friend or relation to lend a supporting hand) have overcome, & I praise God live very contentedly & well, & should be heartily glad of that communication, which this Distance admits of, by letters to hear from you & all friends there   Upon the Exchange in the Virginia walk, you'll meet Mr. John Cooper a Virginia Mercht.[2] who will take care in conveying your & their letters to me, also any Master of a Ship bound to Potomack River in Virginia will do the like, as Capt. Smith Capt. Norrington[3] & others also you may have the same conveniency by Mr. Nicholas Hayward[4] Notary publick near the Exchange in London, your direction may be to me in Stafford County in Potomack River in Virginia. Thus Sir I have given you an account where I live, how to direct, & to enquire for those Masters of Ships who very well know me, & now once again I desire you to give my duty, respects & commends to all friends & relations as aforesd. & from me desire them to write, I am confident you will not fail me your self, and assure them as I now assure you, nothing can or will be more acceptable, than the receiving their & your letters to

Your   W. ff.

Pray be very full & particular in your letter
to Mr. William Fitzhugh Stationer living in
Newgate Market over against St. Martin's
in London

[*LB*, pp. 79-80]

1. This William Fitzhugh was the son of WF's father's younger brother Robert (with whom WF also corresponded). "The Fitzhugh Family," 7 V, 8 V, 9 V, *passim;* 40 V 187-204.
    2. For John Cooper, see ltr. to him, April 4, 1681, note 1.
    3. For Captain Smith, see ltr. to Cooper, May 18, 1685, note 2. For Norrington, ltr. to Cooper, April 4, 1681, note 2.
    4. For Hayward, see ltr. to Samuel Hayward, June 3, 1684, note 2.

To Henry Fitzhugh[1]

Dearest Brother   April 22nd. 1686

   With the same Content & satisfaction as wearyed travellers take up their Inn, or weather beaten Voyagers their desired Port, after a long tedious & stormy Voyage, so did I the most welcome joyfull, & glad news of your health, welfare, & prosperity, which I had from my Sister, Cousin William Fitzhugh & more particularly from Mr. Cooper. Your self would not add to that happiness I believe, doubting too great a repletion, might cause a surfeit, or too great & sudden a joy a suffocation of the spirits. If that hindered you from writing last year, I have prepared by a composed frame, not to fear the one, nor doubt the other, but am ready with all alacrity & chearfullness to hear from your self, of your Condition & welfare. God almighty hath been pleased to bless me with a very good wife, & five pledges of our conjugall affections, three of which he has been pleas'd to call into the arms of his mercy, & lent me two a hopefull boy & girle, & one other that will not suffer so close confinement, is preparing to come into the world. And as he has been pleased to dispense those his choicest of blessings, he hath likewise added a plentifull Dispensation of his favours, in giving me a competent subsistence, to support my self & them comfortably & handsomely: I hear that he has been bountifull in his favours to you, for which I am really glad, & heartily congratulate you therein. By my Sister I understand our poor Mother & dear Sister, have not only tasted, but drank a large draught of the Cup of Affliction, & waded thro' abundance of Calamitys & troubles, which I truly condole, & do think it both our dutys, not only to commiserate, but as far as our abilitys extend, not to suffer one to want, who gave us our being, nor suffer her to strugle to live, who (under God) gave us life here. Charity directs to help those in want & distress, but nature, duty, the Laws of God and Man, not only commands but enjoins, to give the utmost help to a distressed Parent. Therefore I have ordered Mr. Cooper to let you have what money you have occasion for, to the assisting them, if it be the utmost farthing, & if it should not be enough, should be sorry, I had no more there. I refer to your discretion how much to take, & how to dispose thereof. My Mother's age will not admit of such a Voyage, therefore I hope you will take care that she end her days comfortably in her native Soil. But for my Sister if she cannot otherwise better her self, I should be heartily glad of her good company, with an assurance she should never want as long as I have it to supply her. And if her inclination be to come, I would desire & entreat you, that she come out handsomely & gentelely & well cloathed, with a maid to wait on her, & both their passages paid there, if she has it not of her own, out of my money in Mr. Cooper's hands, if so much can be spared from our Mother, & for the Credit of it let her pay the money her self. By Capt. Smith who will not be long before he goes, & a third time this year by way of Liverpoole, opportunity will admit me to write you, & shall then endeavour to put in any thing that I have now omitted, & always assure you I am

Most Dear Brother

To. Mr. Henry Fitzhugh   Your   W   ff

[*LB*, pp. 80-82]

1. Henry, older brother of WF, was baptized at St. Paul's, Bedford, England, April 28, 1650. He was less than a year older than WF. Though the letters to him below indicate that he was probably a captain in the Royal Navy, his name has not been discovered in the extant records in the Public Record Office.

2. Dorothy, who later came to Virginia, was baptized at St. Paul's, Bedford, January 24, 1645. Apparently she had received news of her brother in America through his letter to his cousin William Fitzhugh of May 18, 1685.

3. For this William Fitzhugh, see ltr. to him, May 18, 1685, just above.

4. For Cooper, see ltr. to him, April 4, 1681, note 1.

5. Probably WF's son Henry, who at the age of eleven was to be sent to Bristol to school. The two older children were William, Junior, and Rose or Rosamond (also spelled Rosamund).

6. Mary Fitzhugh, daughter of the Reverend Giles King of Tempsford, county Bedford, was the widow of Henry Fitzhugh of Bedford, woolen-draper. See the letters to her below.

7. For Captain Thomas Smith, commander of the *Constant* of London, see ltr. to Cooper, May 18, 1685, note 2.

To Miss Dorothy Fitzhugh [1]

Dear Sister   April 22nd. 1686

Your two kind endearing letters I have receiv'd, & heartily congratulate; The afflictions & miseries therein mentioned that our poor Mother & your self have gone through, I as truly condole, as the one gives me true contentment in your health & lives, so the other gives me as true a sense of sorrows for your Calamitys & afflictions, which God in his good time I hope will alleviate, if not take off. I thank your care & kindness, in your large & particular account of all friends and relations there. I have taken care with my Brother, according to my Ability, to assist both my Mother & you, who I suppose will be so kind to shew his letter, & in assurance of that will save me some trouble in writing, because to him I must refer you for a more particular relation. Dear Sister I have advised him to perswade you, & now entreat you my self, to come in here (except your fortune be

above it) which your Letter does not signifie where you will be a welcome
& kind Guest both to me & my wife, & as long as I live you shall be assured no want. The methods I have taken for your coming in, I would
advise you by all means to follow, which will give us both credit & reputation, without which its uncomfortable living, & I am assured my Brother
will both assist & direct you in it. I hope the money I have ordered him to
dispense, will fully pay your & a maid to wait on you, your passages, &
have some thing Overplus gentilely to set forth your self. I am tired wt.
writing & business, & do intend to write very speedily again, therefore shall
add no further now, than only to assure you   I am

To. Mrs. Dorothy Fitzhugh   Dear Sister   Your &c.

[*LB*, pp. 82-83]

1. For Dorothy, see ltr. to Henry Fitzhugh, April 22, 1686, note 2, just above.

To Mrs. Mary Fitzhugh [1]

Dear Mother   April 22nd. 1686

My Sister gives me a sad account of your continued misfortunes &
afflictions, for which I heartily grieve, & am really sorry that my distance
will not admit me the happiness of your company, to comfort you in your
afflictions, & that my ability is not as great, as my desires to aid & assist you,
you must accept my letter for my company, & I have taken care with my
brother, to draw the utmost penny that I have in England, to contribute
to your & my Sister's relief, those necessarys that, was designed for, I had
rather be without, than your necessitys should continue, as far as my
abilitys permit. I thank God I live very comfortably with a good wife &
two children now living, five I had in all but three are dead, & my wife is
now with child. Praised be God I neither live in poverty nor pomp, but
in a very good indifferency, & to a full content. My Brother & Sister will
more fully give you a particular relation of me & my concerns to whom I
refer. God almighty I beseech to take off those afflictions, he has been
pleas'd to chasten you with, or endue you wt. a Christian patience to

bear them. I have at present only to add to crave your blessing & continuall prayers for

                                        Dear Mother
To. Mrs. Mary Fitzhugh   Your dutifull &c.

[*LB*, pp. 83-84]

1. For Mrs. Mary Fitzhugh, see ltr. to Henry Fitzhugh, April 22, 1686, note 6, above.

To William Fitzhugh [1]

Most kind Cousin   April 22nd. 1686

   I joyfully receiv'd your kind, courteous and particular letter, & therein receive the full satisfaction & contentment, to hear of the health & welfare of all friends & relations therein enumerated, & particularly your own, & wife, & children. which I pray God continue   I have also to return you my hearty thanks for your courteous trouble in communicating my letter, to the severall relations in your's mentioned, I can't say I'll serve you in the like kind, but can assure you in any thing that lyes in my power, shall think my self happy in receiving your commands, & now intend to give due obedience to your desires in my particular to let you know, that I have been twelve years happy in a good wife, & still continue so, & God almighty has been pleas'd to bless me with five pledges of conjugal affec-tion, three boys & two girls, the eldest girle & two youngest boys, I hope are Saints in heaven, my eldest son named Willm. is now living & his Sister, & I hope e'er long I may have another, to add to the number. I have this year particularly written to my Mother, Brother, & Sister therefore shall not give you the trouble in my behalf of saluting them, but must beg the favour to give my service & due respects to all friends & relations else, & more particularly to your father & mother & my Aunt [   ] [2]: My wife gives her due respects to your self & good wife, & I must entreat you to accept of the same from

To. Mr. Wm. Fitzhugh   Sir Your   W. ff.
Stationer &c.

[*LB*, pp. 84-85]

To Doctor Ralph Smith [1]

Doctr. Ralph Smith   April 22nd. 1686

In order to the Exchange you promised to make for me, & I desired you to proceed therein, to say to Exchange an Estate of Inheritance in land there of two or three hundred pound a year, or in houses in any Town of three or four hundred pound a year, I shall be something particular in the relation of my concerns here, that is to go in return thereof. As first the Plantation where I now live [2] contains a thousand Acres, at least 700 Acres of it being rich thicket, the remainder good hearty plantable land, without any waste either by Marshes or great Swamps the Commodiousness, conveniency, & pleasantness your self well knows, upon it there is three Quarters well furnished, with all necessary houses, ground & fencing, together with a choice crew of Negros at each plantation, most of them this Country born, the remainder as likely as most in Virginia, there being twenty nine in all, with Stocks of cattle & hogs at each Quarter, upon the same land is my own Dwelling house, furnished with all accomodations for a comfortable & gentile living, as a very good dwelling house, with 13 Rooms in it, four of the best of them hung, nine of them plentifully furnished with all things necessary & convenient, & all houses for use well furnished with brick Chimneys, four good Cellars, a Dairy, Dovecoat, Stable, Barn, Hen house Kitchen & all other conveniencys, & all in a manner new, a large Orchard of about 2500 Apple trees most grafted, well fenced with a Locust fence, which is as durable as most brick walls, a Garden a hundred foot square, well pailed in, a Yeard wherein is most of the foresaid necessary houses, pallizado'd in with locust Punchens, which is as good as if it were walled in, & more lasting than any of our bricks, together with a good Stock of Cattle hogs horses, Mares, sheep &c, & necessary servants belonging to it, for the supply and support thereof. About a mile & half distance a good water Grist miln, whose tole I find sufficient to find my own family with wheat & Indian corn for our necessitys & occasions   Up the River in this Country three tracts of land [3] more, one of them contains 21996 Acres another 500 acres, & one other 1000

Acres, all good convenient & commodious Seats, & wch. in a few years will yield a considerable annual Income. A Stock of Tobo. with the Crops & good debts lying out of about 250000lb. besides sufficient of almost all sorts of goods, to supply the familys & the Quarter's occasions for two if not three years. Thus I have given you some particulars, which I thus deduce, the yearly Crops of corn & Tobo. together with the surplusage of meat more than will serve the family's use, will amount annually to 60000lb. Tobo. wch. at 10 shillings ℔ Ct. is 300£ annum, & the Negroes increase being all young, & a considerable parcel of breeders, will keep that Stock good for ever. The stock of Tobo. managed with an inland trade, will yearly yield 60000lb. Tobo. without hazard or risque, which will be both clear without charge of housekeeping, or Disbursements for Servants cloathing. The Orchard in a very few years will yield a large supply to plentifull house keeping, or if better husbanded, yield at least 15000lb. Tobo. annual Income. What I have not particularly mentioned, your own knowledge in my affairs is able to supply, if any are so desirous to deal for the Estate without the stock of Tobo. I shall be ready & willing, but I will make no fractions of that, either all or none at all shall go. I have so fully discoursd you in the affair, that I shall add no farther instructions, but leave it to your prudent & carefull management, & would advise that if any Overtures of such a nature should happen, immediately give an account thereof to Mr. Nicholas Hayward Notary publick near the Exchange London, both of the person treating, & the place Scituation, Quantity & quality of the Estate, who will take speedy & effectual care, to give me a full & ready account thereof, which I hope you will ℔ all opportunitys do to

To Doctr. Ralph Smith in Bristol   Sir Your   W. ff.

[*LB*, pp. 85-87]

1. As WF states below, Smith was a physician, Virginia landowner, and merchant. He died before 1689, for by that date his widow, WF's sister Dorothy, was married to her second husband. 44 V 204.

2. Though all earlier writers on WF have said that his home plantation was "Bedford," Mr. G. H. S. King has given the editor interesting and convincing evidence that the estate here described was that which is now called "Eagle's Nest," which WF bequeathed to his eldest son William. As Mr. King points out, the acreage of "Eagle's Nest," its location in relation to other tracts owned by WF, and the likelihood that the eldest son would have inherited the home place, all point to it as the place where WF spent most of his life in America. "Bedford" seems to have had its origin in a six-hundred-acre tract WF acquired in 1688 (as shown in a complex conveyance of 1708 from Robert Dade to Henry Fitzhugh).

Missing Stafford records for the period might make the matter certain one way or the other. Dr. Thomas Fitz-Hugh has stated to the editor that he saw the grave of Sarah, WF's wife, some years ago at "Bedford." But she might easily have spent her last years with her second son, Henry, who inherited this property. "Bedford," near the present Owens Post

Office, remained in the Fitzhugh family until 1953. "Eagle's Nest" is a short distance farther up the river.

3. These are the tracts in modern Prince William County, including the estate of 21,996 acres later known as "Ravensworth," on the Occoquan in old Stafford. Before he died in 1701, WF had deeded in eight groups several dozen tracts of land in several counties. *Stafford County Deed Book, Grantee, W-Z*, pp. 24, 83, 92, 104; *Stafford County Will Book, Liber Z, 1699-1709*, pp. 24-27, 28-30, 84-85, 92-101.

To Nicholas Hayward [1]

Most Worthy Sir   April 22nd. 1686

I must confess I want abilitys, to polish & adorn my expressions with that Elegance & sweetness of Stile your two letters I this year receiv'd are full freighted with, yet I'll endeavour to supply that defect, with a true sincerity & ardent zeal, to assure you of my most hearty affection, & real propensity which your generous worth obliges & obliging favours binds me to, & shall be always ready to court all occasions to demonstrate the same. I never met a Disappointment with greater chearfullness, than when I was informed of your of your [sic] Purchase of the seat of land contiguous,[2] for my intention of purchase was to have such neighbours on it, as might live quietly & honestly, the contrary of which are in all places ill, but here really pernicious, Your Purchase not only takes away those fears, but adds to my contentment in the assurance of so generous & friendly a Neighbourhood, either by a Trustee for your self, or by some near & dear relation to your self. What service I can do you either in the settlement or farther confirmation thereof, if your kindness will please to communicate my ready obedience shall be fully shewn, in a speedy (& to my skill) full complyance But if you intend for sale, (which I hope not) if you will be pleas'd to give me the Refusal, I will give you the full heigth of the market, because the Interposition of an unknown Neighbour so near, may be vastly prejudicial. Sr. Your generous & kind offer of more vegetables in any condition desired, either in seed, trees, slips or plants, agrees so naturally with my Constitution, & the melancholly Condition of this Country, that I must be of all men the most ungratefull, if I should not meet with so great a favour from so good a friend, with all the chearfulness a tongue is able to express, or heart to think, & should be guilty of a high Ingratitude, (which sin next to the sin of witchcraft I utterly abominate) if I should particularly impose farther troubles, all I have retributed your past favours in

this kind, by a due acknowledgement, & a thorough account of the Essays
therein made, which I hope are now upon Gemination, & by the next I
hope to give you some satisfactory account thereof Your Uncle Porteous
remote habitation ³ & my retirement from publick Concerns, (and so consequently from James Town) admits me not at present that desired opportunity of retalliating your kind favours in the nature & quality desired,
yet with my near Neighbour, & very good friend your brother Sam: ⁴ I
can never forget your desires, (being so correspondent with my own inclinations), in commemoration of your good health there, & by the first opportunity shall fully answer your expectations & my own wishes. Sr. The
inclosed is a copy of Directions & Instructions to Doctr. Ralph Smith ⁵ an
ingenuous Gentleman but an inveterate Whig & one that has good credit
& Interest in Bristol with that party where he lives, & gives me some assurance (by the beating of his own pulse) which he says keeps even stroke
with the rest of that discontented side) of its taking its desired effects, the
humour of that party being to remove & change with difficultys and
hazards, rather than live contentedly & submissively (though plentifully)
under the established governmt. & had rather wrest & cross the express
letter of the Scripture, than suffer that to wrest their inclinations or cross
their Anabaptistical humours. The latter part gives you the reason that I
sent you copy thereof, wherein as in a Mirror, you may see my desires
are now to breath my native air, & to enjoy the fruition of my native soil,
if as it is there proposed it could be done with reputation & Credit, as also
my true station & standing here, which without a firm settlement there I
am resolved not to leave. If Mr. Smith writes you anything relating
thereto, I beg your favour in the examination thereof, or if in the course
of your business, you could meet with such a disconted party, you will
be pleas'd in my behalf to propose the Overture. Sr. The inclosed is a
letter to my brother which I beg the favour of your self to deliver, Mr.
Jno. Cooper I presume will bring you to his company I have sent it purposely open, that you may both see & know the Contents. And I hope he
will (pursuant thereunto) heartily acknowledge, & truly thank you for all
your favours & kindnesses expressed and manifested to me, & for this last
trouble in par- particular [sic], which I'll assure you shall always be
acknowledged by

To Mr. Nichs. Hayward Notary &c   Sir Your   W. ff.

[LB, pp. 87-90]

1. WF's consciousness of "stile" is evident throughout his letters (see "Pen in Hand," in
the Introduction). In an age of rhetorical and epistolary manuals, an educated writer even

in the colonies was quite conscious that he was practicing a literary art, albeit a lesser one. See R. B. Davis, "The Gentlest Art in Seventeenth Century Virginia," *Tennessee Studies in Literature*, II (1957), 51-63.

2. Although this "seat of land" has usually been taken to be the famous "Brenton" or "Brent Town" tract, of which more later, it was possibly a much smaller place, much closer to WF's home than "Brenton" was to be. The date is a little early, for the thirty thousand acres of "Brenton," in the neighborhood of WF's "Ravensworth" property, were granted by the Proprietor on Jan. 10, 1686/87, and acknowledged by WF as attorney for Culpeper in the Stafford Court of July 13, 1687 (Harrison, *Landmarks*, I, 177-96). In view of WF's ltr. to Hayward of Jan. 30 1686/87, however, it may refer to "Brenton."

3. Probably Edward Porteous (d. 1700), merchant and planter, who lived on York River in the upper end of Gloucester County at "New Bottle." He was a vestryman of Petsworth Parish, and in 1693 was included by the Governor in a list of gentlemen suitable for appointment to the Council. His house, later known as "Violet Banks," was still standing in 1905. 1 V 397; 13 V 310-11; Mary W. Gray, *Gloucester County (Virginia)*, Richmond [1936], p. 70.

4. Samuel Hayward's two-hundred acre property lay between WF's "Bedford" and his "Eagle's Nest," contiguous with the latter.

5. For Smith, see ltr. to him, April 2, 1686, note 1, just above. WF's Toryism is evident in this description of his future brother-in-law.

To Henry Fitzhugh [1]

Dearest Brother   April 22nd. 1686

I have under Cover of Mr. Nicholas Haywd. my highly honoured & most esteemed friend, seconded in the same Ship my first under Cover of Mr. John Cooper, only to bring you into his acquaintance, & to beg your assistance to give him my due acknowledgemts. & thanks, for all his past kindness, & continued favours, which without the heigth of Ingratitude, I cannot omit the acknowledgement. I have been so large & particular in my first, I have now little to add, only to tell you that necessity, of business, occasioned me to give a more near & perfect account of my Station here, than either prudence or modesty, would admit me to do in your's, which upon your request, I assure myself he will communicate to you, & if you can do me any kindness therein, I am certain you will contribute your helping hand, towards the effecting thereof for

To Mr. Henry Fitzhugh in London   Your   W. ff.

[*LB*, p. 90]

1. For Henry Fitzhugh, see ltr. to him, April 22, 1686, note 1.

To Thomas Clayton [1]

Mr. Thos. Clayton   April 26th. 1686

The Trade & Dealing that I have had with Mr. Greenhalgh [2] this year, & by that means the Converse, Society, & acquaintance with Mr. Jno. Marshal [3] is fully able, & I suppose will readily inform you, & whose persuasion & advice gives me the opportunity, & you the trouble, of this present Overture for a quick constant, & certain, & I believe advantageous trade, which in my apprehension you have not hitherto hit on. The offers I have to make are but of two sorts. The first for a quick and speedy Dutch Trade. The Second for a quick & sudden Trade, & Dispatch here, & a ready and full complyance to your whole Ships & Cargoe &c. As to the first which is the Dutch Trade, to have a Ship of 200 hhds. burden here, the beginning of October, & to have her whole Loading ready by the 15th. & on board by the 25th. of the same month, that she might be dispatch'd out hence by the 27th. at farthest, & by that means have the first & choice of the Crops here, & the first & best of the Dutch Market there. In which Design I myself would go a quarter, or rather than fail a third part, & engage to have my whole Loading ready by the 10th. of October at farthest, but doubt your own remoteness, & the Indexterity of most of your own Factors in the Course of trading, you are now in, will not admit so ready a complyance, that Concern requires to be profitably carried on, shall be no more particular therein, but refer you to Mr. Marshal, for a more ample account thereof. As to the second, for a quick & sudden dispatch &c. I have this to offer, that at 16.8d. ℙ Cent, I will engage to load a Ship of 200 hhds. after this manner, that is, let her arrive any time by the 10th. November, immediately upon her Arrival, after the 10th. Novr. aforesaid, I will give her Notes for one third of her Loading, as soon as ever she has dispatch'd those Notes & got the Tobo. on board, I will then give her Notes for one third more of her Loading, & when she has dispatch'd them, I will then give her Notes for the remaining part of her full Loading, which beginning the 10th. Novr., may be easily perfected & performed by the 28th. of the same Month, & she ready to sail by the last of the same Month or beginning of December at farthest, Provided the Master be a diligent & Industrious man such a one as I can assure you Mr. Marshal is. And whatever Stay she makes for want of my Notes aforesaid, I will be bound to pay damage money ℙ day to the full of these Ships Charge.

The Conveniency of Tobo. & readiness of getting it on board, Mr. Marshall can pretty well inform you, & I must also tell you, that near one half thereof must come off my own Plantations, near a third more at one particular Rowling house* 4 or landing, & the whole remainder not above twenty miles distance, which in this Country is a very inconsiderable matter. The 200 hhds. at 460 ℔ hhd., which will certainly be the smallest weight of forward Tobo. will amount to 92000lb. Tobo. which at 16.8d. ℔ Cent comes to £776.13.4 half of which money I would have deposited in such hands as I shall appoint, & the other half in goods sortable for this Country Cargoe, the money there deposited, I covet not the disposal of, nor the goods hither sent the possession of, till I have first answer'd my Contract ℔ the Delivery of Notes for good Tobo. Thus I have shortly touched at the Trade proposed, & if you doubt in any thing, I refer you to Mr. Marshal, with whom I have more amply discoursed thereof, & who is fully able to inform you, of my capacity and ability for performance, & the conveniency that will be in it. By this way of Trade, your Ship has no stay, your men a full employment, your goods a certain Sale, your Ship a certain Loading, your selves but one half of the risque by reason one half of the money is left in Engld. no fear of bad or slow Debts, no doubtfull careless or giddy Factors to overthrow the voyage & reckoning the charge of the Ships stay, upon the Course of Trade you are now in, & the bad debts left, the same quantity of Tobo. must needs stand you in a great deal more money, with all the hazards & disadvantages aforesaid. What is before said for the forward Ships arrival & dispatch in November, I have the same to propose in the same Circumstances, & under the same Conditions for the said ship or some other of the same burden, arriving here by the 10th. of february, which may likewise be as suddenly dispatch'd, but the weights of the hhds. round, cannot be expected so great as the first Ships, yet may & I believe will hold out 420 ℔ hhd. which will amount to 84000lb. Tobo. at 16.8d. ℔ Cent is 700£, which money I would have likewise ordered as the former, half there deposited, & half in sortable goods as before, which latter Ship will be dispatch'd before most if not all your Ships, that come hither under the course of Trade you are now in[.] By this means one Ship will readily & easily perform two voyages in one year, the Seamen kept in full employment, & consequently deserve their wages, the Master busily & constantly employ'd & the Ship according to the intent of her building in a continuall Run, & as above all things in certainty, & what loytering time is made, (provided the Master be diligent and dextrous) at my charge, which I believe well weighed & considered,

---

* In pencil, late eighteenth-century hand (?): Rowling House—see IV Henry, *Statutes*.

will deliver Tobo. in Engld. at cheaper rates than it is now purchased, by those that make the cheapest Purchases. If this Method & proposal be acceptable, then care must be taken, to give me for the first year timely & speedy notice, either ℞ the last Septr. or beginning of October at farthest, of the acceptance & continuance for at least three years, provided we live so long, but mortality must separate, because the Contract is personal. Now the Directions that I have to propose for your methods to take therein to give Mr. Hayward Notary publick near the Exchange London, notice thereof who will give me a speedy & sudden account of it, also to pay the money for the first & second Ship into his hands, or else to take such care that shall be to his satisfaction for the payment thereof, together with such Caution for the same as he shall approve of, after notice of the same from him, I shall be ready then to make my full complyance in Tobo. as aforesaid[.]

And for the goods sort then, as if you were to send a Cargoe to purchase your Loading there, (with this Caution that it well bought & with ready money) which is this way advantageous that in case of my mortality, it may suitably fit you towards your Loading, according to your present Course of Trading, & will most properly suit me for my second Ship's loading & such sortable goods in your second Ship, will suitably prepare me for my Summers Market, & your next forward Ships punctual & ready complyance. To Mr. Nicholas Hayward I refer the security & receiving the money payable in England as aforesaid, & therefore expect the application & complyance first to be made to him, who will by the first opportunity & timely enough give notice thereof, to make preparation accordingly, for that reason do expect to receive my first letters from you sub Cover of his, & upon reception of them, shall take care to be provided pursuant thereunto And whereas I have set the sums of money according to the weights of Tobo. I guess at, if the weights of the hhds. fall short bulking may make up the complement, or if it overdoes your matter, order must be large enough, to make an allowance. Also as to the set times of 10th. November & 10th february, for the giving the first Notes, I have set them down because of certainty, & as boundaries to the proceedings, but if the Ship arrives before either of the Times, immediately upon her Arrival she may keep doing, & if I have sufficient Tobo. ready by me, she may get her Dispatch, but if for want of Seasons or Receipts, I should not have Tobo. to make complyance, I may then have as much time given me afterwards, before I pay damage money, as I gave them employment by my notes, before the prefixed time aforesaid. Also if the Ship by contrary winds or bad weather stay longer before her Arrival than the times prefix'd, I do not expect that exactness, of three times for the Delivery of

Notes, but they may have Notes for the whole or the half, according to the time of her Stay immediately upon her Arrival. Now my Intentions being to make a full complyance of 400 hhds. at the time, & under the penaltys, in the manner & method before mentioned, for the money & goods there expressed, if I have been defective in any thing that may relate to your Interest, provided the main Intention be kept good, upon notice thereof, I shall be ready to supply that defect, or if I have been deficient in any particular relating to my own Interests, the main being kept whole, I expect the same Measure, for every particular perhaps may not occur to my memory, in a bargain of this weight & nature, but in the general, if you approve I will make a full & sure complyance, which is the needfull at present from

To Mr. Thos. Clayton   Worthy Gent: Your   W. ff.
& Doctr. Silvester Richmond
Merchts. in Liverpool

[*LB*, pp. 90-95]

1. Thomas Clayton and his partner Dr. Silvester Richmond were Liverpool merchants trading in Virginia. Clayton was probably of the same family as Jamestown attorney Thomas Clayton (see ltr. to H. Hartwell, June 19, 1681, note 2), that is, the Clayton family of Fulwood near Preston, Lancashire (see 1 V 399n).

2. Or Greenhow, a north-of-England name. He was probably also a Liverpool merchant. WF in a letter to George Brent (August 10, 1687) speaks of Mr. Greenhow's ship. The first known immigrant of the name in Virginia was John (1724-1787) who probably arrived about the middle of the eighteenth century.

3. A John Marshall was an active supporter of Bacon during the rebellion. But WF probably refers to the man of this name who in 1692 was captain of the *Olive Branch* of Liverpool, which was in the Rappahannock district at that time. P.R.O., C.O. 5/1306, pp. 105, 119 III, copies in L.C.

4. As the note in the Fitzhugh letterbook suggests, there is a reference to a rolling-house in early statutes (see Hening, *Statutes*, IV, 32-36). It was a tobacco warehouse to which inland planters, or planters without wharves, might roll (with horse and wooden tires or cart) their hogsheads. These rolling-houses were of course located along navigable streams. Jones, *The Present State of Virginia*, pp. 88, 213.

To Doctor Ralph Smith [1]

Doctr. Ralph Smith   April 29th. 1689

    At your Request I have given you Copy of this my Proposal of Trade to Mr. Clayton & Mr. Richmond of Liverpool if you find Merchants or others of your acquaintance in Bristol that are desirous to lay hold thereof, for the time therein mentioned, for three years at least, upon the terms & under the Conditions & circumstances therein specified, you must advise & direct them, to give speedy & sudden notice thereof to Mr. Nicholas Hayward Notary publick near the Exchange London, as also that they take such satisfactory care to make, according to the methods proposed, full complyance & satisfaction to him, & if before their offer, Clayton & Richmond have not proceeded therein, they then may have the opportunity of the offer, & conveniency of first complyance, & assuredly a full return, according to the methods, & pursuant to the Agreement there-therein [sic] mentioned. Thus Sir Att your request I have made this more general, but if it be any way serviceable, the end is answer'd of

To Doctr. Ralph Smith in Bristol   Sir Your   W. ff.

[*LB*, pp. 95-96]

   1. For Smith, see ltr. to him, April 22, 1686, note 1.

To Captain Robert Norman [1]

Capt. Robt. Norman   May day, 1686

   I have at your request given you Copy of this my Proposal of Trade to Mr. Clayton & Richmond of Liverpool, & if you think that you, together with yor friends & Employers may approve & accept thereof I will readily condescend & agree thereto, provided you give speedy & timely notice to Mr. Hayward as therein is directed, & take care in the performance, of the proposals & agreements therein mention'd. And whereas I direct them to Mr. Marshal, for an account of me, my concerns & abilitys for performance of my part, I must refer your friends & Employers to your own knowledge, for an account of my standing and Capacity, to undertake & go through with that affair. And do also farther direct & advise, that if you & your friends accept thereof that if it be possible, you be in this first time by the beginning of October, though it be a small matter more chargeable, for the reasons I more fully render'd you when were together &c. I having

so fully discours'd you in this affair, need add no farther than to assure
you all things here on my part, shall be punctually & fully performd

To Capt. Robt. Norman &c.   by Your W. ff.

[*LB*, p. 96]

   1. Norman is said to be of Belfast, Ireland, in ltr. to N. Hayward, May 6, 1686, below.
Perhaps he was a relative of Robert Norman of Middlesex County, Virginia, who died about
1710. 1 V 404n.

To Nicholas Hayward [1]

Mr. Nicholas Hayward   May 6th. 1686

     Sr.   The above is Duplicate of my former ₱ way of Bristol, dated
April 22nd. 1686. This comes ₱ Capt. Smith but do not think it needfull
to send Duplicate of the inclosed Instructions in that, to Doctr. Smith
about the Exchange therein mention'd, because if that should miscarry
Doctor Smith who is in the same bottom cannot be safe, & consequently
incapacitated to carry it on, but if it should come safe to your hands, I
am well assured of your kindness. The inclosed being a copy of a letter to
Mr. Clayton & Doctr. Richmond of Liverpool, about trade speaks its own
business, & your friendship & kindness, largely expressed and as largely
manifested, embolden me to add this trouble to your former, intreating
you to secure the money therein mention'd for me, if they accept the
proposal, & to give me timely & speedy notice thereof by the first Ships, &
if Ships should not come time enough into our River, by directing letters
for me to be left at Mr. Jno. Buckner's [2] Clerk of Gloucester County in
York River, or to Collo. William Diggs in St. Mary's in Maryland,[3] who
will give them a quick conveyance to my hand & are so conveniently seated
that letters coming into any part of Virginia or Maryland, will suddenly
fall into their hands, or if you know any Merchants in London, will accept
of the terms, I will assuredly make complyance, or if you or they doubt
of my Abilitys for performance, Capt. Thos. Smith or his Mate Burnham [4]
are able to give satisfaction therein. Sr. I have already shewed it to two
Traders here, Mr. Ralph Smith of Bristol, & Capt. Robert Norman of
Belfast in Ireland,[5] who desired Copys thereof, & am verily persuaded

their owners & employers will comply therewith, which Copys I gave them & particular letters (the Copys whereof I have here inclosed sent you) to give a relation to them, although the Original Design was to Clayton & Richmond. Sr. If either Clayton or Richmond, or any of the above mention'd agree to it, or any Merchants in London, will accept thereof, I wholly refer myself to you for the securing the money, out of which I desire you to reimburse your self, for your care, charge & trouble of it the Trade does not take, I shall take effectual care to reimburse your charge, & make you full satisfaction for your trouble, & must likewise thankfully acknowledge it as a farther Addition, to your accumulated favours done to

To Mr. Nichs. Hayward   Sr. Your   W. ff.

[*LB*, pp. 96-98]

1. For Hayward, see ltr. to Samuel Hayward, June 3, 1684, note 2.
2. For Buckner, see ltr. to him, Dec. 3, 1681, note 1.
3. William Digges (d. 1698) of a distinguished English and American family, was a picturesque figure. J.P., captain of horse, sheriff of York County, Virginia, in the 1670's as a bold loyalist during Bacon's Rebellion he had cut off one of the fingers of the rebel Hansford in hand-to-hand fighting. Soon after 1679 he moved to Charles County, Maryland. Several years after the date of the present letter (see Introduction) WF and Digges were accused together of Jacobinism in Maryland. 5 V 68; 9 V 30; 10 V 378; 19 V 357-58; 1 W(1) 141; *Exec. Journ. Council Col. Va.,* I, 282; *Cal. St. Papers, Col., Am. & W.I., 1693-1696,* Item 643.
4. For Smith, see ltrs. to J. Cooper, March 10, 1682/83, note 2, and May 18, 1868, note 2. For Burnham, see ltr. to Cooper, May 18, 1685, note 7.
5. For Ralph Smith, see ltr. to him, April 22, 1686, note 1; for Norman, see ltr. to him, May Day, 1686, note 1.

To Henry Fitzhugh [1]

Dearest Brother   May 6th. 1686.

The above is Duplicate of my former ℔ way of Bristol dated April 22nd. [seven words inked out by writer], what I have more to add now is to tell you, that there will be £20 in Mr. Cooper's hands left to your discretion, to supply my Mother's present wants, & to help fit out my Sister for her Voyage hither,[2] or if she will not come, to assist her in her necessitys there, & to tell you that's all the money I have in England, or can at present command there, please to tell them it is not so much as my desires are, to contribute to their relief, but the whole of what I can at present spare. Also I would desire you to shew them this letter, which will give satisfaction, in which I have omitted writing to them, & save me the trouble of being more particular in theirs. I know nothing that I have farther to add, save the full assurance that I am

To Mr. Henry Fitzhugh &c   Your   W. ff.

[*LB*, p. 98]

    1. For Henry Fitzhugh, see ltr. to him, April 22, 1686, note 1, and other letters to him.
    2. For Dorothy and Mrs. Mary Fitzhugh, see ltr. to H. Fitzhugh, April 22, 1686, notes 2 and 6.

To Miss Dorothy Fitzhugh [1]

Dear Sister   May 6th. 1686

    The above is Copy of my former sent by way of Bristol 22nd. April. I have been so large with my brother, & intreated him to shew you my letter which I am confident he will, that I need not be more particular, than only to tell you that I have ordered him about £20 to be disposed to my mother's & your use, which is all the money I have in England, & would desire you, that if you intend in hither, as I hope & wish you will, that you would prepare to come away in the very first Ships that comes into this River, by which means you may promise to your self a prosperous & quick passage, & make me the sooner happy, in the enjoyment of your good company. Mr. Nicholas Hayward near the Exchange London, & Mr. Jno. Cooper will direct you to a good Ship & a civil Master, if you apply yourself to them, they being my very good friends. And Mr. Hayward will also take effectual care, to send your letter to me, if you deliver them to him, with all speed & expedition, & sooner & safer than you can possibly yourself, therefore would have you deliver what letters you send me to him, Pray convey the inclosed away to my Mother with all expedition, & present my duty to her, & true love & respects to all friends else there, so hoping both to hear from you & see you too, by the first Ships next year   I have now no more to tell you, but to give you this assurance, you shall always find me

To Mrs. Dorothy Fitzhugh   Dear Sister Your   W. ff.

[Pencilled addition in more modern hand:] She afterwards married Doctor Rolf Smith, March 5 1687

[*LB*, pp. 98-99]

1. For Dorothy Fitzhugh, see ltrs. to her above, and to H. Fitzhugh, April 22, 1686, note 2.

To John Cooper [1]

Mr. Jno. Cooper   May 6th. 1686

Sr.   The above is Copy of my former ⅌ via Bristol bearing date 22nd. April last, & do intend this ⅌ Capt. Smith,[2] if he be not gone before I get it down to him. In my former I sent you bills of Exchange & in this send you the second bills, & do think they are so good they will be punctually paid, I have likewise advised in my former letter, to deliver to my brother what money of mine he calls for without limitation, [three and one-half lines inked out in the original hand], I likewise in my former acquainted you that I thought I should consign you some Tobo., but Smith's going away so suddenly hinders that Design, though now I have the Tobo. lying ready by me, & doubt it too late to get freight in any other Londoner for the same, also more bills I have to send, but cannot get them time enough to send by this conveniency, but by next which will be by way of Liverpool, you may expect another, letter, with other bills of Exchange inclosed therein   It not being long before they will sail, I have now no farther to add, than to assure you I am

To. Mr. Jno. Cooper Mercht.   Sr. Your   W. ff.
in London

[*LB*, pp. 99-100]

1. For John Cooper, see ltr. to him, April 4, 1681, note 1.
2. Captain Thomas Smith. See ltrs. to Cooper, March 10, 1682/83, note 2, and May 18, 1685, note 2.

To Nicholas Hayward [1]

Mr. Nicholas Hayward   May 20th. 1686

I have been so often troublesome to you this year, & perhaps impertinently too, about my proposed Exchange, & my offers of Trade, of both which I hope you have already, & will by this receive Duplicates This comes to return you my Cordial thanks for your Almanack, & which is of greater moment, a continued assurance of your constant friendship & kindness, intimated in your Brother Sam's letter, which I as joyfully please myself with, as the most miserly Usurer in the enjoyment of his full bags, & with the same propensity shall endeavour the continuance, as he does his adored golden Mammon. Also in the said letter, you seem to have an inclination, of disposing your new purchase in my Neighbourhood, to some french Hugonots.[2] If your Intentions therein be as well led by charity to help the distressed, as ⅌ advantage to make profit of your Purchase, I believe it may lay in my power, to answer both or either of them for if you are designed for Sale, if you please to give me the offer, & to set your lowest price, I will accept, & make you punctual & good payment either in money or Tobo. And for the french Protestants, I have convenient & good Land enough, to seat 150 or 200 familys, upon one Dividend, wch. contains 21996 Acres, which I will either sell them in fee, at £7 sterling for every hundred acres, or else lease it to them for three lives, paying 20 sh: ⅌ annum for every hundred Acres, & they may have the liberty, of renewing one two or three lives at any time, paying for each life to be renewed, one years Rent, without demanding any fine or other Consideration for their first purchase, & will engage to find them with Corn & meat for the first year, meat at 12/6 ⅌ hundred & corn at 2/6 ⅌ bushel for as many soever as comes in, if it be three or four hundred people & all other necessarys for their money at the Country market price. The Land I offer to sell or lease[3] is scituate in this County, lyes within a mile & half of Potomack River, & of two bold navigable creeks, is principal good Land, & is more proper for french men, because more naturally inclined to Vines than yours or any about our Neighbourhood, & will engage to naturalize every Soul of them at £3 sterling ⅌ head, without any more or other manner of charge, or trouble to them, whereby the heirs will be capacitated to inherit the father's purchase. Sr. I am more afraid of falling upon Scylla to avoid Charybdis, that is, of one side, if I should endeavour to be perspicuous, I should be too impertinent & troublesome, & if I should be very short I doubt obscurity, therefore I'll rather venture a breach of good manners, & a trespass upon your patience (which your repeated letter manifests to be soon tired,) by repetitions, rather than hazard an obscurity in my propositions & intentions, for whereas I have said if so many familys comes, my meaning is, let few or many familys come, not exceeding that number, I am provided, & will certainly seat them, & provide for them upon the Conditions expressed. And if I lease for three lives my meaning is, they shall pay no fine or Purchase, but only their annual Rent, also one man may have 2, 3, 4 or 500 Acres, or as many hundred as he pleases, paying for each hundred 20 sh: annually, & renewing 1, 2, or 3 lives at any time for the full of the yearly rent. Sr. If these Offers be acceptable or pleasing to the frenchmen, or any other of your friends, it will be doubly advantageous to me, first by meeting with an opportunity to serve you through your friends, & secondly, by profitably either selling or tenementing my Land, which till so done, is rather a charge than profit. Sr. What I have farther to add about the proposal of Trade is, that I do not desire to have the money, till they have an assurance of the receipts of their Tobo., provided you shall have such Security, as you shall like for the payment, then also to acquaint you that if more than one should accept of the offer, I am ready & in a capacity, to comply with two Ships forward & latter, that is for eight hundred hhds. in the whole, not doubting but to have pretty near that quantity out of my own stock, & to advise to accept of the first, if you find them fully responsible. Sr. The reason of the repetition of this offer of Exchange, contrary to my Intentions as intimated in my former is occasioned, because our continual news hither, is of higher & greater dissatisfactions, amongst that discontented whiggish Party,[4] & being something acquainted with the disposition of the men, by the knowledge of two I here met with, that parted with such Estates as in mine mentioned, merely upon Discontents, & were bound for Pensylvania, who heartily wished they had had Intimations & Assurance of such a change as I proposed, for they are now throughly sensible, all their money for their Sale, & as much again, cannot settle them in this Condition, as I have offered to Estate any one in, besides the hardships & hazards, they must necessarily go through, that begin a new Settlement, & the losses & troubles they must sustain, before its brought to any maturity or perfection. Sr. In your two former I have desired your assistance, if in the Course of your business, you should meet with such an opportunity which the Criticalness of these times gives me no occasion to despair of, & your universal acquaintance, gained by your skilfull & active Dexterity in your publick Concerns, unites my wishes into some hopes of success, (the relations of those two Pensylvanians I before mentioned assuring me divers were offering to Sale, & preparing for a Remove) which if it should happen would not only bring with it, that great satisfaction of enjoying my native Country comforts & enjoyments, but a large opportunity to retalliate you many signal favours, which this Distance will allow me only the liberty of a gratefull and thankfull acknowledgement. Sr. If understanding a mans self when present, to have been too troublesome, causes a sudden call of the spirits from the heart to the face, by its blushing shews a sence of its guilt, the same thing though absent, this abrupt conclusion will shew you has possess'd

To Mr. Nichs. Hayward　　　　　　Sr. Your W. ff.

P:S: Just as I am writing comes the Commission of the Peace for our County, wherein I find your Brother Sam: a Quorum Justice therein, according to his worth & deserts, but with an assurance of his Clerk's place [5]

[*LB*, pp. 100-3]

1. For Nicholas and Samuel Hayward, see ltr. to Samuel Hayward, June 3, 1684, notes 1 and 2.
2. Although this project of settling French Protestants on Hayward's land probably may originally have been designed for the smaller tract owned by Hayward (ltr. to Nicholas Hayward, April 22, 1686, note 2), the idea was to develop into the famous "Brenton" project of the next year, surely under way during the autumn of 1686. In January 1686/87 the Proprietor made a grant of thirty thousand acres in upper Stafford (now Prince William) to Nicholas Hayward and his partners Robert Bristow, Richard Foote, and George Brent, and on July 13, 1687, it was recorded in Stafford Court. The revocation of the Edict of Nantes (1686) had caused an influx into England of Protestant refugees. Hayward and his associates hoped to encourage them to settle on lands in Stafford. Perhaps he originally had in mind the smaller property he owned already; but his ideas and plans quickly developed into the purchase of the "Brenton" tract for this specific purpose.
   In the winter of 1686/87, a Frenchman named Durand, who visited "Brenton" and WF in his search for suitable lands for himself and his compatriots, seems to have been approached by one of Hayward's associates then in Virginia and to have found the "Brenton" project already organized at about the exact date when it was getting its official patent or recognition from the Proprietor. When Durand returned to Europe, he published in 1687 at the Hague an account of his American adventures, including as an appendix Nicholas Hayward's "Propositions for Virginia," a description of "Brenton" and the conditions for purchase and settlement. See Gilbert Chinard, ed., *A Huguenot Exile in Virginia; or, Voyages of a Frenchman Exiled for His Religion with a Description of Virginia and Maryland* (New York, 1934); Harrison, *Landmarks*, I, 177-96, and *Va. Land Grants*, pp. 70-74; *Prince Wm. WPA*, pp. 19-21 (which locates the "Brenton" property fairly exactly); Patricia H. Menk, "Notes on Some Early Huguenot Settlements in Virginia," 52 V 194-96.
   3. This land, the tract called after 1724 "Ravensworth," was in upper Stafford near the "Brenton" property. WF's tract had originally become his by title in 1685, had been reentered in 1686, and reconfirmed to him by the Proprietor while he and Brent were agents in 1694. See Harrison, *Landmarks*, I, 187. For more of the terms offered by WF to prospective settlers, see the ltrs. below.

4. WF is of course noting the growing unrest in England which would lead eventually to the Revolution of 1688. Though he would now like to capitalize on the English Whigs' discontent by exchanging property with them, for some time he had been growing disgusted with what he considered Whiggish persecution of himself in Virginia. Perhaps he believed everybody might be satisfied by an exchange, for he feared the Whigs were becoming strong in the colony. During late 1685 and early 1686 he had lost a disputed election to the House of Burgesses and been accused of embezzlement for receiving tobacco-salary when "unduly elected" and for demanding and receiving tobacco revenues, as Potomac garrison "provider," beyond his due and right. Though nothing came of these charges of embezzlement, as noted in the Introduction above, WF was for the time disgusted with local politics. *Journals H.B. 1659/60-1693*, p. liii; *Cal. St. Papers, Col., Am. & W.I. 1685-1688*, Items 482, 963, 1729; 5 V 50; Effingham Papers, L.C.

5. The Commission, or body, of justices of a county court nominated at least four of their number as a quorum. One of this inner body and three other justices constituted a valid court. The first named of the quorum was usually the presiding justice (an office held by WF for many years) and the others in order named succeeded in his absence. Thus there was considerable prestige attached to Samuel Hayward's being a quorum justice. His holding this and the clerk's place at the same time was apparently unusual.

To Captain Henry Fitzhugh [1]

Dear Brother   January 30th. 1686/7

If the hearing of your health & welfare gave me such sentiments, as you perceived ℔ my last, the receipt of your's this year, must be sure to admit of reciprocal joys, if you will not admit them exceeded, your picture would have been mighty acceptable, & pleasing to me in your absence, but your Company that is the original according to your own expression, would be infinitely more acceptable & pleasant, would opportunity & business admit it, but at these years & with no setleder fortunes, than we are both at present endued with, will not admit an absence, where opportunity or business calls for one's immediate presence, for in my Opinion none under the degree of a settled annual income, which can be advantageously managed in their absence, can give that Regency & power to fancy & delight, as to neglect Interest or their particular concerns, purposely for a Visit, I do not premise this, either to deter or hinder you from your Intentions, & I am sure you cannot imagine, I would argue against my own height of pleasure & delight, which would be certainly in the pleasant enjoyment of your most desired company, provided it would quadrate with your Interest, & conveniently suite your Concerns. I heartily thank you for your intended, & your Lady's real presents to my wife, son & daughter, & that Steel Seal to myself, had she writ it had been our Coat of arms, I should have allowed the mistake not esteeming her conversant in Heraldry, or skilfull in Coats of Arms, & for your writing it to be so, I must interpret it either to Credulity or mistake [2] I could wish with all my heart, I were able to supply your necessitys or occasions, with twice the sum proposed, without puting you to the trouble or charge of procuring or bringing in servants in return thereof, but Tobo. is this year so low, that I cannot raise one penny of money from it, having now near three hundred hhds. by me, & if I would now let them go all, to procure such a Sum as you propose, I believe I should be hard put to it to obtain it. Last year when Tobo. was a Commodity, I could more easily have procured £100 than this year £10. I understand by my Sister that your Interest and friends are great at Court, by which & their means, I might have the opportunity of seeing, you, & vast advantage to your self, by your coming, if you could get to be Commander of one of the King's Ships, that are appointed to attend here, all profits might fairly be worth to you a thousand pound sterling a year, without being at two pence expence, these two that we have now Allen & Crofts,[3] one is a Sott & the other is a fool, and yet they clear better than 500£ str. a year, one is already in disfavour with our Governor, & the other is falling into it, if you could lay hold of such an advantage, or some that by my next I shall propose to you, you would at once give me the joyfull opportunity of seeing you, & the most acceptable assurance of your future gentile & comfortable being.   I thank God I am plentifully supplyed with Servants of all Conditions, to serve me in all my occasions, therefore would not have you put yourself to the charge or trouble, of procuring or sending me any in, well knowing it lies out of the course of your business & Concerns. But again as I said last year, I should be heartily glad of your Picture, & our Coat of Arms, fairly & rightly drawn, not as on the Steel Seal that came here, if you cannot find an advantageous Opportunity of shewing me the Original.   Since my last God has been pleased to bless me with one Son which not long since was christen'd by the name of Henry.[4] We live here very plentifully without money, & now Tobo. is low I shall be very hard put to it, to purchase £10 for to supply our Mother, which I fully resolve, if possibly to be procured, but could hardly with all my Tobo., & anything I could part with except Negroes, supply you with the sum you proposed, which had I it at Command, should be as readily your's as it is mine. My wife gives here due respects to your self & Lady, & assures your selves both of the same from

To Capt. Henry Fitzhugh,   Dr. Brother Your   W. ff.
at the Pall Mall&c.

[LB, pp. 103-5]

1. For Henry Fitzhugh, see ltr. to him, April 22, 1686, note 1.

2. What were the proper arms for the Virginia Fitzhughs has been by no means clear, for WF confused the situation. The arms and crest WF insisted on were those of the old Barons Fitzhugh of "Ravensworth." It is quite clear that WF and his descendants in the next several generations accepted this because, in addition to WF's letters, (1) the silver sugar bowl, believed to have been WF's own and bearing his name and date of marriage (now owned by Eppa Hunton, IV, a descendant), bears this arms in full; (2) the two saltcellars (owned by Mrs. Robert H. Stevenson, a descendant), allegedly WF's own, bear this crest; (3) the bookplate of the Fitzhughs (eighteenth- or nineteenth-century copy in Va. Hist. Soc.) bears this arms; (4) later generations (at least after 1724) used the name "Ravensworth" for the upper Stafford plantation. The arms are described in 7 V 196-99 as: *Az, three chevrons interlaced in base or, a Chef or.* WF in ltr. to Hayward of June 8, 1688, describes the arms as "A field of azure three chearonells, brased in the base of Excocheon & a Chief Or."

The latest genealogical writer on the subject, however, the Reverend Victor C. A. FitzHugh of Yorkshire (40 V 187), states positively that there was no connection between this family and the Barons of Ravensworth (who are now, incidentally, completely extinct) but that the proper arms (reproduced 40 V 189) are those registered and owned in a painting by WF's cousin William Fitzhugh the London stationer: "Quarterly, 1 and 4 ermine, on a chief gules, three martlets or (Fitzhugh). 2 and 3 argent three chevrons sable each charged with a bezant." The motto here is "In Moderation placing all My Glory" instead of the "Pro Patria Semper" of the Virginia Fitzhughs' bookplate. The Reverend Mr. FitzHugh had the arms registered after careful tracing and documentation on January 17, 1930. William Fitzhugh the stationer had "The Arms from a tablet in Oyl & hanging in Mr. Fitzhugh's house." The Reverend Mr. FitzHugh also seems to be supported by the fact that WF's older brother Henry disagreed as to the family's proper arms, though we do not know what arms Henry did think proper.

As Mr. J. P. Brooke-Little, Bluemantle Pursuivant of Arms of the College of Arms, has recently pointed out to the editor, these latter are the arms of the Fitzhughs of Wilden in Bedfordshire (the Reverend Mr. FitzHugh also pointed this out). Mr. Brooke-Little agrees entirely with the Reverend Mr. FitzHugh's findings: the latter are the proper arms for the Virginia Fitzhughs, and WF was in error. Mr. Brooke-Little points out that WF's error may have arisen from simple ignorance of heraldry, but, more likely, from some ancient family tradition that his Fitzhugh family were descended from the Barons Fitzhugh, though they knew that the relationship had not been proved. The insistence on the use of the former arms and the name "Ravensworth" in another generation of Virginia Fitzhughs would seem to indicate that such a tradition existed. William Fitzhugh's usual meticulousness and scholarship in legal matters would seem likely to have carried over into heraldry, especially in an age when arms-bearing was so important socially.

3. Apparently Captain John Crofts, commander of H.M.S. *Deptford* (a ketch) was the sot. He quarreled with his wife and attacked her with drawn sword. He was drowned eventually (after 1687) in a squall in Chesapeake Bay. Captain Thomas Allen, apparently the "fool," was commander of H.M.S. *Quaker* (also a ketch). He arrived in Virginia in June, 1684, with his mistress or "ward" aboard his ship, and he kept her there. She was delivered of a son shortly before Feb. 14, 1688, upon which event Allen sent Governor Effingham word that he had a son and heir and christened the child with great solemnity. He was very unpopular in both Virginia and Maryland. Effingham despised both men and regularly sent complaints of their misbehavior to the Lords of Trade and the Plantations. Both defied the Governor's authority. WF as a friend of the Governor and a representative of civil power as opposed to military could hardly fail to share Effingham's view. Bruce, *Inst. Hist. Va.*, II, 181; *Exec. Journ. Council Col. Va.*, I, *passim*; *Cal. St. Papers, Col., Am. & W.I.*, *1681-1685* and *1685-1688*, *passim*.

4. Thus this boy, WF's second son to grow to maturity, was born January 15, 1686/87. It was quite clearly this son, and not William, who was sent to England to study in 1698 (see ltr. to George Mason, July 21, 1698). That WF had a special fondness for this son may be indicated by the fact that he first sent him to live with and be educated by a French clergyman in Virginia and then to England for further schooling, that he left him half his study of books, and that he left him half the great "Ravensworth" tract and much more. Henry was high sheriff of Stafford in 1715 and burgess in 1736. His son Thomas built "Boscobel," and it is probably by Thomas that this letterbook was preserved. It may have been copied at Henry's order. This son of WF was known as "blind Henry," and his portrait (probably done from life in 1751) by Hesselius does appear to indicate a squint or cast in one eye. Jonathan Boucher

in 1765 said, in pointing out traits of various American families, that all the Fitzhughs had weak eyes (ltr. of Mr. George H. S. King of Fredericksburg, Va., to Va. Hist. Soc., Nov. 2, 1955). Mr. King says that he has seen Henry's prayer book, with his name on it, in very large type (though one may wonder if this was not a conventional prayer book such as might be used by lay readers or clergy during services). For Henry, see 7 V 317-19; *Prince Wm. WPA*, p. 152; Eubank, *Touring Historyland*, p. 16.

To John Cooper [1]

Mr. Jno. Cooper   June 1st. 1685

In my two former have given you account of the receipt of your two letters this year, & there take notice, that you have not sent me any accot. of the Sales of my Tobo. receiv'd, of my money of Mrs. Bland,[2] nor take any notice of those things, I sent for last year, I hope next year you will mend it. I believe I shall consign you next year thirty or forty hhds., most or all of it will be sweetscented, & of my own Crops, but I desire you to give me an account by the first, whether Oroonoko or sweetscented, yields the best price there, for accordingly I can order my Shiping & my Sales here, for I shall have very good of both sorts at my own Plantations. I expect to hear from you by the first Conveniency. I desire you to take care of the Delivery of the inclosed: I have only in my former sent for 100lb. of Sun dryed Sugar, & about 60 or 80lb. of powdered Sugar. I have no occasion to add farther now, for I will take care for the future, not to overburden my Accot. but to keep a due factoridge

To. Mr. Jno. Cooper   Sr. Your   W. ff.
Mercht. in London

[*LB*, pp. 105-6]

1. For Cooper, see ltr. to him, April 4, 1681, note 1.
2. For WF's client Mrs. Bland, see ltr. to him, June 5, 1682, note 1, etc.

To John Cooper[1]

Mr. Jno. Cooper   April 22nd. 1686

Sr. I received your several letters, that by Chas. Partis[2] with the account of the barrel of sugar, & accot. Currant which came well to hand. also therein take notice of your care & kindness of the Delivery of the inclosed letters to you last year, together wt. answer returned in your's this year, for which I heartily thank you. Missing the conveniency of writing to you by Harris,[3] I take this first opportunity by way of Bristol to acquaint you that my Consignments if any, will be very small this year, this late Act scared us, & the goodness of the Commodity, induced me to sell in the Country, having an allowance of 16 .. 3d. ℔ Cent for 150 hhds. & for what else I sold 13 .. 6 ℔ Cent in goods sortable, & well bought. By Capt. Smith[4] I shall be larger, & do hope if he makes another turn up this River with his Sloop this Voyage, to ship in him 10 or 12 hhds., of very fair & bright large Oronoko Tobo., which from the beginning I designed for shipping, knowing it to be such Tobo. as I might venture a market upon, but my Plantation its made upon is so far above me, & consequently out of my Kenn, that they have not got it ready. Here inclosed you'll find two bills of Exchange which please to receive for my use. In my inclosed letter to my brother, which I desire you to take care to deliver, I have order'd him to call for such money of mine in your hands, without limitation, as his occasions require, which please to let him have though it be the last penny of my former ballance, & the money now sent when receiv'd. ℔ Capt. Smith I shall send you Duplicates of these & I do think some other bills, wherein I shall be fuller, as well in the Disposal of what money I shall then send as in other concerns. And now Sir have only to thank you for your kindness, & expence in drinking my health there, as your letter intimates for the first, I must gratefully acknowledge the favour, & for the latter desire you to take 20 shill: out of my money, either to reimburse your former expences, or else to drink out with my brother when you see him next, & deliver him this inclosed letter. Just now the weather promises a season, if so I shall certainly consign yor. Tobo. ℔ Capt. Smith, till whose Arrival I refer you, & conclude myself

To. Mr. Jno. Cooper   Your W. ff.
Mercht. in London &c.

[*LB*, pp. 106-7]

1. For Cooper, see ltr. to him, April 4, 1681, note 1.

2. For Partis, a ship captain, see ltr. to Francis Partis, May 31, 1681, note 1, etc.

3. Presumably Captain Martin Harris, commander of the *Gerard* of London. See ltr. to Cooper, March 10, 1682/83, note 4, and ltrs. below.

4. Presumably Captain Thomas Smith of the *Constant* of London. See ltr. to Cooper, March 10, 1682/83, note 2.

To Mrs. Mary Fitzhugh [1]

Dear Mother   January 30th. 1687

Your kind religious letter came in the welcome company of my dear Sister, the one gave me much satisfaction, in seeing your religious Conduct & stedfast Patience, in bearing up against the storms of Affliction, that for this long time have & do still impend you, & taking the right sence & measures of them, in esteeming them to be God's Rods, with which chastisements he means to draw you nearer to himself for afflictions mature & ripen the soul for heaven. The other that is the Society of my Sister, was & still is extremely pleasing, & I hope to her satisfaction, for she shall want nothing, that lyes in my power, to serve her as long as she stays with me, & no manner of countenance & encouragement, if any Overtures happen of her advancement. What entertainment she met with at her coming, receives here, & is like to continue she herself can best & most properly tell you. I am sorry to hear so ill a Character of so dear a Brother, & withal to find my expectations so soon disappointed, not only in his own comfortable & gentile Subsistence, but in his assisting you in your low & calamitous Condition. I do design £10 which by the next Ships if I can possibly picture, you may assuredly expect, & if can by any means be procured, I will order it by way of Coz Harris [2] or Coz Wm. Fitzhugh,[3] the reason that I do not appoint it now, & the difficulty this year to procure money, & all other particulars I refer you to my Sister's more particular relation. The great God of Heaven & earth bless, preserve, & keep you is the daily prayers of

To. Mrs. Mary Fitzhugh   Your   W. ff.

[*LB*, pp. 107-8]

1. For WF's mother Mary King Fitzhugh, see ltr. to Henry Fitzhugh, April 22, 1686, note 6, and subsequent ltrs. to Mrs. Fitzhugh herself.

2. Thomas Harris, haberdasher in London, as WF's later letters show.

3. The stationer of London, through whom WF first got contact with his immediate family again. See ltr. to him, May 18, 1685, note 1.

To William Fitzhugh [1]

Most kind Cousin   January 30th. 1686/7

Your very acceptable letters came safe to my hands, the last with the welcome of my Sister, who had a very prosperous & successfull Voyage. I truly condole your self in the sudden death of your two sweet Babes, which loss is easily & cheerfully born, if natural affection be laid aside, & we truly consider as we ought, that they have changed a troublesome & uncertain terrestrial being, for a certain & happy Celestial habitation, & you have this happiness continually to joy you, that you have of your Offspring in Heaven, continually singing Hallelujah's to the most highest, their Regeneration in Baptism washing off all Original Sin, & their fewness of years excusing them from all wilfull & obstinate sins. I as heartily also congratulate the joyfull welcome of your new born Guest, and wish that as he grows in years, he may grow in grace, truly to serve his God, & then without question you his Parents will find him abound with all dutifull observance, & due Obedience. Sr. Your kind offers of friendship & kindness, I heartily accept & thankfully acknowledge, & must give this assurance, that I shall gladly receive, & readily observe any thing, you shall propose in my power to serve you who am, &c   Please to give the inclosed to my Uncle Fitzhugh,[2] & my Aunt Porter [3] a speedy conveyance

To Mr. Willm. Fitzhugh Stationer   Your   W. ff.

[*LB*, pp. 108-9]

1. For William Fitzhugh the stationer, see ltr. to him, May 18, 1685, note 1, and the ltr. to Mary Fitzhugh, Jan. 30, 1686/87, note 3, just above.

2. Presumably the stationer's father Robert, of "the Greenhouse in Bedford." See ltr. to him of this same date just below.

3. She was presumably a daughter of WF's grandfather William Fitzhugh, and of course sister of WF's father Henry, though she may have been WF's mother's sister. 7 V 196-99, 317-19, 425-27.

To [Thomas] Harris [1]

Cousin Harris   January 30th. 1686/7

Your extraordinary civility & kindness to all your Wives Relations & particularly to my Sister, who is now with me, not only invites but obliges me to return you my heartyest thanks, & to desire as near an acquaintance & Communication as this Distance will admit of for kind husbands may be sometimes met with, but to meet with a Concatenation of an Indulgent Husband, an obliging nature, and generous temper in one person is very rare, all which continually Circulate in all your Actions & proceedings, therefore I shall not only Court your Converse, as a Relation, but your intimacy as a friend, & please to think of any Service, wherein I may demonstrate myself to be

Your   W. ff.

Pray give my kind respects to your good wife my Cousin [2]

[LB, p. 109]

1. This is Thomas Harris, haberdasher, who married a cousin of WF, as we note below in ltr. to N. Hayward, July 18, 1687, and in ltr. to Harris of April 5, 1687.
2. Probably a sister of William Fitzhugh the stationer, though there are other possibilities.

To Mrs. Margaret Porter [1]

Dear Aunt   January 30th. 1686/7

My Sisters safe Arrival to me, amongst other my relations, more particularly mentions your most kind remembrance of me, for which reason I take this opportunity to return you my humble thanks for the same, & to assure you that if the Distance would admit, or business permit, I would personally pay you those respects your near Relation to me requires, or your kind remembrance of me Commands. However please to accept the tender of my most due respects, to your self & good husband from

To. Mrs. Margaret Porter &c.   Your   W. ff.

[*LB*, p. 109]

1. She is mentioned in other letters. See ltr. to William Fitzhugh the stationer, Jan. 30, 1686/87, note 3.

To Robert Fitzhugh [1]

Most worthy Uncle   January 30th. 1686/7

Your's under Cover of my Cousin Wm. Fitzhugh came safe to my hand, which I joyfully received, having thereby a full & sure Confirmation, of your and my Aunts health & welfare, which I pray God continue in it you give me the satisfactory account, although not of your wealthy, yet of your contented Condition, which in my opinion far exceeds the other, for its the mark that all drive at, from the Monarch on the Throne, to the lowest Tradesman, without which the Riches of Croesus are not satisfactory, & with it the lowest Degree passes his time away here pleasantly. Sr. My Condition here is in a very equal temper, I neither abound nor want, as I live in, So I have a share of the Government, having for these eight or nine years last past served as the Representative of our County in our Parliament here, with some Reputation in the House, & a full Content to my County I served for. I have now been married this thirteen years, in which time God hath blessed me with six dear Pledges of Conjugall Affections, two sons one daughter I am well assured are Angels in Heaven, & the same quantity & of like quality I now enjoy to my great comfort & satisfaction. My Sister Margaret hath been dead these ten years, lived but poorly, hath left one Daughter behind her, who last year was with me about six months & then left me.[2] I have been thus particular Sir, in answer to your's in hopes it may invite you, to write me again next year there's no greater satisfaction to me in this world than to hear of & receive letters from my Relations & friends. I hope this will find yourself & my

Aunt in the same health tranquillity & content, as that from your self to
me intimates, which assure yourself is the hearty prayers of

To Mr. Robt. Fitzhugh at the   Your.   W. ff.
Greenhouse in Bedford

[*LB*, p. 110]

1. The youngest son of William Fitzhugh of Bedford and younger brother of WF's
father, Henry. Presumably he was the Robert Fitzhugh who was mayor of Bedford from
1656 to 1657, then Alderman (as past mayors always were), and perhaps mayor again in 1679.
He was on the list of Aldermen at the time of his death in 1689. The "Greenhouse" appears
to be something of a mystery. The market house on the green at Elstow, a village near Bedford,
was known as the Green House. It was probably never a dwelling house. There is a small
opening in Bedford known as St. Peter's green. But that is as far as Bedford officials can go.
Ltrs. to the editor from Mr. G. F. Simmonds, Town Clerk, Bedford, May 9, 1958, and from
Miss Joyce Godber, County Archivist, June 26, 1958.

2. Unidentified, though all likely clues have been followed. She was baptized Nov. 12,
1640, at St. Paul's in Bedford. Since WF in his will mentions lands he might become heir to
in Maryland, she may have lived in that colony. She probably had some influence on WF's
emigration to America. 7 V 196-99, 317-19.

To Nicholas Hayward [1]

Worthy Sir   January 30th. 1686/7

Having before me your several kind & Courteous letters, by way of
Gloucester, Pensux & Burnham,[2] I am obliged to return you my hearty
thanks, & acknowledgement for the one part, & retribution for your
trouble & charge on the other part, & do fully agree with you in your
Philosophical sentiments of ye. Simpathy of absent friends, as you in
Laconick expression aptly deliver in your last, for which reason the first
Inventer of letters deserves eternal Commendations, by whose means I
have not only the opportunity, of the first acquaintance with so worthy &
judicious a friend, but a continued Communication & Society, which I as
really enjoy, whilst I am reading your most endearing letters, or answering
them, as if happily present with you   Sr. As I said last year am heartily
glad of the continuance of your purchase, & earnestly wish you both profit
& success therein, & hope for an opportunity, that I may do you service,
both in the Confirmaon. of your Title, & Settlement upon the same, as
yet I know of nothing done, your Brother Captt. Brent & Mr. Massey, told

me of your desire of surveying, having a draught of the said Survey, &
settling upon two of the most convenient places of the Dividend,[3] this I
have been told of, but by none consulted with, neither do I know the
particular directions therein. I should think my self unworthy & ungratefull, if I had stuck at any trouble, or stop at any reasonable charge, would
you communicate your desires & intentions, having myself receiv'd from
you, such obliging favours & been these two years not only chargeable but
troublesome to you. And perhaps my Vicinity together with conveniency
of my Servants, always ready at hand, may give me a greater opportunity
of doing you Service therein, than any you have hither to write to you, I
shall hope & expect your commands, which shall no sooner arrive, than
they shall be readily obeyed. Now Sr. my experience in Concerns of this
Country, especially in building & settling plantations, prompts me to offer
my advice, having had sufficient trial in those affairs, at the expence of
almost three hundred thousand pounds of Tobo. I shall propose no other
than what I would follow my self, that is, if you design this land to settle,
a child of your own or near kinsman, for whom it is supposed you would
build a very good house, not only for their comfortable but creditable
accomodations, the best methods to be pursued therein is, to get a Carpenter & Bricklayer Servants, & send them in here to serve 4 or five years,
in which time of their Service, they might reasonably build a substantial
good house, at least, if not brick walls & well plaister'd, & earn money
enough besides in their said time, at spare times from your work, having
so long a time to do it in, as will purchase plank, nails & other materials, &
supply them with necessarys during their servitude, or if you design to
settle Tenants on it, as your letter purports, in my opinion its needless
for you to be at the charge of building for their accomodations, if you
intend any time, if it is but seven years, for there's several may be found
that for a seven year's Lease, will build themselves a convenient dwelling
& other necessary houses, & be obliged at the expiration of their time, to
leave all in good repair, but if you at your own charge should build an
ordinary Virginia house, it will be some Charge, & no profit, & at the expiration of your tenants time, the plantation will not be in better order,
than the way before proposed. But if you design only to let it from year
to year, not knowing how soon you may have occasion to make use thereof,
then I say its necessary for you to build yourself because no Tennant will
be oblig'd to build, that is but Tennant at Will or from year to year only.
But should not advise to build either a great, or English framed house, for
labour is so intolerably dear, & workmen so idle & negligent that the building of a good house, to you there will seem insupportable, for this I can
assure you when I built my own house, & agreed as cheap as I could with

workmen, & as carefully & as diligently took care that they followed their work notwithstanding we have timber for nothing, but felling & getting in place, the frame of my house stood me in more money in Tobo. @ 8 sh ℔ Cent than a frame of the same Dimensions would cost in London, by a third at least where every thing is bought, & near three times as long preparing, Your brother Joseph's [4] building that Shell, of a house without Chimneys or partition, & not one tittle of workmanship about it more than a Tobacco house work, carry'd him into those Arrears with your self, & his other Employers, as you found by his Accots. at his death. And which I preadvised him before he went about it, workmen of your own, as I at first proposed to you, will take off much of those objections. Thus Sir with all Candour & Integrity, I have given you my sentiments about building & settling your neighbouring Plantation, either for the present or future, & should be heartily glad not only of the Society of the Son of so worthy a friend, but should be ready by all opportunitys I had of serving him, to demonstrate to the world, my gratefull acknowledgement due to the father through the son. Sr. I am sorry I missed the Critical minute in my proposals of Exchange, indeed I had not then thought on, had not Doctr. Smith [5] not only encouraged me, but given me some assurance of its promised effect. However am glad for the generall good, that so plenary and full satisfaction, & assurance is given to all partys, that they may sit safely under their own Vines & fig trees, & pray God to continue the same, though perhaps it may not so fully quadrate, with my intentions & desires continuing the same, to breath my own Country air if it could be done with that advantage & security I proposed therein, & could still accept, though it were for sixty or eighty pound a year less than I proposed in my former. Your kindness gives me assurance, that if disaffections should again happen, I am ready provided of an Overture, & should gladly accept, though in the Country where I am, I desire neither to be better seated, & am plentifully provided, & a Country that agrees well with my constitution & desire, being of a melancholly, constitution, & desire privacy & retirement: these things being thus premised, it will seem strange to you that I am for a Remove to take off that strangeness, I'll give you the reall reasons. Our Estates here depend altogether upon Contingencys, & to prepare against that, causes me to exceed my Inclinations in worldly affairs, & Society that is good & ingenious is very scarce, & seldom to be come at except in books. Good Education of Children is almost impossible, & better be never born than ill bred, but that which bears the greatest weight with me, for now I look upon my self to be in my declining age, is the want of spirituall help & comforts, of which this fertile Country in every thing else, is barren and unfruitfull, which last Consideration bears the greatest weight in my Desires of Exchange & removal, for I well know that such an Estate as I propose, especially now having cut off sixty or eighty pound a year, cannot there live with that great plenty &c, as I can do here, nor gain the third part of the Annual profits as I can make here. Your Brother I suppose will give you a particular account of Lewis his Rascally actings,[6] how diligently it was searched into, & the measures taken therein   He was only suspicioubly guilty, but the diligentest enquirys could bring nothing to light. Before I receiv'd your letter, I endeavour'd to lay him close prisoner at least a month, but with this advice to the Sherriff, to give him all opportunity of flight, in hopes the charge laid so home to him, & no less than an expectation of a trial for his life, would have induced (having an opportunity) to a flight, that the Country might be rid of such a Villain but he, hardened in wickedness, & not valuing his Reputation, staid by it, & having no proof, but Circumstantial, & those not very strong, we must Enmerito Justitiæ discharge him. My proposals of trade I have heard nothing of, neither from Liverpool nor elsewhere. I suppose the lowness of Tobo. gives a stop to those proceedings, for as yet I neither hear nor know of any Liverpool man in the Country, & very few other Ships are yet arrived, those that are here say the lowness of the Commodity, occasions so few Ships & no more are to be expected, but we are apt to believe that bad weather & contrary winds keeps many out,   It would be of mighty advantage to any trader here, if he could have an account of what Ships are bound to Virginia & Maryland, from the most considerable Ports in England, for accordingly he might order his affairs to take the forward or latter Market. Concerning my offers about the French [7] I must necessarily conclude, of the Consequences, by your friendly hints, & a more perfect account of their offers of land in Carolina by their own History, which I have since read, than you, I cannot say its a true account of their Country, but my proposals were as low as any land here with us, is generally patented out at, or lett to Lease. Sir Your great Civility & kindness to my Sister, in assisting her in her affairs, in advising her to a good Ship & civil Master, commands my heartyest thanks, for by your means & assistance, thank God she is arrived safely here, & happily to both our Contentment & satisfaction, & she doth believe & I am well assured, that your Influence on Mr. Burnham [8] largely contributed, to his kind and Civil usage & entertainment during the whole Voyage, for which she also gives you her cordial thanks, & desires to have her humble service presented to your self & good Lady. I thankfully take notice, & longingly expect those choice Plants, mentioned in your letter, & when they arrive shall take great care to plant them in proper places, & at seasonable times, & doubt not their thriving, but how to compensate so great a kindness, I know not, otherwise than furnishing your Plantation with a Nursery of the same. Sir I am glad by you to hear of my Brother's health, which if he drinks so hard, he cannot long continue, & if his acquaintance with so worthy a friend as your self, I must borrow from the latter part of your letter, my Excuse for not repeating your health, so often as my Inclinations lead me, by assuring you that what is wanting at Bacchus Orgyes, shall be supply'd at Jove's Temple, for your good fortunes & successes, neither my brain nor my Constitution will admit me, to go too far in those Bacchanalian Exercises, since my last writing, I have wt. your Uncle Porteous [9] once at James Town, & wt. your brother Sam several times, drank your health but cannot long continue by it, for either of them now exceed me more at that sort of Exercise, than your letter intimates my brother exceeds you, & can sit as much longer by it tho' not for the same reasons. Att Margaret Broderick's [10] earnest Desire & Request, as you'll perceive by her inclosed letter to her father, & as she told both me & my Sister, her friends Desires & inclinations were, that if it were possible she should go to Mr. Hammersly, who is her father's Country man Townsman, & afar off related.[11] My Sister sold her to the said Mr. Hammersly, but with condition to do no Country work, nor work without doors, as by the Condition here inclosed, you'll see, for if he should offer to put her to Country work, or to sell her, then I have liberty to seize her again, notwithstanding the Sale, besides she did resolve that neither threats nor persuasions, fair means nor foul should make her do any thing, if she might not be sold to Mr. Hammersly. If her own Desires, the Desires of her friends, the Condition for her service to do no Country work &c. is not sufficient satisfaction to her friends, to take you from your obligation, then I have agreed to have her again, for I would not for ten times her price, have my friend suffer especially so kind an one as your self. Sr. In August last died a near Neighbour of mine Mr. James Ashton [12] possess'd with two tracts of Land, both adjoining to mine, one joining upon my back line, & did contain about 2000 Acres, but there is some parcels sold out of it, & 100 more, given out to the quantity of 700 Acres, & another parcel of 550 Acres joining upon me up the River, as your's down the River, which said Land he has given to two Gentlemen in England, that part undisposed of, the 2000 Acres, to his Cousin John Ashton Habberdasher living in Russel Street in Covent garden that other of 550 Acres, to his Cousin Jno. Foster of Woodbridge in the County of Cambridge Gent as ℔ Copy of the said Will here inclosed, you'll see which said land I believe those Gentlemen in England will sell, & I would willingly become their Purchaser, because of its conveniency to me, & desire the favour of you to deal with them about it Sr. Your repeated favours & kindnesses gives me the boldness, & the conveniency of the Scituation makes me earnest & sollicitous for the purchase & Draught of the Survey here inclosed & plotted by Capt. Brent in 1681, & now while I am writing.   named by me for your clearer satisfaction, together with a true Copy of the Pattent, Copy'd by my self from the Original, Also Copy of Collo. Peter Ashton's Will,[13] the first Purchaser, wherein you may see how he disposed to his two brothers, the 2000 Acres back land, to his brother Jno. Ashton & his heirs for ever, but with this limitation, if they should not dispose thereof in their lifetime, that then it shall come & accrue to Jno. Ashton Habberdasher abovementioned, & his heirs for ever, what Disposition he made thereof, appears by his Will, the Copy whereof I have sent you, wherein he makes his brother whole Executor, & to the heirs of his body for ever, & if he died without heirs, then to his Cousin Jno. Ashton & to his heirs for ever. I suppose he intended if he had had wit to direct, or his writer skill or knowledge to have drawn it, an Estate in special taile to his brother, the remainder in fee to his Cousin, but for want of knowledge in the one, & skill in the other, I apprehend it undisposed by him, & so ought to descend & come to Jno. Ashton Haberdasher, by vertue of Collo. Ashton's Will, & Mr. James Ashton who esteemed his title good, to the said 2000 Acres by vertue of the said will of his brother John's, hath by his will also given & bequeathed the said land, what part thereof was by him in his life time undisposed, that is about 1300 Acres to his said Cousin John Ashton, by which several bequests, notwithstanding unskillfulness in the one, & uncertainty in another, he has a sure & certain title in fee simple to the sd. land, & therefore without much caution may be treated & concluded with upon the purchase, if he be intended to sell, but it is but an indifferent hand, & lies back & consequently of low value, if it was here to be sold at the best hand, would not yield above 50 or 60£ sterling for that 600 Acres, part thereof sold by Mr. Ashton in his lifetime, was sold at 2000lb. Tobo. ℔ 100 Acres, wch. rises not to much more than I before proposed, & its well known to all dealers, the difference betwixt buying ℔ parcel & by retail &r. the other Trail of 550 Acres upon the River, which by Mr. Ashton's Will belongs to Jno. Foster of Woodbridge in Cambridge Shire, though in its real Value is worth more money, could the title be made as clear as the former, but here is this doubt in it, whether a bequest by Will is such a Disposition in his life time, as shall cut off Jno. Ashton's Haberdasher's Claim, Seeing that a Will hath no force or effect before the death of the Testator, & so consequently before his Death the Estate not actually alienated, & if not conveyed & alienated by James Ashton in his life time, then to descend & come to Jno. Ashton the Cousin, which in my opinion, notwithstanding may give John Ashton a colour to, though not

absolute title of that Tract of land, unless the first bequest to James Ashton shall be esteemed in fee, because its given to him & his heirs for ever, &
its said in that clause wherein Jno. Ashton's remainder is mentioned, if he
do not dispose thereof, which is a Confirmation of his first title, & gives
him liberty, to dispose of that which the former words in the Will made an
absolute fee, & after a fee simple, there can be no remainders or Reversions
expectant Thus Sr. I have clearly Stated the Case to you about the other
tract, & would willingly give sixty or seventy pound sterling for the same,
Provided I might have a sure title, which by the joint Deeds of Foster &
Ashton together would be indisputable, or I would venture to Give Foster
fourty pound for his title, without farther Warranty, & stand trial with
John Ashton, but if Foster should stand upon high terms, & will not take
under sixty or seventy pound for his title, I shall be unwilling to give so
much for a disputable title as his is, but will venture to give Jno. Ashton
15 or 20£ for his title, & stand trial with Foster for the Inheritance. In
the main I leave all to your discreet Conduct & management, & if you find
it will not be performed, without 10. or 15£ more than I have mentioned,
I shall gladly reimburse that with the other. But now Sir it may be
reasonably ask'd after the desire of laying out so much money, where this
money is that must be laid out, & if the Purchase exceeds, to that I must
beg you to add this favour to all your former, to disburse so much money
for me as you shall see occasion, & for your Security to answer you principal & Interest, together with all your charges & trouble. I will find over
the Purchase, & besides as much of my own Estate, as shall be double the
value by Recognizance & Defeazance, till you are fully satisfy'd, & do also
hope by the next Ships to send you some bills of Exchange, to answer some
part thereof, & if this that I have proposed seem not sufficient Security,
make your own proposals, which I am sure will be reasonable, & I will
readily comply with them.   Sir I thought to have sent Deeds ready drawn,
but considering I have sent all the Wills & the Pattent, & the ready way
that is now in practice, by Lease & Release it may be as well if not better
done there than here, taking but this care, that to the Leases Releases
letters of Attorney &c. such Witnesses be present, as will be here viva voce
to attest the same.   Sr. As yet those Gentlemen do not know of their title
to the said Land, for by the Will you'll see, that your Brother John
Harvey [14] & myself are Executors in trust, in behalf of them in England,
& we cannot yet meet & prepare business effectually enough, to give them
a satisfactory account till after our next Court, which will be then fully
done by us all, but doubt that the personal Estate will do little more, if
any thing, than clear the engagements, for in his Estate there was but two
Negroes (which upon the appraisement I helped Mr. Hayward to, upon his

request so that he has in that quality doubled Mr. Stork,) [15] few servants & those few almost free, a pretty good Stock of Cattle, but of household stuff there was hardly the value of £10, the old man left a ruinous Estate & more ruinous Plantation, for there is not one good house upon either Plantation, perhaps the housing & Conveniencys upon the Plantation, may be urged as an increase of the Purchase, but this I give you a full assurance of, that all the Houses upon both Plantations are not worth £5. perhaps it may be urged likewise to buy real & personal Estate together, but that can be neither advantageous to buy, nor proper to sell because it is not certain, what personal Estate there will be left, after all debts & Legacys satisfy'd & if any it will be very inconsiderable, as by the next we shall give them a full account. Sr. If you crave excuse for the length of your most endearing & obliging letters, which are filled with a pleasing Phrase & happy expression, what words must I use to excuse not only my length but Impertinencys, not only my harshness of Stile but badness of expression, but a continued addition of my boldness & trouble, since I cannot find words, I'll beg one more Obligation to all your former to grant a favourable Construction, & a generous Pardon to

To Mr. Nichs. Hayward &c.   Sr. Your   W. ff.

[*LB*, pp. 111-22]

1. For Nicholas Hayward, see ltr. to Samuel Hayward, June 3, 1684, note 2, the Introduction, and various ltrs. to Nicholas himself.

2. Presumably ltrs. landed at his friend Buckner's or some other place in Gloucester County, Virginia, by the sea captains Pensux and Burnham. A Captain Samuel Pensax was in 1655 commander of the *Henry and David;* he was probably a relative of the present man. For WF's good friend Captain Burnham, see ltr. to J. Cooper, May 18, 1685, note 6.

3. George Brent (see ltr. to R. Wormeley, June 19, 1681, note 3) was "brother" only in the sense of business partner. WF, as Brent's law partner, also called him "brother." There are several Stafford county Masseys of prominence. A Captain Robert Massey was a militia officer in 1680. Sigismund Massey was perhaps the best known. Here WF seems to refer to the "Brenton" or "Brent Town" grant (see ltr. to N. Hayward, April 22, 1686, etc., above), and it seems to indicate that the partners had at least tentatively secured the grant long before. Also see 3 V 165; 1 V 251; 9 W (2) 182.

4. A Joseph Hayward was fourteen in 1664 in Virginia. After his death George Brent, as Nicholas Hayward's attorney, showed that "Joseph Hayward late of this county decd merchant" owed Nicholas a considerable amount. Samuel Hayward later (*c.* 1690) wanted quietus on the administration of Joseph's estate. 45 V 178-79.

5. For WF's future brother-in-law Dr. Ralph Smith, see ltr. to him, April 22, 1681, note 1, and other ltrs. above and below.

6. Probably the nephew Philip Lewis, mentioned in Samuel Hayward's will, or the father of that person. Since the Stafford Court records for the period are missing, the matter remains obscure. See ltr. to Samuel Hayward, June 3, 1684, note 5.

7. See ltr. to N. Hayward, May 20, 1686, note 2.

8. For Captain Burnham, see ltr. to J. Cooper, May 18, 1685, note 6. Burnham was a merchant sea captain who handled cargoes and traded for Nicholas Hayward.

9. For Edward Porteus, see ltr. to N. Hayward, April 22, 1686, note 3.

Richard Lee (1646-1715)

Portrait by an unidentified artist, owned by Mrs. Cazenove Lee of Washington.

Francis, Lord Howard of Effingham (1643-1695)

Portrait by Godfrey Kneller, owned by the Virginia Historical Society.

10. Apparently an indentured servant brought over by or with Dorothy Fitzhugh, perhaps as the maid her brother suggested should accompany her.

11. Perhaps Francis Hammersley of Northumberland County, Virginia (see ltr. to R. Smith, April 18, 1686/87; *Journals H.B. 1659/60-1963*, pp. 173, 182). A man of this name also was one of the early lawyers of Stafford. One Francis Hammersley married the widow of Giles Brent and was the guardian for his stepson. Harrison, *Landmarks*, I, 110; 16 V 212.

12. This will was dated August 18, 1686, and was proved Sept. 8, 1686, in Stafford County Court and in the Prerogative Court of Canterbury. WF, Samuel Hayward, and John Harvey were executors. As we have noticed, there were various small bequests. But most of the property was left to English relatives, Ashton's cousin John Ashton, haberdasher of London, the tract that had formerly belonged to James's brother John; and John Foster of Wozbridge, Cambridgeshire, the plantation called "Chatterton" on the river side, and that tract "belonging to my 550 acres." 2 V 27; 10 V 282-83; 7 W(1) 177.

13. Colonel Peter Ashton, who died in 1671, had left to his brother James of Lincoln, England, his estate of "Chatterton," and to John Ashton of Lincolnshire the two-thousand-acre estate adjoining. Both James and John came to Virginia. John had died in 1682, leaving his property to his brother James. 10 V 292-93.

14. John Harvey was in the late 1690's J.P. and member of commission of oyer and terminer for Stafford. 1 V 231. In what respects he was Hayward's "brother" in business or blood is not clear.

15. Nehemiah Storke of Stafford and England, or perhaps Thomas Storke of England, merchant. James Ashton's will mentions Mr. Thomas Storke of London. See ltr. to Wm. Leigh, June 27, 1682, note 2; Harrison, *Landmarks*, I, 112-13; 2 V 30n; 10 V 292; 9 W(2) 183.

To the Honourable Nicholas Spencer [1]

Honoured Sir   February 18th. 1687

The first day of February I receiv'd your's dated 15th. January about Collo. Jones [2] his affairs, I immediately upon the receipt thereof dispatched a Messenger away to him to come to my house, where I apprehended I should have the freer & fuller opportunity, to discourse him in it, & to persuade him to the payment of it, which letter he answer'd me with his company about five days after, which was as soon as he came home from Gloucester, where he had not only account of, but Dunns for several Sums of the like nature protested. I used both my Interest & persuasion, to get him to pay in Tobo. for the money, & agreed to allow him ten shillings ⅌ Cent, & remit the damages, which he seemed willingly to approve of, & would he said use his endeavour to procure that Tobo., & what Tobo. he owed me, which was about five thousand, for his own Crops were already disposed of, in paying Neighbouring Debts, & supplying his family's necessarys, & with such intentions & some assurances he went from my house, & promised to be with me again within four days at farthest, & did not question to bring me a satisfactory answer, he was punctual to his word as to his coming, but with tears in his eyes said, he could not possibly answer either yours or mine, for he said he had neither Tobo. nor effects to procure it, I offered to buy two or three Negroes of him, he assured me they were already made over to the Alderman & his Ship merchants to whom he hath not yet paid one penny, and therefore that way there was nothing to be expected. And I hear since, that night he went away from my house, he went into Maryland & so conclude he is clear gone   Thus Sir I have stated the Case, & given you my Sentiments of the man; I refer to your self to take such measures therein, as may be to advantage his Estate is so shattered & incumber'd with Mortgages Conveyances &c. & his debts so many & great that without a very sudden Course taken it will be impossible ever to recover one penny. If I can be any ways serviceable to you therein, I shall most acceptably & willingly receive your Commands, & diligently therein manifest myself to be

To The Honble. Nichs. Spencer   Your   W. ff.

[*LB*, pp. 122-23]

1. Nicholas Spencer, mentioned many times above, was at this time, as he was until his death in 1689, Secretary of State in Virginia.

2. For Cadwallader Jones, WF's neighbor, see ltr. to R. Wormeley, August 2, 1682, note 2, and other ltrs. above. Bold soldier and Indian trader, Jones had by this time got himself into all sorts of financial difficulties, perhaps through extending himself too far in his trade with the Indians. This may refer to tobacco funds he had received for his Potomac garrison. If so, it was an official colonial matter. But it may be that he owed Spencer personally. Though he stole away at this time, he tried desperately to retrieve his fortunes and credit. Later he was Governor of the Bahamas, and later still (1698) he was again in Virginia. See Fairfax Harrison, "Western Explorations in Virginia between Lederer and Spotswood," 30 V 323-40; *Journals H.B. 1659/60-1693*, p. 127.

To Captain George Brent [1]

Dear Brother   February 25th. 1687

John Simpson [2] brought me your most acceptable letter, ill weather at our appointed time for our last Court, hindre'd me of the real enjoyment of your most desired Company, the purport of your letter, I will affectionately & fully answer, that is of your desired piece of gold, & what Cravats &c. fashionable I have at present, to supply you with, could wish I had more, & they should with the same alacrity & readiness be devoted to your service. By his return from Cullum,[3] & disappointments there, I was not only concerned, but extreamly troubled guessing at your concerns & intentions there, & before your Return a full Consumation &c. In the carrying on all which designs I know you would neither be beholding nor appear to have any occasion thereof to any one in Maryland, therefore I have so far straitned my self as to supply you with all my stock except one piece of eight, which I hope may be enough to carry on your designs as I imagine there &c. or to supply your pocket expence in your journey, which please to Accept, with the same freedom as they are offered & sent. I hear Cullum designs out before our Court, therefore would have you send again before then, that you may not be disappointed of your expected money, & if you think that I may be any ways serviceable to you, please to lay your Commands, & they shall be readily obeyed ~~by~~ Mr. Newton [4] now at my house informs me of abundance of Rum now at Paluxen [5] at 15d. ℔ Gallon and under, please to do in that & all other concerns as for your self. I have about 200 hhds. now by me, the conveniency your self knows. I sent by this Messenger 1 guinea twelve pieces of eight, one Cravat & ruffles, & Sleeves & Cravat strings

To Capt. George Brent at Woodstock   [no signature]

[*LB*, pp. 123-24]

1. Brent, WF's law partner, married as his second wife a stepdaughter of Lord Baltimore (she was the daughter of Col. Henry Sewall). At this time he was on his way to the wedding. Lord Baltimore's ltr. of Oct. 20, 1687, congratulated him on the marriage. 17 V 42-43. WF's lack of money is characteristic of his class and way of living.
2. John Simpson of Acquia in Stafford is spoken of in a conveyance of 1699. In March, 1689/90, WF complained in Stafford Court that John Simpson died owing him 679 pounds of tobacco, but another John is also spoken of here as still living. *Stafford Court Record Book, 1689-1693*, pp. 13, 19; 6 V 311.
3. Unidentified.
4. For John Newton, husband of WF's mother-in-law, see ltr. to K. Chiseldine, June 8, 16[81], note 3.
5. Patuxent Bay and River in Maryland, a frequent anchorage for merchant vessels and later for naval vessels.

To John Buckner [1]

Mr. John Buckner   March 14th. 1686/7

I three days since receiv'd your's of the 7th. March last, & do as truly condole your present affliction & past losses therein mentioned, as I heartily thank you for your kindness & trouble therein expressed, both in the presenting Sir Robert's note,[2] & the return of the three pound bills inclosed I wish both your self & family perfect health & full Recovery. Sr. The inclosed Protest will speak its own business, I have been already so often troublesome to you, & yet continue, that I want expressions to beg pardon, and have no other refuge left, than to assure you if any of your business lies this way, I shall court all occasions to assure you I am sincerely

Your   W: ff.

The protested bill abovemttend is Edwd. Lassels drawn on Capt. Henry Fearnes assigned to me by James Davis [3] the Sum is £4 .. 10.0

[LB, p. 124]

1. For WF's friend John Buckner, see ltr. to him, Dec. 3, 1681, note 1. Buckner was Clerk of the Court, and WF had to do legal business in Gloucester through him. In the present situation, WF may refer to debts owed to Buckner personally by Cadwallader Jones.

2. For Sir Robert Peyton, the person here probably referred to, see ltr. to Captain Francis Partis, June 11, 1680, note 2.

3. Lassels, Captain Fearnes, and Davis are unidentified.

To the Honourable Nicholas Spencer [1]

Honoured Sir   March 14th. 1686/7

As I writ in my last my thoughts of Collo. Jones his Departure,[2] I find since absolutely true but whither I can't yet learn, but I imagine (by some Discourse he let fall at my house) it is for England, to get himself into his Majesty's Army, & since his flight, his wife, (to whom its presumed he communicated his thoughts) has carry'd out of this County all his Estate, that is, all his Negroes, for stock of Cattle, hogs or horses he had none in our County, & has them now with her at Rappak. Therefore there is the place to attack them in   My remoteness from their Judicial Place, & unacquaintedness with their Ministerial Officers, might I fear indanger a miscarriage of the whole proceedings, therefore I have yet stop'd taking out an Attachment, for fear of alarming them, till I had first advised wt.

your Honour, for which I have sent this Messenger on purpose, to inform
of the circumstances, also to propose that an Attachment might come immediately from my Lord, (propter Excellantiam &c) Directed to the Sherriff of Rappahannock & that you would either to Mr. Spicer,³ or some
other knowing & interest person in that County to see the same duely
executed, & fully & discreetly prosecuted. and I will deliver your Instructions & directions therein, with my own hand, to the person directed, &
contribute what lies in my power to their assistance, I wish you may secure
your own, but for my Lord Culpepper's, I look upon it almost impossible
to secure, I am sure improbable, nor can't advise in any measure to be
taken therein, for by all that I can learn there's hardly Estate enough to
answer your debt, which is not particularly & by name bound over, besides
a great deal that is bound over in general terms   Sir Four days since I
receiv'd your's of the 28th. february last, & I hope by this time its too late
to condole your afflicting torment because as its seizure was in (the almost)
conclusion of the month, so do please my self with hopes & expectation
that at least the violence terminated therewith & hope by this time you
are arrived to a full Recovery. Because Mr. [   ] his letter & encouragement from his Excellency, was occasioned first from your Honour's letter
to his Lordship, I advised him to send this letter & petition open to
your hand, to crave your Honour's encouragement & assistance, for if
it be true as Mr. [   ] saith, & can prove by his whole Ship's Company, it is not only bare Robbery, which is only forcing away money
from him without any pretence of Authority, but it is Robbery heightened
& aggravated, under colour of his Majesty's Commission & Authority,
which if not timely prevented, will prejudice his Majesty in his Customs, by the Discouragement of trade, & Ruin of this Country. And indeed it must needs appear, to the Merchants, owners & Employers, in
England a foul Imputation & Scandal to the government, the consequence whereof I refer to your most discerning Judgment. God almighty
preserve your Honour in health & happiness always prayer of

To The Honüble Nichs. Spencer Esqr.   Sr. Your   W. ff.

[*LB*, pp. 125-26]

1. See ltr. to Spencer, Feb. 18, 1687, note 1.
2. For Jones's flight, see ltr. to Spencer of Feb. 18, 1687, note 2.
3. Arthur Spicer (d. 1700), of Rappahannock and later Richmond counties, was one of
the more prominent attorneys of the Northern Neck. He probably was on the other side from
WF in the Wormeley *vs.* Griffin and Burwell case discussed above. The inventory of his library
indicates that he was a man of wide interests and perhaps of learning. Wright, *First Gentlemen of Va.*, pp. 140-43; 2 V 122n; 3 V 258n.

To Captain George Brent [1]

Dear Brother   March 22nd. 1686/7

Your full absolute & perfect assurance in your's, fully perfectly, & absolutely pleases & Contents me, & gives me as great, if not greater satisfaction, than the welcome full bags to the most miserly Usurer or the joyfull & full harvest to the most industrious & thrifty husbandman, & do with the same earnestness wish the Consumation in facie Ecelesiæ, to furnish you with a full enjoyment, & though the Distance will not admit at that happy Day, I shall not then fail to sing Io Paean in your remembrance. Your treaty & conclusion with Collo. Diggs,[2] discourse with Phipperd,[3] & intentions with others therein mentioned on one part shews not only your skill but Activity on the other part a continuance of your friendship & kindness, by admitting me a partner in your best offers, & greatest expectations. I have advice from York that Tobo. is very plentifull, & consequently low, therefore should advise to strike as soon as possible, doubting when this market will be over, whether any more Overtures may happen, for its a general saying, that abundance of Tobo. will be left in the Country &c. As you write in your's you have time enough this week to do business in, so next week I hope you'll have business enough to do, for as your stay is intended but short, I am sure your service both must & will be brisk, your limited time is so short, that to be plain with you, You cannot be wish'd for sooner. Your Intimacy & nearness to that good Lady [4] emboldens me though unknown to request the tender of my humble service to her

To Capt. George Brent at &c.   Your   W. ff.

[*LB*, pp. 126-27]

1. See ltr. to him, Feb. 25, 1687, note 1. WF refers to Brent's approaching second marriage.
2. For Colonel William Digges of Virginia and Maryland, like Brent and WF an ardent Tory, see ltr. to N. Hayward, May 6, 1686, note 3. Digges had established himself in Charles County, Maryland, soon after 1679. Earlier he had lived in York County, Virginia.
3. Probably Captain William Phippard, a sea captain active in Maryland in 1698. A Sir William Phippard appears in the York County (Va.) Deeds and Wills in the 1702-6 period. *Md. Hist. Mag.*, XV (1920), 173; 31 V 275.
4. Brent's future second wife was Marie, daughter of Lady Baltimore by Henry Sewall. She died March 12, 1693/94. Clara, her first child by Brent, "Obit 10 March 1689," according to an inscription in the old Acquia burying ground. 18 V 224-26, 321.

To Captain Henry Fitzhugh [1]

Dearest Brother   April 5th. 1687

In my last sub Cover Mr. Hayward by Spenser,[2] which by this time I suppose is with you, I gave you an account of the receipt, of your two most acceptable letters, & therein a full answer to each part, therefore now shall not need repetition. In my last I advised, that if you intended in here next year, as you seemed to intimate in your letter, how I might have the happiness of your good company & you the profit of so long a Voyage, which was by your Interest at Court, which I hear is Considerable to get to be Commander of one of the King's ships, that gives their attendance here, by which place you might clear 1000£ sterling a year, pursuing such methods as my knowledge in the Country, & acquaintance with trades & traders is able to dictate to you, & you might be assured of, those that are here (viz) Allen & Crofts [3] clear better than 500£ a year a piece, though Sobriety is a stranger to the one, & discretion not very intimate with the other. I also promised in my last to propose another profitable method for your advantageous coming here, provided what I before premised cannot be obtained, which is to get to be keeper of the broad Seal of this Country, with the profits there to appertaining, for you must know, that before our present Governor the Lord Howard came over,[4] the Seal of the Collony was in the Secretary's Office,[5] & all Pattents, Commissions, Proclamations &c. that issued forth came out of his Office & the fees thereof was very small, but since this Governor's time he has taken the Seal to himself, & makes 200lb. Tobo. for every Commission, Proclamation, Pattent, Commission of Administration, &c. which amounts to at least betwixt eighty & a hundred thousand pounds Tobo. ℔ annum without fourty shillings Charge or three days trouble in the year, & in my opinion is not very difficult there to obtain it, & after such a settled Officer & Office the profits would daily encrease & as at present you can obtain the place by no other name than Keeper of the great Seal of the Collony, so in a short time the Chancellor's Place & profits will fall into the same, which will far exceed all places in this Country, except the Governor's both in Reputation & Profit. I could also propose to you the farming the Virginia Dutys, I mean the two shillings ℔ hhd. which amounts annually to about four thousand pound sterling clear, paying all Officers for collecting the same, & I know of no other payments to be made out of it, than 1200£ sterling to our

Governor, 100 to the Auditor in England, Mr. Blithwait,[6] & 300 to our Auditor or rather Deputy Auditor Collo. Bacon [7] (who is very antient & in all probability cannot live long, by whose death there will be the vacancy of a Considerable profitable & easie managed place) & betwixt thirty & fourty pound a year to each Councellor, whereof there's rarely above twelve, never above thirteen, which in the whole amounts to not above 2100 or 2200 sterling ℈ annum, which is little more than half the clear Income, & none of the rest as I know of, (& I have some reason to know by reason I have revised diligently Mr. Auditor's Books & accts.) goes to his Majesty, & I am sure not to the Country's use, so that paying 500£ ℈ annum to some Court Pensioner, & the Governor Auditor & Councils Salary here, there might certainly be cleared communibus annis 1000 or 1200£ a year at least. But it must be supposed that large Security would be expected if it were obtained by the way of farm, which I am affraid would be difficult for you to get, but to have the handling & paying of this money to the respective Officers, as well as the Collection & Disposal of the whole Country's Quitrents, under the name, & by the title & Office of Treasurer of Virginia, could not be less worth than 500 or 600£ sterling a year, & it is a place now vacant & wanting, & I believe there might not be much difficulty to obtain it, using this caution to inform your self of my Lord Howard's interest & friends at Court before you may embark upon any of them, for all my proposals are branches lopp'd from the tree of his Interest, except that of being Commander of the King's Ship, therefore it cannot be for my advantage, to publish from whom you receiv'd this information. What I have now farther to add is a piece of news, that just a month before the writing of this, We sang Io: Hymen at my Sister's wedding,[8] who I think is well matched, having marry'd an ingenious Trader into this Country, a skilfull & quaint Surgeon, as his particular operations here has sufficiently demonstrated, & one of considerable Reputation & Substance in Bristol where he lives, but intends this year, to transfer his whole concerns hither, & here settle his name is Doctr. Ralph Smith, the person that I mentioned in my last years proposals of Exchange & by whose conveyance this letter comes to your hand. As in my last I intimated & desired your Picture, & our Coat of Arms, if you could not get an advantageous opportunity, of giving me your own wish'd for company, so again I must repeat my former desires & wishes either to see you in person, or to see you truly personated by your lovely Picture which would largely contribute to the satisfaction of   Dearest Brother

To Capt. Henry Fitzhugh &c.   Your   W. ff.

[LB, pp. 127-30]

1. For Henry Fitzhugh, see ltrs. to him, above, especially that of April 22, 1686, note 1.

2. This possibly may be Nicholas Spencer or some member of his family. No sea captain of the name has been identified.

3. The two British naval officers (see ltr. to Henry Fitzhugh, Jan. 30, 1686/87, note 3) apparently earned this amount through customs inspections and in prizes from pirates, etc.

4. Francis, Lord Howard of Effingham, arrived in Virginia Feb. 10, 1683/84.

5. That is, Nicholas Spencer's office.

6. For William Blathwayt, see ltr. to Madame Sarah Bland, March 19, 1682/83, note 7. Secretary of the Lords of Trade and the Plantations, Blathwayt was a power in colonial administration from 1682.

7. Nathaniel Bacon, Sr. (1620-1692), who came to Virginia about 1650, was Auditor-General of the colony, 1675-1687, and President of the Council in 1689. He lived at "King's Creek," York County.

8. Dorothy Fitzhugh (q.v.) was now married to Dr. Ralph Smith (q.v.), the Virginia and Bristol trader and physician.

To Nicholas Hayward [1]

Worthy Sir   April 5th. 1687

I have already been so large & troublesome by Pensux,[2] which before this I hope is come safe to hand, & expect to Duplicate with addition by Burnham,[3] that in this I shall only return you my most hearty thanks, for your many & continual favours & expressions of kindness, & in answer to your's shall begin with your last, which I the other day receiv'd by Mr. [   ] wherein you sensibly condole [   ] of that report of your Brother's Dissolution, from whom that Report should arise, or upon what grounds I cannot imagine. Your Brother to this day having not given any occasion by one hours sickness or the least indisposition, & which by this time his letter from Town, I am sure gives you plenary satisfaction in, not only by his perfect health, but new acquisitions of his Reputation, by serving as a Representative in our last Assembly, with sufficient Credit & satisfaction, considering his new Introduction into affairs of that nature, & though that house came off with a special mark from his Majesty, & disreputation from the Governor, yet he so evenly ballanc'd himself, that by all partys he was esteemed an honest well meaning man [4] I speak knowingly Sr. though I did not belong to the House, yet was impeached formally by them, & all methods pursued, as in an Impeachment by the House of Commons in England, but it proved like all the rest of their Proceedings ill grounded & worse managed, & in the end did me no farther damage than the waiting upon them, till my triall was over, keeping me so long (which was almost three weeks) from my pleasant Retirement at my own house,[5] which business your Brother shew'd himself a true man in his Station, & a faithfull fast friend. Sr. This is in haste by Doctr. Ralph Smith, whom I last year mentioned in my proposals of Exchange, who is now more near Related by means of my Sister (who gives your her humble service) for about a month since, that Gordian knot was tyed betwixt them, that nothing but Death will separate, & I believe it not only is but will continue to both their satisfactions & content. In my last I advised that I continue the same in my Inclinations & Desires for Exchange, & have only this now farther to add, that could the Estate to be exchanged for, be procured in Ireland or Scotland I should both like & approve the same. With the Inclosed note Sir I desire you to pay the Arrearages of Post money, & what this now comes to, for really I blush when I consider, the trouble I continually put you to, & am wholly ashamed to add charge to the same reckoning—I shall within these ten days write again by Burneham, therefore now shall add no farther than sincerely to acknowledge my self,

To Mr. Nichs. Hayward &c.   Sir Your   W. ff.

[*LB*, pp. 130-32]

1. For Hayward, see ltr. to Samuel Hayward, June 3, 1684, note 2, and other ltrs. directly to.

2. For Captain Pensux, see ltr. to N. Hayward, April 5, 1687, note 2.

3. WF's sea-captain-friend who visited him frequently at his estate. Burnham had brought his sister Dorothy to Virginia.

4. Samuel Hayward (see ltr. to, June 3, 1684, notes) served in the House of Burgesses from 1685 to 1686, representing Stafford.

5. For discussions of this case, see "Burgess and Politician," in the Introduction above, and *Journals H.B. 1659/60-1693*, pp. liii, 265, 266, 268, 271, 282, 303, 305, 306; also *Exec. Journ. Council Col. Va.*, I, 509, and *Cal. St. Papers, Col., Am. & W.I., 1685-1688*, Items 482, 963, 1729. The three weeks of trial WF refers to were probably of the session of the Burgesses, Oct. 20—Nov. 17, 1686. Actually the records show no real trial, merely repeated charges and requests for investigation and perhaps some questioning. Nor, as noted in the Introduction, was there anything more than the beginning of an impeachment proceeding. WF was not through with the matter, for it appears in the 1688 records again several times. He was right in saying, however, that no real damage was done him by this time. Nor was it later.

To Thomas Harris [1]

Cousin Harris   April 5th. 1687

I have no farther to add now than what I formerly wrote ⅌ Pensux [2] sub Cover Mr. Hayward only to beg the favour of you to deliver the inclosed letter to my Mother, & the money in the inclosed bill of Exchange, to receive & deliver to her, also to acquaint you with my Sister's good fortune in meeting with a good husband, the person to whom she is matched, being a very ingenious & truly honest man, & one of no mean fortune. I do suppose my Sister her self has been more large in the particular Circumstances, therefore refer to her letter. Pray remember my kind respects to my Cousin your good wife & accept the same to your self from

To Mr. Thos. Harris Haberdasher In &c.   Your   W. ff.

[*LB* p. 132]

1. There is an earlier ltr. to Harris of Jan. 30, 1686/87.
2. For Captain Pensux, see ltr. to N. Hayward, April 5, 1687, note 2.

To Mrs. Mary Fitzhugh [1]

Dear Mother

In my last ℣ Pensux I promised to send you £10 if to be procured, by this I have sent a bill of Exchange to my Cousin Harris to receive £3 & deliver it you, which please to accept it being all the money I can at present procure, I design to make this up £10 by the next, if possibly to be procured, but Tobo. is now so extreamly cheap & low here, that money cannot be procured therewith, as my Sister I suppose will more fully inform you in this affair, with what difficulty I got this money that I now send, as also in her own affairs, how suddenly fortunate she has been in meeting with a very good match, which will be to her future comfortable Subsistence & prosperity, all which I wholly refer to her particular relation, & indeed all things else that you desired to be informed of my particular Concerns. I have nothing more to add but Prayers to God almighty for your health & in his due time your Comfort & prosperity   I am

Your   W. ff.

[*LB*, pp. 132-33]

1. For WF's mother Mary King Fitzhugh, see ltr. to Henry Fitzhugh, April 22, 1686, note 6, and subsequent ltrs. to Mrs. Fitzhugh herself.

To Doctor Ralph Smith [1]

Brother Smith   April 18th. 1687

I hope this will find you safe arrived to Bristol, & the inclosed will shew you Mr. Francis Hammersley's [2] care & honesty in delivering your bills of Exchange for the £13 he owes, which he questions not, but will be readily accepted & duely paid. Thank God we are all in as good health as you left us, & one in particular longingly expects your company This is all the needfull at present from

Sir Your W. ff.

[LB, p. 133]

1. For Dr. Ralph Smith, see ltr. to him, April 22, 1686. WF's brother-in-law soon after his marriage to Dorothy Fitzhugh returned to England to look after his affairs in Bristol. They had been married about March 1, 1687 (see ltr. to Henry Fitzhugh, April 5, 1687).
2. For Francis Hammersley, see ltr. to N. Hayward, Jan. 30, 1686/87, note 11.

To John Cooper [1]

Mr. John Cooper   April 18th. 1687

Sir I receiv'd your severall letters, by my sister Capt. Martin Harris & Paine,[2] together with Copy of your Accot. Currant, & also the protested bill in one of your inclosed, if I could have got any freight this year, intended to have consigned you twenty or thirty hhds. Tobo., but there was this year such plenty of Tobo. & scarcity of Ships, that freight was hardly to be procured upon any terms, & I was not very willing to give very high for freight, seeing Tobo. is at so low a rate in England, & as the fullness of ships promises no very Rising Market, about a fortnight ago, I doubted I should have 200 hhds. lying upon my hand, but the greatness of the quantity & the Conveniency of it, did at last help me to a saving Market for the same as this year goes, for I had for it nine shillings & six pence ℔ cent, which I believe is as much if not more, than I could have there expected, though for this three years successively, the two former for the heigth of the Market, & this latter for want of freight, I have not consigned you any Tobo. yet next year I believe I shall & do intend to consign you some, if a rising Market gives encouragement. I intend to write you once again this year, & hope to send inclosed some bills of Exchange, & therefore shall refer all farther discourse till then, & have now only to assure you   I am

℞ Capt Burnham[3]   Sir Your   W. ff.

[*LB*, pp. 133-34]

1. For Cooper, see ltr. to him, April 4, 1681, note 1.
2. For Captain Martin Harris of the *Gerard*, see ltr. to Cooper, March 10, 1682/83, note 4. Paine is unidentified.
3. For Captain Burnham, see ltr. to Cooper, May 18, 1685, note 7, and other ltrs.

To Nicholas Hayward [1]

Mr. Nicholas Hayward   April 18th. 1687

What's before is Duplicate of my former ℞ Capt. Pensux[2] the inclosed letter to Mr. Ashton & Foster[3] together with the papers relating to the same, will I presume deceive their expectations of a great Estate, as they supposed their Cousin here to be possessed with, which their this year's letters seemed to intimate, for besides all those Judgments, there is considerable Sums due to us that are his Executors, besides some in the Country that have not yet brought in their Actions, & Mr. Storke[4] in England to whom we imagine he was considerably indebted, & in this Inventory was his whole Estate, except his stock of horses which are of low value, & could not be brought together to the Appraisement, by which you will perceive what personall Estate will be left, after all debts satisfyed. Sr. In my last by way of Bristol I gave you account of your Brother's perfect health, and new acquisitions at James Town, together with the signification of the continuance of my Desires of Exchange, though it were for an Estate lying in Scotland or Ireland, if it could not be had in England, provided it could be secure for either of thesee [*sic*] answer my reasons for removal as well as in England, though it would not be altogether so pleasing to me. Since the writing of the former I have receiv'd a letter from Mr. Clayton [5] of Liverpool, who writes me that the lowness of Tobo. will not answer to give my settled price therein mention'd of 16 .. 8d. but yet is mighty willing, & desirous to be concerned in a trade with me, & highly approves of the Dispatch, desiring me to propose a lower price, or other Methods, which I have now done as ℔ the inclosed Copy of the letter sent him you'll perceive, & the reason I send the Copy to you is because I continue my Designs (if he approve of any of the propositions therein mentioned,) in lodging what money I can conveniently spare in your hands, & have ordered Doctr. Ralph Smith my brother in Law, by the marriage of my Sister, as I informed you in my last, to direct in the sorting of the goods, & ordering some of the money there to be deposited in your hands. In my last also I sent you A Note from Mr. Saml. Hayward for £20 which I forgot to advise to pay this Postage, & the former arrears which I hope is come safe to your hands. I have now only to beg this favour to pardon this trouble, & therein you will continue your Obligations to

Sir Your   W. ff.

To Mr. Nicholas Hayward Notary publick
near the Exchange London

[*LB*, pp. 134-35]

    1. For Hayward, see ltr. to Samuel Hayward, June 3, 1684, note 2, and other ltrs. directly to.
    2. For Pensux, see ltr. to N. Hayward, April 5, 1687, note 2.
    3. John Ashton and John Foster, heirs of James Ashton. WF was one of James Ashton's executors and wished to buy the lands bequeathed to the two. See ltr. to N. Hayward, Jan. 30, 1686/87, note 12.
    4. For Thomas Storke, merchant of London, see ltr. to William Leigh, June 27, 1682, note 2, and ltr. to Storke, August 11, 1690.
    5. See WF's ltr. to Thomas Clayton and Dr. Silvester Richmond, merchants of Liverpool, April 26, 1686.

To John Ashton and John Foster [1]

Mr. Jno. Ashton & Mr. Jno. Foster

    The inclosed Will of your Cousin Mr. James Ashton [2] who dyed in August last, will give you the reason why this comes from us, as being intrusted in your behalfs, till you come or send, therefore have taken this opportunity to acquaint you therewith, & also inclosed have sent you an Inventory of his whole Estate, with the Appraisements according to Order of Court, & pursuant to Law, together with an Account of the Judgments already obtained against ye. Estate what horses & mares there are belonging to the Estate are not in, because they could not possibly be got together to the appraisement. There is near upon twenty thousand pound Tobo. more due from him to us than the Judgments & charges that we have been at in management of the same, & paying Servants wages, which when you come or send we shall be ready to give you an accot. of. We suppose your best way will be to know of Mr. Thomas Storke what his debt is,[3] which we doubt is very considerable, & make payment of the same to him there, otherwise that debt together with debts already known & justly due, will sweep the whole personall Estate, & yet want effects to answer some debts, we know not what farther to add, having sent you these inclosed Records, which will speak their own business, but hoping to hear from you or see you by the first next year, we conclude & rest

April 18th. 1687   Gentlemen Your   W. ff.

[*LB*, p. 136]

1. For Ashton and Foster, see ltrs. to N. Hayward, Jan. 30, 1686/87, note 12, and April 18, 1687, just above. Ashton was a haberdasher of London. Foster lived at Woodbridge, or Wozbridge, Cambridgeshire.
2. As noted elsewhere, the will was proved in Stafford County Court Sept. 8, 1686, and in the Prerogative Court of Canterbury, July 14, 1687.
3. For Thomas Storke of London, merchant, see ltr. to William Leigh, June 27, 1682, note 2, and to N. Hayward, April 18, 1687, just above.

To Nicholas Hayward [1]

Mr. Nicholas Hayward   May 13th. 1687

In my former ℔ way of Bristol Pensux & Burneham [2] I have been so largely troublesome, that my endeavours shall be to contract my Discourse in a narrow Room, by only telling you that all your friends here are well & in good health, & particularly your brother Sam, with whom about three days since, we heartily & merrily drank your health. Sir I desire you to receive & keep for me, the contents of the inclosed bill, & by the next which I believe will be Sutton, I expect to send you more bills to the value of 40 or 50£ sterling, but am not certain. Sr. I have had it in my thoughts to write a small treatise, or History of Virginia, describing its Scituation, Temperature, & fertility, nature of its present inhabitants, with their method & manner of living, the plenty of Iron Mines, almost everywhere in the Country, & probable conjectures of the Discovery of others (more profitable though perhaps not so usefull) together with the prodigious quantity of wood to manage the same, the plenty of all sorts of provision the easie & profitable living of the people therein. It's regular easie & even Government in its severall Courts of Justice, together with their respective powers & methods of proceeding, with divers other heads too many to be enumerated, & to observe that brevity as I proposed in the first part of my letter. I have only mentioned this to you Sir to desire your opinion, whether a business of this nature might be of any advantage for the persuading Inhabitants hither, and might not be prejudicial to me in my particular Concerns, for I have some rough materials towards the building such a work & could quickly supply my self with the remainder, & have reason & conveniency to finish the same.   Excuse haste

To Mr. Nichs. Hayward   Sir Your   W. ff.

[LB, pp. 137-38]

1. For Hayward, see ltr. to Samuel Hayward, June 3, 1684, note 2, and other ltrs. directly to.
2. Pensux and Burnham are mentioned many times above.

―――――――――――――――――――――――――――――――――

To Thomas Clayton [1]

Mr. Thomas Clayton   April 8th. 1687

Sr.   Your's by Mr. Marshal [2] I receiv'd (though have not seen nor certainly heard where he is) & so consequently not the opportunity of consulting him, nor indeed throughly to understand your meaning, for I find you are very willing to be concerned in a Trade, & approve of the Dispatch, but withall give me a particular account of the lowness of Tobo., & the severall great & incident charges thereunto, from whence you conclude, that unless Tobo. be purchased very low here, in the method of trade you are now in, you cannot possibly advantageously continue the same, in all which I fully agree with you, & must now plainly say, as in my last was intimated, that your purchase had need be very low here, to make a profitable return to you there, when I consider the length of your Stay here, the Charge your Ships lie at, the charges of Storage & Drinkage, the Commissions that you give to your Factors or Agents, the uncertainty of a Market when you arrive here, the many debts necessarily contracted, the difficulty afterwards of getting those debts, when they are due from responsible persons, & many of them never to be got nor any possibility of getting, the hazard of sending in a careless or negligent Factor of your own, or of employing one here, as great an hazard, of meeting with an honest or substantial person, or if your Master has the management of the Merchandizing affairs, as well as the Ships, he must necessarily neglect the one or the other, for each of them requires a whole man, so that if he be Industrious on the Cargoe's account, either the Idleness or carelessness of his own Crew, will give at least a Months stay in the Ship's Concerns, or if he neglects that, then want of employment will hinder as much, all which considered makes me concur with you in opinion, but the method in my last proposed, took off all those inconveniencys, & all things considered, I believe comes as near of purchasing Tobo. almost as cheap, if not altogether, as the other way [But I will according to your Desire make this farther proposal] * especially most years, tho' I must confess this year the scarcity of Ships & plenty of Tobo. causes an alteration. But I will according to your Desire make this farther offer, that upon the same terms & under the same Circumstances, I will let you have the quantity of Tobo. at the times therein limited & mentioned at 12/6 ℔ Cent, which considering the dispatch of the Ship, & indeed the Ship's charge in her stay, I estimate goes a great way in your Purchase, & by this means, she may as easily make two Voyages as one in the year, & at both times after arrival may be in continual & full employment, no arrears left behind, nor no hazard of Negligence, insufficiency, or falshood, being you part neither with money nor goods, till you have full satisfaction for the same But if you are unwilling to give that settled certain rate, then I will make another offer, that is I will make the Dispatch as I before mentioned, for your forward & latter Ships loading, allowing 2 sh: ℔ Cent more than the Currant Market price, at the time of the Ship's arrival, & 15 ℔ Cent Com-

---

* Marked out by writer in manuscript.

mission, bearing all Charges my self, & running the hazard of all debts, every year sending you the full produce of your whole Cargoe, if yet you think that may be uncertain, because of the rising & falling of the market, I will agree the Market price to be 8/6 ₩ Cent, & accordingly will make you your Return yearly, & this way your Dispatch may be in a month or five weeks time at farthest, & should be willing that each Ship or the Ship at each time, could carry 300 hhds., & could as easily dispatch her as the Ship of 200 or 250 hhds. mentioned in my letter last year. If this method still likes you not, I will once again propose that I will fill you two Ships a forward & a latter one, with the same celerity & Dispatch, as I mentioned in my former at 25 ₩ Cent Commission, & 30£ sterling extraordinary for each 300 hhds. & make you full return, according to the Market price, or settled price before proposed of 8/6 ₩ Cent, but you can expect no farther Account of Sales from me, than the Market price or settled price mention'd, because your first ship's loading, must be put on board out of my own Tobo., for before I have sold a penny worth of your goods, or indeed before I desire a penny worth of them in my Custody, according to my method in my last year's letter, I must have given notes for all if not the greatest part your first ships whole Loading, so that the goods may be properly after their Arrival accounted my purchase according to the Market rate, or the price there mentioned, & not sold to procure the Tobo. Upon this last proposal I'll make remark to you 10 ₩ Cent, is the ordinary & agreed allowance for receiving Tobo., 5 ₩ Cent the same for Sales of goods, 3 ₩ Cent it comes to for Storage, & I am sure to deal with our Country Planters, less than 2 ₩ Cent will not afford drinkage, insurance of the whole cannot reasonably be accounted for less than 3 ₩ Cent, & I believe should make no extravagant computation, if I should reckon the Dispatch as I propose with the leaving not one pound of Tobo. behind, tho' in good sure hands, to be worth at least 7 ₩ Cent all which reckoned together, comes to more than I ask by 3 ₩ Cent & better, reckoning the 30£ extraordinary, also, In my opinion if you accept of this last proposal, the better way would be, to let your forward Ship be of about 200 or 300 hhds. & the latter Ship a good fly boat[3] of about 600 hhds. for these reasons. First Such a flight is sailed almost with the same charge, as one of your Country Ships in the method you are now in are, because such Ships are built rather for the profit of Merchants, than the Accomodation of Masters &c. being of a large hold & little Cabbin, & the only Ships indeed for this Country Trade. Secondly I had as lieve fill such a Ship for a latter ship than one of less burden, provided I had timely notice, & assurance of the same, & she might also be filled with the same speed & ease too provided Sloops & flats were provided before hand against her Arrival, by

which easie charge & great quantity of Tobo. carry'd your freight would
be mighty low. But I must thus caution you, that I expect the goods
bought well, & with ready money, & the Custom & other incident charges
particularly mentioned, & not an advancement of the goods, to make up
those charges as is in frequent use & practice   Sir according to your desire
I have once again made you other Offertures, if you like any or either of
them, give but timely & speedy notice to Doctr. Ralph Smith of Bristol,
by whom this is conveyed to your hand, & he will take effectuall care to
give me timely accot. thereof or if you doubt in any thing, or every particular is not so full & plain as you desire I have given him full orders &
Instructions, to make every thing plain & conclude the same with you as
well as if I were there my self, but must desire you to write to him, & sub
Cover of him to me timely to come with the first Ships, though you like
not to accept of any of these proposals & acquaint Doctr. Smith therewith,
he will in my behalf, & according to my Instructions given to him direct in
the suiting of your Cargoes, & what quantity of money is to be ordered
for my use

To Mr. Nicholas Hayward &c.[4]   Your   W. ff.

[*LB*, pp. 138-41]

1. For Clayton, see ltr. to him, April 26, 1686, note 1.
2. For Marshall, see ltr. to T. Clayton, April 26, 1686, note 3.
3. The *Shorter Oxford Dictionary* defines "Fly boat" in England as (1) A fast-sailing vessel, used especially in the coasting trade; (2) A fast-sailing vessel for warlike purposes, voyages of discovery, etc.; (3) A small boat. The first definition fits here.
4. This address to N. Hayward may be a slip of the copyist, for the letter was to go by Dr. Ralph Smith, presumably via Bristol instead of London. It may have had to go via Hayward and London, however.

To Nicholas Hayward[1]

Mr. Nicholas Hayward   July 18th. 1687

   Sir   I have been so large & troublesome in my severall former this
year, that now I think it high time to leave off, only desire to acquaint you
that yesterday there was an Essay made to survey your land, upon the
finishing the first line whereof, at your Corner tree upon Potomack River,[2]

your brother Sam my self & some others drank your health, in Running the second line either the unskilfullness of the Surveyor, or the badness of his Instruments made us come away with the business re infactæ, the particular relation whereof I am sure you will hear from your brother, with this assurance that the next attempt will succeed better, by reason Capt. Brent will effectually perform the same, & that I believe forthwith. Sir Inclosed you'll find three bills of Exchange, one Duplicate of my former upon Capt. Grosman [3] of Liverpool for £5 .. 2 .. 8. another of Mr. Smith's upon Perry & Lane [4] for £6, & a third of Capt. Zachary Taylor's [5] upon his wife for £25, I expected these to be larger & some others amounting in the whole to £80 but the lowness of Tobo. has disappointed my expectations. By this time I presume Sir you know whether those Seats of Mr. Ashton's [6] are to be disposed & upon what terms, if they or either of them sell, then the above money will make part of the payment, & I must request your kindness in depositing the remainder upon the terms & Security as I proposed in my first letter, but if neither of them will sell, then please to lay out my money in the Plate underwritten, Your last letter to Capt. Brent gives us the welcome assurance of your full certainty of your brother's health & welfare [7] the continuance of which to you both is sincerely wish'd you ~~by~~[8] I have charged a note upon you to Mr. Thomas Harris [9] Haberdasher £5 sterling, if he comes with the note, & you have so much money of mine in your hands ready receiv'd or undispos'd, please to answer it. The Plate A pair of middle Sized Silver Candlesticks, A pair of Snuffers & Snuff Dish, Half a doz. of Trenches Salts, the remainder in a handsom Silver Basin marked   WFF

To Mr. Nichs. Hayward &c.   Your   W. ff.

[LB, pp. 142-43]

1. For Hayward, see letter to Samuel Hayward, June 3, 1684, note 2, and other ltrs. directly to Nicholas.
2. Perhaps the "Brent Town" tract, no survey of which has been found. For an outline of its probable boundaries, see *Prince Wm. WPA*, p. 19. For William Byrd's copy of the original grant, see Harrison, *Landmarks*, I, 177.
3. Unidentified.
4. Perry and Lane, apparently the firm at other times known as Hill, Perry, and Randolph, was the best known of the London groups intensely interested in Virginia trade. Micajah Perry Senior and Junior were its leading spirits for several decades well into the eighteenth century.
5. Zachariah Taylor was in 1682 master of the *Augustine*. William Byrd I employed him in 1684 just as WF did. Perhaps he was a son or brother of James Taylor, the ancestor of the American President. James settled in the Mattaponi region in the 1660's. A Zachary Taylor (1707-1768), son of a James Taylor and grandfather of the U.S. President, married Elizabeth Lee. 24 V 229; *D.A.B.; Exec. Journ. Council Col. Va.*, I, 18.
6. For this property, see ltrs. to N. Hayward, Ashton, and Foster, just above.

7. Presumably this refers to Samuel Hayward (q.v.). Samuel did not die until 1696, as WF mentions below.

8. Partially erased in manuscript.

9. For WF's cousin-in-law Thomas Harris, see ltrs. to him from January 30, 1686/87.

To Henry Fitzhugh [1]

Dear Brother   July 18th. 1687

My former letters ℔ Burnham Pensux &c I hope before this time you have receiv'd, & if you still continue your desires & my wishes, of coming here, I am assured you have been busie in negotiating those proposals there mentioned, for your advantageous & credible Voyage, & continued Interest. Tobo. continues still as low as ever, & rather lower for which reason the best of my endeavours cannot possibly procure the sum desired, nor any thing equivalent to it, if I could I would have you assure your self, neither will nor endeavours should be wanting to supply your present occasions. Our Sister has had two or three small fits of a feaver & ague, which now has left her, & so consequently her seasoning over, & her self pretty hearty & well, & only now desires her new husbands company, she desires to have her due respects presented to your self & Lady If you obtain any of those places, I proposed in my former letter, & by that means can give me the wish'd for enjoyment of your most desired company, you had best bring in an ordinary Geleass [2] with you, & I will find you horses to draw it with   I suppose you may easily procure one of some Gentleman of the horse to a person of quality, & by furnishing it with double Gear, it would be a long time serviceable, & that way of procuring little charge-able, this I only advise don't urge. I have nothing at present farther to add than to assure you we are all well praised be God, & the same is hoped for of you by   Dearest &c.

To Capt. Henry Fitzhugh &c.   Your W. ff.

[*LB*, pp. 143-44]

1. For Henry Fitzhugh, see ltr. to him, April 22, 1686, note 1.

2. Probably WF refers to the "Calash" (Caleche, calèche) he mentions elsewhere as wanted for himself. This was a light carriage with low wheels, having a removable folding hood.

To John Cooper [1]

Mr. John Cooper   July 1st. 1687

Sr. I have once by Burnham writ you already, the scarceness of freight this year, would not admit me the opportunity of consigning you any Tobo., which I fully resolved upon, & for that little money the lowness of Tobo., would give no opportunity of procuring. I did not think it needfull to trouble you with the receipt seeing it is there to be paid away by Mr. Nics. Hayward & no goods nor other things to be purchased with it, & therefore have desired him to receive it, for I do not love to create trouble without profit, next year if the commodity gives encouragement, you shall be sure early, both to hear & receive consignmts. from me, therefore pray Sir let me receive advice from you by the first opportunity, & therein you will oblige

                                          Sir Your   W. ff.

[LB, p. 144]

   1. For John Cooper, see April 4, 1681, note 1.

To Doctor Ralph Smith [1]

Brother Smith   July 1st. 1687

I take this last opportunity by way of London to acquaint you that now Praised be God we are all in good health, my Sister has had her seasoning if it may be so called, two or three fits of a feaver & ague, which almost a week since has left her, but yet she is a little indisposed to write, & therefore by this desires to have her true love & due respects presented to you. Sr. I hope you have taken care in that affair of Mr. Clayton's of Liverpool,[2] & Crops this year will be very indifferent, the time of planting according to Act being now expired, & in no places of the Country full Crops pitch'd, & in most places not half crops, make what profitable use you can of this advice, for I can assure you it is very certain. Pray let me hear from you not only by all but by the first opportunity, with what advice, occurence of affairs there offer & therein you will much oblige. Please to mind the things sent for by you, as also to add a large looking glass, with an Olive wood frame, & a pewter Cistern   I am

To Doctr. Ralph Smith &c.   Your   W. ff.

[*LB,* pp. 144-45]

1. For Dr. Ralph Smith, see ltr. to, April 22, 1686.
2. See ltrs. to H. Hartwell, June 19, 1681, note 2, and to Clayton and Silvester, April 26, 1686, note 1. In the latter WF makes his business proposal to Clayton.

To Thomas Harris [1]

Cousin Harris   July 1st. 1687

I take this opportunity of resaluting your self & good wife only for an inclosure of this note upon Mr. Nicholas Hayward for £5 sterling which I presume he will pay upon sight, the money I would desire you to deliver to my mother to assist her in her present occasions. I suppose before this you have receiv'd the three pounds of Mr. Storke [2] & delivered it to her. Pray present my duty to her, begging her pardon for not writing to her at this time, having already four times this year written health & prosperity is wish'd to you & your's.

Mr. Nichs. Hayward. Pay or cause to be paid to Mr. Thos. Harris Haberdasher or order five pounds sterling, & place it to the acct. of W: ff.

To Mr. Thos. Harris Haberdasher

[*LB,* p. 145]

1. For Thomas Harris, see earlier ltrs. to, beginning Jan. 30, 1686/87.
2. See several ltrs. above, particularly that to N. Hayward, April 18, 1687; also ltr. below to Storke of August 11, 1690.

To the Honourable Nicholas Spencer [1]

Honrd Sir   July 4th. 1687

I just now receiv'd your's by your boy, wherein you mention you were pleased to hasten his Dispatch, for the suddener Intelligence of the doubtfull Inroads of the Seneca Indians into our Country, in their Return with their spoils from James River, together with your directions to give notice to the Inhabitants to be upon their Guards,[2] which order I shall readily obey, & I dare say the whole County will thank your Honr. for your early and timely advice, & will accordingly pursue the same, but what measures to take if they should be upon us, further than self preservation dictates & directs, I know not, there being not one Militia Officer in Commission in the whole County, & consequently people best spared can not be, commanded into service, & appointed to guard the remotest most suspected & dangerous places. I intend this day up to Capt. Brent, & with him shall consult what Courses to take in this present Exigence, & accordingly pursue the same. As your Honour has been thus early in your first Notice of the sudden & probable doubts of their Incursions, so I am well assured, upon farther Intimations of the approaching dangers, you will be pleased to give us sudden knowledge, but assist us with your full advice, directions & authority, in what lawfull posture we must stand in Defence, & if occasion be, opposition to their ravenous Spoils, & barbarous Inhumanity. In the mean time I shall take the best care I can, not only to give general notice, but endeavour the best security for the safety of the people in their lives and Estates

Your Honour's Most &c.   W. ff.

To The Honble. Nichs. Spencer Esqr. &c.

[LB, pp. 145-56]

1. Nicholas Spencer, mentioned many times above, was Secretary of State in Virginia. As a resident of the Northern Neck, he would have been personally concerned about Indian raids in his area.

2. By 1680, Virginia was organized into military districts with officers who could bring their militia troops into action within a very short period. In 1685 there had been an alarm that the Senecas were about to descend on Virginia via the head of the James River. In 1687, when a number of murders had been committed in New York near Albany by French and Indians, the Virginia Council immediately spread the news and ordered each commander

throughout the colony to organize his district and stand in readiness to start upon a march at a few hours notice. WF as lieutenant colonel had probably been the ranking militia officer in Stafford since the death of George Mason I in 1686.

That the danger was not a mere rumor seems evidenced by the fact that a party of English hunters had recently been attacked by wandering Indians and some killed and wounded. WF may refer to this group of aborigines and confuse it (as perhaps Spencer confused it) with the Seneca raiders of 1685. He and others thought they were Indians returning north from raids in the James River area. Despite the apparent danger, the General Assembly was strict in punishing those who spread false rumors of Indian uprisings. Bruce, *Inst. Hist. Va.*, II, 94-95.

To Capt. George Brent [1]

Dear Brother   August 10th. 1687

The welcome news of all your healths I receiv'd by Jno. Simpson,[2] which I heartily congratulate, & wish therein continuance, & rejoice again with you, not only in your wishes but kind salute, with the presentation of our humble service to yourself, & good Lady   John Simpson & my self went down to see the Stears in Mr. Ashton's pasture,[3] but they could not be got in, seventeen of them there is full assurance that they are there, having been five times seen, & reckoned since your being here, one I last year killed; but then did not remember that one that was wanting when you was here cannot yet be found, when it can it is at your service. to take or leave, so that there is only at present seventeen to be charged at 600 ℔ head. Twenty Sheep he will bring up with him, what measures we took in delivering the same, Jno. Simpson will give you a particular account of, which are to be charged at 160 ℔ head, there needs no farther or other writing as I know of in that affair. I have also sent Mr. Cannon's books,[4] & thank your kindness in the loan thereof, to whom please give my humble service. I heartily thank your mindfull care, & your Lady's great kindness in those welcome glasses, which came well & safe to hand. I neither have seen nor heard of Mr. Greenhalgh,[5] & if it be his Ship that is come up, conclude you will have the first opportunity of discoursing him, & driving on those affairs we last treated of, in which as in all other mutual concerns, shall be willingly & gladly referred to your most judicious conduct

To Capt. George Brent at Woodstock   Dear Sir Your   W. ff.

[*LB*, pp. 146-47]

1. For George Brent, see ltr. to R. Wormeley, July 14, 1681, note 3 and two ltrs. of 1687 to Brent above.

2. For John Simpson, see ltr. to N. Spencer, June 11, 1683/84, note 2. Simpson lived at Acquia in Stafford.

3. That is, part of the livestock of the estate of James Ashton, of whose will WF was one of the executors. The estate is discussed several times above.

4. If this is a variant spelling of Kennon, WF may refer to one of the Kennons mentioned above. See ltr. to R. Wormeley, July 14, 1681, note 2.

5. For Greenhalgh or Greenhow, see ltr. to T. Clayton, April 26, 1686, note 2.

To Nicholas Hayward [1]

Mr. Nichs. Hayward   August 18th. 1687

Sir This comes only for Cover of John Busford's [2] bill of Exchange for £20 & letter of advice about the same, the money became due for Tobo. I paid for him here, to keep him out of trouble & he gives me the full assurance that it will be punctually paid, which if so, please to receive it for me, & keep it in your hands, till I shall farther order therein, but if it should be protested & you cannot give me timely notice, before his departure from hence, I must then request your favour of prosecuting the protest against him there, for he intends from hence by the first Ships. We are now in daily expectation of hearing from thence, of all your healths & welfare which is particularly wish'd your self by

To Mr. Nichs. Hayward &c.   Sir Your   W. ff.

[LB, pp. 147-48]

1. For Hayward, see various ltrs. to above.
2. Busford is unidentified.

To the Honourable Colonel Richard Lee [1]

Honrd. Sir   January 18th. 1687/8

I heartily thank your kind opinion, & free & full advice by Jno. Newton,[2] which agrees with mine from Mr. Jno. Cooper in the lowness of

Tobo. & inexpectancy of its rise, as to Hill, Perry, & Randolph, I have had an opportunity about five days since, of sending an Intelligent person to feel the pulse of their trade.³ I know you are too well practised in the Topicks of Honour & generosity, to render advice other than fair and Candid, & as certain you are not Yorkshire enough,⁴ to set the Course of your advice by the Compass of your Interest. Sir I shall always endeavour to manage those parts that God Almighty have given me the use of, that the Devil may not have the application, & to be sure to keep honesty & integrity at the helm, when I launch out into any manner of Concerns, & not with North country men thrust them under hatches.

As you were pleased at first, to offer me your advice & Intelligence, I now beg the continuance, which will farther add to the obligaons of

To The Honble. Collo. Richard Lee   Worthy Sir Your   W. ff.

[*LB*, p. 148]

1. For Lee, see ltr. to him, May 15, 1679, note 1, and subsequent ltrs. to.
2. For John Newton, see ltr. to K. Chiseldine, June 8, 16[81], note 3, and other ltrs. to various persons subsequent to this one. Newton was the third husband of WF's mother-in-law.
3. The London firm of Hill, Perry, and Randolph may have been the same firm as Perry and Lane (see ltr. to N. Hayward, July 18, 1687, note 4); almost surely the same Micajah Perry was a leading spirit in both groups. Whether WF sent a trusted friend to London or to some Virginia port like Jamestown is not clear.
4. Though the term *Yorkshire* refers proverbially to "bargaining skill, cunning, or sharp practice attributed to Yorkshire people," (Phrase 1620: "*To come or put Y. on* [a person], to dupe or overreach," *Shorter Ox. Dict.*), it is amusing here that several of WF's correspondents and friends, even a relative by marriage, are Yorkshiremen: Robert Beverley, John Newton, Christopher Robinson, and Lord Fairfax are among them. WF and his friend Nicholas Spencer from Bedford in the Midlands could easily have been a little pharisaical about their northern brethren. The Lees were originally of Shropshire.

To the Honourable Nicholas Spencer ¹

Honoured Sir   January 18th. 1687/8

Yesterday I receiv'd your letter about Mr. Storke & Mrs. Meése's Claims from Majr. Ashton's Estate,² which Claims We that are Executors have long expected, especially Mr. Storkes, for Mr. Ashton in his life time, acquainted me that he was largely indebted to Mr. Storke, but did not mention Mrs. Meese Since the receipt of your letter. I also have overlook'd all the letters & Accots. between him & Mr. Storke, & the last letter & Accot. betwixt him & Mrs. Meese, by which said last mention'd letters & Accots. I find him indebted to Mrs. Meese for Ballance £22.17 .. 7 which said debt Mr. Storke by his letter promises payment of, if Mr. Ashton desire, by letter dated 15 Decr. 1682 in answer to which Mr. Ashton does desire payment by him to be made, by letter dated May 17th. following £20 part thereof was formerly paid by Meese, for which Mr. Ashton was to have a receipt from his Sister, which receipt could not be found, as ℔ Mr. Storke's 19 January 1685, these are all the papers or letters relating to this whole matter as I can find, which said letters & papers I have also sent for your view, therefore can object nothing upon the whole matter against Mr. Storke's debt, but it seems prima facie, upon reading & comparing their Intercourse of letters, that Mrs. Meese's ballance should be included Mr. Storke's debt, but upon farther consideration, viewing Mr. Storke's Accot., (which I also send herewith) I cannot find Mr. Ashton' debited for any such Article, & therefore conclude that the receipt for the £20 suspended the payment, & so consequently the ballance may still be due to Mrs. Meese. Sr.   Considering the trust reposed in us, by the deceased, in behalf of his friends in England, to manage the charge imposed on us, with all   with all [sic] diligence & honesty, also well weighing our dutys as Executors, in the first place to discharge all claims & dues according to Law & Justice, & believing upon consideration of these papers & accots. that those debts are justly due, yet cannot legally be paid (according to the methods & courses of proceedings in this Country) without judgmt. first had & obtain'd for the same, & being also as equally unwilling to retard the knowledge as to sham off the payment of all just dues, in answer to your's have sent this Messenger on purpose with this & the papers inclosed, to assure you that we shall be ready to make punctual payment in Tobo. according to Law for the said debts, so soon as Judgment is obtained for the same (& if your Honour enters the Actions in your name as their Attorney) shall take no [   ] * juris, no punctilios, no exceptions, to the letters of Attorney, entry of Actions, or Declarations or any other matter but shall hold our selves clearly to the justice & Merits of the Cause, & accordingly submit to such Judgment as the Court shall give, immediately upon its first call att our next Court, which is this day three weeks viz february 8th. And lest that time should seem too long to stay without Tobo. in this busie time of Dispatch, I will immediately lodge

---

* Blank in manuscript.

1283olb. Tobo. in your Honour's hands, which comes to both their debts at 10 shillings ⅌ Cent according to Law, which your receiver may come forthwith up & receive, or this bearer would gladly obey your commands and gladly receive it, who has honestly acquitted himself in that affair to me both in the time of his service, & now since his freedom. The Tobo. I shall order by Capt. Brent, whose letter I have also inclosed sent you, that you may see his intentions, both for the goodness & Conveniency of payment. This Claim goes near the whole appraisement, therefore expedition is necessary, for fear of other or future Claims. If you know Sir of any other or nearer way wherein we may be serviceable to you, & you oblige your friends, keeping the integrity of our trust, the Duty of our places, & the Security of our selves, we should be all ready to obey your just Commands in particular.

Sir Your Honrs. &c. W. ff.

To The Honble. Nicholas Spencer Esqr. &c.

[LB, pp. 148-51]

1. Apparently Secretary of State Spencer was acting in a private capacity as attorney for two claims on the Ashton estate made by persons in England. That he was Proprietary agent may also have been his reason for acting here.
2. Thomas Storke (q.v.), London merchant, is mentioned in the Ashton will. Anne Meese, widow of Col. Henry Meese of Westmoreland and Stafford, had removed to England with her husband before his death. Meese, who lived on Potomac Creek in Stafford, was sworn a member of the Virginia Council after Bacon's Rebellion, and before he returned to England. 23 V 397-400; Harrison, *Landmarks*, I, 110.

To the Honourable Nicholas Spencer [1]

Honrd. Sir   February 16th. 1687/8

Herewith comes the Examination about the late Indian murther,[2] taken according to my Lords & your Directions, with the assistance of the rest of the Justices, & in the full view & hearing of the whole County, together with Capt. Brent's particular sentiments & Judicious Contrivance for a full & plenary satisfaction to all Interests & pretences, in so dark & obscure a matter, which appears in probability a surer way, for quieting their jealousies & appeasing their future revenge (it being to be acted according to their Laws) & concurrent with their knowledge & understanding, than a legall & (according to the best Evidence to be gotten) ineffectuall tryal. We have also sent to his Excellency,[3] as your Honr will likewise see, an account of the number of our Freeholders & inhabitants, capable of maintaining a standing Militia of Horse & foot in our County, as we conceived pursuant to the Honourable Boards order, conceiving that a full number with a Soldier like appearance, is far more suitable & commendable, than a far greater number presenting themselves in the field with Clubs & staves, rather like a Rabble Rout than a well disciplin'd Militia We humbly beg your Honour's favour in aiding our Defects, where you perceive the Deficiency, & in the true representation of our (which is a standing Militia) to his Excellency We have also promised his Lordship an industrious Care for the providing Drums Trumpets Colours & other Military ornaments but promise an effectual performance, because of the hazard of the Voyage & indeed more minutely, & particularly of the uncertainty [the word "because" written just above "uncertainty"], & at present lowness of our most despicable Commodity: which we assure our selves your Honr. in our behalfs will favourably recommend to His Excellency. Sir Capt. Brent has got Judgment for Mr. Storke & Mrs. Meese against the Executors in trust of Mr. Ashton for their respective debts,[4] to expect payment in money I believe will not be performed, but if in Tobo. I have taken care to make it ready, by lodging so much in Capt. Brent's hands, which is always ready when your Honour in their behalfs shall require the same, if this Year be slipped the Executors will come in, & consequently our trust ceases, it will be of them altogether as difficult to get money, & perhaps difficult to get Tobo. I submit all to your Honour's Judgment & subscribe my self

Sir Your &c. W. ff.

To The Honble. Nicholas Spencer &c.

[*LB*, pp. 151-52]

1. This ltr. is addressed to Spencer in his official capacity as Virginia Secretary of State.
2. Since the Stafford Court records for this period do not survive, the "murther" escapes us.
3. Governor Francis, Lord Howard of Effingham.
4. Apparently Brent, as an on-the-spot lawyer in Stafford, was acting for Spencer in the Storke and Meese claims. It is possible that Spencer's interest in the whole matter was purely official, though the details do not appear to indicate that this is the situation.

To John Cooper [1]

Mr. John Cooper   May 10th. 1688

  I receiv'd your several fair & kind letters this year wherein you can-
didly give me an account of the lowness of Tobo. & the probability of its
continuance, upon which fair advice I desisted from my Intentions, and
indeed Inclinations of shipping off & consigning to you 30 or 40 hhds.
However since the Market would not give me encouragement for that
Correspondence this year I shall not fail (according to your notion & my
own desires) of a continued & friendly conversation by letters, & hope the
same from you & if there should be war as its rumoured with us here, I
desire you to take me freight for 20 hhds. certain, 30 uncertain, for if
Wars, freight will be difficult to be obtained here, & Tobo. will be a worse
Commodity here than it is now, though it is now at the lowest as ever I
knew it, Crops hardly furnishing the Servants with Cloathes & working
tools that make it. Sir I allow of your Act, & thank your kindness in supplying my Mother with £5 in her present Exigence which she her self gave
me an account of   Here inclosed have sent you three bills of Exchange,
one of Capt. Norrington's & Mr. Vincent Goddard's upon Mr. Richard
Parks of London for £229 sterling, one other of Mr. Jno. Buckner's upon
Alderman Jefferies for £4 & one other of William Smith's for £5.13 upon
Perry & Lane,[2] all which I would have you receive & keep for my use, till
my farther Order, that of Norrington's & Goddard's is the poor produce
of almost 200 hhds. Tobo., which I considered, although very low was
something in certainty, and if shipp'd off might have been lower, or perhaps brought me in debt. Sr. If my Mother be living, & you see her your
self, which I much doubt, because I have neither heard from her self, nor
by any other hand, since the first Ships pay her £10 sterling upon my
accot., & make no other payments, except by my particular Order, nor this
except you deliver it to her your self. I desire you also to pay to Mr.
Nichs. Hayward Notary Publick upon my accot. £80 sterling, if he comes
to demand the same, my next will give you the reason of my ordering him
that, together with full directions, for the disposing, of that & the remainder in your hands or the greatest part thereof   I desire you next year
to be full & timely in your advice. Mr. Newton [3] has I suppose this year
taken care to satisfie you for your former trouble, in his business, & made
you some small Consignments   The above is Copy of my former, I refer

still to the next, for more full orders & directions only now send you Duplicates of the above both which I am sure you will take care of for

Your   W. ff

To Mr. Jno. Cooper Mercht. in London

[*LB*, pp. 152-54]

1. For Cooper, see ltr. to him, April 4, 1681, note 1.
2. For Captain William Norrington, see ltr. to Cooper, April 4, 1681, note 2. For Goddard, ltr. to Captain F. Partis, Dec. 4, 1680, note 4. Buckner is mentioned frequently above. Parks is unidentified. Jeffries and Smith are unidentified.
3. John Newton is mentioned many times above.

To Nicholas Hayward [1]

Mr. Nichs. Hayward   May 10th. 1688

Sir I am in too much haste now to give you a particular answer, to your severall most endearing letters, which by my next I shall endeavour to do. I hurry this away in hast together with one to Mr. Cooper, to whom I have sent bills of Exchange for £238 . . 17 sterling which in case of Mortality &c. I desire you to take into your Custody for my use   I have also ordered him to pay you £80 sterling upon my account if he demand the same, part thereof, which trouble, I give for these two reasons, one that upon accident or Casualties, which all men are subject to, being my Agent & there upon the spot may serve me, the other is, one of the bills of Exchange being for £229 sterling, is drawn here by two persons (the Copy of which bill together with Copy of Judgment I have also sent you) Mr. Vincent Goddard & Capt. Wm. Norrington, Capt. Norrington will be in England, Goddard here,[2] if the money should not be answer'd, I believe it would be a safe Course to prosecute Norrington there, which perhaps Mr. Cooper might not be so forward in, because their Interest & Intimacy as I am informed is great, & being also his chief & principall Owner, for if it should happen to be protested, of which I hope I have no cause to doubt by that method against Norrington there, the business here will be facili-

William Fitzhugh's sugar bowl, showing arms used by the Virginia Fitzhughs
and Fitzhugh's date of marriage.

Owned by Eppa Hunton IV of Richmond.

Large saltcellars, showing the crest used by the Virginia Fitzhughs.
Owned by Mrs. Robert H. Stevenson of Boston.

tated & eased, if Goddard who is here should be insolvent. By my next also do intend to send you an Originall bill with like indorsement, as to Cooper in this, by which means, if the money be paid, you have no more to do but burn it, if it be not paid but protested, you will be better enabled to see it prosecuted effectually, if it be not paid nor protested, you will then be strengthened to proceed in such method, which in your Judgment shall seem best for my security. Sir By my next I shall be more full, & take care both to give you & Mr. Cooper account how I would have the money disposed of. I have it now in my intentions, for all or three fourths at least to be laid out in plate, but yet have not fully resolved, nor time to particularize. Sir I must beg your pardon for this last, which will admit me now to add no farther, but an assurance you shall always readily find me. Pray if Mr. Dorrell[3] be come to you yet, Remember me kindly to him, & if a Collash would not cost above £ six or seven pound I mean an ordinary one, but strong & well geared, that may be drawn with one horse, & Mr. Darrell could bring it in freight free, I could be very well contented, provided my money be paid, to be at the charge of one, & I am sure Mr. Darrell would not refuse the care & trouble, all which concurring I desire to have one bought

To Mr. Nicholas Hayward &c. W. ff.

[*LB*, pp. 154-55]

1. For Hayward, see various letters to above.
2. For Norrington, see ltr. to Cooper, April 4, 1681, note 2. For Goddard, ltr. to Captain F. Partis, Dec. 4, 1680, note 4.
3. Probably Sampson Darrell, who owned land in Stafford, Gloucester, and King William counties. In 1692 he testified in Stafford Court with reference to his frontier plantation at Pimmit's (also Pimmett's), "alias the Upper Spout, Run falling into Potomac River below and near the falls thereof," that is, at the Chain Bridge. Harrison, *Landmarks*, I, 75; *Exec. Journ. Council Col. Va.*, I, 429, 438; 17 V 115; 32 V 70, 339. The "Callash" is mentioned in a ltr. to H. Fitzhugh, July 18, 1687, note 3.

To Nicholas Hayward[1]

Mr. Nichs. Hayward   May 18th. 1688

Sir The above is Copy of my former, who by this have sent you the Originall bill, indorsed according to my promise in my former, & for those reasons there mentioned, also for the Callash if it cost no more than is there mentioned, I would have it sent, though it could not be brought freight free, provided it be delivered directly at my Landing. As in my former I referred to my next so in this I must do the same, this being only the produce of a sudden opportunity for Duplication of the former &c. I shall in the next be largely thankfull, & thankfully large to which I refer. I am secure in Maryland   W. ff.

To. Mr. Nichs. Hayward &c.

[*LB*, pp. 155-56]

1. For Hayward, see various ltrs. to him, above.

To Mrs. Mary Fitzhugh [1]

Dear Mother   June 1st. 1688

Having receiv'd but two letters from you last year, & both of them in one Ship, & in both of them the unwelcome news of your indisposition & weakness, with your own doubts of your continuance in the land of the living, which makes me mournfully doubt the worst, but yet hoping that God in his Mercy has by this time restored you to your former health, I take this opportunity to assure you that my wife, sister, & all our family are in good health, & wish the continuance of the same to you, I have also ordered Mr. Cooper to pay you £10 sterling, which please kindly to accept from   W. ff.

[*LB*, p. 156]

1. For Mary King Fitzhugh, see ltr. to Henry Fitzhugh, April 22, 1686, note 6, and subsequent ltrs. to her.

To Captain Henry Fitzhugh [1]

Dearest Brother   June 1st. 1688

I longingly expected every day this last winter especially by every Ship, the welcome receipt of a letter from you, wherein I might from your self, have the joyfull satisfaction of your good health, I must confess I never doubted your continued & constant love & affection, neither do I still, notwithstanding this Omission, which I was afraid was occasioned by indisposition till Mr. Hayward gave me the welcome assurance of the contrary. I please my self with the hopes of early receiving a line from you this next year, to make satisfaction for this year's failure, which will be most joyfully welcome to   Dear Brother Your W. ff.

To Capt. Henry Fitzhugh &c.

[*LB*, p. 156]

1. For Captain Henry Fitzhugh, see ltrs. to him above, especially that of April 22, 1686, note 1.

To John Cooper [1]

Mr. John Cooper   June 1st. 1688

Sir I was so full in two last by Capt. Bowman & Capt. Conway,[2] that now I shall have little to say, only to give order about the disposal of the money sent home to you, which I would have all laid out in plate by you & Mr. Hayward, because I have ordered him part of the money, which by a particular letter directed to both here inclosed, I shall give full Instructions in & therefore have no more to say than to assure you

To Mr. Jno. Cooper   I am Your W. ff.

[*LB*, p. 157]

1. For Cooper, see ltr. to, April 4, 1681, note 1.

2. Probably Thomas Bowman, commander of the *Henry* of London, a ship carrying in 1690 twenty-two men and twelve guns. P.R.O., C.O. 5/1305, p. 44, L.C. copy. A Robert Conway was commander of the *Prince*, bound for York River, as early as 1676. *Cal. St. Papers, Col., Am. & W.I., 1675-1676, Addenda 1574-1674*, Item 1020. He was probably the seaman who fought staunchly against the Dutch in 1667 (19 V 247; 21 V 125), however, and is probably not the present man.

To John Cooper and Nicholas Hayward [1]

Mr. Jno. Cooper & Mr. Nichs. Hayward   June 1st. 1688

In particular letters to you both I ordered you money, & in my last particular letter I acquainted you that I would have what I had not there expressly dispos'd of, laid out for my use in plate, after having paid your selves the full ballance of your Accts, the plate that I would have bought pray let it be plain & strong, being in these particulars following, if my money will reach to it, but rather leave some out, than bring me a penny in Debt   One dozen silver hafted knives. 1 doz: silver forks   One dozen silver spoons large & strong. 1 Set Castors   One 3 quart Tankard. A pair silver Candlesticks less than them sent last year by Mr. Hayward but more substantiall. One Silver Salvator plate   Four silver porringers   2 indifferent large, 2 small ones   A small silver bason, 1 doz. Silver plates. Four Silver Dishes 2 pretty large for a good joint of meat, & two of a smaller sort, if my money falls short let it be wanting in the Dishes, if there be any remaining let the Overplus be what it will, laid out in silver plates & let it all be thus marked W F S & that Coat of Arms put upon all pieces that are proper, especially the Dishes, plates & Tankards &c. that I have sent inclosed & blazoned in a letter to Mr. Hayward. Pray let it be sent by the first Conveniency, & by bill Loading deliver'd at my Landing

Gentlemen   Your W. ff.

To Mr. Nichs. Hayward & Mr. John Cooper

[*LB*, p. 157]

1. Hayward, WF's friend and advisor and usual purchasing agent, was often asked to confer with John Cooper, WF's tobacco factor and also at times his purchasing agent. WF respected Hayward's judgment more than he did Cooper's, as the reader may gather from at least one letter.

To Nicholas Hayward [1]

Mr. Nicholas Hayward   June 1st. 1688

I have now before me your severall most obliging letters, & continued offers of favour & friendship, more especially those by your Cousin Foote [2] & Capt. Madge,[3] wherein you give me the whole particulars of your unweary'd endeavours in negotiating my affairs about Ashton's purchase, & former Exchange &c, as also the Return of my money in the plate sent for, for all which I sincerely & heartily thank you, & do really wish for occasion to demonstrate my gratitude, as well as barely to acknowledge the obligations. Your Cousin Mr. Foote since his Arrival has not given me the honour of his good company, nor the happiness of any the least of his Commands, nor indeed the least knowledge of his sentiments or intentions, whereby I might have the minutest opportunity, of serving or advising him, which his near relation to you not only obliges but commands, & when ever required or in the least but intimated, shall be gladly receiv'd & readily obey'd. As to the building a small house for the Settlement of a Plantation, backward upon your neighbouring tract, I shall be always ready to assist Mr. Hayward,[4] as also in preparing for & planting an Orchard upon either or both & do intend, upon your first advice this year, of the continuance of your Intentions for that Settlement, to give you the building of such a house, though in my apprehensions cannot see the present profit nor future advantage of such an undertaking, the Tract being too small for so many Scituations, in the method our Country now stands, unless the Design were for a Quarter to settle hands upon, for the larger support of the River side plantation. I cannot understand by your Brother that there is any Defect in your Purchase, & consequently no need of farther advice for the firmer settlement thereof, if ever I perceive the least Defect in that kind, shall immediately undergo my best services, & utmost Endeavours to the closing such a Breach

I thank your kindness in Mr. Durands book & must agree with you, as well as I can understand it, that its a most weak unpolite piece, having neither the Rules of History, nor method of description, & taking it only as a private Gentleman's Journal, 'tis as barren & defective there too,[5] when I come out in print do intend to appear more regular, & therefore as yet am not provided for such an undertaking.[6] Sr. I am glad to hear by you of my Brother's health, which I would favourably think, indisposition or multiplicity of business, has hinder'd him from acquainting me with, for I find by your's that large glassing does not take up so much of his time now. I have sent by Capt. Sutton[7] directed to you, a skin which is esteemed a Lions with us here, killed upon your Town tract, which I would desire you to present in my behalf to him. I have in my two former given you an account of money, sent to Mr. Cooper with relation to your self in taking part, & assistance in laying out the same, which now upon second thoughts I wholly design for an additional supply (except £5 I have charged payable to Brother Smith, which according to the tenour thereof at sight I desire you to pay, & £10 I have ordered Mr. Cooper to pay, & the Callash if you purchase it wt. the freight thereof) for now my buildings finished, my plantations well settled, & largely stocked with Slaves, having added about five more than when I gave you an account thereof, & purchased at least three plantations more than is there mentioned, & being sufficiently stored with goods of all sorts, I esteem it as well politic as reputable, to furnish my self with an handsom Cupboard of plate which gives my self the present use & Credit, is a sure friend at a dead lift, without much loss, or is a certain portion for a Child after my decease, and therefore last year I had a small quantity from you, & about a like quantity from Bristol, & did expect some from Plymouth but that miscarry'd. By thus discovering my thoughts & intentions to you, you may perceive that what plate I design to have purchased, would be strong & plain, as being less subject to bruise, more Serviceable, & less out for the fashion, which I assure my self you will supply me with, as what you sent me last year was except in the Candlesticks. Brother & Sister Smith[8] gives you their humble services, & please to accept of the same from. Sr. The Inclosed is Impression of my Seal & Coat of Arms,[9] the Seal is lost, therefore I request your favour to supply me with another steel one

To Mr. Nichs. Hayward &c.   Your W. ff.

[LB, pp. 158-60]

1. For Hayward, the many ltrs. to above.
2. Richard Foote the younger (1666-1724) was son of a sister of Nicholas Hayward and Richard Foote, one of the partners in the "Brent Town" enterprise. The elder Foote was just twenty in 1652 when he came to Virginia as agent for Nicholas Hayward the elder. Foote returned to London within five years and married his employer's daughter. He himself became a successful merchant. Though WF's later references to the younger Foote are hardly complimentary, the young man did settle in Stafford at "Brent Town" and was by 1700 a J. P. Harrison, *Landmarks,* I, 193; *Prince Wm. WPA,* pp. 21-22; 1 V 371; 7 V 73; 9 W(2) 182; 33 V 159-60.
3. Unidentified.

4. Probably Samuel Hayward (q.v.), though possibly Joseph (q.v.).

5. *Voyages d'un François Exilé pour la Religion avec une description de la Virgine & Marilan dans L'Amerique* (orig. ed. 1687; trans. and ed. by Gilbert Chinard as *A Huguenot Exile in Virginia; or, Voyages of a Frenchman Exiled for His Religion, with a Description of Virginia and Maryland* [New York, 1934]). See Introduction above and notes to certain ltrs., especially to that to N. Hayward, May 20, 1686, note 2. The book concludes with a transcription of Hayward's brochure advertising the "Brent Town" tract as a haven for Huguenots. WF is hardly gracious here (of course he is acquiescing to Hayward's expressed feeling), for Durand gives a favorable and striking picture of WF's own establishment and the way of living of the first Virginia aristocrats such as Ralph Wormeley and WF. Durand does rather dryly remark that everyone in Virginia appeared to want to sell land to the Huguenots. WF was probably among them. But Professor Chinard feels that Durand's account was "admirably calculated to attract the attention of the French refugees to Virginia," and that WF is hardly fair in his remarks to Hayward.

6. Like other educated men of the colony, WF planned a book on the colony. Later he did write an introductory sketch and compiled the laws.

7. Henry Sutton was in 1702/3 master of the ship *William and John*. His name appears frequently in Stafford County records. 33 V 35; *Exec. Journ. Council Col. Va.*, II, 289.

8. Dr. Ralph Smith and WF's sister Dorothy.

9. For discussion of the Fitzhugh arms as WF conceived it to be, see ltr. to Henry Fitzhugh, January 30, 1686/87, note 2, and Introduction.

To Nicholas Hayward [1]

Mr. Nicholas Hayward   June 8th. 1688

Sr. The above is Copy of my former, the inclosed speaks its own business, & is only Duplicate of what I sent to Mr. Cooper in my former. Suppose this together with my severall former letters, will afford you the reason of my joining you in the trouble with Mr. Cooper, & now have only to beg your pardon for all the troubles given you ~~by~~ In my last I sent you the Impression of my lost Seal, desiring you to get me one more Cut, having no more of those Impressions by me, & that but by accident   I have in this sent you the Coat blazoned, wch. I desired you to get fair Cut in Steel, & for fear of loss again, I believe it would not be much amiss to send me another large one upon an Ivory Stand, it is thus blazoned viz A field of Azure three Chearonells, brased in the base of Escocheon & a Chief Or [2]

Your W. ff.

To Mr. Nichs. Hayward &c.

[*LB*, p. 160]

1. For Hayward, the many ltrs. to him, above.

2. For discussion of the proper arms for the Fitzhughs of Virginia, see ltr. to Henry Fitzhugh, January 30, 1686/87, note 2, and Introduction.

To Nicholas Hayward [1]

Mr. Nichs. Hayward   April 1st. 1689

I have receiv'd your severall particular & kind letters this year & congratulate, your new acquisition of part of Mr. Ashton's back tract,[2] though I cannot agree with you, according to the Platt, that it lyes so very contiguous to you & remote from me, but this can assure you, that it is a bargain really worth your money, if it be as cheap as Mr. Darrell[3] represents it. I also thank your kindness, in sending me so much of my Plate sent for, nay more than I could have expected singly from your self without the mortality or resignation of Mr. Cooper, which is safely come into the Country, & has been this month but is not yet arrived at my house, neither the letters above four days since, what the reason is that Mr. Cooper did not join with you, in buying the whole as far as my money reached, nor lay out the money in his hands for the remainder according to my directions, I can't imagine, without the closeness of his nature, made my designs seem extravagant, in which point I have sufficiently writ to him, & withall signify'd to him that he is my Factor not my Adviser, because to him I pay Commission. Now Sir to you to whom I pay no Commission, & by that means under no Obligation, further than your generous & free nature obliges, I must beg excuse that I want expressions, throughly to acknowledge my Gratitude   Sir the inclosed is Copy of my Proposals to Mr. Secretary,[4] which he gives me assurance will take with my Lord Culpepper, therefore beg your favour to negotiate in my behalf with his Lordship, & to get a Confirmation in England, though the drawing deeds, consulting Counsel, & inrolment in Chancery cost twelve or fifteen guineas, your own Purchase of Brenton[5] with the Rentcharge thereof, gives you the manner & method. Your late Acquisition assures me of your Abilitys, & your continued kindness emboldens me to request this, as also another, that you would please to make a piece of Plate of ten guineas price from me acceptable to your Lady by your kind representation thereof, for your Consummation of the same. Perhaps My Lord Culpepper may object that the quantity of land, mentioned within those Bounds (which I have also sent you inclosed to perfect, the business there if it be possible) may be more, but the Rent roll which Mr. Secretary has diligently searched, makes that fully appear, also that the Purchase is too low for so great a quantity of Land, considering that you gave as much or rather more rateably, for your tract of 30000 Acres, which lyes remote to that, it is easily answered your's is a new acquisition, & consequently lyable to the Rents in specie, as my Lord put it, but this whole Purchase that I make, is of Land taken up before the Originall Grant to the first Proprietors of this Northern Neck, & therefore stands under the Conditions upon the first settlement of the Country, & not my Lord's conditions now to be made upon new Purchases & consequently neither by his Lordship himself or any other, to be inhansed or advanced without a generall Disturbance to the People: Also what's now to be taken up, it lyes in his Lordship's power, to put what terms upon the Rent & in what specie he pleases, therefore 1000 Acres of Land, taken up since my Lord's acquirement, is more worth for an annuall advantage or immediate sale of a Rent charge, than 5000 Acres antiently taken up, & all that I propose to purchase within the bounds mentioned, has been a considerable time taken up before his Lordship's Right. And this I dare affirm that if his Lordship was to be Governor himself, he would not be able wt. the greatest Industry, assisted by power to clear from my intended Purchase £20 ster: a year, & if he wants that power, his utmost endeavour will never bring it to above half that Sum, for all the Tennants upon the whole Tract three excepted are not able to pay their Rents in money, being poor needy men, & then the refuge must be by Distress, & nothing will be found to Distrain but Cows & horses, & those to be valu'd by those that look upon themselves to be under the same Mischief, & from thence the Valuaon. may be judged. I must assure you Sr. that if I make this Purchase, I have not the expectation of receiving one penny in money for Rent but being placed in the middle of the Purchase, & Tobo. my method of Dealing, Tobo. will answer my ends & suit my Conveniency, & perhaps in time reimburse me or my Posterity for the money laid out. Thus Sr. I have given you some reasons of my Proposals, which when duely considered, may be conducive to persuade his Lordship to sell, which if, I would not have you stick upon ten or twenty pounds extraordinary in the Purchase, therefore in generall terms shall desire you to act in this affair for me as for your self, & whatever you do shall be thankfully acknowledged. Mr. Cooper intimated to me that the money in his hands was ready at your call, which I desire you to take into your custody, & I shall endeavour to send more by the latter Ships, & what my money falls short if the Purchase goes forward, please to propose your own Security for the payment thereof, with Interest, & I shall take effectuall & satisfactory care to answer it: but if the Purchase should not go on, I still continue my resolutions of purchasing the same pieces of Plate, & particularly the knives which I have already forks for, when they come to hand, which I desire you'll please to purchase for me according to my last years direction, with the addition of a Silver ladle, & send it in by the first Ships. Capt. Brent who is now at my house, has the same designs, but waits the issue of this, for the purchase of almost as great a quantity, above Oquoquan, & intends to propose it in partnership, which will be a far more profitable Purchase, by reason little Land is already Pattented, and what is, must come under your own Conditions, because Pattented since the Granting of this Northern Neck, himself best knows what he does, & the advantage thereby, & therefore to his relation I refer. Sr. What encouragement my poor Endeavours or Interest can give to your pleasing Establishment at Brenton, & a sudden Commotion we have had (under the pretended expectations of Indians [6] in which Capt. Brent has given you a full just & clear relation) gives me the present opportunity not only to assure you the people, but also to satisfie the Government, that were full encouragement given & Immunitys granted to that Town, which might be conducive to draw Inhabitants thither, the Country would be indifferent secure from future alarms, & it would be a sure Bulwark against reall dangers, because either by them or within them must lye the Indian Road, a good Company of Men there settled, would be immediately called, either to keep off the Enemy at his first approach, or cut him short in his Return. Sr. This sudden turn of times in England may perhaps at present give a Check to the Increment of Brenton from your French expectation,[7] but I believe may be additionally supplyed, by those methods Capt. Brent intimates, though not plainly expresses, by being a Refuge & sanctuary for Roman Catholicks, & I dare say let it be encreased by whom it will, our Governmt. will give it all the Indulgences that can be reasonably required, by reason of its convenient Scituation for a watch & Defence agst. Indian Depredations & Excursions, neither do I believe that persuasion will be hindred from settling any where in this Country, especially there, where being Christians they may secure us against the Heathen. I hope to have another opportunity to write to you again this year, therefore have now only to beg your pardon, for this & all former troubles, with this assurance you shall always find me thankfully acknowledge my self. Sr. Inclosed is a bill of Exchange of Mrs. Warner's upon Mr. Thornbush [8] which I desire you to receive for £5

To Mr. Nicholas Hayward &c.   W. ff.

[LB, pp. 160-64]

1. For Hayward, see the many ltrs. to above.

2. Since Samuel Hayward was a co-executor with WF of the James Ashton estate, he may have aided his brother Nicholas in purchasing this property WF so much desired. For the Ashton property, see ltrs. beginning with one to Hayward of January 30, 1686/87, note 12.

3. For Sampson Darrell, see ltr. to Hayward, May 26, 1688, note 3. Darrell may have been attorney in fact for the Ashton heirs.

4. Nicholas Spencer was agent for the Northern Neck Proprietors as well as Secretary of State in Virginia. For WF's proposals, see enclosure addressed to Spencer just below. Though WF did not get the one hundred thousand acres, he and Brent did later become the Proprietors' agents in the Northern Neck.

5. For many references to Hayward's "Brent Town" project, see ltrs. above.

6. For "danger" in 1687, see ltr. to N. Spencer, July 4, 1687, and note 2, above. This is our first reference to "Parson Waugh's Tumult," one of the exciting events in early Stafford history. The whole affair appears to have grown out of the remains of Baconian feeling combined with the struggle in nearby Maryland of extreme Protestantism vs. Jacobinism. In March, 1688/89, Burr Harrison of Stafford saw Indians on their annual hunting expedition south of the Potomac and grew panicky. He brought reports (allegedly from an Indian) that Colonel Pye and other Maryland Catholics were hatching a plot and would soon dip their hands in Protestant blood. The fanatical agitation of Parson John Waugh of Stafford, in sermons and otherwise, directed the emotion against the circumspect and mild Catholic Brents. The Stafford people rushed to arms. Real trouble might have resulted but for the good sense of the three Northern Neck members of the Virginia Council, Spencer, Lee, and Allerton (qq.v.), who had a firm grip on the government. Waugh, Harrison, and John West, a third participant, were arrested and brought before the Council and General Court at Jamestown (see R. Lee's recommendation in Exec. Journ. Council Col. Va., I, 104-6).

WF for a time sheltered Brent at his house. This, and the fact that WF and Brent had got the better of several more evangelical Protestants in Stafford in legal land-cases, turned certain of the populace and Waugh against WF. For WF's troubles with Waugh, see Introduction and ltrs. below.

All these rumors of potential massacre of Protestants in Maryland and Virginia irreparably harmed the project of settling French Huguenots on the "Brent Town" property. Harrison, Landmarks, I, 131; 30 V 31-37.

7. William III (1650-1702) had landed at Torbay on Nov. 5, 1688. He was proclaimed jointsovereign with Mary Feb. 13, 1689. WF saw how the wind was blowing and appeared convinced, by what had just happened in Stafford, that English Catholics might now be persecuted.

8. Madam Mildred Warner is discussed in connection with a ltr. to her, Jan. 1690/91, note 1, below. Thornbush is unidentified.

To the Honourable Nicholas Spencer [1]

Proposals to The Honourable Nicholas Spencer

Esqr. Agent & Attorney in Virginia for the Right Honourable the Lord Culpepper To purchase 100000 Acres of Land at ten years Purchase of the Rent, thus to be deduced 100000 Acres, at 120 lb. Tobo. ℔ thousand, comes to 12000lb. Tobo. out of which must be deducted 20 ℔ Cent at least, for receiving & reducing it into hhds., which is 2400, then remains 9800, & 20 ℔ hhd. allowed, estimated each hhd. at 400 makes twenty four hhds. & half, which comes to 735 again deducted out of 9800 makes the clear Tobo. 9065 which at 5 sh ℔ Cent the utmost value that can be expected, for Tobo. so scattering & remote in the best of times, amount to £22 .. 13 .. at ten year's purchase is £226 .. 10 sh .. but because as in the severall Rentrolls appears, there is not above 84 or at most 86 thousand Acres in our County already taken up & seated, & some thousand Acres part of that, above Oquoquan, & from Okoquan downwards, fully taken up & almost all seated, & it might be doubtfull to my Lord's Interest to go beyond those bounds, because part is there taken up, & greater part lies still in his Lordship's Grant, therefore to take off those scruples and objections, I am willing to become a Purchaser, from the head of Okoquan to Machodock the extent of our County downwards, not exceeding five miles in the Woods from the nearest Landing, that I may be far enough clear from Brenton purchase, & without my Lord's suspicion of getting any considerable quantity of land already untaken up, the said Land from Oquoquan downwards according as the County Runs, & five miles backwards where the County will admit it, which will no where do it till you come to the head of Potomack Creek, & from thence in some places upwards, which said proposed Tract, according to the severall Rentrolls, may amount to about sixty or seventy thousand Acres, but because there may be some surplusage, I am willing to allow it 80000 Acres & pay accordingly, comes to £177 .. 10 sterling, which I will give for that tract, & immediately pay down the money upon his Lordships Order to your Honr. for passing me the said Estate over in fee under these Circumstances to have within the sd. Tract, all benefits of any Escheat, if they fall, & all other Priviledges as his Lordship has by virtue of the first Purchase or last Grant in 1688 except the benefit of all Mines & Minerals, wch. I wholly refer to his Lordship, under the yearly Rent of an ear of Indian Corn if lawfully demanded, to be paid at the feast of the Nativity, & withall that I may have priviledge to take out Pattents or Deeds in my own name (paying the Officer's fees according to the Constitution of the Office here) for any part greater or smaller, or as many as I please, within the before granted Premises, & the Rent to the Respective Pattents to be a grain of Indian Corn. The reasons for taking out new Pattents or Deeds, are first, For Escheats that I may have a right from his Lordship, as well as a Possession, if any fall, Secondly to get the advantage of pretended Rights if any such to be met with, & thirdly to get as much as I can in my own particular name, to avoid future Quo Warrantos. That I may have farther or other Deeds & assurances, as Council learned shall advise, either by Deeds drawn in England, & inrolled in the high Court of Chancery there or otherwise

&c. being at my own particular Cost & Charge. That I may have all the immediate Rents & arrearages, but if his Lordship opposes the arrearages rather than break off I will desist.[2] The land is thus bounded (viz)[3] Beginning at or near some of the falls of Oquoquan Run, ten miles from the mouth of the said River, & on the South West side thereof, & extending by a Line drawn South West & by West, crossing the Runs & Branches of the severall Creeks that Run into Potomck. River, to Wit, Neapsco, Yeasocomico alias Powel's Creek, Quanticutt, Chappawamsick, Oquia & Potomack Creeks, untill the said South West by West Line shall have included the branches of Potomack Creek within the limits within the limits [sic] of Stafford County where the branches that run into Rappahannock River meet & render it the bounds of that County, & consequently that this South West & by West line, by or betwixt the branches of both the Rivers of Rappahannock & Potomack, that is now the known bounds of Stafford & Rappahannock Countys, & from that place or point of Intersection along the said line of Division, untill it reach the most Southern and Eastern parts of Stafford County inclusive, bounded on the South by the head of Machodock River, & so to the mouth thereof, & from thence up along Potomack River, according to the severall Courses thereof, to the mouth of Oquoquan River first mentioned, & from thence up the said River ten Miles to the first Beginning

Mr. Nichs. Hayward Sr. When I made these proposals to Mr. Secretary, did not think to have given you the trouble, as you may see, but upon second thoughts, have thought it my best way, if I can make a purchase to be as quick with it as I can, that I may have the more time to make a firm Establishment thereof, & considering also that you had made a Purchase of the like nature, & consequently experiencedly knowing the Consummation of this, if his Lordship agrees to it, as I have fully writ you in my lettr. I have also got Mr. Brent to lay me down the bounds, so that there's nothing wanting, to make a perfect Deed in England, But if these new troubles, & the great oppressions that from thence we may guess will fall upon the Roman Catholicks in England, should incline them to remove, any place in Virginia, & Brenton I esteem a good Sanctuary for them, I could still be contented to continue my proposed Exchange, though I have added almost a third in Land, Negroes &c. more than when I writ you, & then had rather let alone this purchase, for it is not worth two pence to anyone that is not actually upon the Spot

[LB, pp. 164-67]

1. Nicholas Spencer was at this time agent for the Proprietors of the Northern Neck as well as Secretary of State in Virginia.

2. As noted in a ltr. to Hayward of May 6, 1689, WF soon found out that Culpeper was dead and "desisted" from this ambitious project.

3. This area would have included several of the counties which have since sprung from the Stafford of WF's time.

To John Cooper [1]

Mr. John Cooper   April 18th. 1689

Sr.   I receiv'd your two letters this year, one by Gutteridge the other by Harris [2] in the first you send me no Accot. Currant, & charge me very high for receiving money, & therein promise that my money shall be laid out according to my Order, when it is receiv'd, when in the same letter you acknowledge your self the paymaster by taking Norrington's & Goddard's bargain [3] off of their hands, & consequently your self to be Paymaster, in your last you give me acct. of the receipt of my money, that is to say, your self was then willing to pay it, but withall nothing that I sent for, nor no provision therein, perhaps esteeming that I had been extravagant in sending for those things, & you by your great judgment would moderate by forbearing to send, I must tell Mr. Cooper, it is a Factor, that I require, not a Director or Superadviser & expect one to follow orders, not to dispute the necessity or Inconvenience of them, especially considering it was my own money to be disposed of, & neither desired nor Requested to run in debt for a farthing. I must acknowledge my Employ small & inconsiderable to a Gentleman in your Method & Circumstances, therefore if you are willing to decline please to signifie the same, for as long as I keep clear of debt, I reckon to have a due observance of Orders, as if I was the greatest Merchant Sr. Before I had receiv'd your letters, especially your last (which but two days ago came to hand, though the Ship has been in the Country this two months) I advised & persuaded two Gentlemen Mr. Hayward & Mr. Samson Darrell,[4] to make their Consignments to your self, & when it is worth while should be able also to persuade others, assuring them of your true honesty & Integrity, which yet I am very unwilling to question, from whom by this Ship you'll have some Consignments, & by the next may expect more, as also I have sent a little by this Ship to say seven hhds. as by the bill of Loading, you'll see, which I desire you to dispose for my best advantage. Sr. You write me also in your last that the money in your hands is ready for Mr. Hayward when he calls for it, which please to deliver him, that I may have it disposed by him according to my Directions. I do think by the next Ship to consign you more Tobo., & then shall advise what I will have done with the proceeds, that comes from both parcells.

To Mr. John Cooper   Your   W. ff.

[*LB,* pp. 168-69]

1. For John Cooper, see the many ltrs. addressed to him, above.
2. Nicholas Gutteridge was captain of the *Spencer* of London, a ship of 20 men and 16 guns. This ship left Virginia in the convoy of August 20, 1690, in its voyage of the next year. There are several other Gutteridges in the Virginia records. P.R.O., C.O. 5/1305, L.C. copy; 16 V 70; 7 W(1) 244, 296. Captain Martin Harris is mentioned as early as 1682/83, ltr. to Cooper, March 10.
3. Probably the bill of exchange mentioned in ltr. to N. Hayward, May 10, 1688, note 2. WF is probably sarcastic here in using the word "bargain," for he is clearly furious at Cooper's behavior.
4. Samuel Hayward and Sampson Darrell, WF's neighbors, are mentioned several times above.

To John Cooper [1]

Mr. John Cooper   May 6th. 1689

Sr. In my last by Dorman,[2] I gave my sentiments for not sending my plate according to Orders, & therefore have acquainted you that I have desired Mr. Hayward this year to send me it in, according to last year's Directions, giving him an accot. that you will pay the ballance of my Accompt in your hands for him to lay out in Plate for me according to my particular desires & directions to him this year. I have also by the said Ship consigned you seven hhds. Tobo., which I desired you to dispose to my best advantage, & promised you in this to acquaint how I would have that money disposed of that the Tobo. produced, which I would have paid to my Mother, if she be living as far as ten pound goes, if the Tobo. will reach but if it should yield more, please to keep it in your hands till my farther Order. In my last I also acquainted that Mr. Darrel & Mr. Hayward [3] had each of them consigned you Tobo. by the said Ship, & I believe by Burnham you may expect a greater parcell from Mr. Hayward & perhaps from my self too, I am not yet resolved, I hope to hear timely from you this year, & if I could have news it would be very welcome, especially some abatement upon this great Tobo. Custom, & I should be encouraged to make a handsome Consignment, but as 'tis, there's so money required for clearing Tobo., & the Commission for paying & receiving such a Considerable Sum of money, so high, though it should happen to be in own hands, I mean your self to be purchaser, as it happen'd to you last year, that it is more uncertain for a Planter to get money by consigned Tobo. than to get a prize in a lottery, there being twenty Chances for one Chance

To. Mr. John Cooper Mercht. in London   Your   W. ff.

[*LB*, pp. 169-70]

1. For Cooper, see the many ltrs. to him, above.
2. Dorman, mentioned in three ltrs. of 1689, is unidentified.
3. Sampson Darrell and Samuel Hayward, mentioned just above in ltr. to Cooper, April 19.

To John Cooper [1]

Mr. Jno. Cooper   July 22nd. 1689

Sr. In my last I gave you an account of my consigning you seven hhds. by Dorman, & how I would have the money disposed, that it raised as far as ten pound went, if it should rise so high, & therefore told you I thought I might consign you some more by Burnham which I have also done, & herewith send you a bill of Loading, which please to dispose to my best advantage. Mr. Sam Hayward has also consigned you some before & some now by Burnham, the neat proceeds whereof he desires you to give my Accot. Credit for, which said money whatever it be, I desire you to pay to his brother Mr. Nichs. Hayward, when he presents you with a bill of mine payable to him for £25 .. 10 sterling, as also to pay the ballance of the proceeds of my Tobo. now & formerly consigned after payment of £10 to my Mother, if any thing shall then remain, which I much doubt by reason of the extreme lowness of Tobo. but if my Tobo. should not arise to £10, whatever it arises to, please to let my Mother have it, but be sure bring me not in debt. If Mr. Hayward should upon the presenting the said bill, only require his brother's money out of your hands, because it is money only lent his brother, & perhaps he'll answer for the remainder himself,

& my Tobo. should yield above £10 before Ordered, please to send me in those things, or any part of them my money in your hands will purchase (viz) A home shagged Saddle, two suites of Child bed linnen, shoes & stocking for the remainder, though I assure you I expect nothing of them. We have had so extreme a low & scarce Market for our Tobo. here, that it is but three days ago I disposed of my Tobo. abroad, & at a very mean rate too, I have now by me of my own Crops above 100 hhds. Oroonoko, but freight being high & Tobo. light, & no promising encouragement, I durst not venture to Ship it, therefore have this year planted at severall Quarters sweetscented, not that I expect that will bear a much better price, but for that it will weigh heavyer, & therefore better answer freight & keep better & so not so great danger or loss, if want of freight or a Market make one keep it by him. I hope to hear timely from you, who am

Your   W. ff.

[*LB*, pp. 170-71]

1. For Cooper, see the many ltrs. to him, above. Dorman and Hayward are mentioned in the ltrs. to Cooper of April 19 and May 6, 1689, just above. Captain Burnham is mentioned many times earlier.

To Nicholas Hayward [1]

Mr. Nichs. Hayward   May 6th. 1689

Sr. I intended to have Duplicated my last by Dorman,[2] especially about the purchase from my Lord Culpepper, but since hearing certainly from your self in Capt. Brent's letter that he is dead,[3] I did not apprehend a probability of making the proposed Purchase, and therefore desist, well knowing you being upon the Place can best tell, whether any thing be in prospect to be negotiated in that affair, if those letters come safely to your hands, also since the writing thereof, have been informed by Mr. Darrell, that you esteemed me a jealous pated fool, & gave those two instances, the one of the purchase of Mr. Ashton's tract, & the other for the set price of the Callash,[4] farther adding that you did not care for being concerned for such a person, neither would you advance the limited price a penny, whatever the prospect of advantage might be thereby, both which (to bring me right in your Esteem though I'll promise you not Introductive of a farther trouble, which I acknowledge I have already sufficiently given you, & will promise you for the future to clear in that nature my self of farther guilt) I will clear as to the first Mr. Ashton's Purchase, I proposed as much as the Land was intrinsically worth, & I had rather be without than give more whatever representations may be made thereof, & I am sure it is £20 better to me than any Purchaser else, because of its Vicinity. As to the second, the purchase of the Callash, it was only a recreative project, & if for that Sum proposed, it could be procured, I could willingly have spared it, for the fancy of my present Recreation, but did not think it reasonable, to give my fancy an unlimited allowance. Sr. In my last I sent to you to purchase the Remainder of the plate left behind this year of my Design last year, which I have desired you again to purchase for me, my resolutions still continuing the same for that supply, & would also desire you to send it in by Capt. Gutteridge in the Spencer,[5] who is a carefull Master & in a good Ship & will be early, but if he should not come away early, then I desire you to send it in the first good Ship, that comes for this River or Rappahannock, the money Mr. Cooper has writ me he is always ready to pay, though I last year mentioned the plate, yet now I think it convenient to mention it again (viz) Two Silver Dishes weighing 50 oz. a piece or thereabouts, two Ditto weighing 70 oz. a piece or thereabouts, a Sett of Castors that is to say for Sugar, Pepper and Mustard about 24 or 26 oz. a basin betwixt 40 & 45 oz. a Salver about 30 oz. a pair of Candlesticks about 30 oz. a ladle about 10 oz. a Case containing a dozen silver hafted knives, & a dozen silver hafted forks answerable, what remains if any, let it be laid out in a large Salt, & what else you think convenient. I must again repeat & request you to send me the said plate by the first ship comes out for Rappahannock or Potomack, if Capt. Gutteridge be not as forward as any, for his bringing it will very suite my conveniency. The Ship is just ready to sail that I send this by, & therefore beg pardon that I cannot enlarge about your Neighboring Plantation, & your delighted Brenton, which by my next by Capt. Burnham [6] (who is now at my house while I am writing this) I shall be full of. Sr. I must return you my hearty thanks & due acknowledgements, for your continuall & continued favours, & particularly for your last year's kindness, in the purchase of that parcell of plate sent me & receiv'd. Sr. The ballance of your Acct. last year was 1 sh 10d. if I had time would for your satisfaction have sent you Copy thereof I am with great sincerity

To Mr. Nicholas Hayward &c.   Your   W. ff.

[LB, pp. 171-73]

1. For Hayward, see the many ltrs. to him, above.
2. Dorman is mentioned in the ltrs. to Cooper of April 19 and May 6, 1689, above.
3. Lord Culpeper died January 27, 1689.
4. Clearly WF wanted the Ashton tract, but one would certainly not judge by his ltrs. to Hayward that he was a "jealous-pated fool." The "Callash," a light carriage, is mentioned twice above.
5. For Gutteridge, see ltr. to Cooper, April 18, 1689, note 2.
6. WF's friend Captain Burnham is mentioned many times above.

To Nicholas Hayward [1]

Mr. Nicholas Hayward   July 22nd. 1689

I have already writ you twice this year, wherein I gave you an account of the delivery of the delivery [sic] of my plate, with many thanks for your care & trouble, in the purchase and conveyance thereof, which this Convenience by Burnham gives me the opportunity thankfully to repeat. In my last I desired you to call for money of Mr. Cooper, & to lay it out in plate for me according to direction there given, which was pursuant to my advice last year, only in my last which I question not but before is come to hand, I advised more particularly, & nominated the method for its coming in, which I will so far transcribe as relates thereto, (& would desire you to send it by Capt. Gutteridge in the Spencer,[2] who is a carefull Master & in a good Ship, & will be early, then I desire you to send it in the first good Ship that comes for this River or Rappahk. the money Mr. Cooper has writ me he is always ready to pay you, though I last year mention'd the plate, yet now I think it convenient to mention it again (viz) 2 Silver Dishes weighing 50 oz. a piece or thereabouts   2 Ditto weighing 70 ounces a pieces or thereabouts, a Sett of Castors that is to say for Mustard, Pepper & Sugar about 24 or 26 ounces   A bason betwixt 40 & 45 oz. a Salver about 30 oz. a ladle about 20 oz. a Cace containing a doz. silver hafted knives & a doz Silver hafted forks answerable, what remains if any, let it be laid out in a large Salt, & what else you think convenient, which I believe before I can reasonably expect your receipt of this, you will have shipped off.   Sr.   In mine last year I assured you that my Carpenter should build you a small house upon the clear ground in your Neighbouring purchase, if you continued your resolutions of settling there which before this should have been, but that I had not nails of my own to spare, & could purchase none, but the other day your brother [3] promis'd to supply me with nails for that purpose, & next month I intend to set my man to work upon it, which shall be forthwith finished. In my first this year I gave you the assurance, as also I have done to Capt. Brent here, that if I could do Brenton any service by due Commendations to particular persons or any encouragement from the County, or from the publick, if ever I come to be concerned there you might fully assure your selves of, & still do & shall continue the same. Sr. Herewith will come to your hands from your brother a bill of Exchange for £25 .. 10 drawn upon Mr. Cooper, which he desired me to lend him to pay for the Smith, he spoke to me so late, that I believe you will have disposed my money before this will come to your hand. I advised him to write to you, to charge him in his acct. Debtor for the said sum, which I told him, I did assuredly believe, would be fully satisfactory to you, but he, with some trouble & concern, was unwilling thereto, because he apprehends you esteem him negligent in his business, & careless in contriving you payment for the ballance of his debt already contracted, & so is ashamed to offer a farther debt till this be first cleared, which really troubles him, & he is resol- resolved [sic], to take effectual care forthwith fully to answer it, & toward payment of this has ordered me what money his Tobo. produces that he has consigned to Mr. Cooper, which I have also ordered Mr. Cooper, to pay you, together with what money of mine he has in his hands, if any, for Tobo. is so dull a Commodity, that I look but for a small produce of that little Tobo. I have this year shipt & Consigned to Mr. Cooper, & if my money should be already laid out as I imagine before this comes it will be, & consequently but a small part of that bill paid, I would desire you not to protest it, & next year Mr. Hayward & my self will take due care that the whole remainder be answer'd if you do not think it more adviseable & friendly to charge it to his proper accompt, & by that means give him the assurance of your continued kindness & assistance to him, I ca'nt tell what his debt is already to you, but can give you this assurance, that if it be not extraordinary great his Estate will be largely Solvent fully to answer it, together with what remains unpaid of this, he having four good Slaves with some other English Servants, a large stock of good Tobo., his house well furnished, a good Stock of Cattle horses hogs sheep, & his stock of debts every day increasing by his Clerk's place, & Smith's work [4] together with the addition of his Crops in his own hand, & I dare say not a pound of Tobo. nor a penny of money in debt, in this Country except you reckon this to me. Now Sr. Having given you this account of your brother, I heartily request the favour of you, to give me some account of mine, for he will not be so kind as to give me one line, nor in deed can I learn from any one, any thing of his Circumstances, which I would gladly hear of, as I have been thus free with you about yor. bror. & troublesome abt. mine, please to think of some service, wherein I may deserve your continued favours, & you shall find no one more ready to contribute than

Sir   Your W.ff.

[*LB*, pp. 173-75]

1. For Hayward, see the many ltrs. to him, above.
2. For Gutteridge, see ltr. to Cooper, April 18, 1689, note 2.
3. Presumably Samuel Hayward, mentioned often above.
4. Presumably Samuel Hayward had a blacksmith and assistants at work, probably in making nails.

To Madam Mildred Warner [1]

Madam Warner   January 1690/1

I have throughly weighed & considered your husband's Will, both as to the Demising the severall lands therein mentioned, as also the Distribution of his personall Estate, & do find to the best of my Judgment, that your second son George now as heir to his brother & father will hold & enjoy all the lands, which would also have happened, by the particular bequest & limitations of the said Will, if it had been good, which for reasons that I shall hereafter shew you, I esteem not good, for all the pretension that can be, of a Right to your youngest son Robin [2] by the Will, is only to make good the Remainder, for want of a particular Estate to raise the said Remainder upon, which I must confess if it had been in a Deed would have so operated, but in a Will it is quite otherwise, as I have largely discoursed Mr. Chilton [3] in that matter to whom I refer. As to the younger Children's Right in the personall Estate, I look upon it as good & equall with your self, & any of the eldest children, for where any Will is made, & no filiall portions to some of the Children, nor provision made in the life time of their father, that Will ipso jure is void, & they shall come in for an equall share with the rest of the Children, thatt it is so, reason & naturall Equity will tell you, for if by the Law the father's omission or forgetfullnes, shall not be construed, to the utter ruin & destruction of a Child, as by the settled & agreed Law of filial portions, a fortiori where the intention was otherwise, but suddenly by weakness or death prevented, as in Mr. Warner's case of his latter Will, & though that cannot operate so far as to make the first Dispositions good & valid in Law, yet it concurs with the Law it self to invalidate & make void the first Will, wherein two young Children, what at the time of making thereof, were not known, & are by it wholly & totally unprovided for, & that contrary to the meaning & intent of the Testator, as by the last intended Will appears, for both Law & reason allows, that some suffer a little, rather than that others be totally ruined & destroyed. I must confess it would have been a mighty mischief to your son G. if your son H. had lived,[4] for invalidating the Will would have proved his Disherison, but now there's no such prejudice to be feared, for G. as well by the will as by the Law, has a Right to the whole Lands, in my opinion, as well Rappahannock as else. How this is to be managed & what damage you have sustained for want of more timely proceedings therein, & the nature of your payments already made, will here take up too long a Discourse, therefore Mr. Chilton & I have largely & particularly discoursed that matter, who will give you full advice & informaon therein, together with your particular prejudice for want of your immediate Inventorying the Estate & the present conveniencys & inconveniencys that happen to your self thereby, also measures for your future proceedings therein. As to your father's Deed of 2000 Acres of Land I am inclining to believe the fee simple in your self as Survivor, & consequently the disposall thereof, because the fee is raised after the settlemt. of the longest liver, & so consequently upon the longest liver, but what makes me doubtfull is, whether the word their, has relation to the heirs of the Survivor, or that the first settlement of the fee be upon the heir proceeding from the loyns of both, because that pronoun is in the purall number, &c   Now Madam it will seem very hard perhaps upon your son George, but to have an equal share with rest of the children, & especially the youngest Daughter, but if it be considered withall, that he has all the lands of his father, that will alienate, & farther also considered, that if the Law were not so, the two youngest children were totally ruined & beggared unless by God's providence & your indulgence preserved, from that fatall mischief, Also your son H's death has made little or no alteration, for as his share of the personall Estate is to be equally divided amongst you, so a division of all, makes the same thing as if his land had been separated. For the 10000 lb. Tobo. legacy to Walker Cant,[5] though the condition be joined to the Execution, & not to the Substance of the Legacy, which by all the books speaking, generally makes the Legacy due at the time, though the Legatee live not so long, yet I am of opinion this case of your's is an Exception from the said generall Rule,

& that the Legacy is not due, because the intent & meaning of the Testator seems otherwise, which is the chief guide for the construction of a Will, & here the Testator's intent appears that he shall have 10000 lb. Tobo., if the land demised to his brother Austin [6] did not come to him, by that time he was twenty one years of age, but if he never had the land then the Tobo., & on the contrary if he had the Land or a Right thereto, then no Tobo., but had a Right to the land by his brother's death therefore &c. As to Trotter's Neck I wo'nt be positive, but doubt that the heirs of Cant will enjoy it according to the Will of their Grandfather,[7] & can assure you that if there be severall Demises of one thing in a Will, the last Demise shall take place, though it be otherwise in a Deed or Grant, if any thing gets the heirs of Mr. Warner a Right thereto besides the death of Jno. Cant without issue,[8] it must be upon the incumbent charge imposed upon young Mr. Warner of paying 10000 lb. Tobo. out of his Estate demised, which gives it the countenance of a purchase upon good Consideration, which I apprehend must be the foundation of any of your son's expectations, for the possession & enjoyment of that Seat. Thus Madam I have given you my weak sentiments of your severall queries in relation to the severall Wills & Deeds sent me, according to the best of my skill what is farther to add is to refer to Mr. Chilton for what's defective, who wt. his better abilitys is & I am sure will be willing to supply those Defects, and skillfully to assist in the whole & full management thereof, & to assure you I am   Madam   Your W ff.

To Madam Mildred Warner &c.

[LB, 176-79]

1. Madam Warner was the daughter of George Reade of Gloucester County and the widow of Col. Augustine Warner, Jr., of "Warner Hall." Her husband had been a member of the Council. They had six children, three sons (Augustine, George, and Robert) and three daughters (Mildred, ancestress of George Washington; Elizabeth, who married Col. John Lewis; and Mary, who married John Smith of Gloucester). The sons died without issue and the estate as provided in her 1694 will reverted in 1769 to her four brothers' heirs. Augustine died in 1687 soon after his twentieth birthday.

Madam Warner's husband had died in 1681. His will was dated May 16, 1679. Very little more information appears to exist on this case and these people, for Gloucester wills were all destroyed with other records in fires of the nineteenth century. See M. E. Sorley, *Lewis of Warner Hall* (n.p., 1935), p. 50; 4 V 206; 23 V 395-96.

2. That is, Robert.

3. Edward Chilton, prominent barrister, was later in 1697 with Henry Hartwell and James Blair, author of *The Present State of Virginia, and the College* (see H. D. Farish, ed. [1940 edition; Williamsburg, Va.], pp. xxxii-xxxiii). He returned to England in 1694. From 1691 to 1694 he was attorney-general in Virginia.

4. The "H." here and below may be a copyist's slip for "A," or a copyist's misreading of "A."

5. Major David Cant, who married a daughter of Col. Augustine Warner, Sr., received

several grants of land: on April 2, 1662, 600 acres on the south side of the Piankatank; March 25, 1664, 500 acres in Gloucester, on Piankatank; Oct. 1, 1663, 912 acres in Gloucester, on Piankatank, including 600 mentioned above; Oct. 13, 1663, 100 acres in Lancaster (Middlesex), on Nincock Creek. He had at least three sons: (1) Augustine, who on June 12, 1665, was granted 750 acres in Lancaster (Middlesex) on the north side of the Piankatank, 500 of which were purchased by Col. Augustine Warner and Major David Cant for the use of the said Augustine Cant, and 250 were due Augustine Warner for the importation of five persons; this was regranted in 1678. (2) David, who on June 15, 1675, as son of "Major David Cant, deceased," was granted 1,400 acres on the south side of the Piankatank, in Gloucester, 600 of which were purchased by his father and bequeathed to the said David Cant the younger, and 500 were purchased by Col. Augustine Warner and bequeathed to his grandson, the said David Cant; the remainder was unpatented ground. (3) Walter (or Walker?), who as son of Major David Cant, deceased, received, June 15, 1695, a grant of 500 acres in Gloucester, on the south side of the Piankatank, which had been the property of his father, and by his will bequeathed to the said Walter. John Cant, perhaps another son, was burgess for Middlesex in 1692. 3 V 14n.

6. For Augustine, see note 5 just above. On Jan. 2, 1683/84, Madam Warner had appointed Augustine Cant her attorney to collect debts owing her.

7. The grandfather, as pointed out in note 5 above, was Col. Augustine Warner, Sr.

8. This John Cant may have been an uncle of the three younger Cants rather than a brother, perhaps entitled to some of his brother's property. In the absence of so many records, the situation must remain obscure.

To Christopher Robinson [1]

Sir

January 26th. 1689

I heartily thank your kindness in that affair of Majr. Beverley's [2] that you have generously offered to bring the business to Judgment in your County Court, which will be highly obliging, & to assure you I have no manner of distrust in your Integrity, I have purposely sent you the Will, assuring my self from a Gentleman of your worth to meet with no thing but Candour & fairness, & my small skill in the Law assures me of the truth in your's, that it ought first to be a judgmt. before expectation of payment. I heartily thank you Sr. for your news, & hope by all conveniencys, you will please to continue your kindness in that method, for as we live remote from Court, so now also it is our unhappiness to live as remote from Shipping, which makes us barren in news also. If you would immediately send up a Receiver, or appoint some one here, as Jno. Battaile or Jas. Taylor,[3] I would sell as much goods to Rappahannockers, as would answer that debt of your's if possibly I could, purposely to suite your conveniency, but to purchase Tobo. here, & not to be sure of receiving, or if you do send to receive, liking, would be vastly prejudiciall to me, because clearly out of the course of my business. Mr. Buckner [4] will be so kind as to deliver this, of whom also I have requested a farther trouble, as the presentation of my most humble service to your self & good Lady, which I hope will be acceptable from

To Mr. Christopher Robinson   Sir   Your W.ff.
at his house in Middlesex These

[LB, p. 179]

1. For Christopher Robinson (1645-1693), of "Hewick" in Middlesex, see "Instructions" to John Withers, June 5, 1682, note 7.

2. WF's friend Robert Beverley had died early in 1687 and Robinson, on September 17, 1687, had married Beverley's widow, Catherine, daughter of Theophilus Hone, as his second wife. Beverley's will, dated Aug. 20, 1686, appears in 3 V 47-52. See McGill, *The Beverley Family*, p. 933.

3. John Battaile (d. 1708), of Rappahannock and Essex counties, was captain of rangers against the Indians in 1692 and burgess that same year. His descendant Sarah Battaile of Caroline married Henry Fitzhugh of "Bedford" in 1740.

There were many Taylors in Northumberland and Lancaster counties in this period. But the best-known James Taylor (d. 1698) lived in New Kent, King and Queen, and Caroline counties and died in the last. Another James, perhaps his son, was burgess in 1702 and later. 5 V 287; 34 V 269; 32 V 16-17n; 35 V 213-18; *Exec. Journ. Council Col. Va.*, I, 347; *Journals H.B. 1659/60-1693, passim.*

4. For John Buckner of Gloucester County, see ltr. to him, Dec. 3, 1681, note 1.

To Thomas Storke [1]

Mr. Thomas Storke   August 11th. 1690

Sr. By the perswasion of Capt. Gutteridge,[2] I have consigned you four hhds. of sweet scented Tobo., as will appear by the bill of Lading, which you'll find very good & considerable heavy, please to dispose them to my best advantage, & deliver the produce to Mr. Nichs. Hayward or Order, for the use of   Sir   Your W.ff.

To Mr. Thomas Storke Merchant

[LB, p. 180]

1. For Thomas Storke, see ltr. to William Leigh, June 27, 1682, note 2, and several later ltrs.

2. For Captain Gutteridge, see ltr. to Cooper, April 18, 1689, note 2.

To John Cooper[1]

Mr. John Cooper   July 10th. 1690

Sr.   This serves only for Cover of a bill of Loading for eight hhds. sweet-scented Tobo. which you will find weighs extraordinary heavy, & consequently will help out with the high freight, I desire you to dispose them to my best advantage. Being from home cannot at present give answer to your's, only that part that relates to Collo. Pye's[2] debt, I cannot omit to shew my readiness to serve you upon all occasions, for immediately upon receipt of your letter, I sent to Collo. Pye about it, who made me this return that he would this year take effectuall care for your full satisfaction, which I wish he do, yet doubt, & must advise if he should this year fail, a speedy course is very necessary to be taken, & Mr. Newton[3] will be both willing & active in it to serve you. I do not propose him, as unwilling to serve your Interest, but because of his convenient Scituation, for the prosecution of such an affair, & my own remoteness, for if it must be prosecuted, the Provincial Court, where the Prosecution must be had, is near a hundred miles distant from me, & in a different Country, but very near Mr. Newton   By my next shall be more fully, & therefore shall now only tell you I am

To Mr. Jno. Cooper Mercht. in London   Your   W. ff.
     ⅌ Capt. James[4]

[*LB,* p. 180]

1. For Cooper, see the many ltrs. to him, above.

2. Colonel Edward Pye of Maryland, whose name had been used to stir up trouble in "Parson Waugh's Tumult." He was a brother-in-law of WF's friend Col. William Digges (q.v.).

3. For WF's wife's stepfather John Newton, see many ltrs. mentioning him above, especially that to K. Chiseldine, June 8, 1681. Since John Newton lived in Westmoreland County, Pye must have lived in the part of Maryland just opposite. This he did, for there is plenty of evidence that he was a resident of Charles County, and a March, 1689, letter indicates that he did not leave his house at Port Tobacco in that county for "three

weeks past." *Archives of Md.* (Baltimore 1890), VIII, 91. Port Tobacco is located on an inlet of the Potomac just opposite Westmoreland in Virginia.

4. Probably John James, master of the *Attendance*, bound (in 1692) for Bristol. P.R.O., C.O. 5/1306, 119IV, L.C. copy.

To John Cooper [1]

Mr. John Cooper   July 22nd. 1690

Sr. The above is Copy of my former writ abroad, only for Cover of a bill of Loading for eight hhds. Tobo. Consigned you in Capt. James, which I can assure you by the opinion of the most experienced traders in this Country, is a very good Tobo. & you'll see it is considerable weighty, when it comes to the Custom house Scales, which I hope will yield a good price. Now Sr. In answer to your single letter, which I receiv'd by Gutteridge, & admired you did not duplicate by reason of the dangers of these times, in it I receiv'd my Account of Sales & acct. Currant, both which I approve of. I have here inclosed sent you a bill of Exchange drawn upon your self for £5 from Mr. Darrell, which please to keep in your hands till my farther Order, & because I advised him to consign him to you, I will caution you not to pay beyond his effects, I'll say no more. Mr. Hayward did intend this year to consign you some Tobo. but freight being both scarce & dear, & his Tobo. light I believe hinder'd, next year I believe you may be assured of some more from him. Please Sr. after the Sales of my Tobo. to let my Mother have £10 if she be living, & to convey the inclosed to her safely, I will assure you Sir I look upon my money very secure in your hands, though this last year you were pleas'd otherwise to order it. Sr. I thank your care in the Case & box which came safely to hand, I believe this year shall send you one Tonn of Tobo. more, am not certain, till when I refer, & have now only to assure you I am

To Mr. Jno. Cooper Mercht. in London   Sir   Your W. ff.

[*LB*, p. 181]

1. For Cooper, see the many ltrs. addressed to him, above. Captain James is discussed in ltr. to Cooper, July 10, 1690, note 4, just above. Sampson Darrell and Samuel Hayward, WF's neighbors, are mentioned many times above.

To John Cooper [1]

Mr. John Cooper   August 20th. 1690

Sr. My brother Luke [2] is now coming home in this Ship that this comes to you in, & he has promised me to effect two things, one the getting me an ingenious boy out off the Hospital who can write read & cast accounts,[3] whose passage should be paid & himself doubly cloathed, as Collo. Ludwell [4] has brought in one this year provided he should be continued in an Employ suitable to his Education, upon his Arrival from thence, which would prove a convenient supply to my present occasions, & my business requires a continuance therein, as the Hospital expects & desires, the other is, getting of us, an able, learned, serious, & sober Minister whose allowance here would be large, & comfortable, & his setting forth there would be liberally contributed to, by a twenty pound allowance that is granted to everyone in that Quality that transports themselves to us, by the Bishop of London.[5] What I have to request you is, if he should fail or neglect, if it were not too much trouble, to help his failures & supply his neglects I am Sr.   Your   W. ff.

To Mr. Jno. Cooper Merchant in London

[LB, pp. 181-82]

1. For Cooper, see the many ltrs. to him, above.
2. George Luke (1659-1732), son of Oliver Luke and grandson of Sir Samuel of Woodend, Bedfordshire, was a kinsman and protégé of Secretary of State Nicholas Spencer. His mother was Elizabeth, daughter of Onslow Winch and sister of Sir Humphrey Winch (see below). *The Gentleman's Magazine* ([May, 1824], II, 124 ff.) states that the Luke family became extinct with the death of Sir Samuel's grandson. Presumably this was the George Luke buried at Cople, Westmoreland County, Virginia, in 1732.

As WF's later letters show, George Luke, with a great deal of influence, was basically a ne'er-do-well. About 1700 he was appointed Collector of the Customs in the Lower District of James River, where he got into trouble with his accounts (L. B. Wright and Marion Tinling, eds., *The Secret Diary of William Byrd of Westover* [Richmond, 1941], p. 24 [April 20, 1709]). For Luke's excuse, see *Exec. Journ. Council Col. Va.*, II, 238.

For the circumstances of Luke's marriage to WF's widowed sister Dorothy Smith, see ltrs. below. That Luke married again after the death of Dorothy is evident from a complaint made to England in 1704 that his wife was mistreated and imprisoned at the instigation of Governor Nicholson. *Jamestown 350th Anniv. Survey Reports*, No. 411 (P.R.O., C.O. 5/1314, ff. 45-46).

3. Since this ltr. is addressed to a London merchant, WF means that he wants one of the boys from the charity school, Christ's Hospital, there. Many of the youths were sent to Virginia and apprenticed to different masters. In 1692 the head of the school complained

because the boys never wrote back to him. The result was that the Governor and Council ordered each master to see that the boys wrote back to the authorities at least twice a year. These boys were so well qualified in learning that they actually could have been used as schoolmasters, according to at least one authority. Bruce, *Inst. Hist. Va.*, I, 314.

WF could as well have asked a Bristol merchant to secure for him one of the boys from Queen Elizabeth's Hospital there, for the same sort of training for the same purposes was given there. Many of these boys were apprenticed in Virginia. The school was founded in 1590, and in WF's day was operated by the City of Bristol. Ltr. of March 25, 1958, from E. B. Gillett, Headmaster, to the editor.

4. Col. Philip Ludwell (b. *c.* 1638- d. after 1704) of Bruton, Somerset, brother of Thomas Ludwell, came to Virginia about 1660. Soon he was Deputy Secretary, an office he held for life. He was an ardent supporter of Berkeley and subsequently a leader of the "Green Spring Faction." By 1681 he was a councilor. Of a rash and fiery temper, he was for a time suspended by Effingham. In 1689 he presented in England a petition from the Burgesses to the Privy Council. He was Governor of North Carolina from 1689 to 1694. He married as his second wife the widow of Governor Berkeley. 1 V 174-78; Tyler, *Cycl. Va. Biog.*, I, 145-46.

5. There are records of all sorts of clergy in early Virginia, including several drunkards and many able men. By asking for a "sober" man WF may have been thinking of the unruly Parson Waugh (q.v.). For the condition of the clergy, see Bruce, *Inst. Hist. Va.*, *passim;* Brydon, *Virginia's Mother Church*, I, *passim.*

To Nicholas Hayward [1]

Mr. Nicholas Hayward   July 10th. 1690

Sir.   Your severall letters of the ninth September by way of Pensylvania ℈ Capt. Arnold,[2] of the 4th. January by Capt. Purvis [3] of 22nd. January & indeed that which comprehends all, by Capt. Gutteridge [4] of the 3rd. December I have receiv'd,   I had an account of that by Peregrine Brown [5] & sent a Messenger purposely for it, when I heard of his Arrival, but miss'd, & it is not yet come to hand. I have been thus Merchant like this particular year, because of the uncertainty & hazard of the arrival of Ships, & consequently the letters that are in them,   And now Sr. shall endeavour a full answer to each Paragraph in your's, & shall first begin with that, that I suppose we shall have no farther occasion to mention, that is, about the Ore sent home last year in Madge,[6] wherein I must first tell you, I approve not of your account, for you to charge yourself equall with us & be at that cautious care & great trouble, in the divers Essays & tryals, I think not reasonable neither did I expect it, for indeed the charge ought to have been wholly ours, besides a full acknowledgement for your trouble, which I by this thankfully own, I must confess I had no great opinion at first of the Ore, & considerately turning over Josephus Acosta, in his description of the reall good Ore of Peru,[7] with all the manner & methods of melting & refining, quite damp'd my esteem of this Ore, it has no substance answer-

ing to his account, till again reading a piece I had by me of Mr. Boyle's
called his Scepticall Chymist [8] there in Page 397 & 398, He gives an account of an ingenious Mineralist, who out of American Mineral Earth,
which the publick Sagemasters [9] could not bring to fusion, and esteemed it
useless Earth, by a peculiar flux separated from it near a third part of pure
gold, which was the Occasion that I particularly requested Mr. Boyle
might have the Experiment.   Sr.   I heartily thank your kind remembrance
of my proposed Exchange &c. Really my self had almost forgot it, & in
despair of succeeding, though I am now abundantly better fitted for such
an Exchange, having now about a third more Negroes severall good seats
of Land purchased, besides the absolute securing my great tract of 21996
Acres, which I have now got Deeds for, as good as the Proprietors by their
Attorney Collo. Ludwell do or can give,[10] & which I question not but will
be fully confirmed, if their title should be called in or questioned, as guessing, if at any time the whole tract should be thought inconvenient to be
Cantonized from the rest of the Country, yet what they acted to particular
purchasers will then be confirmed. And now do intend to settle it with
Tennants for three lives, allowing each Tennant 200 Acres, paying twenty
shillings a year or a hhd. Tobo., without any manner of of [sic] fine, & to renew a life or lives at any time, paying one year's Rent for each life so renewed to perpetuity, which is almost as good as giving them the land in
fee simple, & should be ready to supply each Tennant with Corn Provision
& nails for the first year, they repaying me again at the Crop according to the
Market rate, I give you this account of my Intentions for your larger discourse of the Exchange not to propose an offer there, of supplying it with
Tennants, esteeming unreasonable to make such an offer, considering
your Brenton design wants people, which I esteem deserves & requires
your continued care & Diligence, in its supply with Inhabitants, for Capt.
Brent's utmost Endeavours will but make a thin supply here   Sr. I was
well assured of your kindness to act for me, & great abilitys for performance, if my Lord Culpepper's death had not put a full period to that affair,
& also under some assurance from Mr. Secretary [11] of its taking effect. For
your Care Sir in the buying & kindness in sending me my plate I cordially
thank you, which came safely to hand & luckily too, for about 2 or three
days after the receipt of it, I had the honour of the Governor's company at
my House, for 3 or 4 days, who first hansell'd it,[12] also your acct. with it
I both approve & allow of, only blush when I see no Article of gratificaon
for so great a trouble. As to Mr. Darrell [13] I need say no more now than
that I allow of & agree with your Character given him. Sir This year I was
designed to have sent home my eldest son to School there & did intend to
request of your care of him & kindness to him, but accidentally meeting

wt. a french Minister, a sober, learned & discreet Gentleman,[14] whom I persuaded to board & tutor him, which he hath undertaken, in whose family there is nothing but french spoken which by a continuall Converse, will make him perfect in that tongue, & he takes a great deal of pains & care to teach him Latin, both which go on hitherto very well together, only some books are wanting as the french Rudiments of the latin Grammar 3 of them, 3 french common prayer books, a french & latin Dictionary, which I desire you will please to send me: by the first conveniency, discoursing also with him of the Conveniency of a Coach or Collash for this Country, he perswaded me to send for a Chaise Roulant, as he calls it which I can no other ways English, than by calling it a Running Chair, which he told me was altogether as convenient & commodious as either of them, & would be a cheap thing for an Essay upon which I wrote to him to give me an account & description thereof, who by the inclosed letter has largely done it. Therefore Sr. I desire you will purchase me one of them, & send it in by the first Conveniency, I would have one as strong plain & light as I could, for as he says he approves of the lightest sort for this Country. Sr. I have overlook'd all Mr. Massey's letters & accts. & find £106 sterling besides 30000 lb Tobo. of your own & 1000 more of your's & Mrs. Lettens [15] put in to his hands, which has been so ill managed, that I am ashamed to see & ca'nt possibly help, for I find the Acct. mostly made up of rotten Tobo. shipped, & rotten Tobo. left in the Country, & the debts left unpaid, hardly thing to be got, & if it was narrowly sifted, & he severely handled, truly as little to be got that way, for I think your precious factor not worth a groat,[16] I find he has egregiously either plaid the fool or the knave, I believe one may be a little spur to the other, but he has had the greatest share in the first, & for what small use he has made of the last it has done him little good, for he is so poor that nothing can be expected of him if it should be nearly look'd into & discovered, which in my opinion is not worth while, by the next shall send you a particular account, as also perhaps an account of a little Tobo., that I am endeavouring to get shipt for you in Gutteridge,[17] who now lies just at your Landing, the freight is dear, but if I can get him to take it in, I shall put it on board, for then if it will not answer, you have liberty to let it alone, & so lose it for which there is a hazard, but if it should be left in the Country it is then lost wt.out farther expectation. Please Sr. to acquaint Madam Letten that I have receiv'd her goods,[18] & notwithstanding they are unsortable & high charged, I shall use my Endeavour to get them off for her, I am now in treaty to sell them altogether for next year's pay, & by my next shall be able to give her an account, & let her be assured, what I can sell them for, she shall be secured in her payment for them, & have her Tobo. returned to her next year to announce, for the debts that she sent in this year, I think there's but one hhd. that's possible ever to be got, by next shall give her a full & particular answer, with a full assurance that what comes with a Recommend from such a friend as your self, shall studiously & sedulously be endeavoured to be comply'd with, & though it is a shamefull account you'll both have, when it comes to be particularized, yet I am glad of this small opportunity, to shew you how ready I should be upon all occasions, to serve your self or friends, & esteem my self very happy that you think me worthy the title of.

Sr. Since the writing of the above looking over Mr. Secretary's papers in behalf of his Widow,[19] find there in Mrs. Meese's letters, to demand money that had been a long time due to her, amongst other passages she complains to him about the selling of her land here, & returning of her some money, & pretty near in this expression, Since Sr. says she it would yield me some money, & if Parson Waugh cannot in all this time pay one penny,[20] there's little hope he ever will be able, therefore I would have you sell to some other body, that should be able to pay me some thing, from which passages, I gathered two things, one that there's no Sale already made to Waugh the other that now she would willingly abate of her price set to Waugh which was 100 or 120£ sterling, & the tenth of which he is never capable of payment, I presume 70 or 80 or to be sure 100 offered her down, as soon as she has made a firm Conveyance, & by some Attorney in the Country deliver'd possession, might make the Purchase. The title she has to the Land I believe is by her Husband's will. Sr. I request the favour of your management in that affair to make the purchase for me, tho'it be for the highest sum abovementioned, I need not propose you Methods for the Management, your Methods in the purchase of Osborne's seat [21] was so well done that I need say no farther only not to pay the money, till the Deeds are here confirmed & possession here taken, lest Waugh should have any blind Sale or Claim, but to give her Security to answer the money, immediately upon the first advice of the Confirmation of the Sale there. By my next Sr. shall also send you bills of Exchange for £120 sterling, & perhaps something more I am Sr. Your W. ff.

To Mr. Nicholas Hayward &c.

[LB, pp. 182-87]

1. For Hayward, see the many ltrs. to him, above.
2. Either Captain Goldsmith Arnall or the *Friendship* (350 tons, 30 men, 18 guns) or Captain Thomas Arnall of the *Jeffreys* (450 tons, 50 men, 26 guns), both of which were in York River in 1692. P.R.O., C.O. 5/1306, p. 105, L.C. copy; *Exec. Journ. Council Col. Va.*, I, 118-19.

3. Captain John Purvis, master of the *Duke of York* in 1682, of the *Effingham* in 1687, of the *Duke of Gloster* in 1684, was a shrewd sailor who saw the need for printed copies of the Virginia laws and about 1684 without permission had *A Complete Collection of the Laws of Virginia* published in London and brought to Virginia for sale to the planters. The compilation was defective as well as unauthorized. The House of Burgesses requested that it be suppressed and summoned Purvis before that body. *Journals H.B. 1659/60-1693*, p. xlvii, etc.; *Middlesex County Deeds, No. 2, 1679/80-1694*, pp. 29, 260; P.R.O., C.O. 5/1306, 119V, L.C. copy; *Exec. Journ. Council Col. Va.*, I, *passim*.

4. For Captain Gutteridge, see ltr. to Cooper, April 18, 1689, note 2, and other ltrs.

5. Unidentified.

6. Unidentified.

7. José de Acosta, *The Natural and Moral History of the East and West Indies*, trans. by Edward Grimestone in 1604 (London, 1604), pp. 214, 216, and 232 ff.

8. Robert Boyle, *The Sceptical Chymist; or Chymico-Physical Doubts & Paradoxes, Touching the Spagyrist's Principals . . .* London . . . MDCLXI. Here is one of the rare instances in which we know exactly what edition WF was using. For the 1680 edition, the other one of the seventeenth century, discusses the matters to which WF refers on pages 401-2 rather than on 397-98, as this 1661 edition does. There is a copy of the rare 1661 edition in the Yale University Library.

9. Perhaps a miscopying, for the 1681 edition reads "publick Say-masters," that is, assay-masters. See *O.E.D.*

10. For more of this tract, see ltr. to Hayward, May 20, 1686, note 3, and Harrison, *Landmarks*, I, 187.

11. Nicholas Spencer, Secretary of State, died in 1689 and was succeeded by William Cole, who held the office until 1694.

12. This was Governor Francis Nicholson, who had entered upon his office in June 1690. Nicholson reported on July 24, 1690, that in his travel in the country he had seen no militia in proper condition. *Exec. Journ. Council Col. Va.*, I, 114.

"Handsel" means inaugurate with some ceremony or observance of an auspicious nature—to use for the first time, test, try, prove, taste." *Shorter Ox. Dict.*

13. Sampson Darrell, WF's neighbor, appears several times above.

14. Apparently WF had put William in the Frenchman's school earlier and soon placed his second son Henry with the same man (see 1698 ltr. to George Mason below). The French clergyman was probably the Reverend John Bertrand, who with his brother Paul left France during the persecution. Both became clerks of the Church of England. John, the elder, settled in Rappahannock County, Virginia, after having married in London in 1686 Charlotte Jolly, a French nobleman's daughter, with whom he had escaped from France. He died about 1701, leaving several children. He is usually mentioned as of Lancaster County, where he had bought in 1698 the place since called "Belle Isle." He was the rector of St. Mary's White Chapel. His will survives in *Lancaster County Wills &c. Inventories & Wills, 1690-1709*, p. 105. See also *Lancaster County Order Book &c. 1696-1702*, p. 31; *Northern Neck Land Patents, Book 2, 1694-1700*, pp. 293-95; 23 V 430; ltr. to editor of Mrs. Chichester T. Peirce, July 28, 1958, daughter of a rector of the same parish; *Exec. Journ. Council Col. Va.*, II, 13-14. In ltrs. to Hayward of 1692-1693 WF mentions three times bills he has drawn in favor of John Bertrand.

15. Mrs. Susanna Letten, who must have owned land in Virginia, appears in several ltrs. below. Massey was probably Captain Robert Massey, whose widow and executrix was acting for him in December, 1689. 3 V 187; 44 V 204; 9 W(2) 182.

16. The factor for "Brent Town" has not been identified.

17. For Gutteridge, see ltr. to Cooper, April 18, 1689, note 2. The landing may be that of the Ashton estate near "Bedford" rather than a landing for "Brent Town."

18. For Madam Letten and her trade, see ltrs. below.

19. Spencer had died in 1689. Mrs. Meese, widow of Henry Meese. In a ltr. of Jan. 18, 1687/88 to Spencer, WF had spoken of Mrs. Meese's claims on the Ashton estate.

20. In February and September, 1692, WF bought from Parson Waugh three tracts of land in Richmond County, perhaps sold so that Waugh could pay off these debts. There is no proof of this, however, as Waugh was a frequent speculator in land. *Richmond County Deed Book, No. 1, 1692-1693*, pp. 13, 14.

21. Unidentified.

To Nicholas Hayward [1]

Mr. Nicholas Hayward   August 8th. 1690

Sr. The above is Copy of my former which I have before Duplicated for fear of miscarriage, in this I have sent you your precious Account as well as I could get an understanding of it, by the Accompt made up you may see, what you are futurely to expect for your considerable quantity of Tobo. & smart parcell of goods, I have also sent you Copy of his Accompt of Sales, which I hardly think is worth the paying postage money for. I have according to your desire as well as I could make a Distinction between the debts, esteeming & being so informed from Mr. Massey [2] that the list of bills of 29425 is your particular, the book Debts acct. of which goes here inclosed amounting to 11859 have estimated betwixt you & accordingly have framed the Account, the bills that were found & this year sent in Mr. Letten's name have formed the Account to Madam Letten's particular,[3] Wch. also goes herewith inclosed to Madam Letten of which she will find a poor Return, for all the bills except three are certainly lost, & it will be mere accident if any thing of those be got, I shall particularize to her self. I have also sent you an Account of your's & Mrs. Letten's goods unsold undisposed, & still lying at William Tod's [4] which I went purposely to see, & found them so bad that I did not think worth the removing, nor indeed fit to offer to Sale, therefore left them where they are, giving Mr. Tod liberty of making use of any of the things he has occasion for, if he can make use of any of them, but withall have not absolutely given him them, till I hear your farther Orders, which I tell him I believe will be to let them remain where they are, in the Account of the things I have indorsed their qualitys. I have sent you these particular Accounts, but have given him no manner of Discharge, nor no farther allowance of the Acct. than you approve, for I must tell you, was he able I believe he might be forc'd to avast alteration in this Account but he is so poor that I doubt more money would be spent in prosecuting than he would be able to answer, & consequently good money thrown after bad, I give you my sentiments but refer to your self. What I want particularizing in my letter, I hope you will find supply'd in my Indorsement to each respective Acct. I have got three hhds. Tobo. by me for you which Capt. Gutteridge [5] promised to take in, & has Notes accordingly, the particular whereof you have here inclosed, to morrow expect him to give me bills of Loading for them. Mr. Massey assures me they are very good Tobo. & if they come safe may afford you a little Claret, which is more than I perceive you have yet got out of this concern. I have inclosed sent you what particulars relates to Madam Letten, as also her letter open for your perusal, which I request you will seal & deliver her. Herewith comes bills of Exchange from your brother indorsed by me for £12 .. 17. which is part of his debt of £25 .. 10 due to you, the remainder is £12 .. 13.0 place to my acct. & it shall be allowed, it was designed last year for the payment of your Smith, & accordingly he had my bills Exchange but they were lost in Burnham,[6] & I had then likewise an Order from him to Mr. Cooper for the money in part of payment for the sum lent him, which in my letter last year by Burneham, I advised you to take by the said Order, & Credit him your self for the Remainder, wch. would be a mighty obligation to him, & would not be lessened, if you generously do it this year, lovingly to let him see, that as long as he has so kind a brother, he need seek no other nor farther, though, while I am able your continuall obligations, obliges me to move for the service of any related to you. Sr. Inclosed is bills of Exchange from Capt. George Mason upon Mr. Thos. Storke[7] for £4 .. 17 .. 4. which please to receive for my use   Sr. Inclosed also you'll receive a bill of Excha. drawn from Capt. Robt. Hooke Master of the Hanna of Bristol & his brother in Law Mr. Jenkin Harris[8] for 120£, the reason of mentioning it, for the support of the Ship Hannah & dispatch of her Voyage, your acquaintance with trade, & knowledge in the laws belonging thereto, I presume will immediately inform you, that if any accident should happen, it subjects the Ship & Cargoe especially the Cargoe, because the owners to answer or else both lyable to payment & if a Protest should happen, I know you will dextrously meet with the Merchant, Ship & Owners in Bristol &r. Sr. I add no more in this because I am hurry'd away & hard in drinking with two Masters taking their leave I am   Sir   Your W. ff.

To. Mr. Nichs. Hayward &r.

[*LB*, pp. 187-90]

1. For Hayward, see the many ltrs. to him, above.
2. Probably Sigismund Massey, see ltr. to Hayward, Jan. 30, 1686/87, note 3.
3. See the ltr. just above of July 10, 1690.
4. Presumably a relative of Thomas Todd of Gloucester County, Virginia, Ware Parish. This William (1660-1724) may have been the fourth son in the second generation of Todds in Virginia. But there were several William Todds, and this one seems to have lived in Stafford. Martha Hayward, widow of Samuel, in her will left to her nephew Samuel Todd, son of William, a heifer (this was in 1697). Samuel Todd has also been mentioned in Samuel Hay-

ward's will. For Martha Hayward's will, see Washington Papers, L.C.; for Samuel's, Va. St. Lib.; also see 25 V 221; *Stafford County Court Records, 1689-1693*, p. 103.

5. For Captain Gutteridge, see ltr. to Cooper, April 18, 1689, note 2, and other ltrs.

6. Captain Burnham (q.v.) may have suffered a wreck.

7. Captain George Mason II (1670?-1716), son of the founder of the family in Virginia, moved about this time from his father's place at Accokeek in Potomac Neck of Lower Stafford to Pohick. Captain Mason was the grandfather of the George Mason of Revolutionary fame, and the father of two daughters who married two of WF's sons. Harrison, *Landmarks*, I, 74-75. For Thomas Storke, London merchant, see ltr. to William Leigh, June 27, 1682, note 2, and other subsequent ltrs.

8. Captain Robert Hooke of the *Hannah* (ten men, no guns) of Bristol sailed in the convoy of August 20, 1690. Jenkin Harris was probably a Bristol merchant. P.R.O., C.O. 5/1305, L.C. copy.

To Nicholas Hayward [1]

Mr. Nicholas Hayward   Augt. 11th. 1690

Sr. Herewith comes a bill of Loading but for two hhds. of your three receiv'd, I could not possibly get the other on board, am afraid it will be lost, but know not how to remedy, it being so late before I met with the disappointment, that I cannot now dispose of it, & help you to a new one next year, but if I can be assured I shall take that care in it. Brother Luke [2] comes home in this Ship & has a letter of Credit on you for £5 after the receipt of my bill of £120 is answered to you, which then please to let him have if he wants, for he assures me he will very speedily repay it again in your hands, he designs also if his father furnishes him according to his expectation to endeavour the purchase of Mrs. Meese's Land, I have advised him rather to the purchase of Mr. Foster's [3] it being a more proper Seat for him, & more quiet title, but however if he gets effects, & resolves to proceed with Mrs. Meese, I would not have my Concern oppose him, but had rather, if he could, that he purchased Fosters, And Sr. if you can perswade him if he purchases the one or the other, to take a speciall Estate taile, that is for his life his wife's life, & the heirs of their two bodys begotten, the remainder in fee to me & my heirs, I am willing to pay a third part of the purchase, & desire you in my behalf to negotiate & consumate the affair for me. I would willingly be out the money for the expectation of the fee of the other aforesaid, & what money you shall be out more for me than you have in your hands, I shall take care next year fully & honestly to satisfie you, if it should prove so fortunate that I could to the purchase of both wholly my self, I would willingly make the purchases. Sr. I shall longingly expect to hear from you, & shall joyfully & readily receive your further Commands, which shall be with all Chearfulness readily obeyed by   W. ff.

Sr. I have shipped Mr. Storke [4] some Tobo. the produce whereof I have ordered him to pay you, which please to keep for my use. ⅌ Capt. Gutteridge [5] in this letter was the Copy of that by Hooke & that by James on the other side

To Mr. Nichs. Hayward &c.

[*LB*, pp. 190-91]

1. For Hayward, see the many ltrs. to him, above.
2. For George Luke, see ltr. to Cooper, August 20, 1690, note 2.
3. Luke had gone home partly to get money to buy an estate in Virginia. John Foster of Cambridgeshire had been left the estate of "Chatterton" on the river by his cousin James Ashton of Stafford. He did not sell "Chatterton" until 1705. See ltr. to Hayward, Jan. 30, 1686/87, notes 12 and 13. Also 10 V 293.
4. For Storke, see ltr. to Hayward just above, August 8, 1690.
5. For Gutteridge, see ltr. to Cooper, April 18, 1689, note 2, etc.; for Hook, ltr. to Hayward, August 8, 1690, note 8; for James, ltr. to Cooper, July 22, 1690, note 4.

To Mrs. Susanna Letten [1]

Madam Letten   August 8th. & 11th. 1690

By Capt. Gutteridge [2] I receiv'd your letter wch. you are pleas'd to say was occasioned by the Recommends of some friends of mine there, truly I am highly obliged to those worthy Gentlemen the Recommenders, for putting me in the opportunity of serving so deserving a Lady, which I shall with all alacrity & readyness willingly perform. By the same conveyance I receiv'd your bills, the particulars of which I have also sent you an account of, & have in that account indorsed the poorness of their value which now is out of my power to help or retrieve, for there you'll find two already receiv'd. Bruton & Matthews, which you have Credit for in Mr. Massey's account,[3] & I hope will be secured for you next year, almost all the rest are irrecoverably lost, King's [4] is doubtfull whether ever it will be got, Holdings very hazardous for the reasons there mentioned, & only Colilough's [5] pretty certain, as ⅌ the account sent will more particularly appear, also there you have a particular account of what goods are sold, & your whole ballance from Mr. Massey, which I shall take care to secure for you next year, together with an account of those useless damnify'd goods left, the methods I have taken with them I refer to Mr. Hayward's relation. I have also sent to Mr. Hayward which I am confident he will shew you, the Station of the joint accot. betwixt your self & him, as well as I could collect it, & in that too you will find very mean expectation, I will give you this assurance Madam that the best of my Industry shall be used, to make them as advantageous to you as I can. You tell me you have made your letter of Attorney joint to take off cavilling pretences, truly I know of none of those cavills to the debts standing out, nor heard of none of those already recovered, & I find things falls in so square with that remainder that its possible to recover, that I do'nt find it needfull, & therefore wo'nt put you to the charge of Recording your letter Attorney   I likewise by the same Ship receiv'd your goods [6] which with the Costs & Charges amount to £21 .. 15. which because of the unsortableness cannot be retailed out, nor did I think it convenient, without you had taken freight to sell them for ready Tobo. if I could, because freight was both high & scarce & hardly any to be got, & Tobo. purchased & not freighted is as good as lost, therefore have sold them together in parcell for next year's pay, at seven shillings ₱ hundred to Mrs. Massey's sister in law to Mr. Sigismund Massey,[7] which amounts to 6214 lb Tobo. which shall be assuredly secured you, for which you may certainly take freight in England, provided this year there be Crops made, as likewise you may take uncertain freight for the ballance of Mr. Massey's account of 2485 which I shall endeavour to secure too, I will assure you Madam I have acted in your affairs as if it were really my own, & have hitherto put you not to a penny charge, & hope shall so finish, for yor. kind acceptance is the full of the expectance of   W. ff.

To Mrs. Susanna Letten in London &c.

[LB, pp. 191-93]

1. WF wrote to her twice, and she is mentioned in some six other ltrs. She may have shared cargo exports to Virginia with Nicholas Hayward.
2. For Gutteridge, see ltr. to Cooper, April 18, 1689, note 2, etc.
3. There were Brutons in York County in 1655. Thomas Mathews (q.v.) was WF's friend and client. Sigismund (q.v.) is probably the Massey referred to. 2 V 181, and ltrs. above.
4. On Nov. 12, 1690, Sigismund Massey as attorney for Nicholas Hayward complained that the late Robert King of Stafford had owed two thousand pounds of tobacco to Hayward at the time of his death according to a signed note of July 16, 1689. King probably owed Madam Letten in similar fashion. 45 V 171.
5. There are several Colcloughs, Coliloughs, or Cocloughs in Stafford at this period. The

estate of John was inventoried Jan. 13, 1702. In 1689/90 a Benjamin had complaints before the court. *Stafford County Court Records, 1689-1693*, for March 10 and 14, 1689/90; *Stafford County Will Book, Liber Z*, Jan. 13, 1702.

6. Apparently WF was going to act as agent for her cargo in somewhat the manner, but not on so ambitious a scale, as he had earlier proposed to various merchants that he would like to do for theirs.

7. In December, 1689, Mary Massey was the executrix of her husband's (Captain Robert Massey's) estate. She was born Mary Dade, daughter of Francis, and married successively Gerard Lowther, Robert Massey, and Rice Hooe. Sigismund Massey's own will was probated May 10, 1692. 1 V 251; 3 V 165; 44 V 204; 46 V 131; 9 W(2) 182, 185.

To Oliver Luke [1]

Honoured Sir   August 15th. 1690

Your Son which I had always an Esteem for as a Country man & friend,[2] by his own endeavours in complyance with Mr. Secretary Spencer's advice & by the perswasion & solicitation of Mr. Secretary himself,[3] as they have both assured me, & as Mr. Secretary himself informed me, is of a friendly Country man more nearly concerned by an Alliance which together with what you have heard from Mr. Secretary, he will inform you of that whole affair, at whose instance & request this now comes, he being coming to pay his Duty to you, & to crave your blessing & your advice, direction & assistance now to launch him out into some happy subsistence in this world. I have told himself, that if you could furnish him with a handsom farm in your part of your Estate there, it would be a comfortable subsistence, & which I believe would better sort with his Desires, now he has seen the trouble of travelling & settling, but if your conveniencys & occasions or indeed inclinations do'nt agree to such a Settlement, & that you continue your resolutions of settling him here, as Mr. Secretary told me you always designed, then Sr. I will presume at his Instance to give you the best method for such a Settlement, which is by lodging in some Merchants hand in London 150 or 200£ for the buying, a good convenient seat of land, which upon so much ready money some may in a short time be purchased, & then about such another sum lodged in the hands of some of the Royall African Company who for that will engage to deliver Negroes here at 16 or 18 or to be sure at £20 ℔ head, which purchase so made of Land & Negroes, the dependences upon a Settlement, so made, as horses Cattle, hogs &c. are easily purchased here to begin with, & continually raised for a future support. Sr. A Settlement thus made, will make a handsom gentile & sure subsistence, & if there be any thing of Care & Industry may be improved, but cannot well be mischiefed Whereas if he should have three times the sums above mention'd, its certain it will yield him a great deal of Tobo., but if either neglect carelessness or unskilfullness should happen its all brought to nought, & if the best husbandry & the greatest forecast & skill were used, yet ill luck at Sea, a fall of a Market, or twenty other accidents may ruin & overthrow the best Industry   I am   W. ff.

To Oliver Luke Esqr. at Woodend in &c.

[*LB,* pp. 193-94]

1. Oliver Luke, Esq., Bedfordshire, England, was the son of Sir Samuel Luke (supposed "hero" of *Hudibras*) and grandson of Sir Oliver Luke. He married Elizabeth, daughter of Onslow Winch, of Emerton, Bedfordshire.
2. For George Luke, see ltr. to Cooper, August 20, 1690, note 2. Since Luke was born in 1659, he was fourteen years younger than his first wife, WF's sister Dorothy.
3. A charter was granted to the Royal African Company in 1662, with the exclusive right of importing Negroes into the British possessions, the number to be introduced annually not to fall short of three thousand. It received a new charter in 1672, and lost its monopoly in 1700. As late as 1681 Culpeper declared that the Company had not brought any slaves into Virginia. He may not have been wholly accurate. After 1682 the Company was the principal agency in increasing the African population of Virginia. After that time slaves were brought directly from "factories" on the African coast to Virginia. As noted below (ltr. to Oliver Luke, July 21, 1692), WF believed in ordering from merchants in London who were agents for the Royal African Company such Negroes as one needed. Bruce, *Ec. Hist. Va.*, II, 77-84, 246.

To Nicholas Hayward [1]

Mr. Nichs. Hayward   Novr. 3rd. 1690

The inclosed speaks its own business which I would request the favour of you to get copied over, & deliver to Collo. Ludwell,[2] who is interested for the Lord Culpepper's heirs [3] & now in London; The reason I would not have it appear in my own hand is, because the Government at present is bent against it, for what reasons is best known to themselves, for my shallow apprehension ca'nt reach them. My Lady Berkly,[4] I dare say will be very free in communicating the same to you, wherein you will see, to the reputation of your brother,[5] the fair & full Record of Stafford County, & likewise to add to its lustre the disjointed & irregular Record of our chief or generall Court.[6] It much concerns me, perhaps as much in Reputation as Interest, it being the first law suite I ever had in my life,[7] & therefore am mighty solicitous not to miscarry therein, esteeming the well manage of this, the prevention of many others, as also the thing itself requires it, for the land in Controversie is really worth £300 sterling your friendly assistance is desired by   Your   W. ff.

Collo. Ludwell either lives or may be heard of at Mr. Berry's. Brother Luke [8] I dare say will contribute his assistance

---

State of the Case betwixt Fitzhugh & Dade upon an Appeal the said Dade had from Stafford Court against a Judgment the said Fitzhugh ob-obtained [sic] against him for the possession of land, the said Dade claimed to descend to him from his father   One Dodson [9] takes up & pattents 1300 Acres of land lying in Westmoreland, at the time of taking the same up, but upon Division of the Countys it was in Stafford, which said land the said Dodson sells to Jno. Smith father of this Dade, by a sort of Deed, on the back side of the Pattent, by the right whereof the said Smith sells again to Hugh Dowding,[10] by another Deed upon the back side of the said Pattent, by vertue of which Sale the said Hugh Dowding takes possession & seats & manures the said land, & parts with one hundred Acres, part thereof, to one Blacgrave, & the moiety of the Remainder disposes to Jno. Buckner,[11] the other half which is 600 Acres keeps for his own use, & lives upon the same, & by his will disposes thereof to his son Hugh Dowding & his heirs, and one third thereof to his wife for life & dies, Hugh Dowding the son dies before he attains the age of 21, after whose decease Richard Dowding brother of Hugh Dowding, the father & Uncle to Hugh Dowding comes in, & claims the Inheritance of the whole as heir, & after possession thereof, assigns to the Widow of Hugh Dowding the father one third part thereof according to her right by the law, & her bequest by her husband, & the other two thirds keeps in his own possession, after wch. the said Richard Dowding dies, without heir or Will or any other wise disposing of the same, by means whereof the said land Escheated, upon notice whereof the said Fitzhugh petitions for & obtains the Escheat thereof from Mr. Secretary Spencer Agent & Attorney for My Lord Culpepper, only Proprietor & Owner of the Northern Neck, who by his severall Deeds had the right to the same, & who did by his Attorney Mr. Secretary Spencer aforesaid, upon the sd. Fitzhugh's paying a large purchase for the same, grant the sd. Fitzhugh a Deed for the said Land, drawn up, as he himself said in his letter to Mr. Secretary Spencer, by the advice of the ablest council in England, by vertue of which Deed the said Fitzhugh was possess'd of the

two third parts that were in the actuall possession of the sd. Richard
Dowding, & waited the death of Hugh Dowding's wife for the present
Right & immediate possession of the other third part, who during her life
made a lease of the same to the said Francis Dade & died in May 1690,
after whose decease the sd. Fitzhugh by vertue of his Right aforesaid, demanded the possession, & forewarned the said Dade from the same, upon
whose refusall of Delivery, the sd. Fitzhugh brought his action of trespass
against the said Dade, to Stafford County Court, where the land lay, &
sets forth fully in his Declaration, as is above express'd, to which the sd.
Dade by his Attorney, pleads a speciall justification, & maintains his
Right by descent from his father Jno. Smith, though it appears fully, that
his father's departure from the same was more authentick, than his Right
by his purchase from Dodson, upon which plea Stafford Court adjudged
he had no title there & gave time till the next Court for the said Fitzhugh
to produce his title at which time the said Fitzhugh produced the Deed
granted by Mr. Secretary Spencer as aforesaid, upon view & Consideration
of which Deed & the Invalidity of the pretensions of the said Dade, they
order the possession of the said third part, then held by the said Dade, as
aforesaid to the said Fitzhugh, from which judgment the said Dade Appealed to the first day of the next Generall Court, there by the Governor
& Council to be heard, at which sixth day aforesaid, the said Fitzhugh appeared, to answer the Appeal aforesaid, & waited there the 6th. 7th. 8th.
& 9th. day of the Court aforesaid, & then found no Appeal Returned, but
finding a Petition entered for a speciall Justification as aforesaid, without
any Appeal Returned, put in an answer to the said Petition, & therein
prays that the Judgment of Stafford Court aforesaid might be confirmed,
for that there was no Appeal returned according to the day nor three days
after, the said Fitzhugh conceiving as he then humbly offered to the Court,
that an Appeal made to such a day of the Court is in the nature of a
Process, to call the Appeal to answer the Determination of better & more
learned Judges, also conceiving that if it did not appear at the time, the
Appellee had reason to suppose, the Appellant was satisfied & contented,
with the Judgment of the inferior Court, especially in this particular
Case, when the Appellant himself in the Essence of the said Fitzhugh
undertook the timely & safe Return thereof, as is fully set forth in the said
Fitzhugh's answer to the said Declaration. And the said Fitzhugh farther
urged, that the Generall Court could neither Arrive to the Cause nor
proceed to Judgement, without the Return of the Appeal aforesaid, no
more than they could come to tryall upon a Writ, where the Writ was
either not served or not returned, notwithstanding which the sd. Dade by
his Attorney, puts in a Petition & prays that he may be heard notwith-

standing there was not Return of the Appeal, which the Court immediately granted, from which proceeding the said Fitzhugh offered to Appeal to be heard before their Majesties in Council, & tendered security then at the Bar, but was not admitted, which being overruled, the said Fitzhugh then moved, that as the said Dade had pleaded a speciall Justification, he might affirm his title, & desired the Judgment of the Court upon his title, which the Court would not admit neither, but declared the sd. Fitzhugh's title to be Null & void, though so authenticated as aforesaid, when at the same time they had no Return of an Appeal from the Clerk as aforesaid, & made void the Order of Stafford County County [sic] Court, & adjudged the said Fitzhugh to pay all Costs, from which Judgment the said Fitzhugh moved again to Appeal to be heard before their Majesties in Council, because the Copy of his Deed sent in hither by my Lord Culpepper was (as he said) drawn & methodized by the advice of the learnedest Council in England, which was likewise refused him, though the said Fitzhugh had laid his Action for £300 sterling, upon wch. the said Fitzhugh moved that he would undertake nakedly to State the Case with the approbation of the Lieutenant Governor & Council to the Justices of the King's Bench, & be at the Charge & trouble of remitting it to them, & would wholly submit to their Determination, which was also denied him, And now as it appears in the Order there is a Jury appointed to inquire whether the third part which is the land in controversie be worth £300 pound sterling, that the said Fitzhugh may have his Appeal, which in plain English is, he shall have no Appeal & consequently be kept out of his land, that he has honestly bought & justly & largely paid for, by one that pleads he holds by a Right, which the Court itself would not approve though put to them, & the said Fitzhugh adjudged to pay all Costs of Suit, though he has so fair & so full a Right as aforesaid, to one that has no Right nor pretension of Right, to one that has no Suite nor pretension of Suite, by reason of the failure of the Return of the appeal to one that in all probability has let fall the Suite as aforesaid, by reason of the failure of the Return of the Appeal, he undertaking to perform the same. Memorandum In my Lady Berkley's Packets goes the true Copy of the whole Pattent, the Deed from Dodson to Smith, the Deed from Smith to Dowding, Dowding's Will, the fair & full & in my Judgment regular Record from Stafford Court, in which most part of the Station as I have put it fully appears: After that you'll see Dade's petition without an Appeal returned, (which is like a Declaration without an action, or a suite without an Arrest) to which you'll see my answer with some reasons why he ought not to be heard, after which follows a Petition without any reason for a hearing & that granted, & upon the same Judgment granted against me, that have a title to one that has none, though he has pleaded a speciall Justification that is, Stood upon his title, I adjudged to pay all Costs, & left remediless for want of an Appeal, &c. All which will come fully authenticated from the respective Records

[*LB*, pp. 194-99]

1. For Hayward, see the many ltrs. to above.

2. See ltr. to Cooper, Aug. 20, 1690, note 3. He was at this time in London presenting petitions against Effingham to the Privy Council.

3. Ludwell was appointed agent for the Proprietors (Margaret, Lady Culpeper; her daughter Catherine, who in 1690 married Lord Fairfax; and from about 1690 Lord Fairfax; until 1694 Alexander Culpeper, one-sixth owner) about 1690 and served until 1693, when George Brent and WF succeeded him. Harrison, *Va. Land Grants*, pp. 82 ff., and Introduction above.

4. Ludwell had married the widow of Sir William Berkeley about 1677. She retained her title and the name that accompanied it.

5. Samuel Hayward (q.v.), Clerk of the Stafford Court from 1665.

6. WF's troubles before the General Court in such cases as those of Beverley and Wormeley and several lesser clients are mentioned in ltrs. above. The records of the General Court of this period do not survive, though from the records of the House of Burgesses and the Council a certain amount of information concerning the Court may be gleaned.

7. The whole case of Fitzhugh *vs.* Dade appears in surviving Stafford County Court Records reproduced in 44 V and 45 V, *passim,* beginning March 13, 1689/90. Fitzhugh complained that Francis Dade was trespassing on property ("Simmes' Plantation") on Mochodoc Creek in Stafford, that Dade had been warned off, and that he continued to "detain" the same. This suit is in WF's own language, with learned allusions to Coke and other legal lights. Lowther, Dade's attorney, got a deferment from one Court to the next. Dade eventually lost, but appealed to the General Court of September 9. WF himself in these ltrs. gives all we know of the final disposition.

8. George Luke, then in England or on the sea.

9. See 44 V 302-11 and 45 V 11-15, 247. Gervais Dodson had sold the tract to (John Smith) Dade on Aug. 17, 1658. 20 V 326.

10. On July 15, 1659, "John Smith" (alias Dade) sold this land to Hugh Dowding, and on June 12, 1667 Mrs. Behethland Gilson, "by name the late relict of" Major John Smith, relinquished her interest to WF obtained by conveyances from Dowding. Dade stated that he was the lawful son and heir of Major John Smith, but claimed the deed to Dowding had not been legally executed. For this and more, see 20 V 326.

11. John Buckner was WF's friend of Gloucester County who owned property in Stafford and other counties.

To George Luke [1]

Brother Luke   James Town Octr. 27th. 1690

Because you shall see I will miss no opportunity I take this from James Town by the latter Ship, to acquaint you that when I came from home both your & my family were well & in health. Just this day I minded Mr. Secretary Cole [2] in your behalf, about the Sherriff's place, who still promises fair, time   Time [sic] must give an account of his performance You have a fair Opportunity to serve your self there by his Lordship,[3] to whom before this I hope you have applyed your self & given him from me my most obedient service. And withall I would have you be actively Industrious about the Collector's place of our River, more particularly for the upper District, which was divided from Pope's Creek upward & from thence downwards, & was always formerly in two Collector's hands, which made it more easie both to Master & Merchant, & more advantageous to the King's Interest, & more satisfactory to the People.[4] Whereas now, as you of your own knowledge know, for want of a Collector for the upper District (as indeed in James River, there is two Collectors where the River is not so large) abundance of the Tobo. in our parts is carried in to Maryland, & some ships that would trade with us when they are up here, but are so discouraged at the remoteness of the Collector, that they choose to go clear away into Maryland, as you know two or three did this last Summer, whereby the King loses his Dutys here, the Governor his advantages, the People the opportunity of goods & trade, this might easily be remedy'd if there were two Collectors as formerly, & as it is now in James River. I would have you be diligent wt. my Lord Howard in this affair, & obtain the place either for your self or me, for if I have it, it shall be as convenient to you & easie for trade as if you had it your self, I ca'nt imagine you will miscarry in it, if his Lordship has the disposall thereof as Governor, considering there is no prejudice done to any, by reason it was two distinct Districts, & the greatness of the place requires it, I believe also its advisable for you to shew this to Mr. Nicholas Hayward our very good friend, in whose pleasing Society, I question not but before this time you have had a delightfull enjoyment, who will if he embarks therein, effectually I dare say manage & and [sic] obtain, especially if you be to him full in your Relation, giving him an account of my commodious Scituation for such an undertaking, & withall the the [sic] conveniencys & inconveniencys thereof, wch. I question not but you will fully manage, & rather than miscarry I would have you concern your Uncle Sr. H. Winch [5] [   ] If you find at last that no Collector's place can be obtained, without it be to the person of a Councellor, then you must desist, I know nothing else can oppose an ingenious management. I must beg you to supply my defects in this concern, by your own more ingenious skill & knowledge. Sr. Since your going I have undertaken the manage of the Division betwixt you & Harry Meerest,[6] & have already had the Orchard divided, & intend the rest upon my return from Town, which will give quietness to my sister in your absence, & to your self upon your return, if you do not better supply your self there. The Conclusion of Parson Waugh's business, is, He has made a publick & humble acknowledgemt.[7] In the Generall Court, by a set form drawn up by the Court, & ordered there to be recorded, & is appointed to do the same in our County Court, as soon as I come home, with a hearty penitence for his former faults, & a promised obedience for the future, which he sincerely prays for the accomplishment of, & for the sake of his Coat so do I too. Sr. You know some of the newest books if they be ingenious will be mighty acceptable, as will likewise a full account of the News. David Shore's business,[8] Arthur Spicer [9] & I have agreed to determine betwixt you, Mason's business [10] appeared with such a Report from the Referrees Allerton & Lee (back friends to us both as this Court then found) that there was neither word nor Argument to be used, when I see you I shall be more full &c. Sr. The above is Copy of my former sent by Norrington,[11] which I now thought not inconvenient to Duplicate, because these wars make so great uncertainty of the safe arrival of Ships About a month since I received one single letter from you, which I believe came in Burnham,[12] where I congratulate your safe Arrival, & kind reception by your friends,   In it there was one to my Sister, which is the only letter also that she has receiv'd, which I immediately carry'd her myself & therein had a larger account of news than in my own, I suppose you will have a full answer of that from her self by this conveniency, And now Sr. I will give you a full answer to mine. And begin as you begin first with the Sherriff's place, which to accomplish according to your Desires, & for your advantage, (though I must tell you I had no such information from the inclosed as your letter directs nor nothing farther of it than barely your writing so) went immediately to Arthur Spicer's, shewed him your letter just as he was going to Town, desired him to apply himself to Mr. Secretary Cole to whom I also writ acquainting him with your information, who promised faithfully a diligent pursuit of the same, from thence I applyed my self to Collo. Allerton,[13] shewed him likewise your letter, who gave me his assurance to use his utmost endeavours therein   the result is not yet arrived to me, because the Assembly is sitting, & no Commissions come out, which now I every day expect. I am heartily glad you are so well esteemed & in such good respect with your Uncle Sir Henry Winch, & have so good an Introduction to renew your former acquaintance, and advance your Interest with my Lord Howd. which I do'nt question but you will so discreetly & wisely manage that they will find great Satisfaction not only in continuing & heaping their favours, both to your future advantage & reputation, & both have Cause to rejoice, one in so hopefull a Nephew, the other in so discreet a friend: I find also that now you are in a hopefull way of managing that concern of the Collector's place, especially now because Collo. Lee, in whose hands it now is, by, refusing to take the appointed oath to be taken to King William &c. it is said has made himself uncapable of bearing any Office or place,[14] & consequently the place not to be compleatly supplyed, till my Lord Howard's particular appointment, which luckily now gives you a full opportunity for performance, which opportunity I assure my self you will dextrously manage. I must acknowledge my self highly obliged, by your means to your Uncle Sir H. Winch, for his nomination of me to that honour, your letter mentions of being added to the Council, & under great obligations to his Lordship for kindly hearkening & almost agreeing to it, which I never did, nor yet am not so ambitiously foolish, as to think of,   Pray Sr. therefore be so kind as to fit my humble and hearty acknowledgements, for so great a favour, in a suitable stile & fit expressions for their acceptance. Collo. Ludwell's being at my house last summer when you brought him has occasioned me some ill thoughts, from our Lieutenant Governor, which he has declared to severall, some of whom has been so kind as to inform me. He being informed that I joined with him in opposing the Government about the Northern Neck, & that I was principall Officer under him in the management of that affair, & divers other things which raised a very great prejudice against me,[15] in his & some of the Council's opinions, & I know not but may be so represented to my Lord Howard in England. How clear I am of those aspersions your self very well knows, being at my house the whole time of his being there, & as well know that I was no way concerned, either in one thing or other, with him or any manner of his affairs, though I gave him the Civility of my house & had a sufficient trouble thereby as you are very sensible of. Pray Sr. endeavour to know of my Lord, whether there be any such representations made, & if there be please to clear them to his Lordship, & manifest my Innocency, which you may be able to testifie, as being an Eye & an Ear witness during his whole stay. But I think I am as well fitted for that as for my former trouble, when I stood in the gap & kept off an approaching Rebellion,[16] to my no small charge & trouble as you fully know, being sending almost every day for five months together, & writing with my own hands above three quire of paper to quash the raised storys & settle their pannick fears, having my house most part of the time constantly thronged, & in daily expectation of being plundered by the Rabble, & once of being treacherously murdered, for all which charge & trouble, I being out as you well know about £25 sterling, particularly for Messengers sent severally up & down, besides the purchasing the powder & shot for our men in Arms, for all which I thought at least I deserved thanks if no Retalliation, but thank God I have miss'd them both, & can do it with chearfullness, too but to be disregarded nay & slighted too, & to see those mischievous active Instruments as you well enough know Waugh & Mason &c, the only men in favour, & the only men taken notice thereof, grates harder than the non payment for powder shot & other disbursements I thought good to intimate this to you, that you may give my Lord a particular account of that whole affair (wherein his Lordship as you know from those persons miss'd not his share of the scandall &c.) & fully set forth to him the wickedness of Waugh & Mason &c. the at present grand favourites, but I hope upon his Lordship's arrivall the Scene of affairs may be changed. Please to bring me in if you can meet with it, Rusworth's third part of his Historicall Collections which begins from the Parliament in 1640,[17] and carrys transactions on to the year 1653. Also Cornelius Agrippa's occult Philosophy in English if it be procured, if not then one in latin.[18] I hope to see you in early at the fall, when I shall be able more fully to discourse all matters with you & to assure you I am

Sir   Your W.ff.

Brother Luke   May 20th. 1691

I write this particularly by itself, & make a Conclusion in the former, because if you have occasion & see convenient, you may let any one see it, & save your self some labour of discoursing some matters, that are discoursed upon for your manage. I have sent Hawkins[19] up & down to every house to look about your Tobo., who renders me a very vile account thereof, some gone, some hogbeds, & some damnify'd, & that that remains good, there is such plenty of new Tobo. there's no disposing a pound thereof, for Mr. Harrison[20] neither look'd after it him self, & discouraged Hawkins in the looking after it. I hope you remember the Hospital boy,[21] that I desired you to bring in, as also to perswade a Minister in, if you can with a sober, serious learned one. I suppose my Sister will be large with you, about your family affairs that I need add no farther I am with sincerity Sr.   Your W. ff.

To Mr. George Luke at &c.

[LB, pp. 199-205]

1. For WF's brother-in-law George Luke, see ltr. to Cooper, August 20, 1690, note 2.
2. William Cole succeeded Nicholas Spencer as Secretary of State by patent of Jan. 17, 1689/90. Cole seems to have combined the Collectorship of the Lower James River District with the Secretaryship. 20 V 11.
3. That is, Lord Howard of Effingham, who had returned to England in 1689 but re-

tained the Governorship until 1692. Apparently WF's advice was followed. In 1691/92 Luke and his influential friends got the ear of Effingham or someone else having power in the colonial administration from London. For on April 21, 1691/92, Lieutenant Governor Nicholson asked the Council whether they approved of Luke to be sheriff of Stafford "as his Excellency proposed." The Council's answer was that the recently appointed George Mason should be continued in the sheriff's post. *Exec. Journ. Council Col. Va.*, I, 528.

4. What Luke eventually received was the Collectorship of the Lower James River, but he was not appointed until 1700. *Exec. Journ. Council Col. Va.*, II, *passim*.

5. Knight and Baronet, Winch was one of the Commissioners of the Foreign Plantations as early as the 1670's. 19 V 352.

6. Henry Meerest appears several times in the 1689/90 *Stafford County Court Records*. On July 9, 1690, George Luke made humble petition to this Court showing that "your petitioner by virtue of a grant to him made by Coll. Wm. Fitzhugh doth hold and Enjoy the two thirds in three parts to be divided with Henry Meerest in Right of Mary his wife of a certain Dividend plantation and Tract of Land in this County of Stafford Therefore your petitioner humbly prays division of the said premises according to Law in that behalf made and provided." The petition was granted, Meerest to have first choice of his third, "together with the housing orchard and pasture ground." Apparently Luke had sailed in August.

7. See ltr. to Hayward, April 1, 1689, note 4. Parson Waugh defied the first order (1689) of the General Court that h₂ appear, but finally gave in. As already noted, a year or two later WF was buying tracts of land from him. Beverley Fleet, *Va. Col. Abstracts, Richmond County, 1692-1704* (Richmond [1942]), XVI, 4, 10; *Exec. Journ. Council Col. Va.*, I, 104, 519, 522; Harrison, *Landmarks*, I, *passim*.

8. Unidentified.

9. See ltr. to N. Spencer, March 14, 1686/87. Spicer (d. 1699), of Rappahannock (afterwards Richmond) County, was one of the distinguished lawyers of the Northern Neck.

10. Though the business has not been identified, George Mason II, Isaac Allerton, and Richard Lee have all appeared in WF's correspondence several times before.

11. For Norrington, see ltr. to Cooper, April 4, 1681, note 2, etc.

12. For Burnham, see the many references to above.

13. For Col. Isaac Allerton, member of the Council, see ltr. to Spencer, Nov. 2, 1680, note 6.

14. For Richard Lee II, see ltr. to him, May 15, 1679, note 1, etc. Lee, Allerton, and Armistead of the Council refused (before April 21, 1691) to take the oaths appointed by Act of Parliament to be taken instead of the Oaths of Allegiance and Supremacy. Christopher Wormeley was appointed Collector in Potomac River instead of Lee May 11, 1691, and the Lieutenant Governor was asked to give Wormeley his commission. In 1697 Lee was appointed Naval Officer and Collector for the Upper Potomac River, the river having been divided. *Exec. Journ. Council Col. Va.*, I, 172, 177, 200, 526; see also *Exec. Journ.*, II, 22, 62, 107, 294, 456; "A List of Ships & Vessells Which Have Entered & Cleared in ye Upper District of Potomack River from ye 25 March 1697 to ye 25 March 1698," HEH, Blathwayt Papers, Box IV.

15. Philip Ludwell had been quite autocratic as Northern Neck agent for the Proprietors and had brought about another conflict between the colonists and his agency which was to culminate in the petition of the Burgesses of May 21, 1691 *(Journals H.B. 1659/60-1693*, pp. 370-72) to the King that the Crown take over the Proprietary. Lord Fairfax, the chief Culpeper heir by this time, was able, however, to get a new grant or charter for the whole.

Francis Nicholson was with the Burgesses in this petition and even may have engineered it. He might easily have had "ill thoughts" of WF, who with Brent succeeded to the agency in 1693/94, and who was apparently always on good terms with the Ludwell faction or party in Virginia. Curiously there is plenty of evidence too that WF was a favorite of Effingham.

16. Effingham was still titular Governor of Virginia and in a position to influence many things in the colony. WF refers to his own part in quashing "Parson Waugh's Tumult," the Protestant panic of March 1688/89. At the request of the Northern Neck members of the Council, he had protected Brent at his own house and consequently been labelled a "papist." As militia officer he had got his men organized in case the situation grew worse.

17. For *Rushworth's Historical Collections*, see ltr. to R. Wormeley, August 2, 1682, note 3. The Third Part in two volumes, licensed Nov. 11, 1691, was published in 1692. It covers only 1640-1644. Part Four covers 1645-1648. This reference is puzzling. Perhaps WF had heard that Part III was to be published, and that it was to cover all the years he suggests

that it does. Perhaps circulars announcing intended publication had been received. At any rate, here is an English colonial asking for a book two years before it was published.

18. *Three Books of Occult Philosophy...Translated...by J. F....*(London, 1651). The original was *Henrici Cornelii Agrippe...de Occulta Philosophia Libri Tres....*(Cologne, 1693), etc.

19. Unidentified.

20. Perhaps Burr Harrison of Stafford, who had participated in the stirring up of "Waugh's Tumult." There was also a Thomas Harrison (1665-1746) of Chipawamsic, a son of Burr Harrison. Harrison, *Landmarks*, I, 76.

21. For these hospital boys, see ltr. to Cooper, Aug. 20, 1690, note 3; and for the clergymen, *ibid.*, note 5.

To Nicholas Hayward [1]

Mr. Nicholas Hayward   May 20th. 1691

Sr. Your only & single letter dated 18th. Novr. came to hand about a month since, wherein I find the welcome news of your good health, & continuation of your often repeated favours which were both extreamly welcome to me; your Brother has not yet receiv'd one line which miscarriage something troubles him, not doubting but you have often written. Your kindness about the money for the Smith is extreamly welcome to him, I suppose he will by this conveniency thankfully acknowledge it. As I must with all sincere affections imaginable, acknowledge your most obliging favours, about the care & conduct of my son,[2] if I had sent him thither, which nothing but that present conveniency that I fortunately met with should have hindred, for he rather exceeds than comes short of my expectation. My wife accepts the same with an hearty zeal, & desired me to return your self & Lady her sincere thanks & humble service. Sr. Your continuall favours prompted me to add that to the rest of the purchase of Waugh's tract, which if it be not done before this Return will now be facilitated, for he is now making promises to Mrs. Meese of payment, as he has done eleven years already to Mr. Secretary Spencer without performance of a penny,[3] & so his begining will appear to her, for I suppose upon his promise of Consigning Tobo. towards the payment of it, she took freight, or Mr. Storke in her behalf for him, which he had neither thoughts nor capacity to comply with one hhd. of when it came to him, I question not but he will find this year a pretension for that failure, but I dare venture to give her my Lugs, if in ten years he comply with £20 of the purchase.[4] I thank your kindness about the Chaise Roulant & the books, & doubt not their reception this year, the present dangers only excepted. Sir I truly condole your unsuccessful (though chargeable & vigorous) proceeding about Brenton [5] the unsteadiness of the times [6] since the first undertaking, has been a great hindrance thereto, when or whether they will end, for your advantageous perspect & Interest in that concern, I believe is uncertain, to you that are there upon the Theatre where those bloody tragedies are acted (& which occasions such burdensome & ruinous losses to one or other dayly) much more to us at this distance: I am glad your Hudson's Bay Interest makes you some compensation. Sr. Am extreamly troubled that Madam Letten took no care for freight, when I gave her the Assurance her Tobo. would be all ready, & positive directions to take it, which made receive her Tobo. long before the arrivall of any Ships, which now I fear will be much worse for lying. I have now above 100 hhds. of my own, which I can neither sell nor get freight for, the greatest part of wch. I doubt will be much damnified, & some part of it utterly lost. Please to assure her Sr. the same care I use about my own, as in sending to the particular houses severall times to view it, the same I shall take about her's. Doubting the year I receiv'd none but for the Sale of the goods, for which I writ for certain freight, which your Brother can inform you I could not avoid receiving, & employ'd his Clerk & Receiver to receive the same, under an assurance of freight, so that your & her Arrears that little that it is, lyes for a better time, if time don't waste it, by the death, runing away &c of the Debtors. Truly I look upon myself the Principall in being your Factor, for really the thanks are acknowledgements you are pleas'd to give me, are of more value than that whole Concern as it now stands. In my former I gave you the assurance & still continue the same of my utmost service towards the settlement of your Contiguous tract, & can also assure you that your Brother has been carefully diligent, in providing & graffing trees for orcharding there truly effects are not answerable to the services done, for want of care in the Inhabitant there, for without a constant care & diligent Eye, a well made plantation will run to Ruin, what a new made plantation will arrive where that's wanting, (which hitherto has been your unfortunacy in this Country concerns) I leave your self to judge, And what in my former letter I severall times inculcated. Sr. Preparation for an Orchard is soon made, & that as soon planted, but without a constant care & continuall residence thereupon, the labour & care of seven years is destroyed in as many hours. Capt. Gutteridge & Brother Luke very well know the man that has the management of your plantation, please to enquire of them your expectaon from the above premises. Sir I heartily congratulate & Emulate also my Brother's Lukes fortunacy in the enjoyment of your good company, & as heartily thank your kind remembrance of us (in this War times) [7] almost deserted people here, for we have hardly supply sufficient here to make you return. My Orchard I must confess, contributes largely to my present supply, & gives me from its loaden boughs a promised assurance of a future gratification which I'll assure we never chearfully pass about yor. self unremembred. I once thought this year to come upon you of a sudden, but the dangerousness of the Sea, & troublesomeness of a Prison, took me quite off that inclination, continually pleased my self with the full opportunity I should have in acknowledging your many & manifold Obligations & favours, & thankfully my self appearing to be. I hope Sr. You have receiv'd my money of Mr. Storke for the produce of the Tobo. consigned him in Capt. Gutteridge, I have drawn a bill of Excha. upon you for £11..10 payable to Doctr. Clark,[8] if it comes to hand please to let it have acceptance. This Duplicated & triplicated

To Mr. Nicholas Hayward &c.   [no signature]

[*LB*, 205-8]

1. For Hayward, see the many ltrs. to him, above.

2. Though Henry did go to England to school in 1698, this probably refers to William. Henry was only five at this time.

3. WF as attorney for George Luke, and Luke as attorney for Anne Meese of London, on November 10, 1692, entered suit in Stafford County Court against Waugh for retaining the land and house lying upon Potomac Creek in Stafford which belonged to Mrs. Meese. Waugh lost (though WF's political enemy Martin Scarlet dissented from the majority decision) and his attorney appealed to the General Court. Captain George Mason II became Waugh's security. See ltr. to Hayward, July 10, 1690, notes 19 and 20; also *Stafford County Court Records, 1689-1693.*

4. An interesting usage. *Lugs* is Scottish and northern English for *ears,* and by the seventeenth and eighteenth centuries was used in jocular fashion, as WF may be using it here. But also by this period it was used as a name for the lower leaves of the tobacco plant, or as the lowest grade of tobacco (Bruce, *Ec. Hist. Va.,* Item, 442). WF is apparently, either way, "betting his bottom dollar" here.

5. With the rumor of Catholic and/or Protestant persecution, neither group came to "Brent Town" to settle.

6. This apparently refers to the former Ashton property near WF's home place.

7. The War of the Alliance (1689-1697) between Louis XIV and Spain, the Empire, Great Britain, and other states. From 1689 to 1691 the Jacobite cause was fought to an issue in Ireland. At sea, English and Dutch commerce were attacked from 1689 to 1692.

8. Gutteridge and Thomas Storke appear frequently above. Doctor Clark is unidentified.

To John Cooper [1]

Mr. John Cooper   April 25th. 1691

Sr.   Your's of Decr. date last I receiv'd by Capt. Gutteridge, & therein inclosed your letter of Procuration about Collo. Pye & his Acct. Currant, at the receipt whereof he happened to be at my house, I then shewed him his Acct. Currant, & the power I had, which he seemed then not to be displeased with, but objected there was not altogether so much due, & that he had sent you bills of Exchange drawn upon Mr. Samuel Groome,[2] for your full ballance by the last Shipping to which I returned answer, that let him tell me what he said was his just due, & his bills for upon said Groome, & I would take such bills of him with letter of advice to pay, if not already paid, the debt he said was thirty odd pound, but could not remember the particular Sum, which he has promised me faithfully to perform, & for the remainder of the ballance we have agree'd to leave that open till we hear from you next year, & that you by your Acct. clear the same, upon which he has promised payment of that also. Thus Sr. I have acted for you as for my self, esteeming it better to get the better three parts of four, & leave the quarter disputable, than clash for the whole & endanger all. Sr. I received the inclosed bill of Loading with the things therein mentioned, though I must tell you part of the things were damnified, the Coarser sort of Diaper extreamly Coarse, & the finer sort not very fine I could have wished both sorts a little finer, for when I send for goods I would have a medium used, neither too fine nor too Coarse. I have by this Ship the John & Margaret Capt. Philips Commander [3] Consigned you four hhds. sweet scented Tobo., which please to dispose for my best advantage. I heartily thank your care for endeavouring to take me freight, but am heartily glad you met with a fool to deny you, as by the freight you may see, & now I hope to get else where. I approve of your payment of £10 to my mother last year, & desire you to do the same this, & by the first conveniency to send me my Acct. Currt. Inclosed have sent you a bill of Exchange for £49. 8.7 drawn upon Jno. Marsh & Robert Ruddle [4] which if you have not already receiv'd please to receive, for in my last by the Ship Hopefull of Novr. date I sent a former of those bills, which perhaps may become safe to hand before this: In my next perhaps may be capable of consigning you some Tobo., & remitting you more bills, till when I shall conclude myself

To Mr. Jno. Cooper   Sr. Your W. ff.

[*LB*, pp. 209-10]

1. For Cooper, see the many ltrs. to him, above. Captain Gutteridge appears many times also. Col. Edward Pye of Maryland is mentioned in a ltr. to Cooper, July 10, 1690, note 2.

2. Perhaps a son of the Samuel Groome, whose ship the *Dove* had been in Virginia waters from 1658 to 1666/67. 18 V 157; 19 V 174; 15 V 274.

3. Captain George Phillips was in command of the *John and Margaret* (two hundred tons, twenty-four men, sixteen guns) of London when that ship sailed from Virginia in the convoy of July 1692. P.R.O., C.O. 5/1306, 119V, L.C. copy.

4. Marsh is unidentified. A Robert Ruddle of Bristol was overseer of a 1702 will (proved 1709). 17 V 403.

Petition to County Court, June 10, 1691 [1]

[As printed in *The Virginia Magazine of History and Biography*, XLV (April 1937), 184-86.]

Fitzhugh's Petition. Lieut. Coll. William Fitzhugh being by the Sheriff called into Court and by the Court desired to Sit he then refused but delivered a Petition to the Court in these words—

Worshipfull Gent :   I have now Sat amongst you Seven years and as much above as Since November last. Five years of which time I have Sat as first in Commission and consequently as Judge in your worshipfull Society and the two former years in Truth Coll. Mason [2] was first in Commission but was Sherriff if I doe not misremember one of these two years and being therefore next in Commission to him had the first place in your Society during his said Employment and the remaining part of his time tis well knowne to yourselves that he seldom or never Sat and when he did Sit he was pleased modestly and kindly refer the giving the charge to the Jury and opening and summing up the whole pleadings of the Attorneys to me with what faithfulnesse and Integrity I then managed the affairs of our Countie soe committed to me as afsd and since his death when it fell upon me of Course to perform the same duty I refer your Worships and desire your Worships Censure and approbation because at an Election I was publickly Taxed by Mr. Martin Scarlet that neither Law nor Justice had been admrd in this County Since I Sat upon the Bench nor nothing was Law or Justice but what I said was soe, how farr that reflects on yourselves as well as me I refer to your worships more Serious consideration and because the words were said in the full hearing of the freeholders and Inhabitants of this County then met at the Election of Burgesses purposely to make me Scandalous to them and to yourselves. I humbly conceive not very credible. I therefore request that you will publickly read this Letter of mine in the full hearing of the Inhabitants at the next County Court and that you would yourselves if you can or direct any person there present if he be able to Tax me with any falseness or Irregularity injustice or any other illegal proceedings during the time of my Seven years Sitting amongst you as aforesaid but if nothing appears as I am in hopes and am assured nothing will Then I hope your Worships both for your own reputation as well as mine will take effectual care that the same may be Truly represented that such malicious asperors may receive condign Punishment and that those in Authority may with alacrity and cheerfulness perform the duty of their places   I rest your worships my humble servant

William Fitzhugh

Scarletts Answer. In answer to which Mr. Martin Scarlet put in his answer in these following words—

May it please your Worships here and elsewhere hath been a great Stir made by Coll. Fitzhugh in pretence of Vindicating his reputation I could heartily wish that pride ambition and malice were both by him and me and all others laid aside. our reputacons would be in less danger and sooner repaired if prejudiced. I cannot tell what he would have unless my life or Estate the one I fear not if fairly Struck at and the other is not worth his acceptance   I have lived in this County of Stafford near thirty years long before he did and why I must not live peaceably and enjoy the Lawes and Liberties of a Subject now I know not I have dealt falsely or perfidiously or to my knowledge defrauded any man of his right or been Litigious among my Neighbors or a Talebearer among the people let them Shew me wherein I will make double Satisfaction. I boast not as if I had not failings too many which I pray god to pardon tho' I thank god my greatest crimes are openly known to the world so that I fear no mans Just discovery of my faults as to Coll. Fitzhugh I hope I shall never be so obstinate as to persist in Errors, if I have done him any wrong I am sorry for it, I am confident not by any Private or Clandestine means as hath been done by me, to the end to ruin me, which is unknown to many which I pray god forgive willingly and to pass by all former abuses soe that I might live in peace and Quietness as a Christian ought and in Charity with all men which if I may Embrace. But if I cannot live quietly I must otherwaies as long as it is determined and endeavour to defend myself and interest as I can to my power but rather it was other waies —

Fitzhugh refuses to Sit. And the Coll. Fitzhugh being by the Court again desired to Sit and the oaths tendered to him which were enjoyed by act of Parliament he refused to Sit or take the same until he was Justly cleared of the unjust aspersions laid upon him by Mr. Martin Scarlet and that the Court had fully Vindicated him from the Same.

1. This petition is almost self-explanatory. Perhaps it marks the culmination of the long rivalry, political and personal, between WF and the Whiggish Martin Scarlet. For the long background of this petition, see Introduction above.

2. Colonel George Mason I (1629-1686), founder of the family in Virginia, had been sheriff, burgess, and colonel of militia. A Mason family tradition asserts that he gave the county its name, calling it after his native Staffordshire. Rowland, *George Mason,* I, 1-8; *D.A.B.,* many entries in Swem, *Va. Hist. Index.*

Letter to County Court, November 10, 1691 [1]

[As printed in *The Virginia Magazine of History and Biography,* XLV (July 1937), 253-56.]

At a Court held for the County of Stafford November the 11th 1691. Present: Capt. Malachy Peale

Mr. John Withers	Mr. Edward Maddocks
Mr. Matthew Thompson	Mr. Martin Scarlet

Justices

Fitzhugh's Letter

Gentlemen, My Longe absence now this four Courts together occasioned as most of you know, or I dare say have been creditably informed, through occasional absence or Violent Sickness all but the first Court in

June, and why I did not then sit my Letter to the Court   I hope fully clears and Mr. Scarlets acknowledgment and sorrow which he sent me by Mr. Hayward, for his Passionate words made me immediately forget the same and did design to have resigned my Place which fell out to be the Second Wednesday in August but before that time my business called me to the head of the bay, from whence I returned not till the last of August accompanied with a Raging feaver constantly attnded with curd vomitings which without Intermissione violently held me till the Court in September was over, afterwards I had some intermissions and hopes of Recovery but these hopes were soon over for my distemper reseised me again as violent as ever, so that the latter end of the week before your October Court and the week your Court was, I was againe so ill as not to venture out of my chamber nay for some days hardly out of my bed, now thank God its pretty well over and I find myself hearty and Strong considering my Late Circumstances, and therefore I know you'll think it reasonable to Expect me at this Court, and Truly I should gladly wait on you and Joyne with you in discharge of that Service we all owe to their Majesties and the Countrey, but I am deterred by an Information that I had not by uncertain report but by a general and Credible Relation of a most mischievous and dangerous Riot committed by Parson Waugh to your faces and to the judge in Cathedras, telling you as you were a sitting Court the Countrey then in the Court House as you were then Taxing him for his ill behaviour in soe rudely and violently Siding with and defending that Fellow Darnell [2] and some other great Enormities that he had committed in the Court House yard, he immediately answers not regarding that you were then their Majesties Court and then Sitting and the Country Present Expecting your dispatch of their business that he came there to Correct the Irregular Proceedings of your Court, then which I think a greater affront and Indignity was never Put upon a Court also he said in full hearing of your wor'ps as I am informed and of the Countrey then Present that I was a Papist and did not deserve the Kings Protection which you know is enough to set the Rabble to do a mischief to the Person so Taxt besides many other violent and ill behaviours of his during the whole days first Sitting which violent actions of his were neither then Punished nor by the Court represented to the Lieut. Governor and Council not to the Attorney General, but Perhaps you may say the Lieut. Governour has had a relation thereof and I'me apt to believ so too, that they may be reported to his honour, But it may Please your worships you must think and I have such honourable thoughts of him, as I cannot think otherwise than that he would in all his actions Proceed Legally and think rightly and Justly of every man till the contrary be proved either by record or evidence and not give any great heed to uncertain Reports, well knowing that Reports are made according to the affections of the Party relating as if from an Enemy a little fault will be aggravated to a very great crime, and if from a friend a great crime made a very small fault for he cannot reasonably nor honourably think otherwise of the Lieut. Governour upon the hearing of this relation if he has heard it, but that he must argue to himself or Perhaps to the Council too, this must be a malicious Report. Perhaps the Parson might speak a peevish word and his Enemies have aggravated it to this height which a Bedlamist would never have committed, noe noe he will say I can never believe it, what for a man of Reason, a man of Learning and a Clergyman too and one that not long since has been at considerable charge and Trouble for Passionate Expression of a farr inferior nature to this, certainly the relation is uncertaine; and besides may he say it may reasonably supposed it is not soe for surely I should have then heard of his Punishment and by the greatness thereof have Judged of the heinousness of his crimes, or if the Court had omitted or doubted to inflict a present Punishment on him they would certainly have represented it to me or to me and the Council or at least to the Attorney General to have a vindication of soe great an Indignity   Especially being their Majesties Justices and then Sitting in Curia though they might have passed it by in their private Capacities. But passing with Impunity there and noe representation made here, nor application made to the Attorney Generall makes me believe the report as hyperbollical as generally reports are carried up and down here. Thus I apprehend the Lieut. Governour and Councils Sentiments must be Supposed if they have heard of it, and now Gent. to come and apply it   Particularly I must tell you my thoughts that I doubt your Quiet Sitting your Selves, for myself such words as he spake openly of me, may Endanger to throw me upon the Fury of the Rabble, but to be sure can never admit in a Quiet Sitting and to maintain the dignity of the Place I sit in as I ought and will, or will never sit, for he that went so farr without committing a crime, for crimes are known by their Punishment may boldly dare to Proceed further, for the Trouble of which I pray God keep you and him from the wickedness of Perpetrating   Thus Gent. I have rendered you the occasions of my former absences and the reasons that I cannot be Present with you at this Court according to my wishes I beg Pardon for my Length & Conclude myself your Worships ready and obedient Servant

November 10th, 1691   Will. Fitzhugh

Courts order thereon — Foreasmuch as Coll. William Fitzhugh did Send a Letter to this Court wherein he rendered the reasons of his not coming to Court, and Sitting Accordingly. It was therefore ordered by this Court that the said Letter of Coll. Wm. Fitzhugh to the Court afsd. Should by the Clerke be fairly Transmitted and Put upon the Records of this County and that a Fair Copy of the same shall be alsoe Transcribed and Sent downe by the Clerk to the Right honourable the Lieut. Governour at the First opportunity.

1. This "Letter" is as self-explanatory as the preceding "Petition." Waugh's "congenital intransigence" prevented his subsiding after the "Tumult" arrest and disciplining. As far as there is evidence, WF never reappeared on the bench. Therefore it may be assumed that Waugh was never punished for his wild language. See Introduction above.

2. In Stafford Court in March 1690/91 a complaint was filed by Captain Nicholas Goodridge (see ltr. to John Taylor, July 18, 1692, note 3) of the ship *Spencer* that in exchange for some of the trade goods he carried one David Darnell of Freestone had paid him with tobacco full of ashes and dirt and sand, much of which had to be thrown overboard. Darnell was convicted of being a cheat and a knave, condemned to pay damages and stand in the pillory for an hour. The crime was to be fixed on his breast in capital letters by the Clerk of the Court. Harrison, *Landmarks*, II, 392-93.

To John Taylor [1]

Mr. Jno. Taylor   April 25th. 1692

This comes for a Cover of a bill of Loading for six hhds. sweet scented Tobo., by the advice & perswasion of your good friend & mine Mr. Samuel Chue [2] who will satisfie, as to the sort & goodness of the Tobo. he having before approved the same, & to whom for that part I refer. Also in the same bill loading, you will find one small Cask clear of freight which with the six hhds. I am well assured you will dispose to my best & most advantage. Please to give my humble service to your honoured father & acquaint him that the last time I spoke with Esqr. Wormley about his debt,[3] he assured me he would take effectuall care with himself to satisfie him, which I hope he has done   I am

To Mr. John Taylor   Sr. Your W. ff.

[*LB*, p. 210]

1. This appears to be, from subsequent ltrs., the John Taylor who was the son of a London merchant named Thomas Taylor.

2. Samuel Chew (1660-1718) of "Herrington" on Herring Bay in Maryland, owned lands in Virginia and carried on business in the colony. His father or grandfather John had arrived first in Virginia in 1620. *Archives of Md.*, I, 396; *Md. Hist. Mag.*, XXX (1935), 157-75; 1 V 87-88, 197; 3 V 58; 7 W(1), 306.

3. Ralph or Christopher Wormeley (qq.v.), both members of the Council.

To Samuel Chue [1]

Mr. Samuel Chue   April 25th. 1692

Honoured friend   Upon second thoughts I have thought convenient, to treble two hhds. promised by making them six Consigned to Mr. John Taylor, to whom I hope & am well assured that according to your promise you will give it a due Commend, for what I value is the future Estimation & Expectation not the present profit, & am confident will answer the Character you know best to give thereof. I have also farther enlarged my first promise by four hhds. more consigned to Mr. John Cooper, which are all now in the Sloop,[2] the six consigned to Mr. Jno. Taylor are thus marked & No. (viz) WF No. A WF No. 12 3, 4, 5. & a little barrell WF No. 0. which the mate promised me freight free, the four Consigned to Jno. Cooper are marked & numbered (viz) 6, 7, 8, & 9   I have been thus particular, because you might not mistake in the bills of Loading. Please Sr. by the first conveniency to send me two bills loading of each, & inclose one of each sort into Mr. Taylor's & Mr. Cooper's letters John Taylor's I have sent open for your perusal, that you might pursue your promised methods accordingly, which I know you'll inclose & seal up, Sr. According to your desire shall write effectually to our Collector for clearing your dues here, I hope to see you e'er long, & then shall make you full satisfaction for some goods I had of the Mate, & shall have full opportunity to assure you I am   Sr.   Your W. ff.

[*LB*, pp. 210-11]

1. For Chue or Chew, see ltr. to John Taylor, April 25, 1692, note 2.

2. The sloop was the small vessel of relatively shallow draft used to take the hogsheads from the plantations whose wharves were inaccessible to the larger port of call at which the ship would be anchored.

To Cornelius Serjeant [1]

Mr. Cornelius Serjeant   June 21st. 1692

 Sr. Hearing so fair a Character of your honest & punctuall dealing, by Capt. Jno. Moore Commander of the good Ship the Assurance of Bristol,[2] in which you are a Considerable Owener both of Ship & Cargoe, & with all considering your present trade of a Tobacconist, I have sent you three hhds. Sweetscented Tobo. all ready stemmed & fit cutting without any manner of loss or trouble I suppose you will presently understand the goodness of your Tobo. by your Taste & the method of trade you are now in, also Capt. William Jones & Capt. Robert Hooke two of your own Country Masters,[3] can inform you of the goodness & esteem of the sweet-scented Tobo. made upon my plantao in former times in Bristol, they having purchased some thereof from me, I desire you Sr. to sell the same for my most advantage, & make me return thereof by the first Ship bound out of your parts for Potomack River in Virginia, with bills of Loading to be delivered at my landing viz in Kerseys Cottons, & Bedminster Cottons,[4] coarse Canvas, Ironware & shoes, thread & silk, also a hundred of Gloucestershire Cheese, & what else you think convenient for this Country's use, so expecting to hear from you by the first opportunity I rest. I would have you also send if you could with conveniency & early send me in four Spinning wheels to spin flax with I would have them East Country wheels

[no signature]

[*LB*, pp. 211-12]

 1. This is the first of a series of ltrs. to Serjeant, who was a merchant of Bristol.
 2. On June 15, 1691, the *Assurance* cleared Rappahannock River with a cargo of 382 hogsheads of tobacco and 13,484 pounds of bulk. She was a ship of 150 tons, 22 men, and 11 guns. P.R.O., C.O. 5/1306, 119V, L.C. copy.
 3. In 1690/91, William Jones was in Virginia waters in the *Potomac Merchant* (14 men, no guns) and in 1692 in the *Expectation* of Bristol (150 tons, 18 men, 16 guns). P.R.O., C.O. 5/1305; *ibid.*, C.O. 5/1306, 119V, L.C. copy. Robert Hooke of the *Hannah* was bound for Bristol on Aug. 20, 1690. P.R.O., C.O. 5/1305, L.C. copy.
 4. *Kersey* (now rare) was a kind of coarse cloth, woven from long wool, and usually ribbed (from Kersey in Suffolk). *Bedminster cottons* probably got their name from the town in Somerset adjacent to Bristol.

To Captain Robert Edgecomb [1]

Capt. Robert Edgecomb   June 15th. 1692

Sr. I have by your own Ship consigned you one hhd. of Sweetscented Tobo., & one small barrell stemed, upon freight as you'll see by bill of Loading, wch. I would desire you to dispose to my best advantage & send or bring me in the effects in coarse goods (viz) Kerseys Cotton blue linnen, nails & shoes for the product, I have only to caution you that perhaps neither the Tobo. may answer your expectation in a generall Market in your Port, because there they may not generally be used to such Tobo., but if I might advise I believe it wou'd be the best way to take some out of the small barrell & make a present to some considerable Gentleman your friend, which I am confident would give the whole parcell a good & profitable Market. However leave the thing wholly to your own discretion, I have no more at present to add, but to wish you a prosperous Voyage, & if it be for your advantage a good return here again where you will be most acceptably welcome to

                                        Sr. Your W. ff.

To Capt. Robert Edgcomb
        at Plimouth

[LB, p. 212]

1. Robert Edgcomb was master of the *Jane* (180 tons, 6 men, no guns) of Plymouth, which sailed in the 1692 summer convoy. P.R.O., C.O. 5/1306, 119V, L.C. copy.

To John Taylor [1]

Mr. John Taylor   July 18th. 1692

Sr. By this Ship that this goes in the John and Margaret Capt. Philips Commander [2] I formerly sent you a letter, with bill of Loading for six hhds. sweetscented Tobo. & a small barrell freight free, as by the letter & bill of Loading you may fully see. I second this by the same Ship with the same Tobo. (which I suppose Mr. Saml. Chue has given you a full account of) as by the inclosed bill of loading for two hhds. you will see, which also I would have you dispose to my best advantage. In my next by Capt. Goodridge,[3] I shall be more large, & shall ordr. the disposall of the money produced thereby   W. ff.

To Mr. John Taylor Merchant in London

[*LB*, p. 213]

1. For John Taylor, see ltr. to him of April 25, 1692, note 1 above.
2. Captain George Phillips was commander of the *John and Margaret* (two hundred tons, twenty-four men, sixteen guns) bound for London in the 1692 convoy. P.R.O., C.O. 5/1306, 119V, L.C. copy.
3. Nicholas Goodridge, master of the *Spencer* of London, had in 1690/91 brought a large cargo of trade goods into Potomac River. He had been cheated by the Darnell mentioned in WF's "Letter" of November 10, 1691, note 2 above.

To Cornelius Serjeant [1]

Mr. Cornelius Serjeant   July 11th. 1692

Sr. The above is Copy of my former by Capt. Moore of the 21st. June 1692, I send this by Capt. Jas. Scott in the Mountjoy,[2] & in it inclose a second bill loading & also inclosed have sent you Capt. Scot's bill of Exchange upon Mr. George Mason[3] for £22..0..0 & Richard Walters[4] Doctr. of Moore's Ship his bill of Exchange for £7 sterling both which I would desire you to receive for my use, & send me it in also in goods, as is above expressed   Now Sir I have given you a particular account of what goods I would have you send me by the very first Ship bound for this River of Potomack in Virginia, & desire you to take care therein, but if I have expressed more goods than my money will reach I would have you make a proportionable abatement out of the things sent for, or if my money comes to more than will purchase the aforesaid goods, I would have to make a proportionable addition to the goods. I must request you also if you can to save me the freight, because if my Tobo. proves according to expectation, I design to consign you more next Shipping, & shall be willing to freight it in the Ship that brings in my goods, Also I expect some goods by Capt. Moore, which I would have yet amongst those for saving Charges. It would be of great advantage to me could I have those goods come to me by Christmas next, which I hope a short passage to this Ship might effect I rest   Sr. Your W. ff.

To Mr. Cornelius Serjeant Duplicated by Goodridge [5]

[*LB*, pp. 213-14]

1. For Serjeant, see ltr. to him, June 21, 1692, note 1. For Moore, the above ltr. to Serjeant, note 2.
2. Scott had cleared the Potomac District on May 7, 1692, with one hundred hogsheads of tobacco and seventy thousand pounds bulk for Bristol. The *Mountjoy* of Bristol was a ship of eighty guns. P.R.O., C.O. 5/1306, 119V, L.C. copy; "A List of Ships . . . 1697 . . . 1698," HEH, Blathwayt Papers, Box IV.
3. George Mason II, two of whose daughters were to marry two of WF's sons, is mentioned several times above.
4. For Dr. Walters, see two ltrs. below to Serjeant of July 23, 1693, and July 20, 1694.
5. For Goodridge, see ltr. to John Taylor, July 18, 1692, note 3.

To John Taylor [1]

Mr. John Taylor   July 4th. 1692

Sr. By Capt. Philips in the John & Margaret I have sent you two letters one of the 21st. April past acquainting you of six hhds. Tobo. sweet-scented, consigned you at the freight in the bill loading mentioned, together with a barrell of stemmed Tobo. freight free, the other of the first July last giving you an account of two hhds. more sweetscented Tobo. consigned you in the same Ship, as by the severall bills of Loading, in the respective letters & the Duplicates inclosed, in this you will fully see I have also in my former letter referred you to Mr. Samuel Chue, for an account of the goodness & esteem of my Tobo. which about three days since in his letter, he assured me he had performed, I hope the goodness of the Tobo. will answer its Character, & I dont doubt but your honest skill & ingenious Dexterity in dealing, will fully answer my expectation, & give me encouragement to continue a future trade, & correspondence with you. If my Tobo. comes safe to your hand, please Sr. to send me these following goods for the produce thereof if the money will reach it but let me not be a farthing in Debt (viz.) Those goods Sr. I would have you send me by the first Ship bound for Potomack River in Virginia & to take a bill Loading to be delivered at my landing & I would have all but the Iron ware, pack'd in good Saleable Chests & trunks, which though it be dearer in the first Purchase, yet considering their usefullness & Conveniency for Sale, renders the less loss in the Conclusion, if the money for the produce of my Tobo. should not reach to the goods mentioned, please to make a proportionable abatement of the goods, if it overdoes, please to keep the Overplus money in your hand till farther Order of   W. ff.

To Mr. John Taylor Mercht. &c.

[*LB*, pp. 214-15]

1. John Taylor, Captain Phillips, and Samuel Chew are all mentioned in ltrs. above of the year 1692.

To John Cooper [1]

Mr. John Cooper   July 4th. 1692

Sr. The above is Copy of my two former in Philips of 25th. April & first of July last dates. Inclosed in this you will receive the second bills Loading for the said Tobo. also inclosed have sent a letter to my mother, which I desire you to take for its safe delivery. I can yet add no farther about Collo. Pye having not yet one scrip from him, but hope before Goodridge go I may accomplish what I have above intimated, & by him also you may expect some more Tobo, & perhaps a small bill of Exchange or two, I would have you send me in these following goods, by the first conveniency. provided my Tobo. come safe, & you get money of mine in your hands, & not trust to him or them that you purchase them of, for I will assure you he that packed up the diaper last year, cheated you to my loss, for the damage upon them was before their packing up. The things I would have sent are these following viz

[no signature]

[*LB,* p. 215]

1. Cooper is addressed in many ltrs. above. Phillips and Goodridge were sea captains referred two in earlier ltrs. of 1692. Colonel Edward Pye of Maryland is mentioned in several ltrs. beginning with one to Cooper of July 10, 1690, note 2.

To Nicholas Hayward [1]

Mr. Nicholas Hayward   July 14th. 1692

Sr. Brother Luke & Capt. Goodridge brought me the welcome news of your good health, & both your letter of the 1st. Decr. 1691 together with the french books sent,[2] for which I heartily thank you, as also for your trouble in Mrs. Meese's business,[3] inclosed also received all the protests except Mason's, which miscarried last year, though I have made a shift to get the money of him without it, Doctr. Clarke's bills [4] I have answer'd here, therefore they will never come to your hands, but I believe you will have presented a bill of mine. payable to Mr. Bertrand [5] for £14, which when it comes to hand be pleas'd to give due acceptance. Mrs. Letten's business [6] Sr. really troubles me, that I should be so unsuccessfull for her, for as in my letter I assured her the Tobo. should be all ready, & desired her certainly to take freight, which omission of her's, has occasioned the Tobo. to lye all this year under her mark (& so did great part of my own too, for want of freight or a Market) whereby she will receive great loss & damage, how carefull & earnest I have been to do her service, I hope yor. Brother will inform you,[7] And this year again I had not one line from her to direct me in the management thereof. However freight being plenty & not very dear, I ventured to take freight for all her Tobo. that was good, already receiv'd. & what more could get in Capt. Goodridge, which I hope will come safe to her hands. I hope she wo'nt be so unchristianly as to judge things by the success, but will weigh the misfortune in the Scales of reason, & then I hope Sr. you will be my advocate for I protest the damage was unavoidable, according to the measures I assured her I should take. By Capt. Goodridge I shall send her a letter & bills Loading, for what Tobo. is shipp'd for as yet I am not ascertained of the quantity. Your Brother Sam Hayward & my self shall duely pursue your orders as to Mrs. Lewis & Mrs. Tod's Interest.[8] I wish you much joy & happiness in your late purchased Villa & hope you'll reap abundance of Satisfaction & content there, being such a Distance from the noise of the Town & trouble of business   Your W.ff.

To Mr. Nicholas Hayward &c.

[*LB*, pp. 215-16]

1. For Hayward, see the many ltrs. to him, above. George Luke and Captain Nicholas Goodridge are also mentioned many times above, especially during the years from 1690 to 1692.
2. The books WF wanted for the use of his sons in school.
3. For Mrs. Meese's business, see various ltrs. above to N. Spencer and Hayward 1687/88-1690, especially to Spencer, Jan. 18, 1687/8, note 2, and to Hayward, July 10, 1690, notes 19 and 20.
4. Though mentioned in ltr. to Hayward of May 20, 1691, Clarke has not been identified further.
5. John Bertrand, the Anglican minister of French origin and upbringing who may have been tutor to WF's sons Henry and William. See ltr. to Hayward, July 10, 1690, note 14.
6. Mrs. Letten's business concerned the sale of cargo she had sent. See ltrs. to her of August 8 and 11, 1690, and several ltrs. to Hayward of the same period.
7. Samuel Hayward (q.v.)
8. This is a reference to the mothers of the nephews Samuel Hayward mentions in his will of 1684 (proved 1696), Samuel Todd and Philip Lewis. Probably the two women were sisters of the Haywards. They probably lived in Virginia, for Samuel Hayward's widow Martha in her will of 1697 bequeaths to her sisters-in-law Mary King (perhaps Mrs. Lewis remarried?) and Sarah Todd a man or woman servant with at least four of five years to serve. No connection between the two women and the Todds of Ware Parish or the Lewises of "Warner Hall," both Gloucester County, has been discovered, though there probably was a connection. For Samuel Hayward's will, see Va. St. Lib.; for Martha Hayward's will, Washington Papers, L.C.

To John Cooper [1]

Mr. John Cooper

Sr.   The above is Copy of my former by Capt. Scot in the Mountjoy of Bristol. Now I have to acquaint you of severall Consignments out of

Our County, indeed all the Consignments that goes from hence, & because they are come by my recommendation: I must give you a particular account of the men, Capt. Brent if he has encouragement may consign yearly, as likewise Mr. Jno. Taliafero of Rappahannock,[2] & who will never draw more than he has or will immediately have effects to answer. Capt. Mason may consign again but pay no more money than he has effcts for in your hands, Mr. Matthew Thompson is a warm wary person & his bills are good for £200 Mr. Hayward is an old Consigner, & I believe every year will consign some. What others do not occur to my memory, if you please to take my advice, pay no more money for them than you have effects to answer. Inclosed you have a bill of Exchange drawn by John Sandford upon his brother Thomas Sandford, & indorsed by Patrick Mickleroy[3] for £25 sterling, which pray receive for my use, also inclosed you will have a bill Loading for four hhds. sweetscented Tobo. which please to dispose to my best advantage, & a barrell Stemmed Tobo. freight free. If you could send me a Shoemaker or two with their tools as, lasts, tacks, awls, knives &c. with half a hundred of Shoemaker's thread, & about twenty or thirty gallons train Oyl, & some proper colourings for leather, I having this year set up a Tan house, it would be of great advantage & convenience to me. Inclosed Sir according to Collo. Pye's[4] promise & my former advice you will receive a bill of Exchange for £31 sterling upon Mr. Samuel Groome[5] with letter of advice to pay if not already paid, by which you may see his integrity & care to comply with what he concluded your due, & is yet ready to pay, what farther you can fairly & fully manifest which he expects to be by a generall Acct., & withall wonders that you should be so earnest in your demands by a second hand, & not be so kind as to give him one line from your your [sic] self therein, for as he saith his continuall pressures, might a while perhaps take it out of his thoughts, & for some time incapacitate him, but his generous honest principles will push him always forwards to make full allowance to all just demands. This Sir was done in his presence, & pursuant to his letter to you, & in that has promised what I told to make complyance of the Remainder upon a full account   I believe a lawsuit might not have procured it so readily, & as I said before I have taken such measures for you as if it had been my own concern. Here's a seat of land adjoining to me called by the name of Clatterton [Chatterton] Court 550 Acres belonging to Mr. John Foster of Wisbick in the Isle of Ely,[6] & who is willing to sell, but will not to me, though I have formerly endeavoured the same, therefore I would desire you to enquire out the man, & endeavour to buy it as for your self, & take your Deeds by lease & Release in your own name, & the very same Deeds transcribed with alteration of the Names, may repass it again from you to me, which if you should effect & not have money in your hands, upon shewing this letter of mine to Mr. Nicholas Hayward, I am sure he will immediately disburse the money for me, The value is worth 60 or 70£ but I had rather give 120£ than be without it, also Mr. Hayward I dare say will give full Instructions & directions in the management thereof I wish you as successfull in this for me as I fancy I have been for you in Collo. Pye's affair, which with a little drink & trouble of my house, I have brought out of another Country, & performed at my own door without one penny charge to your self, before you consumate consult Mr. Hayward who has been formerly engaged therein. Mr. Storke is now declining in Consignments here, as you may see by your & Capt. Goodridge's intending to leave this Places trade, a Conveniency lyes open for your self to send a Ship of three or four hundred hhds. which might soon be loaden if she brought a Cargoe for one half thereof, the other half thereof I believe might be as soon made up with freighters, & the Consignments to your self which is Capt. Goodridge's opinion, also in which design, Capt. Goodridge & his Jeremy would go a part, if Jeremy might employed as Master, & I my self would go a sixteenth of the Ship & Cargoe, if I could come in for about £50, & could manage the whole affair here. I am capacitated & under what Circumstance's I offer it I refer to Capt. Goodridge's relation, to whom I have fully discoursed thereof & whose partnership procuring an advantageous prospect

To Mr. John Cooper   [no signature]

[*LB*, pp. 216-19]

1. For Cooper, see the many ltrs. to him, above. Captain Scott, Captain George Mason, Samuel Hayward, Thomas Storke, and Captain Goodridge are mentioned several times above in the 1690-1692 ltrs. For Matthew Thompson, ltr. to Wormeley, Aug. 2, 1682, note 4.

2. John Taliaferro (d. 1715) of "Snow Creek" was sheriff of Essex County in 1701 and burgess in 1699. Probably he was the son of the frontier soldier Robert Taliaferro who owned lands in Gloucester and Rappahannock and died in 1682. John married Sarah, daughter of Lawrence Smith of Gloucester. Harrison, *Landmarks*, I, 34; Tyler, *Cycl. Va. Biog.*, I, 336; *Journals H.B. 1695...1702, passim;* 10 V 199.

3. There are a John and Thomas Sandford in Fothergill, *Westmoreland Wills*, pp. 103, 133. Patrick Mickelroy and wife "of the County of Westmoreland" appear in *Stafford Court Records, 1689-1693* (April 7, 1690) and in *Westmoreland Deeds & Wills, Book 2, 1691-1699* (January 27, 1691, and Feb. 11, 1695/96).

4. Colonel Edward Pye of Maryland is first mentioned in ltr. to Cooper, July 10, 1690, note 2.

5. For Groome, see ltr. to Cooper, April 25, 1691, note 2.

6. For "Chatterton" and its owner, see ltr. to Hayward, Jan. 30, 1686/87, notes 12 and 13. *Chatterton* still appears on the 1958 Virginia Department of Highways map of Stafford County.

To the Honourable Sir Humphrey Winch [1]

Honoured Sir   July 21st. 1692

    By my inclosed letter formerly sent to Mr. Luke by his son, the Copy whereof I have sent you purposely open, you may see your former informations were mistaken, for two things I can positively assure you, first, That the match was totally made & concluded, by Mr. Secretary Spencer's mediation & sollicitation, together with their own concurrance, without any partys consulting me for a confirmatory agreement, not that I believe any one slighted me in that affair, but guess Collo. Spencer thought I might interpose for an absolute settlement upon his Cousin, before the full fastening the Gordian knot.[2] Secondly she was a Widow, & not left inconsiderable by her former husband,[3] having Dower in a seat of land & a good stock of servants, Cattle, hogs, Mares & horses &c. & a large stock Tobo. in good debts (her former husband being a considerable dealer here and an able practitioner in Physick, both laudable & profitable employs) besides a house plentifully furnished, where those materials are & a Widow to be courted, I believe you hardly hear of consultations for marriage portions. The Cause being thus truly & genuinely as I have stated, I presume you will accordingly esteem of your former information, I mean as to some of the Circumstances, but as to the match & his Scituation near me, & upon my land, that is really true, & so do intend shall continue till he betters himself, though under no obligation but pure affection, The plantation of mine he is upon, is a pleasant seat & a fair Orchard, & designed for one of my younger sons.[4] Sr. I do in my brother & Sister Luke's behalf, humbly & heartily thank your great & obliging favours to them, in the purchasing Mrs. Meese's seat,[5] which is a fair convenient tract, & I hope in a little time will be quietly settled, none of my endeavours shall be wanting in the management thereof, which by the next conveniency I hope you will hear is fully determined. Had not my losses Sr. been considerable in these Wars & the foundering a Ship at Sea, wherein I had a considerable stake (having within this three years lost two whole crops) I should have been able to have given them a larger assistance, than at present I am capable of, Yet to help to retrieve his late loss, & to join with you in kindness to them, I will contribute what I can, & what shall not be mean, in Negroes towards his full settlement upon that tract. I wish heartily that the measures about land & Negroes had been taken, as in mine to his father was advised, rather than to have brought in goods here to an uncertain Market, to deal for a bulky commodity in these doubt-full times, but since such methods are taken, the best care must be used If your Curiosity leads you to have an account of our poor Country, or your desires for any thing may be procured here, please freely to Command   Honourable Sir   Your W.ff.

To The Honble. Sr. Humphrey Winch Knt. & Bnt.

[*LB*, pp. 219-21]

1. For Sir Humphrey, see ltr. to George Luke, Oct. 27, 1690, note 5. For Oliver Luke, see ltr. to him, August 15, 1690, note 1.
2. Here is evidence of Luke's kinship with Spencer.
3. Dr. Ralph Smith (q.v.)
4. For a list of WF's holdings at the time of his death in 1701, see *Stafford County Will Book, Liber Z, 1699-1709*, pp. 92 ff., and Va. State Lib., *General Index of Deeds, etc., Stafford County, Va.*, chronologically arranged, p. 675.
5. Col. Henry Meese (q.v.) had established himself on Potomac Creek in Stafford in 1665. Harrison, *Landmarks*, I, 110. The tract the Lukes lived on may have been that for which Luke and WF complained against John Waugh as trespasser in Stafford Court on Nov. 10, 1692. 47 V 25-26; *Stafford County Court Records, 1689-1693*, p. 311.

To Oliver Luke [1]

Honoured Sir   July 21st. 1692

Your Son with his most acceptable company brought me in your kind & obliging letter, wherein you are well satisfied with Mr. Secretary Spencer's Character of my Sister, I hope she will endeavour to continue the same by her prudent manage & obedient behaviour: Also therein are pleased to intimate your former order, to Collo. Spencer about purchasing a plantation for your son's settlement, but admire to hear joined with it, my giving the like to my Sister, when at the time of intermarriage she was a Widow, & had all things suitable for this Country settlement, as Servants, horses, mares, Cattle hogs &c. a house plentifully furnished with houshold stuff, of all sorts, & a good stock of Tobo. her chief want being land & Negroes, which Mr. Secretary assured my Sister before the Consummation, & me after should of his Cousin Luke's part be supplyed, & that he had then by him an Order for 150 or 220£ from his father to purchase a convenient seat for him, this he told me three days after the conclusion of the wedding, that being the first of my Arrival after the same; Collo. Spencer proceeding earnestly therein, & in the performance of the Ceremony was a father to the Bride, it being acted at his own house, I being never materially consulted. I presume Sr. if it were otherwise, or as you are pleased to intimate in your letter, that I on behalf of my Sister was to perform such a part, I should have either given it from under my Hand, or acknowledged before some person or other, especially considering the person to whom I should have been obliged, to Collo. Spencer, a person of great parts & throughly acquainted with business of all sorts, & one that had sate in a Judiciall place, & that very considerably for so many years, & thereby had the opportunity of seeing all the falsitys & knaverys in all Contracts, Again that he should not urge me in half a years time, so long he lived after, for some acknowledgement, also considering I was no parent, & my self so often in that time urging him, & that before good company of good Rank & Quality, that there might be a speedy & ready complyance, of what he had in his power to perform, (viz) the plantation, And a desire to hasten what was farther to be performed by the first conveniency, which he as often assured should be performed. Now Sr. I say again does it seem probable, that I should so often urge him to performance, & he not mind me once of such a promise if he had gone no farther. This Sir I do'nt hereby say, but can make it manifest by good testimony, & res ipsa loquitur, the whole Circumstances speaks it, for I had not to deal with a fool nor an inconsiderable person, one that would be pleased with words; or a friend to prosecute, but one of great abilitys & as great authority, by the one, able to prepare matters, & by the other able effectually to prosecute the same, if any such thing had been, I take God & his holy Angels to witness that the above premises is wholly & in every tittle true, & shall have it to your self to draw the Conclusion. What services I have done him since his intermarriage, I had rather you should hear from himself, or any other hand, than from me, yet this much I must say (he not liking his seat belonging to his wife in right of Dower, nor indeed to be out & make conveniencys, upon that which perhaps he might lose to morrow) has lived upon a Plantation of mine, furnished with a good house a Considerable Orchard, & supplyed with all conveniencys without a penny Disbursement, & which would indeed have yielded me 2000 or 3000.lb Tobo. ℔ Annum, which I have freely let him enjoy, & yet shall do till he is well fixed upon one of his own or my son that I design it for comes of age a boy of five years old, have hitherto & yet shall continue to give him my best advice & assistance in management of his Tobo. & and other goods, have been open handed to him upon all occasions, & have severall times not only assisted him with my advice but purse too, & that freely. And now since his Arrival, poor Gentleman, himself & wife have had a violent & tedious fit of sickness, I took care to get them to my house, & to have the best help & means the Country afforded for their Recovery, which now thank God is perfected. I refer to Sr. Humphry Winch his relation, what I design   I design [*sic*] about his supply with Negroes, according to my poor ability. I hope Sr. by this I have shewn you the steps to the match, the agreement before & after it, & my behaviour hitherto, & future intentions, & I presume cleared, that it is pure affection & respect, & not any obligatory promise or engagement. I could heartily Sr. have wished, that the money bestowed upon goods & brought in with him, had been lodged in some able Merchants hand in London, ready for a purchase of Negroes, or laid out with some of the Royal African company for such an intent, according to my letter last year, for as you say in your trading by sea is very difficult & uncertain in these War times, for a Trader, to day he may be worth 1000£, & to morrow not worth a groat. I speak experimentally by my own losses within this 3 years at Sea. I hope Sr. you'll be so kind as to continue your correspondence by an early letter next year, which will highly oblige & honour   Worthy Sr.   Your W. ff.

To Oliver Luke Esqr. at Woodend &c.

[*LB*, 221-23]

1. For Oliver Luke, see ltr. to him, August 15, 1690, note 1. WF is still at some pains to justify the marriage, concerning which the father may well have had misgivings, especially considering the disparity in age of the married couple.

To Nicholas Hayward [1]

Mr. Nicholas Hayward   July 23rd. 1692

Sr. In my last by Capt. Scot of Bristol [2] I return'd you a full answer to your's, & therein acquainted you with bills Exchange drawn on you for £14. payable to Mr. Bertrand, [3] which I would have you accept when they arrive to hand, also I have given you a miserable account of Mrs. Letten's expectations, which upon examinaon & diligent review of her Tobo, now comes under such circumstances, that indeed I am ashamed, there being but nine hhds. fit to ship her, the rest being damnifyed & stolen, as to that damnified, its irretrievable as to the stolen I shall endeavour it if I can, and what's to be got secure for her another year, if any, as to her old debts not a penny to be got this year, Tobo. being worth something & most or all these debts worth little or nothing. I have sent the letter to her self inclosed & open, purpose for your perusal, I guess upon seeing it & her bills of Loading she may passionately fly out against me, till she has either well weighed things her self, or is moderated by your reason, which in Justice I must expect from you, because I entered into her service merely upon your Command, & gave her an assurance her Tobo. should or would be ready, which I accordingly performed & he not taking freight (though positively desired) was the occasion of this present loss & damages, & I am a more considerable sufferer of my own then lying upon my hands, by the disappointment of freight & want of a Market. Sr. As your late purchased Villa gives you the happy opportunity of a retirement, so it gives at the same time the secret & pleasant enjoyment of your self & a true Epicurean contentment, that is, a reall satisfaction of the mind, which I heartily & sincerely wish you. In my last letter last year I sent for a good Still of about fourty gallons, of which I doubt your reception, because you mention nothing thereof in your's, if that letter has miscarried, pray let this supply its place, in repeating my request for such a Still, as also to send me in one of the lightest & cheapest Callashes,[4] you can meet with, to be drawn with one horse, for so it will be oftenest used, though I would have furniture for two at the least. Sr. As your Country retirement takes me off from the expectation of much business from you, so it adds to my desires of having of receiving some moral Essays from you which would be extreamly welcome to

To Mr. Nichs. Hayward &c.   Your   W. ff.

[*LB*, pp. 224-25]

1. For Hayward, see the many ltrs. to him, above.
2. For Captain Scott, see ltr. to Serjeant, July 11, 1692, note 2.
3. For John Bertrand the clergyman, see ltr. to Hayward, July 10, 1690, note 14.
4. WF had been trying to secure this carriage for several years.

To Mrs. Susanna Letten [1]

Madam Letten   July 23rd. 1692

    I admire that I should not receive one line from you, neither this
year nor last, considering I gave you a full account of the disposal of your
goods, the sum of Tobo. they amounted to, & assurance that it should be
all ready & receiv'd to comply with freight, which I directed should be
certainly taken, I being so positive in mine, did not question but you
would have taken care accordingly, & pursuant thereunto recd. the same,
which ever since has lain under your mark, & now upon the plenty & rea-
sonableness of freight, Sending to have it open & reviewed, some of it was
stolen & some damnified, so that all the good Tobo. I could raise for you
amounted but to ten hhds., for some of your old debts, I could not get
in a pound this year, & coming aboard Capt. Goodridge's Ship [2] when
some of those ten hhds. came on board, I had a desire to take a farther
view of them myself, & found one of the number that I looked upon,
though indifferent good, that I thought it more for your advantage to have
it carry'd on Shoar, than to run the hazard of shipping of that which in my
opinion would not answer freight. Now Madam having thus clearly laid
down the matter to you, I must request you to call reason to the helm before you give your Censure, & consider where the fault lyes, & withall to
consult Mr. Hayward of the nature & method of our Dealing, & the bulki-
ness distance & uncertainty of our Tobo. lying here, & then I don't question though you are the loser, you will clear me of blame. I intend to use
my endeavours to get some of that is stolen, & if I do you shall have an
account thereof next year, as also what more of your debts I can get for
you next year, & what I can get I will contrive to send you by the first
conveniency. Here inclosed you'll receive a bill of Loading for nine hhds.
which I hope will prove good, come safe to hand, & produce such a market,
that may help to answer some of your losses, which is heartily wished by

To Mrs. Susanna Letten in London   Your W.ff.

[*LB*, pp. 225-26]

1. For Mrs. Letten, see ltr. to Hayward, July 10, 1690, note 15, and others subsequent to it.
2. The *Spencer* of London. See above, ltr. to John Taylor, July 18, 1692, note 3.

To George Mason [1]

Mr. George Mason   July 20th. 1693

Sr. Here inclosed comes bill Loading for two hhds. of my sweet-scented Tobo., I am made to believe by all that have hitherto had any of it, both here & in England that it produces pleasing smoak, & I am sure the weights are good, I desire you to dispose of it to my best advantage, & keep the money in your hands till my farther Order. Mr. James Scot's information [2] gave me assurance that you would not take this as trouble, & that a future correspondence will not be unpleasing to you, if you please to signifie the same by the next opportunity, it will be thankfully acknowledg'd

To Mr. George Mason   by Your W.ff.

[LB, p. 226]

1. This is not WF's neighbor George Mason, II, but the Bristol merchant adventurer. See McGrath, *Records, passim.*
2. Captain Scott (q.v.) of the *Mountjoy* of Bristol.

To Cornelius Serjeant [1]

Mr. Cornelius Serjeant   July 23rd. 1693

Sr. In my former by Capt. Totterdell,[2] I gave you an account of four hhds. sweetscented Tobo., that I had there shipped & consigned you, (here inclosed I send you a second bill of Loading) which I am sure of you'll dispose to my best advantage, in that also I gave you an account that Walters his money [3] cannot be gotten here, therefore request you to sue him there, if he refuses payment of his debt, £7 the Originall bill 15 ₱ Ct. by the Laws of the Country for damages upon protested bills of Exchange, which comes to twenty one shillings & for the protest mo money paid by you five shillings, which makes in the whole £8 .. sh 6. which if he should refuse to pay, you must if you can get him arrested, & withall tell Capt. Moore to use some care to make the Doctr. pay it otherwise he knows he is lyable himself as being the Doctors security,[4] with that money & what my Tobo. produces, please to send me in these things following, or as much of them proportionably, 5 or 6 ℔s. Bedminister Stuffs, 1 ℔s. of Kersey 6 ℔s. blue linnen, a bayle of Canvas, or the same quantity of English canvas 30 ells of Sheeting holland, & some nails of divers shorts & hoes & axes to make up the money, but I would have you let alone the Ironware, rather than any of the above things   I expect to hear timely from you   I am   Sr. Your W. ff.

To Mr. Cornelius Serjeant Tobacconist

[*LB*, pp. 226-27]

1. For Serjeant, see ltr. to him, June 21, 1692, note 1, and others subsequent to this one.

2. Henry Tatterdale, master of the *Factor* of Bristol, cleared his ship from the Rappahannock District on March 1, 1691/92. He had a cargo of 350 hogsheads of tobacco and 97 of bulk. P.R.O., C.O. 5/1306, 119III, L.C. copy.

3. Walters is mentioned in a ltr. to Serjeant, July 11, 1692, note 4.

4. For Captain Moore of the *Assurance* of Bristol, see ltr. to Serjeant, June 21, 1692, note 2.

To George Mason [1]

Mr. George Mason   July 31st. 1693

Sr. This comes only to second that by Capt. Scott with a second bill of Loading also for the two hhds. sweetscented Tobo. consigned you in him, if it proves according to expectation & the good esteem that it has hitherto lain under. I believe every year I shall send you some, I question not your carefull disposall thereof to my best advantage, & what money it produces, as I said in my former I desire you to keep in your hands till my farther order, but doubting if the London fleet should again fail us, or the Ships where my expected goods are should miscarry, I desire that you will order Capt. Scott, or whom else you shall employ for your Merchant in our parts, that if I have occasion for any necessarys that he bring in, that I may have a small parcell not exceeding my money, to be sure at the first cost with the allowance of as much advance as the Insurance from thence hither comes to, for till I have advice from London I know not what to send for. I hope I shall hear from you by the first conveniency.

Your W.ff.

[LB, p. 227]

1. For George Mason, the Bristol merchant, see ltr. to, July 20, 1693, note 1.

To Nicholas Hayward [1]

Mr. Nicholas Hayward   July 31st. 1693

Sir I cannot miss this conveniency of saluting you, wishing you all health happiness & quiet in these warlike & tempestuous seasons, which hinders us from having that frequent & pleasing conversation, we formerly enjoyed & hope speedily to have renewed. I have this year drawn some bills of Exchange upon you (viz) thirty pounds payable to one Jno. Thomas [2] fourteen pounds payable to Mr. Jno. Bertrand,[3] & four pounds payable to Mr. John Newton [4] if all or any of them comes to hand, pray let them have due acceptance, & be placed to my account. I hope long since you have received all my letters sent last year, & will be so kind as fully to answer my expectation therein   I was almost overperswaded by some of my friends to have sent you by this opportunity, a small piece that I have written giving a summary account of Virginia, & a succinct digest of our laws,[5] but thinking it adviseable first to communicate the same to our Governour, & if I can to get his concurrence & approbation thereto, which I now design within this day or two, to go to him about, & hope may be early enough to send it in this fleet, though not in this ship, or to be sure at farthest, it shall suddenly follow the heels of this; All your friends here are well, which I believe by their respective letters they have signified themselves. Expecting to follow this so suddenly with a second in this fleet: I shall add no more than to give you the full assurance I am

Sr. Your W. ff.

[LB, p. 228]

1. For Hayward, see the many ltrs. to him, above.

2. Probably the sea captain of this name who signed a petition for a convoy June 20, 1691. He was master of the *Bristol. Exec. Journ. Council Col. Va.*, II, 162, 171.

3. For John Bertrand the clergyman, see ltr. to Hayward, July 10, 1690, note 14.

4. For John Newton, WF's wife's stepfather, see many ltrs. above.

5. There is much more concerning this manuscript in later letters. Also see Introduction, under "Pen in Hand."

Speech from Burgesses to Council, November 13, 1693 [1]

[H. B. McIlwaine, ed., *Journals of the House of Burgesses, 1659/60 . . . 1693*, Richmond, Va., 1914, p. 490]

[Coll. *ffitzhugh* from ye Comittee appointed to prepare an answer to the Councills message relateing to *New Yorke* Reported, yt ye Sd Comittee had accordingly prepared an answer wch he read in his place & then delivered it in at the table, where being again read, & some few alteracõns made therein, the same was agreed to as followeth.]

May it please your Honors

Your Honors message relateing to an addres of this house grounded on his Excys Speech concerning *New Yorke* came this day wth yor Honors observacõns thereon to be duly considered by them, who were & now are of Opinion that the affaires of yt Governmt are not under such hardships & necessities as they were represented to her Majty & that what her Majty has commanded relateing to that Governmt ffowes purely from what has been represented from that place and that *New Yorke* has not so great an influence upon this Governmt as they set forth, wherein your Honõrs concurre with them, is perspicuous by our great distance & ye interposõn of Severall Governmts

Yor Honors are farther pleased to take notice of an assertion from this house, that this Governmt neuer had any defence from or dependance upon any other plantation, in wch Opinion they yet continue for that altho Coll. *Kendall* Coll: *Littleton* [2] were imployed from hence as agents to settle & confirme a peace with the Indians in amity wth *New Yorke* & in order thereto made application to yr Governmt to be a means to obtain the Same, yet neither these agents nor any other ever moued for money or men from them, and this house find that all agencies thither have proved so ineffectuall that this Country has been as much as euer infested with those Indians wth whome the peace was concluded, & that euer since the first agencie thither this Country has been at an anuall charge, wch has proved very considerable in some Millians of tobacco to defend & protect themselues from ye rapines & insolencies of those Indians, and notwithstanding all their endeavours many haue been destroyed. And as to that part of your Honors message relateing to the Governor of *New Yorkes* letter concerning Six hundred pounds of that Country money transmitted thither in Aprill last, they humbly take leave to say that they conceiue the same was issued by his Excy out of their Majts Revenue here pursuant to ye Queens comands to the end their Majts affaires in that Governmt might not Suffer.

1. WF is voicing the majority Virginia opinion that that colony owed nothing to the northern colonies in the way of assistance against the Indians.
2. Colonel William Kendall (d. 1685) of Northampton County had been a commissioner to treat with the Five Nations. Colonel Southey Littleton (d. before 1680) of Accomack was a partner in this "agency." 19 V 10; *Journals H.B. 1689/60-1693, passim; Exec. Journ. Council Col. Va.,* I, *passim.*

To Nicholas Hayward [1]

Mr. Nicholas Hayward   Decr. 19th. 1693

Sr. Your two letters bearing date the 24th. January one by Purvis the other by a York Ship I have receiv'd together with the Callash & Still therein mentioned, which considering their long stay on board, are well & safely arrived, & as acceptably received: I observe by the bills of Loading, that I am to pay the freight here, which I like exceedingly, which bill of Loading I receiv'd in an inclosed from Mr. Sam: Richards,[2] the payment of my respective bills to Bertrand for £14 & to Newton for £4

I approve, they being all with my own hand. I esteemed as good as if you
had had a letter of advice.   Sr.   By my last in the Bristol fleet,[3] I gave you
an account of a bill of Exchange of £30 payable to one John Thomas,
which I hope before this is come to hand, & I question not but paid:
Having the opportunity of a good bargain from one Mr. Daniel Parkes[4]
I ventured to draw upon for £100 sterling, I am sensible if the last bill of
£30 be arrived & accepted: I have not so much money of mine in your
hands; Yet by no means would have the same protested, therefore have
sent inclosed towards the making up the Sum good sure bills as I think
of Willis upon Perry & Lane for £7 sterling, I believe I shall be able to
send you more bills speedily but if I be not, there is Jno Taylor son of
Collo. Thomas Taylor hath the produce of some hhds. of sweetscented
Tobo. of mine in hand, which I shall order you; The reason that makes me
so earnest is, I would by no manner of means have a protest, but never yet
so branded, nor indeed did I ever yet before this time, draw bills for more
money that I had in his hands upon whom I drew.   Sr.   I heartily thank
your kindness in Mrs. Letten's affair, & am glad since the Circumstances
have been so unfortunate, that I had to do with one, that judged of the
manage of affairs, by reason, & not by success. I have sent the inclosed to
Mr. Jno. Taylor open for your perusal, whereby you may see the methods
I have taken about my money in his hands, if it be not already disposed.
In my last by the Bristol fleet I gave you an account of my design to send
you a summary discourse of Virginia, & a full & methodicall digest of our
Laws which were then not prepared, but are now fully ready, & only wait
a convenient passport to get them to your hand, without the great charge
of Postage, when I send them, I shall be more large in delivering some
methods about them. All health & happiness is wish'd you by

To Mr. Nicholas Hayward &c.   W. ff.

[*LB*, pp. 228-30]

1. For Hayward, see the many ltrs. to him, above. Captain John Purvis and John Taylor
also appear several times above. For John Thomas, see ltr. to Hayward, July 13, 1693, note 2.
Mrs. Letten's business is also mentioned many times above.

2. Unidentified.

3. Ships had been sailing for some years in convoy as protection against "legal" enemies
in war and against pirates.

4. Probably Col. Daniel Parke II (1669-1710), father-in-law later of William Byrd II, "a
complete sparkish gentleman," noted for his temper, his illicit loves, and his debts. Brave and
dashing, he carried the news of the victory at Blenheim from Marlborough to Queen Anne.
He was murdered while Governor of the Leeward Isles. In 1692 he was burgess and in 1692-
1697 councilor. 14 V 175; 20 V 373-75, etc. WF may be referring, however, to the English
merchant Daniel Parker mentioned by Bruce (*Ec. Hist. Va.*, II, 334) as one of the principal
traders in Virginia at the time.

To John Taylor [1]

Mr. John Taylor   Decr. 19th. 1693

Sr.   I receiv'd your's bearing date 15th. febry by what Ship I know not, & therein you give me an account of the receipt of my eight hhds. & barrell of Tobo., the barrell & one hhd. you give me account is sold, the rest waits a market, which I hope may find a good one, because all Informations give an account of the rising thereof, not one Londoner coming into our River of Potomack this year, and Tobo. plenty where they Ride, there was no possibility of shipping any more this year, or else perhaps you might have heard more effectually from me by this time. The last year I ordered the produce of my Tobo. to be sent me in goods, according as I there mention'd but if you have not shipped or purchased the goods before this letter arrives, I would have you desist from purchasing any goods for me, but, to pay the money due to me, to Mr. Nicholas Hayward or his order, when he shall call for it. Pray let me hear from you by the first Conveniency, that so I may be able better to order my affairs, towards a farther Correspondence   I rest   Sr. Your   W. ff.

To Mr. Jno Taylor Merchant in London

[*LB*, p. 230]

1. For John Taylor, see ltr. to him, April 25, 1692, and other subsequent ltrs.

To John Cooper [1]

Mr. John Cooper   Decr. 19th. 1693

Sr.   Your severall letters of the 20th. January & 10th. March dates came safe by the fleet, wherein you give me an account of the lowness of Tobo., & that therefore you have not yet sold that six hhds. of mine, that is come to your hand, I hope your delay therein may be of some advantage to me, now in the time of a rising Market. I see by your letter & return to Mr. Matthew Thompson it had been of great advantage to me to have sent treble the quantity of Oronoko; which that would have yielded me, but Markets both here & there are so uncertain, that no certain measures can be taken; I designed you some more Tobo. this year, & intended to try of both sorts Aronoco & sweetscented, but we had not one London Ship in our River of Potomack of neither side, from head to mouth thereof, & Ships have no necessity upon them to come round from other Rivers, when they may be supplyed where they lye. As it happened I am glad none of the goods I sent for, came in last year, & now I would have you send me none till my farther Order. As to Collo. Pye's affair I gave you a full account thereof by the Spencer Capt. Goodridge, and therein also sent you his bills of Exchange drawn upon Mr. Groome, together with his letter to you, which I presume before this time are come safe to your hand, he promising extreamly fair, & I hope I shall bring him to act as fair, but till the arrivall of your next in answer to those by Goodridge, I can't fairly proceed vigorously, for there in his letter you may see he promises to pay to the utmost penny, what you shall justly make appear to be due from him upon the station of Accounts: Notwithstanding I have sent your letter to him, & shall hold him in fair treaty, till I receive full & farther Orders, & shall both now & then act & do for you as if it were my own concern. The long detaining the letter was almost as much prejudice to us here, as the damage or loss of our Tobo. &c. Not having one Ship amongst us this year there is fair field open, for a London merchant to strike in with a brisk & full trade here, & if any Londoner had happened to send a Ship he might had large consignments. Sr. The box sent me by my Mother with the letter typed to it, never reached me, nor do I know by what ship it came, if any more lettrs for the future come to your hand, inclose them in your's, the Postage is nothing be the packet never so big. I receiv'd a letter bearing date the 12th. March from Capt. Goodridge out of Ireland, wherein he gives a particular account of his great loss, but with all writes me word that my four hhds. & barrell Tobo. I had in him are safe got on shoar & put in a Warehouse, without any manner of damage, for my Tobo. was stowed in the Hatchway between Decks, of which I suppose you have had full advice by this time, therefore I need say no more, as to that at this time; Your Consignments this year, had there been an opportunity of freight, I believe would have been more than they were, I know no further I have to add save to assure you   I am

To. Mr. Jno. Cooper Mercht. in London   Sr. Your   W. ff.

[*LB*, pp. 231-32]

1. For Cooper, see the many ltrs. to him, above. For Matthew Thompson, ltr. to Wormeley, Aug. 2, 1682, note 4; for Colonel Edward Pye, ltr. to Cooper, July 10, 1690, note 2; for Goodridge, ltr. to John Taylor, July 18, 1692, note 3; for Groome, ltr. to Cooper, April 25, 1691, note 2.

To Captain Roger Jones [1]

Dear Sir   At James Town I receivd about the 3rd. Novr. & a small time after, Capt. Brent & my self receiv'd the powers and Instructions from the Proprietor,[2] of which we gave you an account, by a Ship then ready to go out, which I hope by this time you have receiv'd. At my coming home which was about the last of Novr. I receiv'd two more from you that came by Capt. Jones in the David of Bristol,[3] wherein you are pleased to repeat your kindness, in your kind Recommends to the Proprietor, for which I heartily thank you, & shall endeavour so to serve & accomodate their Interest (which really at present lyes under very great confusion & Distraction, by reason of the incapacity of Collo. Ludwell's Deputy & the opposition of the Government very ill managed)[4] that I hope they may suddenly reap profit thereby, & your self no disreputation for your kindness. As to Mr. Sherwood's business Capt. Brent & my self appeared for you in the Generall Court, & cast him making it manifest that the debt claimed by him was never assumed by you, by which means you are cleared from that clamour, but you had not so good success in Capt. Mason's business,[5] the reasons I suppose Capt. Brent will write you at large, to that shall refer. As to shipping Tobo. we have not one London Ship in our whole River, so no possibility of getting freight, which I earnestly endeavoured but could not, Capt. Braines whom you depended upon for freight came no nearer us than James River, where Tobo. is not so scarce as to invite him to send up to us for Tobo. We are just now fitting & Marshalling out our Receivers about the Quit Rents,[6] & if we can get any Tobo. ready before Jones is full,[7] shall endeavour to get what we can in him, & consign it to you, this I do'nt absolutely say but only hope within this month or six weeks, we shall be able to give them some account of their affairs, in which we have never been idle since impowered. When I have told you your success against Sherwood,[8] the Privateer's Ingratitude will better pass. Pray Sr. by the first conveni   Conveniency [sic] let me have the happiness of hearing from you, together with the full of all news, as you may assure your self shall by all opportunitys, Pray in your next direct me where directly to direct to you   I am

To Capt. Roger Jones   Your   W. ff.

[LB, pp. 232-35]

1. For Captain Roger Jones, now mercantile agent in London, see ltr. to, Jan. 8, 1682/83, note 1, etc. He is said to have recommended WF and Brent for the agency mentioned in this ltr. 1 V 276n; Freeman, *George Washington*, I, 487; Bruce, *Inst. Hist. Va.*, II, 179-81.

2. In granting the power of attorney as Northern Neck agent to his son William Fitzhugh, Jr., WF mentions that he has been "lawful agent" of the Proprietors of the Northern Neck by date of "6th January 1692[3]." *Stafford County Will Book, Liber Z*, pp. 24-27. For an account of the Fitzhugh-Brent agency, 1893-1701, see Freeman, *George Washington*, I, Appendix, 447-513; Harrison, *Va. Land Grants*, pp. 84-93, 125-27.

3. Both John and William Jones were captains of Bristol ships in the 1690's, the former of the *Richard and John* and the latter of the *Expectation* and *Potomac Merchant*. Whether one of them for a time commanded the *David* has not been ascertained. Later WF specifically alludes to Captain Jones of the *Richard and John*. McGrath, *Records, passim*; McGrath, *Merchants*, p. 272; *Journals H.B. 1659/60-1693, passim*; P.R.O., C.O. 5/1305, 1306; HEH, Blathwayt Papers, Box IV.

4. Philip Ludwell actually had two deputies who lived within the Northern Neck, Nicholas Spencer, Jr., and Francis Wright, the latter the elder Spencer's nephew and county sheriff in Westmoreland. Richard Whitehead of Gloucester County was in charge of the land office of the Proprietors in Westmoreland. Harrison, *Va. Land Grants*, p. 82.

5. William Sherwood and George Mason are mentioned several times above, but since the General Court records for the period do not survive, the cases WF alludes to must remain obscure.

6. WF and Brent did not open their office until Oct. 1, 1694. They probably appointed collectors of quitrents by counties. Such an appointment of the year 1700, by William Fitzhugh, Jr., as attorney for his father, was made in Richmond County, empowering George Glascock and Charles Barber "to receive collect demand & when received to give discharge for quitrents etc." *Richmond County Misc. Records, 1699-1724*, Oct. 20, 1700, and March 6, 1700/1; also Harrison, *Va. Land Grants*, p. 90.

7. Presumably either Captain William Jones (see ltr. to Serjeant, June 21, 1692, note 3) or, more probably, Captain John Jones of the *Richard and John*, a ship and master mentioned several times below. Captain John Jones was in Potomac River on July 21, 1698, in this ship, described as "Sqr sterned" and carrying 300 guns. As WF's Inventory of Will indicates, he and John Jones were partners in 1701. "A List of Ships & Vessels ... in ... Potomack River. ..." HEH, Blathwayt Papers, Box IV.

8. For William Sherwood, prominent Jamestown attorney who owned property in Stafford, see ltr. to him, June 11, 1679, note 1. The case and the reference to "the Privateer's ingratitude" remain obscure. "Your success against Sherwood" may mean, however, that the Proprietors, as represented by Jones, who was clearly their agent, had compelled Sherwood to acknowledge and settle for his quitrents due for the Doegs Island property in Potomac River. For the new grant made in acknowledgement of this "attorning," see original document in L.C. and *Va. Col. Abstracts [James City County, 1634-1904]*, Series 2, IV, 17.

To Roger Jones [1]

This is Copy of my former I know not what further to add having not long since joined with Capt. Brent in writing to you, & giving you our sence of the present posture of the Proprietor's affairs which now I look upon just in the Crisis, and must be vastly prejudiciall to them, if they do not take care to steer us in the impending storm, purely occasioned by the ignorance folly & Negligence of those formerly employ'd, if they now

326 / LETTERS OF WILLIAM FITZHUGH

support us according as we have directed, by influencing of us in the Governmt. & to the Governor, all things will be facile & easie. Your self knows Mr. Secretary Spencer's great parts was not the occasion, it was easie to him, but his power & influence in & upon the Government made the management facile, after the rate it was managed.[2] I know I have spoke enough to you & our joint letter being so full, I have no farther to add than to assure you I am

To Mr. Roger Jones Merchant &c.   Worthy Sir Your   W. ff.

[*LB*, p. 235]

1. WF was certainly right that Proprietary affairs were at this moment (autumn 1694?) in crisis. See "Proprietary Agent," Introduction above; Freeman, *George Washington*, I, *passim*; Harrison, *Va. Land Grants*, *passim*. The crisis was to continue, however, until after Robert Carter's attack on the agents and Proprietors in the General Assembly in 1695.

2. That is, no one dared question Spencer, for he was so powerful as Secretary of State that his word when he was Proprietary agent was taken as law. WF seems to be saying that because of Spencer's prestige, and despite the poor management of his deputies, he got along pretty well. He seems to be blaming Spencer's deputies and those employed by Ludwell mentioned above, N. Spencer, Jr., and Francis Wright, who had probably continued from the elder Spencer's administration.

To Nicholas Hayward [1]

Mr. Nichs. Hayward   July 9th. 1694

Sr.   In my former of the 19th. Decr. & 15th. June I gave you an account of some bills I had upon you, the last for £10 to Mr. Danl. Parkes [2] if come to hand I assure my self they are answered. This comes now purposely to accompany what I then promised viz a short description of Virginia, & a methodicall Digestion of the Laws thereof, which you will herewith receive all my friends here perswade me that it will be a very usefull acceptable book, & sell well affirming every one that can read both here & in Maryland would have one, if their guesses prove true, some thousands will be suddenly vended, especially if Traders in England should think them worth their perusal, if so the Printer or Bookseller, if you think it worth the offering, might be induced to give something liberally for the Copy of it, for if they should sell so well as these Gentlemen fancy, it would deserve abundantly more, than is given for the Copy of the ordinaryest Play book, which is twenty shillings a sheet. I shall refer the whole matter to you, only in this particular must advise, that I would not have the Impression neither in my name nor at my charge. If they be printed they had best be in Quarto, (without any blank paper at the end as Purvis in his books foolishly & uselessly devised) [3] which will make them more portable & less chargeable. I need not direct about the divers Characters that it must be put in, both in the book & in the Margin, supposing every Printer knows properly how to direct therein. The next thing to be considered if it be thought worthy the Press, is, for the Printer or Publisher, to get it licensed, which without difficulty or charge will be easily obtained. Also the Printer or Publisher may in some measure, arrive to the value & usefullness of the book, if he takes this Coppy of mine, & procure one of Purvis printed books, Intituled a complete Collection of all the Laws of Virginia which are sold by Thomas Mercer at the sign of the half moon the Corner Shop of the Royal Exchange in Cornhill,[4] & go with both to some learned Lawyer, who will be able presently to inform them therein,

That I have not mentioned any thing of Brenton [5] is easily answered, because nothing is said of James Town but naming the place, this being only a short Introductory discourse, to usher in the account of the Laws, but if this forlorn should come off successfully, then perhaps I might be encouraged to write a larger discourse of the Country; Brenton should not then fail of its due Commends, which future time will see fully manifested. What I have divers times wrote before, was giving an account of the receipt of the Still & Callash sent by Purvis & of three bills charged upon you, one to John Thomas for £30 one other to Mr. Daniel Parkes for £100 & another to the said Parkes for £10, together with an Order upon Mr. Jno. Taylor for my money in his hands, all which I hope are safe come to hand, & I hope the money paid according to Direction. I know not what further I have to add than to assure you I am

To Mr. Nichs. Hayward &c.   Sr. Your   W. ff.

[*LB*, pp. 235-37]

1. For Hayward, see the many ltrs. to above.
2. For Colonel Daniel Parke II or Daniel Parker, see ltr. to Hayward, Dec. 19, 1693, note 4.
3. For the circumstances of publication of Captain John Purvis' *A Complete Collection of All the Laws of Virginia Now in force. Carefully copied from the Assembly Records* ... (London [1684?]), see ltr. to Hayward, July 10, 1690, note 3. Of four copies examined, two in the Virginia State Library and two in the Library of Congress (the latter two in the Jefferson Collection), three of the four were bound with a number of blank pages, or pages once blank, but now containing further records, chronologically, of the laws of the Virginia Assembly. The Virginia State Library copies once belonged respectively to Nathaniel Bacon (Sr.) and

the Bolling family; the Library of Congress copy with MS additions to John Page of Rosewell, whose grandfather Mathew Page was one of the 1699 committee on revisal. The marginal notes in the last may be in Mathew Page's hand. See E. M. Sowerby, ed., *Catalogue of the Library of Thomas Jefferson*, II (Washington, D.C., 1953), 244-45. Since these additional sheets do not bear the watermarks of the printed sheets, they probably were added by the binders for the convenience of the user.

4. This imprint appears on Purvis' title page.

5. There are several ltrs. to John Taylor, London merchant, above and below. There was a John Thomas in Stafford County born about 1644. There was also a John Thomas and Company, Barbadoes, mentioned in William Byrd I's correspondence. Then there was a sea captain in the 1691 convoy, in 1701 master of the *Bristol*. 5V287; 25V251-3, 361; *Exec. Journ. Council Col. Va.*, II, 162, 171.

To George Mason [1]

Mr. George Mason   July 20th. 1694

Sr. Your's I receiv'd by Capt. Scot[2] together wt. an account of the Sales of my Tobo,   I have wrote by Capt. Jones in the David,[3] who I hope is safe arrived, & by him have consigned you two hhds. Tobo. which I assure my self you will dispose to my best advantage   By Capt. Scot I have sent a large Packet directed to Mr. Nicholas Hayward of London Notary public, which is a little too chargeable for Postage, therefore he has promised to send it by the Carriers as directed, if he should not, or your curiosity makes you inclinable to take a view of it, being a short account of his Country & our Laws, which I know traders hither may be desirous to know, you may if you please take a view of, your self but let nobody else see it, & take effectuall care forthwith to let it be delivered as it is directed. I thank you Sr. for your half dozen of Claret, & should have in gratification returned you a hamper of Cyder, but upon examination found none worth my sending or your acceptance, for want of a Racking at the spring, the less having prick'd it, therefore that I may not be under the like misfortune next year, I desire you to send me a thing to rack hhds. of Cyder, which Mr. Scot tells me they make both of Tin & pewter, & has taken a Memorandum thereof,   I do not mean those many Devices the wine Coopers have as bellows &c. I hope if you do not rightly understand me Capt. Scot will inform you. If you can in Bristol meet with Cornelius Tacitus works Annals & History in English, & Polybius history in English, please to buy them & send them in I am   Sr. Your W. ff.

To Mr. George Mason Mercht. in Bristol

[*LB*, pp. 237-38]

1. For this George Mason, see ltr. to, July 20, 1693, note 1.
2. For Captain James Scott of the *Mountjoy* of Bristol, see ltr. to Serjeant, July 11, 1692, note 2. For Captain Jones of the *David*, see ltr. to Roger Jones, n.d., *c.* 1694, note 3.
3. There were many editions of Publius Cornelius Tacitus available to WF. One two-part edition was printed in English as early as 1598. *The History of Polybius ... Translated by Sir H. S[hears]. To Which is added a character of Polybius and his writings by Mr. Dryden* was published in two volumes in 1693. There are earlier editions, as one of 1634.

To Cornelius Serjeant [1]

Mr Cornelius Serjeant   July 20th 1694

Sr.   The last that I sent you was a letter of advice with bills of Exchange drawn upon you for £13 sterling payable to Joseph Newton [2] which please to pay, before that I gave you an account of four hhds. Aronoko Tobo. shipped you in the David Capt. Jones [3] Master which I hope are safe arrived. If Doctr. Walters [4] be in Choptank, as I have heard nothing whether he is or no, is more convenient to me to come at him there, than if he were at Bristol because of the often opportunitys of sending to the one, & the difficultys attending the other   To hear you say you wanted a power Attorney when you are my Assignee upon the back side the bill Exchange, & that Register'd, or should be in the Notary publick's Office, I cannot but admire, therefore pray Sr. if Walters be there, take care to get it of him, if not truly Capt. Moore [5] must answer it, for he is effectually bound thereto, which please to inform him of. I have now sent for nothing, because I know not how my effects may answer, if there be anything comeing sort in coarse goods I am

To Mr. Cornelius Serjeant Tobacconist   [no signature]

[*LB*, pp. 238-39]

1. For Serjeant, see the several ltrs. to him, above.
2. Probably the second son of John Newton (q.v.) by his second wife, Sarah (nee Butler). Joseph may have been born as early as 1666. 37 V 90-91.
3. For Captain Jones of the *David*, see ltr. to Roger Jones, n.d., *c.* 1694, note 3.
4. For Dr. Walters, see ltr. to Serjeant, July 11, 1692, above. If WF really means Choptank and not Chotank (his own parish in Stafford), he refers to Choptank town and river on the Eastern Shore of Maryland, on the Chesapeake.
5. For Captain John Moore, see ltr. to Serjeant, June 21, 1692, note 2.

To Nicholas Hayward [1]

Mr. Nicholas Hayward   July 25th. 1694

Sr.   I have now sent you two Copys of the account of Virginia, &
Digest of its Laws [2] by two Bristol Ships, one is the Mountjoy Capt. James
Scot [3] Commander, the other is by one Capt. Heyden in a Brigantine
bound to the same place, one I have directed to Mr. Cornelius Serjeant
Tobacconist in Wine Street, & the other Capt. James Scot has promised to
send it up by the Carrier, or to deliver it to Mr. Mason [4] who will take
effectual care so to send it up to you, & so will likewise Mr. Serjeant, for
the Packet is too big to send by the Post, & here was never an opportunity
to send it directly by a London ship   In each of the Packets you will find
a letter directed to you therein. I had thoughts also to send you the
Journall of our last Assembly, by which you might have seen plainly how
acceptable my Method was to their intended Revisal but am not at present
provided: [5] if your Curiosity leads you to take a desire thereof at the
Plantation Office at Whitehall kept by Mr. Blaithwaite [6] you may there
with ease have a sight of one: Your brother [7] & all friends here are well &
now drinking your health as at all opportunitys doth. If you should receive
the Packets at the arrival of the fleet one letter to Bristol would hasten
them up if the Ships miscarry not

To Mr. Nichs. Hayward &c.   Your W. ff.

[*LB*, p. 239]

1. For Hayward, see the many ltrs. to him, above.
2. This is WF's manuscript for publication as a book.
3. For Scott, see ltr. to Serjeant, July 11, 1692, note 2. Though nothing has been found
about Heyden as a seaman, a John Heyden in 1701 patented 190 acres in Pamunkey Neck.
Journal H.B. 1695 ... 1702, p. 282.
4. George Mason of Bristol, mentioned several times above, and to whom several ltrs. are
addressed.
5. WF was burgess for the last time from Oct. 10, 1693, to Nov. 16 of the same year. For
his active part in the affairs of this Assembly, including his chairmanship of the committee
for revisal of the laws, see Introduction above and *Journals H.B. 1659/60-1693, passim*.
6. For William Blathwayt, see ltr. to Madam Sarah Bland, March 19, 1682/83, note 5.
7. Samuel Hayward (q.v.)

To John Cooper [1]

Mr. John Cooper   May 17th. 1695

Sr. Two letters this year I receiv'd one by Capt. Trucket,[2] but know not in what Ship the other came, as for your letter mention'd to come under cover of Jno. Corbin's [3] I receiv'd none, & if you send twenty under such Covers I never expect to receive one but believe if you directed to my self by any Ship bound for Mary land or Virginia, it might as soon come to my hand, as Corbin's will come to whom he directs. By Capt. Trucket I have shipped eight hhds. of good weighty Aronoco Tobo. which I hope will come to a good market, all hands concurring that Oronoko Tobo. is daily rising. I desire you Sr. to send me my Account Currant by the first Ships, & send me two or three duplicates for fear of miscarriage, for not knowing how my Account stands, I dare not send for goods though my wants are very great & pressing. I have not had a line from my mother now this two year & upwards, I believe some miscarriages have happened, therefore be pleased when she sends any more letters let them come under Cover of Your's. I am heartily sorry for her pressing necessity Intimated by you, & could as heartily wish that she were near me, that I might be daily contributing all that lyes in my power to her present occasions, or that Tobo. the only thing we have here to raise money by, were such a Commodity that we might certainly depend to raise money upon the same, & then it would be easie for me to obviate her present Difficultys, but howsoever please to let her have sixteen pounds a year & pay it quarterly, that is, four pounds each quarter, & I shall take care justly to answer you. Pray Sr. let me hear from you by the first & all opportunitys. If you receive my wife's letter for to call for £5 let it have due acceptance I am Sr.

To. Mr. John Cooper   Your W. ff.

[LB, p. 240]

1. For Cooper, see the many ltrs. to him, above.
2. Captain Trucket or Tricket has not been identified.
3. Probably John Corbin of St. Mary's Parish, Richmond County, who on Feb. 21, 1692, bought some land in what is now Brunswick Parish, King George County. He conveyed part of this land to his son John Corbin II. 34 V 358. The Corbins were one of the Northern Neck's prominent families.

To Cornelius Serjeant [1]

Mr. Cornelius Serjeant   May 16th. 1695

Sr. Your two letters one by Opy the other by Capt. Jones in the Richard & John [2] came safe to hand, to gether with your Account Currant. I had not then consigned you such light Tobo. last year, if I had not been deceived by a knavish Receiver, but I shall this year mend it, for I have in Jones the Richard & John put on Board ten hhds. Tobo. of my own sweet scented & consigned to you, as by the bills of Loading which you will suddenly receive will appear, I dare confidently say, the goodness of the Tobo. will fully answer the market, & the weights I am as confident, will make the freight easie, & am well assured of your honest care in the disposal thereof. By Capt. Jones & another Ship I shall write you more at large, & in those shall inclose bills of Loading, for the Tobo. above mentioned, if you approve of the Correspondence my Consignments may I believe yearly increase   Pray receive the within inclosed bill of Mr. John Read's [3] for six pounds drawn upon Sr. Hugh Owen & Company in Pembrokeshire South Wales I am   Sr. Your W. ff.

[LB, p. 241]

1. For Serjeant, see the several ltrs. to him, above.
2. For Captain John Jones of the *Richard and John,* see ltr. to Roger Jones, n.d., *c.* 1694, notes 3 and 7.
3. John Read was one of those accused of being of "Popish principles" in 1699. *Exec. Journ. Council Col. Va.,* I, 435.

To George Mason [1]

To. Mr. George Mason   May 17th. 1695

Sr. I receiv'd your single letter by Capt. Jones [2] in the Richard & John, & therein you intimate of a Note & receipt for certain books sent, but in it I could find neither Note nor receipt nor did there any books come in Capt. Jones as he solemnly protests, how the mistake or miscarriage happens I know not, but I believe its necessary that you get full satisfaction therein. I thank your care & kindness Sr. in sending up that Packet to London as directed, & assure your self when it lyes in my power to serve you here it shall not want a retalliation. I had not the vanity to think that we could outdo much less equall your Hereford Shire Red stroke,[3] especially that made at particular places as at the Lord [   ] &c. which is made with so much care judgment & Caution, but only thought that was indifferent, because of the place from whence it came, might there be acceptable, & give you the opportunity in the drinking of it, to discourse what future advantages, this Country may be capable of I have already put on board Capt. Jones six hhds. of my own sweetscented Tobo. the weights I am sure will well answer the freight, & I dare say the goodness will bring it to the heigth of the market which I am assure my self of, having so good a hand to dispose it by, I shall take care according to your directions to send another of Capt. Scot's [4] bills for six pounds with the letter of advice, belonging thereto in Capt. Jones & the third I shall keep for Capt. Scot when he comes in. Add to the books Virgil in English, Horace in latin & English Juvenal & Perseus in latin & English.[5] I hope you will take care to send the books with the things before spoken of, & that you will by all opportunitys let me hear from you which will be very acceptable to

To Mr. George Mason &c.   Yor. W. ff.

[LB, pp. 241-42]

1. For George Mason, the Bristol merchant, see ltr. to, July 20, 1693, note 1.
2. For Captain Jones, see ltr. to Roger Jones, n.d., c. 1694, notes 3 and 7.
3. Redstreak or Redstroke apples were used for making cider at least as early as 1671, the *Shorter Oxford Dictionary* tells us.
4. For Captain James Scott, see ltr. to Serjeant, July 11, 1692, note 2.
5. These were available in several editions. WF wanted them for William, Jr., to study.

To Mrs. Mary Fitzhugh [1]

Dear Mother   May 20th. 1695

I have earnestly expected to receive a letter from you now this two years, but could receive none, & if it had not been by your letters to my sister Luke, should not have heard of you, her husband receiv'd one from you this year, which I saw from him, her self being dead almost eight months, for she departed this life the first day of October last, at which time I was so extreamly ill, that it was hourly expected when I should expire, but God Almighty by his great goodness, was pleased to restore me again, to prepare myself for his service here, & for eternall Beatitude here-after, to whom be the glory thanks & praise & I hope God almighty will be pleased to store me with such a stock of his Grace, that I make make a pious & profitable use of his abundant mercies towards me. I heartily grieve & with the bowels of Duty & compassion lament your present Calamity, & do with my soul wish that you were here, or that I was nearer you there, that I might be throughly capable of contributing such help as my Duty commands & your necessity requires. I had taken care with my Sister to send you both money & other necessarys, which she promised faithfully to perform, but death disappointed her, & the foolish little knave her husband,[2] though she declared the same to him upon her death bed, & by her last dying words entreated & desired him to perform the same, which was to send you the money so prepared, & the greatest part of her cloaths linnen & silks, which were both considerable, I fear will hardly perform any thing thereof, though often by my self & wife urged thereto, I guess he will write you that he wants conveniency, though I offered him the ready conveniency by a Ship bound directly to London, & the Master would carefully have performed the same, for he has already sold some of them, & will suddenly sell & fool the Remainder, though he knows it was her dying desire that the money & greatest part of the things should be sent to you, should be given to my Daughter[3] which he alike performs, therefore from him I dare say you will not have the least tittle, nor he himself now she is dead, be worth a groat within this twelve month, I dare say his unkindness & foolery shortned her days, for she has often with tears to me lamented the same. I have ordered Mr. Cooper to pay you sixteen pounds a year, & to pay it Quarterly, that is four pound each Quarter, & have ordered him to continue the same without farther orders from me for fear, as has already happened of the miscarriage of letters this War time, that it is a thing almost impossible for us here to raise money in England, for there is so much hazard & danger in shipping home Tobo., & the price is so low when it comes there, that 2000 lb Tobo. is more easily paid here than £10 in money there. I question not but you make a true use & due application of God almighty's present afflictions upon you here, that by this fire of Calamitys here your earthly dreggs may be purged & refined, & in his appointed time you may come pure & clean into his everlasting Kingdom, which is continually prayed for by W. ff. When you write to me get your letter inclosed in Mr. Cooper's or Mr.

Hayward's letters, & then they will come abundantly safer, than if they come single I had almost forgot to tell you that about a month since I heard by accident of a box sent by you, & then I came to open it most of the things were spoiled, let Mr. Cooper take bill of Loading for any things hereafter sent

[*LB,* pp. 242-44]   [no signature]

1. WF's mother Mary King Fitzhugh and his sister Dorothy, who married George Luke as her second husband, are mentioned many times above.

2. For George Luke, see ltr. to Cooper, August 20, 1690, note 2. Luke's grandfather, the reputed butt of Butler's *Hudibras,* was a man of very small stature.

3. WF's only daughter to live beyond infancy, Rose or Rosamond, married Willoughby Allerton of Westmoreland. His father, Col. Isaac Allerton, was a son of Isaac Allerton who came over in the *Mayflower* and was a grandson of Elder William Brewster. Willoughby Allerton, later a particular friend and associate of William Fitzhugh, Jr., died in 1724. He had then a second wife named Hannah. Rosamond probably died before her father, and without issue. See Fitzhugh Family Trees, Va. State Lib.; *Westmoreland County Deeds & Wills, Book 8, 1723-1738* (will of Willoughby Allerton); *Westmoreland Deed Book, 1698-1705,* p. 59a; W. S. Allerton, *A History of the Allerton Family in the U. S. 1585 to 1885....* (Chicago, 1900), pp. 19-35; I. A. Greenwood, *Allertons of New England and Virginia,* repr. fr. *N. E. Hist. & Gen. Reg.* (July, 1890), p. 5; 6 V 394-95; 8 V 171-72; Meade, *Old Churches,* II, 193.

To Nicholas Hayward [1]

Mr. Nicholas Hayward   May 30th. 1695

Sr.   Your three letters the first of 3rd. february 1693/4 the second duplicated of the 15th. Nov. 1694 & your last of the 15th. Decr. 1694 I have receiv'd & have this first opportunity of answering. I remember no more bills than your letters mentioned, & must acknowledge your favour in answering all my bills as your second letter mentions. I hope by this time your Intentions of selling Osborne's tract [2] is over, because I find no mention thereof in your second & last letter, I neither desire nor wish for a better Neighbour; & I hope in time you will find in advantageously convenient, though I must confess, if I must charge my Neighbour, I would rather [   ] myself than have a bad one. Mr. Hewet's [3] business I have discoursed both with his Widow & Capt. Brent, the Widow says she has paid it, Capt. Brent says, he has never receiv'd it, one is my Neighbour & a Widow, the other is my particular friend, therefore cannot arrive at the truth of the story, & for that reason cannot do you nor Mrs. Lewis [4] that service therein, as my obligations & inclinations require. Your Brother Mr.

Samuel Hayward assured me he would be full to you in Mr. Peyton's business,[5] therefore about that I need say no farther. Sr. I thank your kindness in speeding away my letter to my Mother, often miscarriages has occasioned her present necessity, which would not have been if Mr. Cooper had rightly understood my former letters, but now I have taken a course with him about her supply, without farther hearing from me, which I hope he will perform. Your letter to my brother Luke [6] he receiv'd but the meaning thereof my sister being dead, he will not be made to understand at present, & is so great a fool, that in one years time he will be incapable of serving himself or friends, therefore I advise if he owes you anything, you take the first opportunity, while he has something left, to get it out of his hands. I reckon upon my account with you by your Accts. Currant, therefore never remember'd the two Goodriches [7] bills, if you can get any thing of them it will be so much money saved. I have inclosed sent you Capt. Thomas Emmes [8] Bills of Excha. for £28..5..6. drawn upon Mr. Joseph Jackson of London Merchant,[9] which I dare say will be punctually paid. I shall longingly expect to hear from you the same news, that I can now assure you of that we are here all well. Please to send me if you can meet with a Conveniency, new Geers for my Callash the old ones being almost rotten. Duplicated by Capt. Jones [10] in the Richard & Jno. of Bristol

To Mr. Nichs. Hayard   I am Your W. ff.

[*LB*, pp. 244-45]

1. For Hayward, see the many ltrs. to him, above.
2. Unidentified.
3. A Hewet was a J.P. of Stafford in the seventeenth century, and a William Hewet witnessed a will there in 1702. Meade, *Old Churches*, II, 206; 38 V 375.
4. For Mrs. Lewis, perhaps the sister of Samuel and Nicholas Hayward, see ltr. to Hayward, July 4, 1692, note 8.
5. Major Robert Peyton of "Isleham," Gloucester County, is mentioned in "Instructions" to John Withers, June 5, 1682, note 10, and elsewhere. Valentine Peyton was a member of the Westmoreland bar in 1684. He is said to have settled along the "Aquia River" in 1654. Bruce, *Inst. Hist. Va.*, I, 583; Horace Edwin Hayden, *Virginia Genealogies* (2nd ed., Washington, D.C., 1931), pp. 487, 492.
6. For more on WF's opinion of Luke, see ltr. to Mary Fitzhugh, May 20, 1695, note 2.
7. Apparently Gutteridge and Goodridge were one and the same. Nicholas of the *Spencer* is mentioned many times above. Paul Gutteridge of the *Benjamin* was in Virginia in 1702. 16 V 70.
8. Captain Thomas Emmes of the *John* (150 tons, 28 men, 18-2 [*sic*] guns) was in the convoy for London of July 1692. P.R.O., C.O. 5/1306, 119V, L.C. copy.
9. A Joseph Jackson was admitted member of the Merchant Venturers of Bristol, not London, in 1688. McGrath, *Records*, p. 32.
10. Captain John Jones of the *Richard and John* appears in the ltr. to Roger Jones, n.d., c. 1694, notes 3 and 7.

To John Cooper [1]

Mr. John Cooper   June 3rd. 1695

    Sr. The above is Copy of my former of May 30th date by way of
Plymouth, this comes farther to acquaint you that I have in Capt. Emmes
in the Preservation of London, consigned you 20 hhds. Oronoko Tobo.,
which I assure my self will come to a good Market, & am sure that you
will use the same to my utmost advantage, about £20 worth of coarse
goods would come very acceptable to me, provided the Market will keep
me out of debt & answer what I have already ordered. I refer all to your
self, but with this Restriction bring me not in your debt, lest you then
claim, what I will now freely offer without compulsion to be

To. Mr. John Cooper &c.   Your   W. ff.

[LB, pp. 245-46]

    1. For Cooper, see the many ltrs. to him, above. For Captain Emmes, ltr. to Hayward,
May 30, 1695, note 8.

To John Cooper [1]

Mr. John Cooper   June 10th. 1695

    Sr. I have this year sent you divers letters, & therein given you
account of what letters I received from you, this is only written because a
present conveniency offers again, to acquaint you, that I have in Tricket
in the Ship Margaret consigned you eight hhds. Tobo. I have also in the
Ship Preservation of London Capt. Thomas Emmes Master Consigned
you twenty hhds. Tobo. I have likewise in the Ship Tower of London
Consigned you thirty seven hhds. Tobo. by all which Ships I have also
sent letters & bills of loading, which I hope will all come safe to hand, &
that the Tobo. will yield me a good price, as good to be sure as any other

Oronoko Tobo. is sold for, which our Oronoko Merchants here are under large expectation, & has been the Inducive means to perswade me, to ship so much for England this year, more than in one year I ever did, & I hope well timed. The quantity Consigned to you is 65 hhds., which surely will yield me a great deal of money, & encourage me for the future to large Consignments of Oronoko. My sweetscented you sold as cheap again, as it was sold any where that year, that I consigned it to you, though your parcell if there were any difference was the best. I admire at your account to see full Commission both to your self & your Bristol Merchant Dudlestone,[2] Tobo. had need be high sold to bring any money in the Planter's pocket after such charges. Inclosed is a second bill of Loading for the thirty seven hhds. in the Ship Tower of London Capt. James Kirke Commander, & belonging to Mr. Peter Renew Merchant in London, if this letter comes to your hand before his Arrivall I would advise you if you could, to sell the Tobo. at so much Tobo. ℔ hhd. clear, because it is but light & perhaps it might be the profitablest way of selling the same. I have been so large in former letters, & those Duplicated that I know not what farther to say, than to desire your account Currant, & to hear from you by the first conveniency I am   W. ff.

To Mr. John Cooper Merchant in London

[*LB*, pp. 246-47]

1. For Cooper, see the many ltrs. to above. Captain Tricket has not been identified further. For Captain Emmes, ltr. to Hayward, May 30, 1695, note 8. Captain Kirke and Renew have not been identified further.

2. Sir John Dudlestone (created knight in 1690; baronet, 1692) was one of the most prominent of the Merchant Venturers of Bristol. McGrath, *Records, passim; Merchants, passim.*

To John Taylor[1]

Mr. John Taylor   June 11th. 1695

Sr.   My last was by Capt. Emmes in the Preservation for Cover of a bill of Loading for thirteen hhds. Tobo. there shipped & consigned to you, which I hope will come to a good Market, this comes now to desire you to send me in goods for what I shall have in your hands, after the sale of the said Tobo. let it be in nails, hoes, axes, kersey, Cotton & other coarse goods. In your's I find my Charge very high for freight, which the Master Capt. Tricket told me was all that was paid for my goods. Joshua Doynes & Ralph Smith's goods [2] I leave your self to Judge, what reason I have to pay for their goods, & I rather believe it a mistake, & assure my self upon this Information you will regulate it

To Mr. Jno. Taylor Mercht. in London   [no signature]

[*LB*, p. 247]

1. John Taylor, Emmes, and Tricket are discussed in ltrs. of the 1690's just above.
2. Ralph Smith, WF's sister Dorothy's first husband, had died in 1688 or 1689. He had been a trader on a fairly extensive scale. Doyne is unidentified.

To George Mason [1]

Mr. George Mason   June 15th. 1695

Sr. Having met with a Conveniency of some black walnut plank, & meeting with an opportunity for the freight thereof in Capt. Jones,[2] I thought you the fittest to consign it to, because I find you just in my former Correspondence, & understanding you are now building, Your self might afford as good a price, & suit your conveniency with the same. Inclosed is a bill of Loading for the same, which I hope will come to your hand from

To Mr. George Mason Merchant &c.   Sr. Your   W. ff.

[*LB*, p. 247]

1. George Mason, Bristol merchant, appears several times above.
2. As the ltr. to him of this same date shows, this refers to Captain William Jones. See ltrs. to Serjeant, June 21, 1692, note 3, and to Roger Jones, n.d., *c.* 1694, notes 3 and 7.

To Captain William Jones [1]

Capt. William Jones   June 15th. 1695

Sr. This comes only for Cover of a bill of Loading for 22 hhds. Aronoco Tobo. its weighty & as I am told bright, but I dare not assure you it will answer a Dutch Market. I believe & so shall advise if it be possible that you sell it at the Mast according to your Phrase there, the money that it produces keep in your hands till my farther Order, if it should come to a good Market it would contribute well towards an Intention I have of being Interested in part of a Ship for your Port, Pray let me hear from you by all Conveniency & therein you will oblige

To. Capt. William Jones Mariner &c.   Sr. Your   W. ff.

[*LB*, p. 248]

1. For Captain William Jones, see ltr. to Serjeant, June 21, 1692, note 3. A William Jones had been admitted to the Merchant Venturers of Bristol in 1675 and by 1688 was a very prominent member. McGrath, *Records*, p. 32.

To Colonel Henry Hartwell [1]

Worthy Sir

Your's from London dated the 18th. January 1695 I received by the fleet which arrived here the beginning of August last, by their long stay here the scarcity of Tobo. will be guess'd at there, & accordingly I suppose govern the Market, for Crops were so extreamly small last year that the fragment of a West Country fleet carry'd greatest part away, & this Crop being smaller this year occasions the fleet to stay for the perfecting of this Crop, & yet will hardly come home fully. The latter fleet now under expectation of the straggling Ships dayly arriving must most of them at least patiently wait the next Crop to compleat their Loading which makes me conclude that Tobo. must needs be scarce & consequently high, I had designed you a small Consignment of Stemmed sweetscented, but was deceived of my freight. I am glad my Endeavours about Scarlet's debt [2] was effectually serviceable to you if it had not been timely performed your debt had been lost by his death, who dyed suddenly after the Draught of the said bills. I thank you heartily for your news in your letter, & should have been glad, had your present Distemper of the Gout (which I heartily Condole & agree with your advice given that the best remedy is to let it alone only applying some good Anodine, for present Ease, not hindred to be received the same large & fuller, which I hope by the next return you will supply, And if you add thereto twenty or thirty shillings in some of the choicest pieces Tryals or Votes of Parliament Sr. I shall make you punctual payment thankfully. Your Care & kindness I'll assure you Sr. is thankfully receiv'd about the Escritore, but I had one last year come into me according to my mind for price & goodness, therefore have no occasion to add a second trouble to you about that. Two days since Capt. Brent was here & desired when I writ to give you his humble service which I hope your self & Lady will kindly accept from

To Collo. Henry Hartwell &c.   Your   W. ff.

[*LB,* pp. 248-49]

1. For Hartwell, see ltr. June 19, 1681, note 1. In June, 1695, Hartwell departed for England and never returned. He died in 1699. He seems to have gone to London on "affairs of state." H. D. Farish, ed., *The Present State of Virginia, and the College,* by Hartwell, Blair, and Chilton, pp. xxviii-xxix.

2. Martin Scarlet, WF's old rival and Assembly colleague, had died in 1695. Scarlet died during a term in the House of Burgesses, but his name is not connected in the 1695-1696 records with the draft of any bills in the legislative session.

To John Cooper [1]

Mr. Jno. Cooper   March 10th. 1696/7

Sr.   I received your two letters the first by the Bengall by way of Bristol of the 15th. Novr. date the other by Bagwell in the Benjamin [2] of the 27th Decr. 1695 the first by the Bengall was extreamly welcome to me, bringing me an early accot. of the safe Arrivall & good sale of all my Tobo. Together with an Account of all things of Import there your last brought me my account of sales & account Currant only there's two Articles that perhaps one may be a mistake, the other an omission, that of three pounds five shillings of Flemings I do not remember a word of which is charged so much to my Debt in your acct. Currant, the other of the Omission is about a barrell of Stemmed Tobo., Custom for which was paid in Bristol, & the land Carriage for the same to London & both charged to my former Acct. but no Credit for the produce thereof, in this, both which I assure myself you will by your next clear or else make an allowance accordingly. I agree with you that you sold my Tobo. extreamly well, Considering the lightness & ordinaryness thereof, in great part of which I was abused my self by my Receivers, and had it not been so promising a year for a Market, should not have ventured it. I approve of your Consideration & Conduct about the stopping the £20 goods, which I gave a Gentleman order for, & as you supposed so I found goods to be easier purchased here, & therefore now desire you not to send me a penny worth goods till my further Orders. Inclosed is a letter to my Mother, which I hope you will take care in the Delivery of, as also to be punctuall in the performance of my former orders in relation to her affairs. Sometimes freight is high, & then some to be had but not worth while presently its lowering again & then none to be got, so that at present I can not tell what Tobo. I shall ship for London this year, but be sure I shall ship some having a little on board, & dayly in expectation of putting more, another week will settle that affair. Inclosed is bills of Loading for four hhds. Tobo. in the Ship Endeavour of London, Capt. Nathaniel Davis [3] Commander, which I am well assured you will dispose to my best advantage. Sr. I know not at present but Mr. Nicholas Hayward in the management of my affairs, now directed to him may have occasion to use a hundred pounds more than he has already of mine in his hands, if he calls upon you for the same let him have it, & it shall be allowed in your Account I rest

To. Mr. Jno. Cooper Mercht. in London These   Your W. ff.

[*LB,* pp. 249-50]

1. For Cooper, see the many ltrs. to him, above.
2. A Captain Bagwill, in another ship, was in the Virginia trade in 1700. 14 V 179.
3. In 1692 the *Robert,* Captain Nathaniel Davis, commander, left Virginia in the convoy, bound for Beaumorris. His ship then carried 138 hogsheads of tobacco and 38 bulk hogsheads. P.R.O., C.O. 5/1306, 119V, L.C. copy. In 1700 he commanded the *Sarah and Susannah* of London, with eight men and three guns. P.R.O., C.O. 5/1310, L.C. copy.

To Nicholas Hayward [1]

Worthy Sir   [Spring, 1697?]

The method of business would require that I should give you an account of the receipt of your letter & then proceed, but the occasion that I have to Condole the loss of your most dear brother,[2] & my intirely beloved & good friend, makes me change that method, who dyed about the middle of August last, His distemper had no symptoms of Death in it, being a small feaver without other ill Circumstances as his last breath was expired, as 'twas thought in an easie fainting fit, I left him not three minutes before his Death with the assurance from himself of having the happiness of his Company at my house within four days, after my Departure, but within half an hour his wife sent me astonishing News of his Death. His Will together with all other Matters relating to his affairs [3] his Widow will send you at large, & Mr. Foote who is now coming home [4] will be able to give you a full & fair accot. of otherwise should have been more full. As I can not believe but his death at first hearing will be troublesome & grievous to you, so I think when you consider that he dyed full of days &c. of an untainted reputation, it will be a great ease to your sorrow & a great solace to your at present disturbed mind, your constant repeated favours, & the intire friendship that I always held with your brother, not only injoins but commands me, to make you a tender of all the Service in my power, towards the management of your business here, which I heartily offer, the Will that he left was made before his last going for England. Sr. I receive'd your single letter of the 26th. Decr. 1695 date, ⅌ the fleet, together with Mr. Hugh Newman's bookseller Inclosed [5] which arrived about the beginning of August, since when here has been no opportunity of answering till now, by reason of a generall Embargoe, therefore as I desired I desire again that you will please to send me my Account Currant for I know not till then how all stands betwixt us. I hope frequent opportunitys next year will present, that I may have the happiness of oftner hearing from you. Sr. I am so very sick at this present [6] that I am not able further to enlarge, tho' I have a great deal to say both to my own concerns & Mr. Newman's too, which I hope shortly to be able to perform, & with this fleet too I ca'nt hold my pen further than to give you the assurance that   I am   Sr. Your   W. ff.

Inclosed is these bills of Exchange which I desire you will please to receive for me & Dispose as I shall after direct (viz)

Arthur Spicer's on Mr. Thos. Ellis	6 .. 00 .. 00
William Lister upon Mr. Arthr. Bayly	4 .. 00 .. 00
Nic: Bolling upon Mr. George Lapthorn	4 .. 00 .. 09
Jno. Watson upon Mathias Partis Esqr.	03 .. 05 .. 00
Thos. Blake upon Mr. Richd. Burlue	20 .. 00 .. 00
William Jones upon Mr. Arthr. Bayly [7]	3 .. 00 .. 00
	40 .. 5 .. 9

In my next shall write at large have nothing to say farther, more than to desire you to buy me two large Silver Dishes, one dozen Silver plates a pair large Candlesticks, snuffers, & stand, two bread plates, & two small Silver chafing Dishes, what money you want towards their purchase I have wrote to Mr. Cooper to supply, who will be sure to do it upon your demand thereof, & please to send me them in by the first Conveniency to Potomack or Rappahannock. I need not tell you to have the Coat of Arms on it as formerly. I know you will do it, but am first to tell you that I have lost my Steel seal & want a new one

To. Mr. Nicholas Hayward   [no signature]

[LB, pp. 250-52]

1. For Hayward, see the many ltrs. to above.
2. Samuel Hayward (q.v.). His will (see photostat in Va. St. Lib.) was proved Nov. 11, 1696.
3. His widow was Martha, sister of John and Lawrence Washington. Her own will of 1697 survives in the Washington Papers, L.C.
4. This is Richard Foote the younger (1666-1729), nephew of the Haywards and agent for the "Brent Town" owners. Foote was established on a grant in Kidwell's Neck. He and his descendants for three more generations lived within the "Brent Town" tract on the original town site. Harrison, *Landmarks*, I, 193; *Prince Wm. WPA*, pp. 21-23.
5. Hugh Newman was a bookseller in London from 1692 until 1703. He was located first at the King's Arms, Poultry, and second at the Grasshopper, Poultry. His first entries in the term catalogues appear in Easter, 1692 (*The Life of Richard Baxter* and a poem called *The Jacobite Chronicle*), and last in Trinity, 1703. H. R. Plomer, *A Dictionary of the Printers and Booksellers who were at work in England, Scotland, and Ireland From 1668 to 1725*, ed. by A. Esdaile (Oxford, 1922).
6. WF was to die in about five years, though supposedly from a flux contracted from Huguenot refugees.
7. Arthur Spicer and William Jones are identified above. Arthur Bailey's name appears frequently in Northern Neck records (e.g., 18 V 47, 82, 85, 158). Thomas Ellis leased land in Stafford County from William Brent in 1700 (17 V 196). On June 19, 1700, WF and Captain William Jones relinquished a mortgage to Major William Lister (23 W[1] 201). This Captain William Jones is perhaps the burgess from Northumberland in 1692 (*Journals H.B. 1659/60-1693*, pp. xv, 415, 432, 442, 444). Thomas Blake and John Watson appear in Isle of Wight,

Va., records before 1670 (7 W[1] 249, 302; 19 V 31; 24 V 383). Mathias Partis was probably a relative of Captains Charles and Francis Partis (q.v.). Bolling, Burlue, and Lapthorne are unidentified.

To Nicholas Hayward [1]

[April, 1697]

Sir   What went before is Copy of my former, this follows to say some thing in relation to the Copy of the Laws &c. Sent you, which you are pleased to write you have communicated to Mr. Newman Bookseller,[2] I dare say an Ingenious man in his Profession, I must thank your kindness that you have not discovered my name to him, which your writing the superscription to his letter manifests His offer of £20 for the purchase of the Copy I think well enough & shall willingly accept it, & in books too at booksellers rates, to have them thus a dozen handsomely bound, half a dozen of which I would beg your acceptance of, & the remainder one half ordinarily bound, & the rest stitch'd. I am not so skilfull as to know what number there will be, but as to that refer totally to your self. I am not so fond of the matter as to perswade the printing thereof neither will I of my self say, they will be advantageous to Mr. Newman, but I believe his best Course will be to say that he has accidentally met with such a Copy together with the Laws now inclosed sent (which I have not had time to Digest into the former method nor indeed if I had time could I not having a correct Copy by me) to some of the Virginia Merchants there as Mr. Henry Hartwell Mr. Roger Jones younger, Mr. Byrd Collo. Byrd's son who belongs to the Temple,[3] or others that you may please to nominate to him, but pray let him nor them know anything of my hand therein, & as I said before let him give out that it was a Copy that he got by Accident. Your Brother Samuel had so good an opinion of it that he believed a full impression would be sold at a good rate in a year's time. His own Profession after discourse with those or other Merchants will be his best Informer. I have inclosed sent you my letter open to Mr. Newman, which I have not subscribed because I would not be known to him at present further than being your friend, for which freedom I beg your pardon. I begin to be doubtfull Sr. that since you begin to decline your business, & have [in?] * part made a retirement from the noise & hurry of the Town,

* Worn page edge.

this as well as my former may be troublesome to you, therefore desire you will be free and plain with me therein, & I shall avoid the same for the future, but must desire that you will give me the liberty yearly in a short letter not cumber'd wt. business to make my acknowledgements that I am[.] Just as I had finished this I was acquainted with Mr. Footes weak resolutions of staying in the Country this year notwithstanding his fathers Command & desires & your advice joined thereto,[4] from whence he had those Counsels I know, but could wish I had known it sooner, I should then have endeavoured [to] alter his resolutions, or else should have been more full about your brother's affairs, which I referred [to?] his relation, & now have time to retrieve the same

Mr. John Cooper   April 29th. 1697

Let Mr. Nicholas Hayward have what money he calls for to the value of a hundred pounds if he has occasion for it, & shew this note, he having direction from me to make use of money for the management of my affairs   I am

To Mr. Nichs. Hayward &c.   Sir Your   W. ff.

[LB, pp. 253-254]

1. For Hayward, see the ltrs. to him, above.
2. For Newman, see ltr. to Hayward, (Spring, 1697?), note 5.
3. Hartwell is discussed in ltr. to him, June 19, 1681, note 1.; see also ltr. to him (Autumn, 1696, or Spring, 1697?). For Roger Jones, the several ltrs. to him, above. William Byrd II (1674-1744) was at this period (1692-1696) a student at the Middle Temple. He was admitted to the bar in 1695 and in 1696 elected a member of the Royal Society. His father William Byrd I (c. 1653-1704), a leading Virginia merchant and planter, was from 1687 until his death Auditor-General.
4. For Richard Foote II, see ltr. to Hayward, (Spring, 1697?), note 4.

To Hugh Newman [1]

Mr. Hugh Newman   [April, 1697?]

Sr.   I receiv'd your's sub Cover of Mr. Nicholas Hayward's, wherein you advise that you have seen & approve of the Copy of the Laws of Virginia &c & would give £20 for the same under Condition [that?] you were sure of a Chapman that you would take off five hundred of them at bookseller's rates. The best way to be assured of that will be to advise & consult your Virginia Merchants there, which Mr. Hayward can acquaint you with if you are a stranger to them, who perhaps may give such assured encouragement that may forward your proceeding therein. Mr. Hayward will be willing on my behalf to take the money proposed to me in books as you can agree to whom I have wholly referred that matter. Sir the fairest & best Copy was taken into France,[2] this that Mr. Hayward has if I were there might easily be made perfect & Correct but for want of that you well know some small Erratas will happen will happen [sic] under the greatest Care & Diligence, which if this Impression sells well will be easily corrected in the next. As to your opinion of printing them in Octavo I submit to your better judgmt. & shall leave the same to your self. Herewith comes inclosed the Acts of Assembly made since which if I had had a perfect Copy by me of my former, I would have Ranged in the same order the former are, but for want of that cannot do it, but suppose you may easily do the same, or may at least put in those that are in force at the full length at last, & those that are expired obsolete &c. you need do no more than just name their titles, which I have pursuant thereunto marked Your own Profession & Conversation in a matter of that nature will be your best Director therein. As for the Preface & Postscript I advise & desire that they be both laid aside, only retaining the Laws therein, & to write a new preface there as from your self, the Printer giving an account of the Casuall meeting with the Copy & the reasons of the further additions since 1693 which those together with these laws now sent you will fully direct you therein. And likewise be sure fully in your Preface to explain the meaning of those so often repeated expressions in the Margin. In the Intended Revisal which the Postcript pretty well clears to you, but lest that should not be manifest enough to you, I must acquaint you that after that Digest was written an Assembly being called, agreed to a Reformation & Methodicall Digestion of the Laws, & the Lower House which is here called the House of Burgesses, had agreed to perform the same in the same Method those were in, & had of their parts throughly performed the whole, which they called by the name of a Revisal of the Laws, but the upper House which is the Council, concurring to the whole almost though not in all, caused a disagreement first & a Rupture afterwards of the said Assembly, to a generall dissatisfaction, & therefore it is called an Intended Revisal.[3] Therefore I say out of that Postcript & Preface & out of what is now said, you may form a suitable Epistle Dedicatory to open the nature of the thing, the advantage thereof together with it's usefullness & conveniencys, but be sure let it be so writ, as if it were an accidentall Copy & no Author known thereto, & be sure let the former both Preface & Postscript be totally laid aside as is before express'd, except the Laws in the one, & what you think convenient out of the other. Your Profession Sr. together wt. your letter, gives me the full assurance, that you are fully capable of managing an affair of this nature, far better than I can direct, therefore shall refer all wholly to you, & had not now said so much, but that the nature of the thing, & the Distance we are at would not admit less from. Which with what went before & these Acts now sent you have all the Laws in Virginia now in force   Mr. Newman Sr. Herewith comes the Acts of two Assemblys which has happened since the writing of my Postscript,[4] wherein there is three or four Laws of that Assembly, those are well enough remarked by the Postscript, those I have remarked at the end of each Law, by which you may guide your self, if you go forward with printing the Copy but lest the smallness of the hand, being confined to so little room, should not to you be legible, & my Distance too great to supply that defect, I shall now go over again & write plainer what is their done. And to begin the first Assembly of the 18th. Apr April 1695, wherein is contained six Acts,[5]   The Remarks upon the severall Acts of that Assembly are at the latter end enter'd viz. Upon the first, This Act is word for word with the former of short continuance & therefore need not be minded. Upon the second. This Act is private & may be either printed or let alone it only relates to that particular County. This Act is wholly expired & now null & Void. Upon the fourth. The Act is Determined by the former, & therefore the title need not be mentioned. Upon the fifth. This Act is in full force, & ought either to be printed at large or suitably ranged. Upon the sixth. This need not so much as be mentioned the Act determining with the year. And now to proceed to the second Assembly begun the 24th. Septr. 1696 wherein is contained fourteen Acts. The severall Acts at their respective latter ends remarked thus viz   Upon the first may either be right ranged in the place of those repeated or printed at large according to its title & time for it is a standing Law & will be in dayly use. Upon the second. This is a private Act, relating only to that particular County, & may be either printed at large, or ranged amongst the former relating thereto, or let alone according as you please. Upon the third   This should be either printed at large or properly Ranged it being now & likely to remain in force. Upon the fourth. This should be printed at large, though if it were properly ranged it would not be amiss. for it will assuredly hold. Upon the fifth, This should be enter'd at large, & if it could be properly Ranged & those repeated Acts left out it would be very well. Upon the sixth   This is to be fully enter'd, unless it could be properly ranged because it will be a standing binding Law. Upon the seventh, This must be enter'd at large, unless it could be properly ranged, for unless it could be properly ranged, for this is a good binding lasting Act. Upon the eighth, This Act is particular to that County, & its indifferent whether it be printed or no. Upon the ninth, This Act must be printed fully & at large according to the time of its making, for this is a new Law & will be of long Continuance, Upon the tenth, This Act must be printed at large, if it could be Ranged in the place of those repeated it would be well. Upon the eleventh, If this can be ranged in the place of those repeated it would be well, otherwise let it be enter'd at large. Upon the twelfth, If it be possible, range this in its proper place, & take away the Acts there repealed hereby, & let this be fully enter'd for its a lasting advantageous Law. Upon the thirteenth, The Title of this need not be enter'd. Upon the fourteenth, This need not so much as be enter'd. Now Sr. What I mean by saying let them be properly ranged in the place of those repeated, that those repealed Laws should be laid aside, & these entered in their place & after the same Method. And where I say let it be entered fully & at large, I mean that it should be enterd in ex- press words, & in its place according to its time, which will be a surer way to enter all these Laws now sent, you being not conversant nor acquainted with our Country methods, though one Law I would earnestly perswade to be properly ranged, & the former repealed thereby left out, if you dare with certainty undertake the same. Our distance together with the diffi- culty of the thing, & my wanting a Correct Copy by me makes me thus prolix, choosing rather to use three words & perhaps impertinent too, than to use only one word though pertinent & leave the matter dubious, or subject you to mistakes I am

To Mr. Hugh Newman   Your W. ff.

[LB, pp. 254-58]

1. For Newman, see ltr. to Hayward, (Spring, 1697?), note 5.
2. Probably carried to France inadvertently. It is unlikely that WF wanted a printing bid from France.
3. See *Journals H.B. 1659/60-1693* and "Burgess and Politician," Introduction above. WF had been the chairman of the committee for revisal of the laws. That he did most or all the detailed work himself is without question. On Nov. 15, 1693, the Council sardonically informed the Burgesses (*Legisl. Journals*, I, 206), "As to the 10 800li of Tobacco presented to Coll *ffitzhugh*, for his great trouble, in Collecting & preparing the Laws in Order to a Reuisall, We think fitt that, that be likewise rejected, for if Coll *ffitzhugh* thereby has meritted any thing from the Countrey ye reputation wch he will Accquire therein, is a Sufficient & Ample Sattisfaction for his Seruices...."
4. The 1695-1696 Assembly met in two sessions, April 18—May 18, 1695 and April 23—April 30, 1696. What WF calls the "second Assembly," was really the opening session of the 1696-1697 Assembly. It convened September 24, 1696.
5. For these six Acts, beginning with "An Act appoynting Rangers att the heads of the four great rivers," see Hening, *Statutes*, III, 126-31.

To James Bligh [1]

Mr. James Bligh   April 8th. 1696 [7?]

Sr.   Your's of the third of January Date 1695/6 I receiv'd the beginning of August 1696 by Capt. Bickford's own hands,[2] together with
the goods sent according to Invoice, which were all safe delivered. The
Tobo. I confess was both light & very ordinary, & consequently all things
considered well sold, but I have now by Capt. Peter Baker [3] Consigned
you a very good parcell of very good Tobo. & weighty as by the inclosed
bill of Loading you will see, three of them are Stemmed sweetscented very
weighty as you will find when they come to be weighed, & as good sweetscented as any is made in York, which I have found by my Returns for
divers years both from London & Bristol, equally sold with the best
stemmed sweet from thence, the three sweet hhds. are Numbered A. B,
& C. the Remainder is Aronoko some of it very good & some very heavy,
but all of it both better & heavier than the best last year, which I assure
myself you will take very good care to make a good Market of Now inclosed is a second bill of Loading for for thirteen hhds. Tobo. I question
not their meeting with a good Market under your Conduct   I would have
sent for the Effects thereof, a good ordinary Surveyor's Instrument fit for
our Country's use, & the remainder in ordinary Linnen Woolen,[4] shoes
& Iron Ware, Such & so sorted as may make a Cargoe fit to trade with up
the River, you know best how to suit it according to the money in your
hand, & therefore shall refer the same to you. Inclosed is a bill of Loading
for twenty hhds. of my Lord Fairfax but directed to you till his Lordship's farther order, therefore I would advise to send immediately to
London a letter to my Lord Fairfax [5] to be left at Mr. Perry's [6] Mercht. in
London & then you will have speedy advice how to proceed

Your W. ff.

[LB, p. 259]

1. Bligh was probably a London merchant.
2. Two Bickfords, Hugh and Paul, had ships in Virginia in 1692. Hugh was commander
of the *Daniel and Henry* (two hundred tons, eighteen men, six guns) and Paul of the *Rebecca*
(fifty tons, seven men, no guns, carrying forty-seven hogsheads of tobacco and thirty-three
hogsheads of bulk), P.R.O., C.O. 5/1306, 119III and 119V, L.C. copy.

3. Unidentified.

4. Probably linsey-woolsey, "having a linen warp and a wool woof," a cloth for heavy duty or everyday wear. *Shorter Ox. Dict.*

5. Thomas Fairfax (1657-1710), fifth Lord Fairfax of Cameron and nineteenth in the recorded descent of his family, lived at Leeds Castle in Kent and in Yorkshire. He married the daughter of Lord Culpeper. She brought with her as dower most of the Northern Neck Proprietary. His son born in 1693 was to be George Washington's friend who died in the eighty-ninth year of his age. Freeman, *George Washington,* I and II, *passim;* 34 V 32.

6. Micajah Perry (d. *c.* 1721), of the great firm of Perry and Lane, had a brother Peter in York County, Virginia, and a nephew Micajah Lane in Charles City County. 14 W(1) 264-67; Harrison, *Va. Land Grants,* p. 158. Perry left his Virginia business to his grandson of the same name.

To John Taylor [1]

Mr. John Taylor   April 27th. 1697

Sir Last year I shipped & Consigned to you thirteen hhds of Tobo. in Capt. Thomas Emmes, the Ship I am sure arrived safe, & the Tobo. was both good & well delivered to you, according to bill of Loading, but to this hour have not heard a word from you. I am yet so charitable to think that your letters sent to me miscarried, but I ca'nt imagine that a Merchant of your Port & Dealing, but would so Methodize your business to give due & proper answers to all Correspondents & Dealers, but perhaps your little Conveniency this way might occasion the miscarriage: therefore I have ordered Mr. Cooper of London, Merchant, with whom I have had a long & punctuall Correspondence, & to whom I send this letter open, to receive my dues from you, which I am well assured upon the sight of this you will readily and punctually comply with, & accordingly pay him what is justly due from   Sir   Your W. ff.

To Mr. John Taylor Mercht. in London

[*LB,* p. 260]

1. For John Taylor, see many ltrs. to him, above. For Emmes, ltr. to Hayward, May 30, 1695, note 8.

To Captain Roger Jones [1]

Capt. Roger Jones   May 11th. 1697

Dear Sr. This comes for Cover of a bill of Loading three hhds. Stemmed sweetscented Tobo. both very good & pretty heavy, which are consigned to your self, & hope will come well to your hands, & then I question not as good a Market as others. My design was for a greater quantity but could not get freight this casually happened. Also in this Ship is sent to you a bill of Loading for four hhds. of the Proprietor's Tobo. as you will see by the inclosed bill of Loading, what Tobo. we have sent them before, (for this Tun accidentally met with: Capt. Brent being in Maryland) [2] you will see by our large letters & Papers Duplicated & now on board the fleet if they come safe to hand which we have endeavoured, by which our Masters & your self will see what a hard Game we have to play the contrary party that is our Opposers, having the best Cards & the Trumps to boot especially the Honor   Yet would my Lord Fairfax there, take his turn in Shuffling & Dealing the Cards & his Lordship with the rest see that we were not cheated in our game, I question not but we should gain the Sett, tho' the game is so far plaid, but if we be not as we have now & always urged, supported from thence not only our Masters money will be lost, but we shall hardly be able to keep our just & legall standing. [3] Their Interest I hope will spur forward the first & the Last I am well assured their Honour will oblige them to the Support of. for Sherwood and Spicer both say that their little appearance has been infinitely injurious to them, if we then guess at ours, therefore either let us be supported from thence, or be called to an account & fairly render up our trust. [4] Your Distance perhaps may make this that I write now seem Apocriphal, but if you were here upon the spot you would see plainly that it was Canonical. Sr. Please after you have sold my Tobo. to say the three hhds. stemmed sweetscented, out of the Produce thereof, Send me two Suits a Winter & Summer Suite ordinary & Decent the measures you may guess at, their shoes stockings & two Carolina hats of the largest size in the head, a handsome quantity of fruit & spice, the remainder in Nails, a few four pennys two thousand two pennys some sixes & the rest in single tens & eights no double tenns. I shall expect your answer by the first Conveniency, & if you will put in your own News or printed News to the value of twenty or thirty shillings it will be very acceptable to   W. ff.

To Capt. Roger Jones Mercht. in London

[*LB*, pp. 260-61]

1. For Roger Jones, London agent, see the ltrs. to him, above.

2. A tun was usually two pipes or four hogsheads. Since WF was agent *with* Captain George Brent, he was shipping this on his own recognizance.

3. See "Propietary Agent," Introduction above, and Freeman, *George Washington*, I, Appendix. The agents beat off the attack of Robert Carter, but the going was hard. What WF wants is for Lord Fairfax to exert some influence upon the Lords of Trade in London, for the burgesses had petitioned through the same group for the return of the Proprietary grant to the Crown. Holders of grants acquired before 1649 held that the quitrents should go to the Crown and not to the Proprietors. WF argued a great deal about this and other resistance.

4. Apparently the attorneys William Sherwood and Arthur Spicer found themselves unpopular for having ventured to support the agents and their point of view. As observed above, Sherwood also had recently "attorned" for his own Northern Neck holdings. WF knew that he and Brent as agents had made themselves unpopular with certain elements in the colony.

To Cornelius Serjeant [1]

Mr. Cornelius Serjeant   July 1st. 1698

Sr. About a week since I receiv'd your's by James Scot, in the Mountjoy wherein you give me an account of the lowness of Tobo., but withall that mine is not yet sold which I hope lyes for a better Market, for as money grows more plenti-   plentifull [*sic*] Tobo. as well as all other foreign Commoditys must rise, for the lowness of Tobo. I have advice from London was only occasioned by the want of money. Now Sr. To give you advice about Tobo. this 'tis here are great Crops under expectation, God only knows what accidents may happen if none, I shall be in hope of making you considerable Consignments this year, & shall not be wanting to advise others to you, Capt. Brent to whom I gave your respects resolves to send send [*sic*] you some if he can possibly meet wt. freight since you are concerned in severall Ships to come this year for Virginia. I shall desire you to secure me in one of your Ships two Tunn & a half at least to make a Merchant like sum according to your letter, & ten hhds more uncertain, also Capt. Brent would have a Tun & half secured for him, & some more uncertain. When a good Market for Sales though a large time is given for payment if it be in secure hands refuse not the offer, for I am at present in hopes not to have a present occasion for the money. By my next which I hope will not be long after this perhaps I may say more

To Mr. Cornelius Serjeant   Your W. ff.

[LB, pp. 261-62]

1. For Serjeant, see the many ltrs. to him, above. Captain James Scott of the *Mountjoy* also is mentioned several times above.

To Samuel Foote [1]

Mr. Samuel Foote   June 6th. 1698

Sr. I believe you are a totall stranger to me not yet hearing of my name, & to receive not only this large letter, but a large Packet too perhaps may at first view be surprising. I will assure you Sr. Whatever I am to you, fame has made you known to me, with a very fair Character, & that has been augmented by my long intimate conversation & Correspondence with your two Uncles Sam & Nick Hayward, & your poor brother here in the Country, who deserves your pity & regard,[2] what I can serve him he shall freely command. Sr. The Copys of the letter herewith sent will acquaint you with the full business betwixt Mr. Hayward & my self, therewith you will find what bills of Exchange I have sent to him, I cannot yet understand any of them have been presented, & Consequently none paid, therefore Sr. I request you to overlook his papers, make Presentation of the Respective bills, & get payment, & please to keep the money in your hands till your further order, I am sure it cannot be doubtfull & I hope it will not be troublesome to lodge so much money in your hands which I look upon sure & safe. Mr. Newman's[3] business you will fully see in Mr. Hayward's & his letters & observations, if it were not too much trouble I would desire to negotiate & finish that affair, with Mr. Newman just in the same method & in all particular Circumstances.   Sir   Had I not known you to be a man of parts, throughly paced in business, I should have been longer in my Directions, till my next I take leave to subscribe. My next will be fuller this Directs only to a Roll of papers in Mr. Nichs. Hayward's Office Study what you call it &c. Sr. After concerting Mr. Hayward's papers if you please to be so kind as to be full to me it will be the highest obliga-tion can be put upon   Sir   Your W. ff.

To Mr. Samuel Foote These

[LB, pp. 262-63]

1. One Samuel Foote (1659/60-1697) was the son of Richard Foote the elder, brother-in-law of Nicholas Hayward. Apparently Nicholas Hayward had died since WF's last ltrs. to him of 1696/97. See ltr. to Cooper, June 30, 1698, below, and 7 V 3-4.
2. That WF had a low opinion of Richard Foote II is evident in his ltr. to Nicholas Hayward of (April, 1697), note 4.
3. For Newman, see ltr. to Hayward, (Spring, 1697?), note 5, and ltr. to Newman, (April, 1697?).

To William Dains [1]

Sir William Dains   June 7th. 1698

Sr.   M. Auditor Byrd's [2] Request & Invitation together with Mr. Mark-ham's handsome & gentile Character,[3] gives the occasion of this letter & this present Consignment, I assure my self you will dispose thereof to my best advantage, & if you see arising Market, stop my Sales till the heigth thereof for I have no occasion of money nor goods. Please to be frequent & familiar in your letters, & what news you think conveniently to com-municate shall be taken acceptably & punctually paid   Please to receive the inclosed bill of Mr. Henry Martin's [4] for £16 .. 17 .. Sterling & keep it in your hands till my farther Order. Sr. Now we are come to the seventh of July, & I send the above as Copy of my former this comes now to inclose a second bill of Loading, & a second bill of Exchange for £16 .. 17 .. 00 ster: which I am sure you will manage to my advantage. I have also in-closed sent you a bill of loading for two hhds. in Capt. Thomas Opy junr.[5] if you mind the bill of Loading the Tobo. is here shipt by Opie him self, & to be Deliver'd me to contain a Thousand weight at least of Neat Tobo. when it comes to your hands to whom I do by this Order & assign it, & question not but to come to a good Market by your Conduct, in my next

I shall say more & believe consign you more Tobo. & therefore will only say now that I am   Your W. ff.

To. Sr. William Dains Merchant in Bristol

[*LB*, pp. 263-64]

1. Sir William Dains appears frequently in the records of the Merchant Venturers of Bristol. He seems to have been knighted in 1690. In that year he and other Bristol merchants petitioned Parliament to allow them a share in the American-African slave trade. They attacked the Royal African Company's monopoly. McGrath, *Records*, pp. 26, 33, 95, 153, 163, 231, 264.

2. William Byrd I (q.v.) was Auditor-General of Virginia. See ltr. to Hayward, (April 1697), note 3.

3. There was a Captain Markham of the *Cuthbert and Spranger* in Virginia in 1703. A Lewis Markham was sheriff of Westmoreland in this period. WF generally got his "characters," however, more often from sea captains than from planters. *Exec. Journ. Council Col. Va.*, II, *passim;* 6 V 81.

4. A Henry Martin's will was proved in 1705. He lived on the Dividing Creek Branch of Choptank River, (Md.?). There was a Henry Martin of Bristol, England, with a seventeen-year-old son in 1728. 24 V 322; 10 W(2) 320.

5. The will of Thomas Opie of the City of Bristol, mariner, was proved in 1703 in Virginia. In 1701 he was master and part owner of the *Adventure,* in 1692 master of the *Constant Love.* He wished to be buried in the grave of his grandfather, the Reverend David Lindsay, in Northumberland. He ordered his executrix to secure a tombstone from England to put on his grave with his grandfather's on top. P.R.O., C.O. 5/1306, 119V, L.C. copy; 18 V 90, 91; *Exec. Journ. Council Col. Va.*, II, 172.

To John Cooper [1]

Mr. Jno. Cooper   June 30th. 1698

Sr.   Your two letters both of the 24th. Decr. Date I have receiv'd, & Inclosed a letter from my Mother, together with the box, in it the welcome bible   Instead of three pounds let four Pounds be the purchase if she be now living. I thank your kindness in not suddenly disposing my Tobo. when the Market was low, I hope since it is risen; to my advantage, your kindness about Tobo. Intended to be presented, requires my thankfullness, which I heartily give you. You know Mr. John Taylor's business as well as I can inform you, Pray use your own Discretion in the Procedure therein, & be earnest both to get his Account & my money into your hands. Just as I am writing this I received a letter from Mr. Taylor, wherein he gives me an account of the Sales of my Tobo., & tells me he has paid freight & Custom for the thirteen hhds. which he pretends to you was lost, if lost why the freight & Custom paid, if there, why not my Account Credit for it; he tells me in his letr. that one Joseph Jackson [2] shipped it off on his Account, pretending that he had one of same Mark, further he writes me that the freight & custom is paid by him for the same, as I have told you above which to me is a Riddle, & further assures that the clear Produce is £13 sterling which I conceive & hope you will see to it, to be added to my money in his hands, which I desire you to get at him, for must I seek for a Man that has upon bare pretensions taken away a hhd. Tobo. Deliverd to him, and for which he paid freight & Custom, & consequently was possess'd therewith, I hope you will manage it to my advantage. Inclosed comes herewith a true Copy of Taylor's letter, account of Sales, & Account Currant, as you will see how he comes to pay freight & Custom, & another man take his Tobo. I cannot imagine but by his letter he makes it clear to me that that was a good hhd. let the others be what they will, for though the others do not clear much yet I find that which looks with a prejudiced Countenance upon me, here is a considerable deal of money I shall once again desire your Conduct, Diligence & care in this affair, & to give me a full account by the first conveniency My last letter to Mr. Nicholas Hayward comes herewith, together with a letter Directions to Mr. Newman Bookseller in London, by Mr. Hayward's letter you will see partly how our Circumstances stood, the Copy of his last Acct. Currant I have not yet sent, but perhaps may in my next. I cannot understand by any hand that the bills sent him as there you will see has been presented, & consequently if so not paid. I heartily thank your former care & trouble in that affair, & now must earnestly require & press you not only to continue the same, but to use your utmost endeavours, that I may not be so great a loser as the present prospect of Affairs renders doubtfull, for his debt to me was before that unhappy addition of those last bills of Exchange, Mr. Newman's business so fully speaks it self, that I shall say no more than to desire you to pursue, as Mr. Hayward if he had lived would have done, I had almost forgot one thing to tell you that I have already writ to a Nephew of Mr. Hayward's, Mr. Samuel Foote,[3] & inclosed sent him the same Copys as I now send you because it was rumoured here, that he had the management of his Uncle's Estate & business in behalf of Mr. Hayward his cousin Mr. Hayward's son, whether so or no, or whether he will negotiate my affair, please to give me a full account by your next. That I have not consigned you any Tobo. this year, you may wonder at, but in truth Sr. Oronoko Tobo. was generally sorry, & of that that was good I could get none for myself, Neither do nor have made any thing but sweet for some years, but with you it seemed inconsiderable & unvaluable, therefore have sent you none, though to whomsoever else I send it I never fall short, sometimes exceed York sweet price, & at Plymouth last Decr. had £23rd. sterling a hhd. clear, indeed the weights were considerable. Sr. Please to be frequent & full to me by all opportunitys, & earnestly request you to send me in my Account Currant, which will be a mighty satisfaction to   Sir   Your W. ff.

To. Mr. Jno. Cooper

[*LB*, pp. 264-66]

1. For Cooper, see the many ltrs. to him, above. For Taylor, the same.
2. For Joseph Jackson, London merchant, see ltr. to Nicholas Hayward, May 30, 1695, note 9.
3. Samuel Foote is addressed in a ltr. of June 6, 1698.

To Mrs. Mary Fitzhugh [1]

Dear Mother   June 30th. 1698

I heartily condole your present sickness and Indisposition, which your age now every day contracts, & God's grace will make you bear patiently to your comfort, his glory, & your own eternall salvation. I cannot enough thank you for your present of your choice Bible, your money that you say you had present occasion for, I have ordered Mr. Cooper to enlarge, & you will see by his letter has ordered it to be doubled. Before I was ten years old as I am sure you very well remember, I look'd upon this life here as but going to an Inn, no permanent being by God's [will] I continue the same, good thoughts & notions still. therefore am always prepared for my certain Dissolution, wch. I ca'nt be perswaded to prolong by a wish. Now Dear Mother if you should be necessitated for £8 or 10 extraordinary, please to apply to Mr. Cooper, & he upon sight of this letter will furnish you, & it will be as acceptable as if done to.   W. ff.
My Sister died a true penitent of the Church of Engld.[2]

[*LB*, pp. 266-67]

1. For WF's mother Mary King Fitzhugh, see ltrs. addressed to her, above.
2. Since Dorothy's first husband Dr. Ralph Smith had been a Whig and probably a dissenter, and her second husband George Luke a ne'er-do-well, Mrs. Fitzhugh may have asked an anxious question about her spiritual state at the time of her death.

To Captain Roger Jones [1]

Capt. Roger Jones   July 7th. 1698

Sr.   About five days since I receiv'd your letter to Decr. Date Inclosed in other letters that you may be sure were very welcome, because writ in a stile so kind & obliging, & all things therein charged so plain, & manifest fate throwing upon the Reading those letters first made me conclude my own particular would not be very acceptable, & accordingly I found it I have made no other Tobo. than stemmed sweet at none of my Quarters for some years past, & always have shipp'd all, have had full prices from London & every Port I sent it to, & from the City of Bristol sometimes exceeding the York Market, but always it had a fair Character, which makes me think you may be mistaken in your guesses of the foulness of that small parcell sent to you when Capt. Allison [2] brought me the things sent, I was surprised not to see Letter, bill of Loading, or Account of the purchase of the things sent, how to reconcile it I could not tell, but the receipt of your letter came to hand, has made me easie therein, for by that letter & its companions, I guess that my own particular business was not worthy your notice to one that had been such a knave &c: To the Proprietors & are gladly willing to render a full & fair account of our whole manage & minutest action in their affairs, to any person authorized to receive the same, which their Interest requires speed in, else this year's may be endangered thereby, for men under our Characters, cannot be expected now reasonably vigorously to prosecute. Sr. I shall proceed no further, either in observations or reflections, but hope in my own particular business you will mend your last mistake, & send me in by the next conveniency the account of Prices of the things sent, my acct. of Sales & Account Currant. Capt. Allison in whom goes the Proprietor's Tobo. will be able to give some manner of the account of the Diligence used in their affairs who has been every where in their Territorys, & is sufficiently knowing in my trouble & charge therein, as also may be seen by discoursing every Sherriff (who must be Collector think you what you will there) how mightily we have cheated them & secured the best Tobo. for our selves, I shall earnestly expect the particular answer to my own particular business by the first opportunity   Come let me tell you ways that you have to arrive at our knavery To the Proprietors the first by Allison who knows the affair almost as well as our selves, having generall orders to the Sherriffs our Collectors to take all receipts on board his ship, know of him whether any of them said our Notes were unreasonable, having shipped off or sold the greatest part of their Tobo., which be sure must be told him if it had been so or any thing like it, the second is for their next Agent to apply himself to the Collectors, & to know what Tobo. received, & how disposed this I will promise you is friendly advice. The above is Duplicate of my former, & now Sr. we are arrived to the 22nd. July I have little farther to say than only this, that if your good friend [   ] ³ that drunken sottish inhospitable fellow if he had lived to come in, should not have had one hhd. on board any Ship that he was concerned in, neither of mine nor of the Proprietor's unless their express orders had so commanded, for that Rascall had such hospitality at my house, that I never saw him sober, what sober time he had he applyed to perswade Bagwell ⁴ from the Proprietor's service, & was as great a Villain as lived in that affair. As to the Proprietor's business have said enough, when you come in which I could wish or any one else & account, then the easie credulity of you there, the maliciousness of our enemies & our own Integrity will appear   I am   Your W. ff.

[*LB*, pp. 267-69]

1. For Roger Jones, the London agent, see the ltrs. to him, above.
2. Perhaps the commander of the *Traveller*, which carried ltrs. to Perry and Lane in 1691. 27 V 287.
3. Why the copyist of the letterbook omitted the name here cannot now be determined.
4. In 1700 a Captain Bagwill was commander of the ship *Levitt*. See ltr. to Cooper, March 10, 1696/97; also 14 V 179.

To George Mason ¹

Mr. George Mason   July 21st. 1698

Sr.   By my last in the Mountjoy their haste would give me no further opportunity, than only to write congratulatory, & to assure you of our healths here; And by this Conveniency of the Richard & John I have time enough to tell you, that I have receiv'd your's from Capt. Jones his own hands dated the 28th. Decr, & now must tell you in your own expression plainly, I was cheated in them eight hhds. Tobo. in the said Richd. & John, for I trusted to the man's word that paid them to me both for weight & goodness, heavy weights & choice Tobo. he render'd account to me, but by your letter & account of Sales, I am well assured I was abused, but the man died before your letter arrived, therefore that is at an end. Truly as to your taking & giving me Credit for that 8 hhds., I do'nt fault it, but must for the future desire you to expose my own stemmed sweetscented out of my own Crops, which I know to be good, to the view & Sale of the Market, for really my account there methinks looks very low, of which I hope hereafter you will take care, that is my own stemmed sweetscented. I shall never trouble Bristol Market more, with any Walnut plank, the reason of my sending this, was I heard you were your self building, & I thought it might suite your conveniency, for Mr. Blaithwaite being building some where about your parts, has two Inch black Walnut plank from Capt. Brent, & the Governr [2] who buys it for him pays six pence a foot here in the Country, Capt. Jones I think has carried home two or three turns for him, & has now a turn home with him, therefore I say though your Bristol price did not answer my expectation, yet I thought my design at first well grounded. As to your fringe it came safe & was welcome, though my wife had one better & richer by her, being a thick close large fringe half Silver half gold & so no necessity for this   Sr. By this comes a large & dear Consignment from me, the Consignment of a son to your care & Conduct,[3] I am well pleased & assure my self of a carefull & Ingenious manage, if you will please to undertake it, the generall good Character of your most vertuous Lady, who I must esteem the Cape Merchant in the Adventure, puts me under the assurance, that he will be as well, if not better, under your Conduct there, than he can be possibly with us here. He is furnished with cloaths only for his Sea Voyage, for I thought it was needless to make him up cloaths here for his wear there, because it might be there better & more suitably done, therefore I shall refer to you for furnishing of him with what is fit & decent, as befits an honest Planter or farmer's son, not with what's rich or gaudy, I shall refer that to yor. own discretion. Now Sr. to tell you that he is eleven years & a half old, & can hardly read or write a word of English might make you believe that either he was a dull boy, or that I was a very careless & neglectfull Parent. Indeed its neither carelessness in me nor dullness in him, for although he cannot read or write English, yet he can both read, write & speak french, & has run over the Rudiments of the Latin Grammar, according to the french method, for he has been a considerable time with a most ingenious french Gentleman, a Minister who had the Government & tutorage of him, & indeed did it singularly well, but the unhealthfullness of his Seat & the sickliness of the child, occasioned his remove from thence.[4] Therefore if it could be as Capt. Jones tells me it may, I would have him put to a french Schoolmaster, to continue his french & learn latin,   Now Capt. Jones tells me there is such a School or two, about three or four miles from Bristol,[5] & if it could conveniently be done, I would have him boarded at the School-master's house. Now Sr. I have told you my mind & how I would have him managed if I could, I must at last say in generall terms, that I refer the whole to your discreet & prudent manage, assuring my self that if you are pleased to undertake the trouble, you will do by him as if he were a Child or relation of your own, & shall without more saying, refer him wholly to your Conduct, & hope within a week after his Arrival you will contrive him to his business, what's necessary for him, either for books, Cloaths or now & then a little money to buy apples plums &c. is left solely to your self & all charges shall be punctually answer'd you & thankfully acknowledged. Herewith comes inclosed a letter open to Mr. Cornelius Serjeant [6] together with a note upon him to pay you £85..01..8. which I am sure he will punctually pay   Sir I desire you by the first good conveniency to send me these things following viz Two large Silver Dishes containing about 80 or 90 ounces each dish. A Dozen of Silver plates. Two silver bread plates, A pair of Silver Candlesticks large & fair. A pair of Silver snuffers & Stand. I cannot tell whether these things are to be bought in Bristol but from London I have had of the same sort, from Mr. Richard Smith & Mr. Elias Spinkes very substantiall & very good Silver, but refer the same wholly to your self, both where & to buy of whom only this I must tell you, that I would have no letters engraved upon them nor Coat of Arms, having a Servant of my own singular good Engraved, & so can save that money. Also I would have you send me a Callico quilted morning gown for myself, & a black Crape gown & petticoat for my wife. Now it is time to leave off sending for any more things this year & to tell you that if the things sent for, together with the necessary charge you must be at about my Son shall have drained your pockets dry already of my money in your hand, & now ordered you by Mr. Serjeant the effects of the little Tobo. I shall now consign you, I shall take care forthwith to pay what remains, & to lodge more in your hands, but if that should not be satisfactory, however pray fail not of sending me in the things according to Directions, & I am in hopes Sr. William Dains upon sight of this my letter will answer it, but if my expectations there should be short too, I am sure Capt. Jones or Mr. Markham will be Security that you shall be fully answer'd, & that timely   Inclosed you will have a bill of Loading for a Tun of Stemmed Tobo. of my own Crop, which I assure my self you will dispose to the best advantage   My wife & self request you will make our humble services acceptable to your good Lady by your kind presentation.

Mr. Cornelius Serjeant   July 21st. 1698

Pay or cause to be paid to Mr. George Mason of Bristol Merchant or Order the sum of Eighty five pounds one shilling & eight pence sterling, make good payment & enter it to the account of   Sr.   Your W.ff.

To Mr. George Mason

[*LB*, pp. 269-72]

1. George Mason, Bristol merchant, appears several times above. The *Mountjoy* and *Richard and John* (the latter commanded by Captain John Jones) are referred to several times above. William Blathwayt, Secretary of the Lords of Trade, and George Brent, WF's law partner, are also mentioned frequently.

2. Sir Edmund Andros was "Lieutenant and Governor Generall," September 20, 1692, to December 9, 1698.

3. WF's second son Henry was born Jan. 15, 1686/87, and died Dec. 12, 1758. In 1715 he was high sheriff of Stafford. He married Susanna, daughter of Mordecai Cooke of Gloucester County. For more on Henry, see ltr. to Henry Fitzhugh, Jan. 30, 1686/87, note 4.

4. As mentioned above (ltr. to Hayward, July 4, 1692, note 14) this tutor was probably the Reverend John Bertrand, who was the rector of St. Mary's White Chapel in Lancaster.

5. In Bristol in this period were three schools, the Grammar School, Queen Elizabeth's Hospital (q.v.), and the Cathedral School, no one of which would fit WF's description. No trace of a Frenchman's school outside the city remains.

6. Cornelius Serjeant and Sir William Dains are addressed in ltrs. above. The Captains Jones are referred to frequently above. Markham is discussed in ltr. to Dains, June 7, 1698, note 3.

To Edward Hayward [1]

Mr. Edward Hayward   July 21st. 1698

Sir   You were pleased to promise me punctually & without fail, to send me in by the first conveniency what books I sent for by you if to be had in Bristol or London, therefore assuring my self & depending wholly upon your promise I have neglected all other conveniencys to send for these books following by you viz. All the Statutes made since the twenty second of King Charles the second to this year.[2] The 2nd. Part of Rushworth's Collections in 2 Volumes   The third part of Rushworth's Collections in 2 volume [3]   Doctr. Thos. Burnet's Theory of the earth in English [4]   All the works of the Author of the whole Duty of man in one Volume.[5] The Lord Bacon's Remains.[6] Cotton's exact Abridgement of the Records of the Tower [7]   Buchanan's de jure Regni apud Scotos [8] if to be had in English. Mr. Boyle's letter to a friend concerning specifick Physick.[9]

A large fair printed bible in quarto. A large common prayer book in folio. The secret History of King Chas the 2nd. & King James the 2nd.[10] A Continuation of the secret History of Whitehall to Abdicaon &c [11] An Historicall account of the memorable actions of King William the third.[12] These are the books I desire you without fail to send me, I am sure you may have all but one, & that is Buchanan   I cannot say whether ever it has been Englished the rest are every day to be had in London to be sure, some part in Bristol, therefore do not send me word some of them are not to be had, but what I need I say for I know you will not be so unkind to

To. Mr   Hayward   Your W. ff.

[*LB*, p. 273]

    1. Presumably the son of Nicholas Hayward.
    2. There are various editions of the *Statutes*.
    3. *Rushworth's Historical Collections* are discussed in ltrs. to Wormeley, August 2, 1682, note 3, and to George Luke, Oct. 27, 1690, note 17.
    4. *The Theory of the Earth: containing an account of the Original [sic] of the Earth, and of all the General Changes which It Hath Undergone, or is to Undergo, till the Consummation of Things*. (London, 1684), 2 vols. There are other editions of 1691, 1687, etc.
    5. [Richard Allestree? J. Fell? R. Sterne? Lady Pakington?] *The Works of the Learned and Pious Author of the Whole Duty of Man* (Oxford and London, 2 vols. in one, 1684 [other editions, as 1704]).
    6. *The Remaines of the Right Honourable Francis Lord Verulam . . . Being Essayes and severall Letters to severall Great Personages, and other Pieces of various and high Concernment and not heretofore published. . . .* (London, 1648).
    7. Sir Robert Cotton [or rather, William and Robert Bowyer], collector, *An Exact Abridgement of the Records of the Tower of London, from the Reign of King Edward the Second, unto King Richard the Third. . . .* 1657.
    8. *De Juri, regni apud Scotos. Or, A Dialogue, concerning the due Priviledge of Government in the Kingdom of Scotland. . . . Translated . . . by Philalethes* (London, 1680 [first English ed.; others 1689, etc.]).
    9. *Of the Reconcileableness of Specific Medicine to the Corpuscular Philosophy . . .* (London, 1685).
    10. *The Secret History of King Charles II and King James II* ([London?], 1690).
    11. *A Continuation of the Secret History of Whitehall from the Abdication of King James . . . to . . . 1696, by* _____ *late Secretary Interpreter to the Marquess Louvois . . . Published from the Original Papers together with the Tragical History of the Stuarts from . . . 1068, down to the Death of her late Majesty, Mary, by D. Jones* (London, 1697).
    12. *An Historical Account of the Memorable Actions of . . . William III.* N.d.

To Cornelius Serjeant [1]

Mr. Cornelius Serjeant   July 21st. 1698

    I receiv'd severall letters from you last year. & the last by Capt. Jones wt. acct. of Sales and acct. Currt. inclosed therein, the acct. of Sales of my

Tobo. I do not at all like, for I must esteem you by your letters & the Sales there made to be but a very ordinary Marketman, for if all the Tobo. I had sold about that time which was not inconsiderable, both at Bristol London, Plymouth & Liverpoole, ordinary Tobo. yielded me as good & some a better price, my own stemmed sweet scented so far beyond, that I have hardly patience to look upon your Acct. You charge me in your Account for a Charter party drawing,[2] & give me notice of the same in your letter, & on the back side of your letter there's a draught of a Charter party with my name mentioned therein, but why I must be charged for a Charter party & not have it, I can't tell, but this I can tell, that if freight had ruled here above the rate taken by the Charter party, it was at the Master's courtesie to let me have any for I am sure for want of it, I could neither compell him nor protest against him, nor indeed discreetly or legally demand it, what you kept the Charter party there for I can't imagine, for if it were complyed with, the Charter party is useless & void, if not complyed with, their Charter party would be produced against you for damages so that your keeping the Charter party, if it were not ignorantly done, was only to bring me under the necessity of paying freight, if freight was high here: However, because I do not love trouble I have comply'd with the certain freight, though to my damage, I have also charged a note upon you to pay Mr. Mason[3] £85 . 1 .. 8. which pray let be answered him   I am

Your W.ff.

To Mr. Cornelius Serjeant Tobacconist &c.

[*LB*, 273-74]

1. For Serjeant and Capt. Jones, see the many references above.
2. A "charter party" was a charter or deed made between owners and merchants for hire of a ship, and safe delivery of the cargo. *Shorter Ox. Dict.;* also see Bruce, *Inst. Hist. Va.,* I, 578.
3. Presumably George Mason, the Bristol merchant.

To Henry Hartwell [1]

Honoured Sir   July 21st. 1698

I receiv'd your single letter of the 10th. January date, & heartily congratulate your hopefull expectation of recovery from your unwelcome tedious & most uneasie companion the Gout, which I pray God may fully answer your hopes. As to your wonder that I have never been troubled therewith I'll tell you Sr. I never much frequented Bacchus Orgyes, & always avoided Adoration to Ceres shrine, & never was one of Venus Votarys: To speak plainly to you, I never courted unlawfull pleasures with women, avoided hard drinking as much as lay in my power, & always avoided feasting & consequently the surfeits occasioned thereby, tell your Doctor this, & he will conclude I am not near being his Patient yet. I thank you Sr. for your generall news in this letter, & have been & am now longingly expecting your particular news in your letter yet to come, which now would be most gratefull & acceptable, & so will be for the future, if you please & think it not too much trouble to hold this kind correspondence by yearly letters. Indeed did I know your mind, I believe I might consign you a little sweetscented Tobo. yearly, which pray by the next let me know. The tenth wane is always the worst, therefore fearing the last effects of your Distemper may be troublesome enough; without my Impertinencys, I shall only request you to make my most humble service acceptable to your good Lady, & to desire your self to receive the same affectionately from   W. ff.

To. Mr. Henry Hartwell Merchant in London

[*LB*, pp. 274-75]

  1. For Henry Hartwell, see ltrs. to him, June 19, 1681, note 1, and (Winter, 1696/97), note 1.

To John Cooper[1]

Mr. John Cooper   July 26th. 1698

  Sr.   I have writ you formerly very large both as to Mr. Nicholas Hayward's business & Mr. Jno. Taylor's which I hope will come safe to your hand, & then I assure my self you will use your [utmost] endeavour to secure my Interest with them within this four or five days I hope to send the Duplicates thereof, for fear of miscarriage   This comes in haste to inclose a bill of loading for thirteen hhds. of Stemmed sweetscented Tobo. two more unstemmed sweet scented in all fifteen hhds. in Capt. Allison [2] which I am well assured will prove good Tobo., & hope you will get a good market for the same. Pray be sure by the first conveniency to send me a full account of my whole business & my Account Currant also by this ship I have sent you also ten 3 inch black walnut plank, which comes freight free, & hope it will come to a good market. Pray by the first conveniency of a London ship bound for this River send me in these things following (viz) 2 quilts A Side Saddle. A large silver salt. A pair women's gallooned shoes, A Table, Pair of Stands, Case Drawers, & looking Glass answerable. Two large leather Carpets. Two gall: Florence Oyl. A Set of Dressing boxes answerable to the Table & Stand &r. A box of glass in quarries with lead answerable in Diamond Cut containing about 80 or 100 feet. Six three quartered lacker book frames for pictures well burnished. About 40 or 50 shillings worth of colours for painting wt. pencils Walnut Oyl & Lynseed Oyl proportionable together with half a doz: 3 quarter clothes to set up a painter. Sr. Fail not of sending me in the goods, according as is directed on the other side & once again I desire you to send me in my Acct. Currant by the first conveniency. If Capt. Allison comes to you with protested bills of Exchange of Mr. Henry Wharton's drawn upon Capt. Thomas Wharton [3] for £5 pay the £5 & send me in the protested bills of Exchange, if he gives you a full and plenary & legall power to get them here otherwise pay no money. If I have any more to add I shall take the next conveniency, but pray be mindfull of all the affairs now & formerly sent for. Send me my goods in a Ship bound for Potomack if possible but take the bills of Loading to be deliver'd at my Landing let the freight be what it will. otherwise I had better have no goods

Your W.ff.

To Mr. Jno. Cooper

[LB, pp. 275-77]

1. For Cooper, Hayward, and Taylor see the many ltrs. to them, above.
2. For Allison, see ltr. to Roger Jones, July 7, 1698, note 2.
3. A Thomas Wharton was executor of an estate in Calvert County, Maryland, in 1695/96. A Thomas Wharton in 1704 owned 270 acres in New Kent County, Virginia, and in 1705 signed a tobacco petition addressed to the Queen. Robert Brent, son of Robert Brent of Woodstock (George Brent's brother), married a daughter of Henry Wharton, only son of Governor Jesse Wharton of Maryland. 19 V 206; 31 V 329; 3 W(2) 251.

To George Mason [1]

Mr. George Mason   August 24th. 1698

Sr. This comes only for Cover of this small bill of Exchange for
£3 .. 14 . 0 sterling drawn by Capt. Joseph Luffe [2] upon Mr. Gotley [3]
which please to receive for my use. I have writ you largely by Capt. Jones [4]
who I hope will be with you before the receipt of this, & therein you will
find my whole desires & affairs, which I hope you will pursue & give me
notice thereof, by the first & all conveniencys which I shall longingly expect, & you may assure your self will be most acceptable to
                                        Sir   Your W. ff.

To Mr. George Mason Mercht. in Bristol

[*LB*, pp. 277]

   1. For George Mason of Bristol, see the several ltrs. to him just above.
   2. Luffe is unidentified.
   3. Richard Gotley or Gostley, Bristol merchant, is discussed in ltr. to Wm. Hardidge,
June 19, 1681, note 4, and ltr. to Stephen Watts, March 30, 1681, note 3.
   4. For the Captains Jones, see several ltrs. above.

To John Pemberton [1]

Mr. John Pemberton   April 26th. 1699

Sir   That I have been quiet with you so long has been because I had
no opportunity of freight to your Port, this opportunity by Mr. Rymer,
gives me the opportunity of renewing my acquaintance by letters & Dealings, & now have sent you four hhds. of choice sweet scented stemmed
Tobo. & weighty for which I hope & expect a good Market, but if at the
first Landing Tobo. be low, & if there be any probable expectation of a
higher Market within a twelve month following rather keep it by you than
sell it at an under rate, for I have no occasion to charge bills or send for

goods, till I have account from you of the Sale of my Tobo. Inclosed is the bills of Loading for the same which I am sure you will take care to dispose of to the best advantage of   Sr. Your W.ff.

To Mr. Jno. Pemberton Mercht. in Bristol

[*LB*, p. 277]

1. Both Pemberton and Rymer are unidentified.

William Fitzhugh's Will and Inventory

William Fitzhugh's Will and Inventory

THE WILL

["At a Court held for Stafford County 10th. Decr. 1701
present
His Majesties Justices for the said County]

In the Name of the Father Son & Holy Ghost Trinity & Unity Unity & Trinity three Persons & one God blessed for evermore Amen. I William Fitzhugh of Stafford County in the Colony of Virginia Gent being by Gods Grace bound for England and knowing the frailty & uncertainty of Mans Life and being at present in perfect health and memory do now ordain Constitute and appoint this my Last Will & Testament Revoking all other former or other Wills this 9th. day of April 1700.

Imprimis I recomme[n]d my Soul into ye. hands of God through the mediation & Intercession of my Blessed Saviour and Redeemer hoping by the meritts of his Death and Burial to have my Sins washed away in his Blood nayled to his Cross & buryed in his grave and by his meritts and Passion to obtain everlasting Life & therefore now do dispose and Bequeath such Estate as it hath pleased God in his mercy to bestow upon me after this manner following after they have disposed my Body to decent Interment without noise feasting drink or Tumult which I not leave but injoine my Exect. or Exects. hereafter named to see decently Ex[ecuted?]

Item I give and Bequeath to my Eldest Son Wm. Fitzhugh all those Tracts of Land following(Vizt.) All that Tract of Land known by the Name of Vauly Land lying & being in Westmoreland County containing 6000 Acres also that Tract or parcel of Land that Escheated from Oliver Griffin Lying in Nomony in Westmoreland County containing 475 Acres also one other Tract of Land joining upon the above sd. Land of Vauly his Land before devised taken up & Pattented by myself containing 2197 Acres Also one other Tract bought of Patrick Mickelroy lying at the head of Popes Creek in Westmoreland conta. 250 Acres also the one half of another Tract above Ocquaquan in Stafford County pattented by myself containing 21996 Acres all which said Tracts & dividends of Land as above expressed I give to the said William Fitzhugh to have and to hold the said Tracts and parcels of Land to him & the heirs of his Body Lawfully begotten for ever and for want of such heirs then to my son Henry Fitzhugh and the heirs of his Body lawfully begotten and for want of such heirs to my son Thomas Fitzhugh and the heirs of his Body lawfully begotten and for want of such heirs to my son George Fitzhugh and the heirs of his Body lawfully begotten forever and for want of such heirs then to my son John Fitzhugh and the heirs of his body lawfully begotten and for want of such heirs to my right heirs forever   *Item*   I further Give and Bequeath to my said son William all that tract & Parcel of Land I now live on in Stafford County Conta. 1000 Acres to be equally divided betwixt him & his mother equally halves & after her decease then I give & bequeath the said Tract wholly to the said William Fitzhugh & the heirs of his Body lawfully begotten & for want of such heirs then to Henry Fitzhugh and the heirs of his Body lawfully begotten & for want of such heirs then I give it to Thomas Fitzhugh & the heirs of his Body Lawfully begotten and for want of such heirs then I Give the same to George Fitzhugh and the heirs of his Body Lawfully begotten and for want of such heirs I Give the same to John Fitzhugh & the heirs of his Body lawfully begotten and for want of such heirs then to my right heirs forever   *Item*   I Give & Bequeath to my son Henry Fitzhugh all those Tracts of Land following (vizt.) the other Moyety or half lying above Ocquaquan in Stafford County pattented by myself containing 21996 Acres whereof I have given his Brother Wm. one half, also one Tract of Land conta. 600 Acres known by the Name of the Church Quarter Land also another Tract of Land lying at the head of Potomack Creek in Stafford County conta. 6000 Acres known by the name of Wilkinson's Pattent all which said Tracts & Dividends of Land above Exprest I give to the said Henry Fitzhugh to have and to hold the said Tracts & Parcels of Land to him and the heirs Lawfully begotten of his body forever and for want of such heirs then to my son William Fitzhugh & the heirs Lawfully begotten of his Body and for want of such heirs then to my son Thomas and the heirs of his Body lawfully begotten and for want of such heirs then to my son George & the heirs of his Body lawfully begotten and for want of such heirs then to my son John & the heirs of his Body Lawfully begotten and for want of such heirs then to my heirs forever   *Item*   I Give & bequeath to my son Thomas Fitzhugh all these Tracts & Parcels of Land following (vizt) all that Tract or parcel that I bought to Mr. Waugh conta. 400 Acres lying upon Rappahannock one half thereof being now Leased [to] William Yates also another Tract of Land conta. 1090 Acres bought of Parson Waugh lying [in] the Forest betwixt Rappa. & Potomack Creek & nigh the head thereof   Also another Tract conta. 200 Acres that I bought of Parson Waugh & now Leased to

John Martin & Kitt Herring also one other Tract conta. 350 Acres Lying upon Rappahannock River Escheated from George Sheppard, Also another Tract of 350 Acres bought by me of John Chadwell lying upon Rappahannock River, Also another Tract containing 1248 Acres which I bought of John Clendenny in Rappahannock Forrest also one/other Tract containing 1246 Acres wch I bought of Richard Sheepy & lying also in Rappahannock Forrest all which Tracts & dividends of Land as above Exprest I give to the said Thomas Fitzhugh to have & to hold the said parcels & Tracts of Land to him & the heirs of his Body lawfully begotten forever & for want of such heirs then to my son Wm. Fitzhugh & the heirs of his Body lawfully begotten and for want of such heirs then to my Son Henry Fitzhugh and the heirs of his Body Lawfully begotten and for want of such heirs then to my son George Fitzhugh & the heirs of his Body lawfully begotten and for want of such heirs then to my Son John Fitzhugh and the heirs of his Body lawfully begotten and for want of such heirs then to my right heirs forever *Item* I Give and Bequeath unto my son George Fitzhugh all those Tracts & Parcels of Land (vizt). all that part or parcel of Land that I bought of Mr. Carey joyning upon Mr. George Brent Mr. Mathew Tompson and others upon Acquia & Choppawomsick Creeks in Stafford County containing 2100 Acres and the first Choise of a Dividend of Land containing 6000 Acres pattented by the said Carreys father & another named ———— [*sic*] who by survivourship has lost all his right Title Propertyship therein as by the Pattent will fully appear but his heir ———— [*sic*] has promised to be at all the charges of the survey & the particular Division & hath further promised to allow unto the Division 400 Acres to be joyned to that 2100 Acres aforesaid and the first Choise to be given after a full survey & division as aforesaid made the said survey and division as aforesaid to be made at the proper Cost & charges of the said ———— [*sic*] then George or his Guardian hereafter Named to take the first Choise but if the said ———— [*sic*] should not Lay out & make Partition upon his own proper Cost & charges, I give the said 2100 Acres & all the Right & Property to the said 3000 Acres as aforesaid as shall be hereafter Exprest provided he the said ———— [*sic*] follows not the agreement of allowing 400 as above Exprest & pay all charges as aforementioned that then my said son George aforesaid have all my right Title & Interest thereunto, also I Give another Tract of Land conta. 500 Acres lying upon Quantico Creek in Stafford County Escheated from Henry Walker also another Tract lying near Quantico in Stafford County being the 1/9 of 800 Acres Escheated by Capt. George Brent and myself from one Mary Heslington the moiety thereof being 400 Acres though all falls to me by survivorship yet we agreed in our Lifetimes not to take advantages but he that survived should have the whole tract Laid out & divided at the Cost & Charges of the Exects. or Admts. of the divident & then the survivour should take his first choise which I now agree to accordingly and will not take advantage of survivourship if they perform the Conditions aforesaid also another Tract lying at the Head of Quanticoe in Stafford County being the half of a divident of 2150 Escheated by myself and Mr John Newton from one Henry Walker the Moiety being 1075 Acres though all falls to me by Survivour yett we agreed in our Life times not to take advantage but he that survived should have the whole Tract laid & divided at the Cost and Charges of the Exect. or admt. or those that pretend claim thereto either of the Dividents or those that have right by his beques[t] and then the survyvor to take the first choise which I now agree to accordingly and will not take advantage of Survivourship if they or any of them perform the Condition aforesaid also another Tract lying near the falls of Occaquan in Stafford County containing 1000 Acres pattented by myself and where once a Tanyard was made by Mr Rice Hooe's father also another Tract of Land lying between Hollowing [sic] Point & Dogges Island in Stafford County within two miles of Colo Mason containing 500 Acres Escheating from one Mary Ireland all which Tracts & Dividends of Land as before Exprest I give to the said George Fitzhugh to have and to hold the said parcels or Tracts of Land to him & the heirs of his Body lawfully begotten forever And for want of such heirs then to my son William Fitzhugh & the heirs of his Body lawfully begotten and for want of such heirs then to my son Henry Fitzhugh and the heirs of his Body lawfully begotten and for want of such heirs then to my son Thomas Fitzhugh & the heirs of his Body lawfully begotten and for want of such heirs then to my Son John Fitzhugh & the heirs of his Body lawfully begotten & for want of such heirs then to my right heirs for ever *Item* I Give & bequeath to my son John Fitzhugh all those Tracts & Pracels of Land following (vizt.) all that tract & Parcel of Land I bought of Doctor Richd. Bryant lying in Paspatanzey Forest containing 200 Acres being now leased to sd. Doctor Bryant also one other Tract of Land containing 150 Acres which I Escheated from Charles Ansell Lying upon the Back of my dwelling Plantation being now leased to John Mee & Stephen Sebastion also one other Tract conta. 200 Acres which I Escheated from Oliver Bokeh [Booker?] his heirs nigh Chotank Creek in Stafford County and in the possession & Lease of Richd. Broad also one other Tract conta. 548 Acres which I bought of John Mathews lying upon Paspetanzy Forest and now part thereof in the Tenancy of one Phillip the Taylor also one other Tract conta. 400 acres which I bought of Joseph Newton lying near Machotick Dam and a little distance from my dwelling Plantation & Tenanted by

Nicho. Savin Joel Striplin Richd. Wall also one other Tract containing
one hundred Acres which I bought of Richd. Ellkin lying near John
Grigsbys & now leased by Stephen Sebastion also another Tract conta. 175
acres which I bought of Thomas Porter lying in the Forrest betwixt Rappahannock & Potomack & now Tenanted by Robt. Jones also another
Tract containing about 400 Acres which I bought from one Edmund
Peirce lying upon Machotick Dam & a little distance from my Dwelling-
house now tenanted by George Downing Charles Martyn & Wm King also
one other Tract containing 100 Acres which I bought of John Colckley
lying near and adjoining to William Bumburys [sic] now Tenanted by
Emanuel Hum all which Tracts & Dividends of Land as before Exprest I
Give to the said John Fitzhugh and the heirs of his Body lawfully begotten for ever and for want of such heirs then to my son Wm Fitzhugh
and the heirs of his Body Lawfully begotten and for want of such heirs
then to my son Henry Fitzhugh and the heirs of his Body lawfully begotten and for want of such heirs then to my Son Thomas Fitzhugh and
the heirs of his body lawfully begotten & for want of such heirs then to
my son George Fitzhugh and the heirs of his Body Lawfully begotten and
for want of such heirs then to my Right heirs forever *Item* whereas I
have given to my Dear & Loving Wife Sarah Fitzhugh the one moiety or
half of the Plantation & tract of Land that I now live on together with the
use & benefit of the Still thereon equally to be divided betwixt my son
William & her in lieu of all Dower & Right & title of Dower to my Lands
before mentioned which will not only be a manifest a due respect to me
when reduced to Dust & Ashes but a preservation and assistance to
theresidue [sic] of my Poor young Orphans left behind that she will take
& accept of that in lieu & full title of Dower of all my Lands before
bequeathed which are not take [sic] the due thirds of each in equivalent
value to compence in profits with the half of this Seat and by her Title
cannot be improved during her Life because an Estate in Dower will not
reach to further nor future Improvements but if this be unkindly or
rather shall I say unnaturally refused then I must say and must give her
& do by these presents give her full thirds of all my Lands each third to be
taken out of each dividend that all my Children may bear their equal
proportion in such an unkindness which I do assure my self will never
happen *Item* whatsoever Lands Tenements or Plantations belonged
to me in Virga. or what Rights or pretensions I may have to any Lands in
England or the Province of Maryland I Give to my Son Wm. and his
heirs forever *AND* as for what Personal Estate God Almighty hath
been graciously pleased to Endow me with I Give and bequeath as followeth *Item* I Give to my Dear and well beloved wife seven Negroes—

(to say) Harry & his wife Katherine Kate Will and his wife Peggy, Hanna & her youngest Child to her & her dispose forever but still with this Intercession & Request to my Dust in the Ground either when she dyes or before a second Marriage that she would secure the three Youngest of the said Negroes to my three Youngest Children or to which of them best pleaseth her by their dutifulness & obedience to them & their heirs I Give to my said beloved Wife one silver Bason three silver Plates one of the Lesser silver Candlesticks a silver Salt half my silver Spoons in the house the second Best silver Tankard a silver Porringer & a large silver Ladle the Great silver Tumbler to her & her heirs forever with this request & desire also that if Necessity do not enforce her to sell the said Plate in her widowhood or before a second marriage that she would be so kind that my two youngest sons George & John to have them Authenticly secured [before?] her Death or if she please before a second marriage but I say be the things to her alt. & her own disposa. *Item* I Give and Bequeath to my Eldest & well beloved son Wm Fitzhugh 8 Negroes to say Giles his Wife & sons Children to say Susan Ned Giles & Joe Tomlin & Peter and a ninth I Give Mulatto Betty to have & to hold to him & his heirs for ever *Item* I Give to the said William Fitzhugh 2 Silver Dishes one the largest & the other the smallest Dish 6 Silver Plates of those that come [*sic*] in the last year from Mr Mason one Large Silver Salver Jappan one small Salver or Bread Plate one Trencher & one Larger Silver Salt one Silver Porringer of the Largest sort a pair of Large Silver Candlesticks with Snuffers Snuff Dish & Extinguisher Together also the Great Silver Tankard & a sett of Silver Castors to him & his heirs for ever *Item* I Give to my Son Henry Fitzhugh 7 Negroes (to say) Daphne & her 4 Children (to say) Phill. Dick Johnny & Jone Cesar & Johnney Black Peggs Son To have & to hold to him & his heirs for ever *Item* I Give & Bequeath to my aforesaid son Henry Fitzhugh 2 Silver Dishes one of the Largest & the other the smallest Dish of those that came in last year from Mr. Masons one small Salver or Bread Plate one Silver Trencher Salt one Silver Porringer of the Largest Sort a Silver Candlestick with Snuffers & Stand to him & his heirs forever *Item* I Give to my Son Thomas Fitzhugh & his heirs forever 7 Negroes (to say Mulatto Pegg & her young Child Will [or Willbey?] boy Mulatto Peggs George black Bettys Youngest Child & her Eldest Child named Frank & Black Betty herself *Item* I Give to my sd. son Thomas Fitzhugh after his Brothers Wm. & Henry are served as before I have Exprest one silver Dish 3 silver Plates a silver Porringer a silver Salt & a silver Candlestick *Item* I Give to my son George Fitzhugh & his heirs for ever 7 Negroes (to say) Black Prue & her 4 Children (vizt.) George Jemmy Moll & Johnny Mulatto Sarah & her young Daughter

Diana *Item* I Give to the above George Fitzhugh after his brothers William Henry & Thomas are served one silver Dish three silver Plates one silver Porringer if one left a Silver Salt a silver Candlestick & the smallest silver Tankard *Item* I Give to my son John Fitzhugh & his heirs forever seven Negroes (vizt.) Mulatto Sarah's 2 Children Esop & William black Sarah's 2 children left yet undisposed Billy & Betty Hannahs Daughter Clory & 2 of Hannah's Children Rose & Robin *Item* I Give to my aforesaid son John Fitzhugh 1 silver Bason 3 Silver Plates a silver Salt a small Silver Tumbler 6 silver spoons to him & his heirs for ever *Item* I Give to my Eldest son Wm. Fitzhugh before named 2 large silver Dishes that are now coming out of England but not yet arrived under Condition that he pays when he receives them 10£. Sterl a piece to each of my other four sons or if he refuses that then the said Dishes when they arrive Equally to be divided betwixt my sd. five sons *Item* I Give & Bequeath to my said Eldest son Willm. Fitzhugh 200£. Sterl out of my money in England & to my Dear & Loving Wife Sarah in part & lieu of her Dower as is said before in my other Legacys 120£. Sterl and to each of my sons Henry Thomas George & John 120£. Sterling to each of the aforesaid Children to be paid them by my Exect. hereafter named as each arrives at 16 years of Age & what remt. or overplush money I shall have in England after the Legacies aforesd. paid I give to my two sons Wm. & Henry Fitzhugh which said William & Henry Fitzhugh I appoint my Exects. to this my said Will & Testament to Execute & do all things therein as before I have ordered & devised *Item* As to my horses & mares I Give my Riding horse Tickler to my wife & all ye Remainder to my son Wm. Fitzhugh desiring him not commanding him that if his kindness will Extend thereto to Each of my 4 other Sons Henry Thomas George & John each of them a good young horse or a good young mare *Item* as to my Beds & furniture sheets & Table linnen I Give & dispose them equally betwixt my Dear & Loving Wife and my son William after they have sett apart for each of my younger sons Henry Thomas, George & John One good feather Bedd & furniture 3 pair Good sheets to each & a Dozn. Diaper Napkins to each which I do by this my Will give them out of the same *Item* I Give my son William my own & wife's pictures & the other 6 Pictures of my Relations together with the Large Mapp in my Study also I give to my Sons William & Henry my Study of Books equally to be divided betwixt them remt. of the Pictures & Mapps I give to my Wife *Item* as to my Goods & Merchandise that is now lying in my two stores I order that Provision thereout for the support of the whole family for 2 years after so much being laid aside then I Give and bequeath all the remainder to my Eldest Son Wm. with the Proviso & Condition that he pay to each of my younger Children Henry Thomas George & John 50£ Sterl: to each as they arrive to the Age of 16 years *Item* I Give to my sons Henry & Thomas my stock of Sheep Cattle & Hoggs equally to be divided betwixt them at my Church quarter Plantation & to my son Wm. & my Loveing Wife I Give all my Stocks of Sheep Cattle & Hoggs to be equally divided betwixt them

Richard Fossaker	John Washington	⎫		
Thomas Gilson	Wm. Andrews	⎬ W Fitzhugh	[*seal*]	
Alexander Spense	Jno Nicholson.	⎭		

[At a Court held for Stafford County. 10th. Decbr. 1701.
Present
His Majestyes Justices for sd. County.]

[The Last Will & Testament of William Fitzhugh Gent. was Exhibited to the Court by the Exects. therein named & proved by the Oaths of Rd. Fossaker John Washington Willm. Andrews Clk Alexander Spense & John Nicholson and that the said Testator was of Perfect sense *&* Memory at the sealing & Delivery of the same John Washington & Richd. Fosaker did depose they saw Thomas Gilson witness the same at the sealing & delivering of the same and a Probat is granted to William Fitzhugh Exectr. therein named giving security according to the will of said Testator.]

Codicil to sd. Will

Item my Will farther is that my son William Fitzhugh have Charge & Care of my 4 sons Henry Thomas George & John of their Estates Real & Personal which by my Will I have given them till they & as they & any of them arrive to the Age of 18 years to deliver them their said Estates & be accountable to them for the same and that he have Power by virtue of this Codicil to Lease their Lands in their Names & for their Use according to the form of my Leases already Lett or as he shall see convenient till they arrive to the age of 18 years at which Age each of them are respectively to have their said Estates delivered them in kind & the profits of the same deducting what my said son William Fitzhugh hath been out towards their maintenance & schooling during there said term of there arrival to the age of 18 Years And it is my will that my Estate may not be brought to appraisement but that a just and true Inventory of the same be rendered and that my said son Wm. Fitzhugh may give Security to be accountable to mysd. four sons Henry Thomas George & John to deliver to them respectively their said Estates as they respectively shall come to the age of Eighteen years this Codicil dates the 20th. October 1701.

William Andrews   W. Fitzhugh   [seal]
Alexander Spense
John Nicholson

[At a Court held for Stafford County 10th. December 1701
Present
His Majestys Justices &c.]

[The first Codicil to the said Will was proved by the Oaths of Wm. Andrews Alexr. Spense & John Nicholson who did depose they saw the said Testator seal & Deliver the said Codicil & that he was of Perfect sense & Memory at the same time to the best of their knowledge.]

The second Codicil to said Will

Item I give and bequeath to my servants John Nicholson Henry the Carpenter & Thomas the Glazier one year of their Times by Indenture for their Tendance on me in my Sickness as a gratification for their Trouble & Care therein *Item* I Give & Bequeath to my Cousin David Abbot his time by Indenture being seven Years *Item* I Give & Bequeath to Mrs. Ann Odonell two stuff Gowns and Petticoats *Item* I Give unto my Mother Newton as much broad Flannell as will [make her] a pair of sheets & as much Flannell as will make her two waistcoats & Petticoats or all the Narrow Flannell. *Item* My Will is at the Request of my Dear Wife that Sarah Negro Woman for a particular respect has to her be exempted from working in the Ground but be imployed in such other works as they who she belongs to shall think Convenient to put her to *Item* I Give and Bequeath to my Dear & Loving wife Sarah Fitzhugh & my son Wm. Fitzhugh both my Coaches Horses & Gear *Item* I Give to Mr. John Nicholson Clk 5£. to buy him a Ring *Item* I Give & Bequeath to Mr W. Andrews ~~Gill~~ five pounds to buy him a Ring   *Item*   I Give and Bequeath to Doctor Spense 5£. to buy him a Ring in Lieu & Satisfaction of their Trouble   *Item*   I Give and Bequeath to Doctor Spense his wife 20s. to buy a Ring.   *Item*   I give to my two sons George & John a Dozn. Silver Spoons I brought out of England with me   *Item*   I Give to my son Henry Fitzhugh my Silver Moonteeth Bason which I brought out of England   *Item*   I Give to my son Thomas Fitzhugh my Silver Chocolate Pott which I brought out of England   October 20: 1701.

Wm. Fitzhugh   [*seal*]

Signed Sealed & Published in Psence of us

Wm. Andrews   Alexr. Spense   Jno Nicholson

[followed by same oaths, etc. as followed first Codicil]

AN INVORY OF THE ESTATE OF COLLNL. WM. FITZHUGH DECD

Negroes belonging to Madam Sarah Fitzhugh Relict of Colle Willm Fitzhugh

Will Black Pegg Billy her son Harry Cato Catereno Beck and Hannah. Eight in Number, Negroes belonging to Wm. Fitzhugh . . Giles Lucy, Sue, Ned, Joe, Ben, Betty Tomline and Peter. . . . 10. Negroes belonging to Henry Fitzhugh. Daphne and five Children, Cæsar, Johnny Black Pegg[s] Son. . . Negroes belonging to Thomas Fitzhugh . . Mulatto Pegg her young Child Sarah and one born since named Nanny & her son George Will boy & _____ Black Betty & Bettys 2 Children Harry & Frank _____ Negroes belonging to George Fitzhugh. Black Sarah and five Children George Jenny Moll & Cate Jenny Mulatto Sarah & her Daughter Diana[.] Negroes belonging to John Fitzhugh _____ Esop, Tom, Mat. Sarah Children Billy & Betsy Black Sarah Hannahs Children Clary Rose & Robin & Black Peggs son Harry—in all fivety one Negroes & Mulattoes   51

PLATE

Six silver Dishes 2 silver Basons 2 dozn. Silver Plates 4 Silver Porringers 3 Casters 3 Salvers 3 Silver Tankards 3 pair silver Candlesticks 1 small writing Do. 2 pair Snuffers & Stands 1 Silver Extinguisher 6 Silver Trencher[s] Salts 1 Table Salt 1. Dozn. Silver hafted Knifes 1 Dozen Silver Forks 1 Silver Ladle 2 Tumblers 1 Dozn. Silver Spoons 1 Silver Tobacco Box 1 Silver headed Cane 1 Silver Cork Screw 2 Silver Dishes 1 Doz: Silver Spoons 1 Bason or Bunch Bowl 1 C[h]ocolate Cup 3 Silver Salts. in all 122 pieces of Plate

Divided between the Widow & Children as by Will. . . .

GOLD

One Gold Snuff Box two Gold Rings./Dividd. between the Widow & Exec^{r}

GOODS & MERCHANDIZES *in both Stores*

Five pieces & Remnants of Linnen pretty Course Quantity 115 yards— 1 Remnant Jeans qt. 18 yards 1 Remnant Fustian qt. 6 yards 2 Ends Fustians 1 End Ticking qt. 15 yards 1 End Do. qt. 9 yards 1 Remnant of Coloured Dimety 1 piece Striped Ditto 1 Remnant Dowlas qt. 25 yards 5 Ends of white Fustians 1 Remnt. Dowlas qt. 22 yards 1 Remnant Sacking qt. 6 yards 1 Remnant Cotton Quantity 17 yards 4 pieces Ditto 1 piece Ozimbriggs qt. 55 yards 10 pieces Course West Country Linnen 1 Remnant of the above sort qt. 21 yards 1 piece of the above Linnen qt. 55. 5 pieces of Irish Linnen qt. about 105 yds 1 piece of Garlick Holland qt. 25 yards 2 Remnants of Dowlas 1 piece Course sheeting Linnen qt. 60 yards 1 Remnant Dyed Linnen 2 Bedd Tick 4 pieces of Canvis 2 peices of Rowled Linnen 1 piece Rowled Double Canvis 27 1 piece Do. qt. 30 yds. 1 piece Rowled Canvis qt. 37 yds. 2pd. Remnts. of Dowlas 1 Remnt of Red half thick 1 Remnt. Serge 2 Remnts. of [Beys?] 5 Liverpool Coverlets abt. m 50 [*sic*] 8 dozn. plain shoes 2½ of Mens Womens & Childrens 1 Dozn. or thereabts of Course Felts two fine Casters

HORSES & MARES

Two Mares and two Colts 1 horse called Whistler One Stone [*sic*] horse at the Church Quarter.

ENGLISH SERVANTS

James Jameson about 2 yrs. to serve Henry Borec 2½ years to serve Thomas Barlow the same John Nicholson the same. Thomas Cave about 6½ to serve Margarett an Old Woman about 2 years.

CATTLE AT HOME PLANTATION°

the whole divided between the widow & Exectr. fourty four head Numberd.

SHEEP AT THE HOME PLANTAO°

The whole Divided between the widow & Exec. twenty four head

HOGGS AT HOME PLANTATION

The whole divided between the widow and Executor twenty head

Cattle at the Church Quarter belonging to Henry & Thomas Fitzhugh 8 Cows 1 killed 2 heifers 3 young stears 6 Cow yearlings 4 Calves sheep being at the Church Quarter belonging to the said Henry & Thomas Fitzhugh—9 Yews & 6 Lambs Hoggs. 7 Sows Shoats & Barrons. Do 3 Breeding Sows

HOUSEHOLD FURNITURE

Henry Fitzhugh has 1 Bed of feathrs. wth. Bolster three pair sheets 1 pr. Blankets 1 Quilt 1 Pillow 1 Dozn. Napkins 1 Table Cloth Thomas Fitzhugh has 1 Bedd Bolster and Pillow 1 Blanket & Quilt 3 pair sheets 1 Dozn. Napkins & Tablecloth George Fitzhugh has 1 Bedd Bolster & Pillow 1 Blanket 1 Rugg 3 pair sheets 1 Dozn. Napkins & Table Cloth John Fitzhugh has 1 Bedd Bolster & Pillow 1 Blanket Rugg three pair sheets 1 Dozn. Napkins 1 Table Cloth The Remainder of the Household stuff to be divided between the widow & Wm. Fitzhugh the Exectr. 8 Feather Bedds Bolsters and Pillows 4 pair Blankets 2 Dozn. old leather 2 Dozn. Kaine Chairs 1 Dozn. Turkey Workt Do. 4 or 5 Tables 4 or 5 old Chests 2 Chests of Drawers 5 Standing Bedsteads 2 Truckle Ditto 2 large looking Glasses 1 Scrutore [sic] 1 small looking Glass 2 pair Brass Tongs with Shovel & Bellows 2 pair Iron Do. 4 Dozn. & 4 Napkins 2 Table Cloths 2 Leather Carpets 2 Turky work't Carpets 1 old Do. 8 pair Andirons 20 Pewter Dishes 5 Doz & 4 Pewter Plates 1 great Brass Dish 1 Copper Sistern 1 Pewter Bed Pan 1 Close Stool 4 Chafing Dishes 1 Copper. Chocolate Pott 2 Skillets or stew pans 2 Possnets 2 stands to set Plates upon 10 Brass Candlesticks 2 Kettles 4 Iron Potts 4 Spitts 6 old Kettles 1 Brass Mortar 1 stone Do. two warming-Pans A Parcel of Pewter a parcel Tinware 1 parcel of Earthware about 2 Gross Glass Bottles a parcel of uncurryed Leather 20 pair sheets 6 Table Cloths 5 setts of Curtains and [6 allins? or Callins?] 4 Ruggs 2 Coverleds 2 Quilts 4 pair Blankets 12 Cushions 1 Iron Punch Bowl 1 Monteeth Copper Bason 1 pair Playing Tables 1 Iron Driping Pan

Cash or Ready MONEY

One Guinea one Mill Shilling Jewels unknown being in the Widows Possession together with her Apparell & Side Saddle.

A Study of Books to be divided between Wm & Henry Fitzhugh. One old Brass Clock 1 old Watch 5 old Trunk a parcel old Cask 1 Calash & Gear with 2 horses a Parcel of Rum & Sugar. Inter Partnership John Jones & Testator the Acct unsettled yet, Whenever it is there will be little coming to the Estate also About 7£ worth Goods the 16th. part of a Ship & Cargo the Account not yet settled when ever it is shall be rendered

W m. Fitzhugh

Henry Fitzhugh

The above Inventory presented into Court the 11th Augt. 1703 p Sworn to by Major Wm. Fitzhugh one of the Exectrs thereto subscribed

[*Stafford County Will Book, Liber Z, 1699-1709*
Will and Codicils, pp. 92-102.
Inventory, pp. 180-83.]

Index

Index

After proper names, page numbers in italics indicate location of letters addressed to these persons. In variant spellings of proper names, each spelling is listed with cross reference if it appears twice. Otherwise the variant appears in parentheses after the more frequent spelling. In the case of married women whose names change, page listing is given under the most frequent surname, with cross references. The title of *Captain* is used only before names of ship captains. Military titles ranging from *Captain* to *Colonel* are omitted, for they change frequently in the course of the letters and mean little more than courtesy to militia officers.

If entry is mentioned in both text and note, the page number will appear only once, with the *n* appended. If there is doubt as to whether a correct first name has been suggested for the surname in the entry, page numbers involved are followed by question marks.

398 / INDEX

150, 150n, 164, 165, *209-10, 212-13*, 215, 217n, *232*, 235n, *235-37, 237-38*, 248, 251n, *251-53*, 270, 279, 281, 282, 288n, 290, 310, 311-13, 325n, 326n
Spencer, Nicholas, Jr., 324, 325n, 326n
Spencer, Mrs. Nicholas, 272
Spense, Alexander, 380, 381
Spicer, Arthur, 13, 32, 88n, 108n, 213n, 286, 289n, 344, 352, 353n
Spinkes, Elias, 362
Statutes at Large, 50, 66n, 72, 129-32, 133n, 152-59; *Statutes at Large in Paragraphs*, 159n; Statutes, 363
Storke, Nehemiah, 122, 123n, 208, 209n
Storke, Thomas, 122, 123n, 208, 209n, 221, 222n, 223, 231, 235, 236, 237n, 238, *265*, 275, 277, 290, 292, 309
Striplin, Joel, 377
Sutton, Capt. Henry, 246, 247n
Swinburne, Henry, *A Brief Treatise of Testaments and Last Wills*, 153, 159n

Tacitus, Publius Cornelius, 49, 328
Taliaferro, John, 308, 309n
Taliaferro, Robert, 309n
Tatterdale (or Totterdell), Capt. Henry, 316, 317n
Taylor, James, 228n, 264, 265n
Taylor, John, 299, 300n, *302-3, 304-5*, 321, 322, *327*, 328n, *338-39, 351*, 356-57, 366
Taylor, Thomas, 300n, 321
Taylor, Capt. Zachary (or Zachariah), 228
Thomas, Capt.? John, 318, 321, 327, 328n
Thompson (or Tompson), Matthew, 70, 71n, 124, 125n, 296, 308, 322, 375
Thornbush, Mr., 250
Thorne, George, 95
Tobacco, growth, sale, shipment of, 18; attempts to improve cultivation, 20; "charter party" in connection with, 365n; rolling house, 180-83n; plant-cutting, 113-14, 114n-15n, 118n, 127n, 129-33. *See also* WF, *Tobacco planter and businessman*
Todd, Samuel, 275n, 307n
Todd, Mrs. Sarah, 307n
Todd, Thomas, 275n
Todd, William, 274, 275n
Towns, making of in Va., 82n, 134, 135n
"Trotter's Neck," Cant-Warner estate, 263, 264n
Trucket (or Tricket), Capt., 331, 337, 339
Tucker, Mr., 115, 116n

Tucker, Gerard, 11n
Tucker, Rose. *See* Rose Newton
Tucker, Rose (dau. of Rose Newton Tucker). *See* Blakiston
Tucker, Sarah. *See* Sarah Fitzhugh

Van Sweringham, Garett, 33
"Violet Banks," Edward Porteus estate, 179n
Virgil, 49, 333
Virginia. *Church in:* gifts to parish, 167n; possibility of probate court under, 168-69; need for sober clergy, 168. *Counties:* Accomac, 23, 320n; Arlington, 14; Caroline, 265n; Charles City, 351n; Essex, 265n, 309n; Fauquier, 14; Gloucester, 21, 23, 28, 32, 82n, 106n, 114n, 118n, 120n, 121n, 123n, 132, 185, 201, 209, 241n, 261-63, 263n-64n, 325n, 363n; Henrico, 28, 32; Isle of Wight, 344n; James City, 28, 95n, 166n; King and Queen (*see* New Kent); King George, 137n; King William, 106n, 120n, 241n; Lancaster, 109n, 273n; Middlesex, 28, 78n, 85n, 88n, 89n, 120n, 123n, 132, 133n, 149n, 185n, 264n, 265n; Nansemond, 23; New Kent, 122, 123n, 265n, 367n; Northampton, 23, 320n; Northumberland, 79n, 100n, 101n, 102n, 104n, 209n, 265n, 344n, 356; Prince William, 14, 74n; Rappahannock (Old), 22, 120n, 124n, 265n; Richmond, 22, 32, 325n; Stafford, *passim* (more than 50 refs.); Westmoreland, 20, 22, 28, 66n, 76n, 78n, 79n, 82n, 90n, 95n, 97n, 101n, 109n, 120, 121n, 137n, 146n, 164n, 165n, 191, 192n, 266n, 281-84, 325n, 336n, 356, 371-79; York, 21, 28, 186n. *Education in* (*see* WF).
Virginia, The Complete Collection of the Laws of (1684) (*see* also *Purvis*), 273n, 327n; *The Lawes of . . . Now in Force* (1662), 155, 159n
Virginia, laws of edited by WF. *See* WF

Walker, Henry, 120n, 375, 376
Walker, John, 119, 120n
Wall, Richard, 377
Walters, Dr. Richard, 303, 329
Warner, Augustine, Jr., 261-63, 263n
Warner, Christopher, 103, 104n
Warner, Henry, 262
Warner, Mildred, 250, *261-63*, 264n
Warner, Robert (or Robin), 261, 263n
"Warner Hall," Augustine Warner estate, 261, 263n